Dyslexia

A Practitioner's Handbook

Fourth Edition

Dyslexia
A Practitioner's Handbook
Fourth Edition

Gavin Reid

WILEY-BLACKWELL
A John Wiley & Sons, Ltd., Publication

This edition first published 2009
© 2009, John Wiley & Sons Ltd.

Wiley-Blackwell is an imprint of John Wiley & Sons, formed by the merger of Wiley's global Scientific, Technical, and Medical business with Blackwell Publishing.

Registered Office
John Wiley & Sons Ltd, The Atrium, Southern Gate, Chichester, West Sussex, PO19 8SQ, UK

Editorial Offices
The Atrium, Southern Gate, Chichester, West Sussex, PO19 8SQ, UK
9600 Garsington Road, Oxford, OX4 2DQ, UK
350 Main Street, Malden, MA 02148-5020, USA

For details of our global editorial offices, for customer services, and for information about how to apply for permission to reuse the copyright material in this book please see our website at www.wiley.com/wiley-blackwell.

The right of Gavin Reid to be identified as the author of this work has been asserted in accordance with the Copyright, Designs and Patents Act 1988.

Library of Congress Cataloging-in-Publication Data:

Reid, Gavin, 1950-
   Dyslexia : a practitioner's handbook / Gavin Reid.—4th ed.
      p. cm.
   Includes index.
   ISBN 978-0-470-76040-6
1. Dyslexic children—Popular works. 2. Dyslexia—Popular works. I. Title.
   RJ496.A5R45 2009
   616.85′53—dc22

2009013395

A catalogue record for this book is available from the British Library.

Typeset in 10/12.5pt Times by Laserwords Private Limited, Chennai, India.
Printed in Singapore by Markono Print Media Pte Ltd.

2   2010

Contents

About the Author

Dr Gavin Reid, Ph.D., M.A, M.App.Sci, M.Ed., B.Ed, AMBDA, Assoc. F. B.P.S
www.drgavinreid.com

Dr Gavin Reid is a consultant on learning disabilities at the Centre for Child Evaluation and Teaching (CCET) in Kuwait, working on teacher education, psycho-educational assessment and intervention. The aim of the CCET is to remove barriers to inclusion and to empower individuals with learning disabilities to achieve their full potential.

He is also an independent educational psychologist in Vancouver, Canada. Dr Reid was a visiting professor at the University of British Columbia (UBC) in Vancouver, Canada in 2007 and a guest lecturer at UBC running a graduate course in learning disabilities.

He is a co-founder and director of the Red Rose School for children with specific learning difficulties in St. Annes on Sea, Lancashire. He was a senior lecturer in the Department of Educational Studies, Moray House School of Education, University of Edinburgh from 1991 to 2007. He wrote and developed the first Masters course in dyslexia in the UK in 1993, which became the basis for the current Open University course Difficulties in Literacy Development. He has been a consultant for the OU since 1999.

He has made over 800 conference and seminar presentations in over 50 countries, including Norway, Denmark, Germany, United States, New Zealand, Australia, Hong Kong, Singapore, Iceland, Poland, Republic of Ireland, Slovakia, Croatia, Ljubljana, Estonia, Greece, Cyprus, Thailand, Austria, Slovenia, Malta, Israel, Egypt, Gambia, Canada, Dubai, Kuwait, Hungary, Italy and Switzerland.

He has currently 22 books in print in the area of teacher education in the fields of dyslexia, literacy learning styles and motivation and classroom management. Many of his books are used as course texts in courses throughout the UK and in many other countries. These include: *Dyslexia: A Practitioners Handbook* (3rd Edition) (Wiley, 1998, 2003), *Dyslexia: A Complete Guide for Parents* (Wiley, 2004), *Dyslexia and Inclusion* (2005), *Motivating Learners in the Classroom: Ideas and Strategies* (2007) and *Learning Styles and Inclusion* (2005). He is the co-author with Shannon Green of *100 Ideas for Supporting Pupils with Dyslexia and Dyslexia: A Teaching Assistant's Handbook and Effective Learning: Ideas into Action: (2009).*

Some of his books have been translated into Arabic, Polish, French, Italian and Greek.

He is the co-author of a computer aided diagnostic assessment and profiling procedures (Special Needs Assessment Profile—SNAP) which has received three national award commendations and was winner of the Special Needs Category at the NASEN/TES book awards in Birmingham, UK in March 2006.

He has been invited to be external examiner at fifteen universities worldwide for PhD candidates and masters courses. He was a member of the British Dyslexia Association Teacher Training Accreditation Board from 1996 to 2007 and was overseas patron for the Learning and Behaviour Charitable Trust in New Zealand. He is the international consultant for the Canadian Academy of Therapeutic Tutors and advisor to the IDA board (BC Branch) and consultant to the parents' organisation—All Special Kids (ASK) in Geneva, Switzerland.

Gavin Reid has used his experiences as a teacher, educational psychologist, researcher, university lecturer and most importantly as a parent in the preparation of this book.

Other Books by Gavin Reid

Reid, G. and Green, S. (2008) *Dyslexia: A Guide for Teaching Assistants*. Continuum, London.

Reid, G., Fawcett, A., Manis, F. and Siegel, L. (eds) (2008) *The Sage Dyslexia Handbook*. Sage, London.

Reid, G., Elbeheri, G., Everatt, J. and Wearmouth, J. (eds) (2009) *The Routledge Companion on Dyslexia*. Routledge, London.

Reid, G. (2007) *Motivating Learners in the Classroom: Ideas and Strategies*. Sage, London.

Reid, G. and Green, S. (2007) *100 Ideas for Supporting Students with Dyslexia*. Continuum, London—also published in Arabic and French.

Reid, G. (2005) *Dyslexia and Inclusion*. NASEN/David Fulton, London.

Reid, G. (2005) *Dyslexia*. Continuum, London—published in Polish and in Arabic (2nd edn 2007).

Reid, G. (2005) *Learning Styles and Inclusion*. Sage, London. Also published in Polish.

Reid, G. (2004). *Dyslexia: A Complete Guide for Parents*. Wiley, Chichester, reprinted 2004, 2005 (3 times), 2006 (twice)—also translated into Italian.

Reid, G. and Fawcett, A. (eds) (2004) *Dyslexia in Context, Theory and Practice*. Whurr, London.

Reid, G. (2003) *Dyslexia: A Practitioners Handbook* (3rd edn). Wiley, Chichester, reprinted 2004, 2005 (twice), 2006, 2007.

Peer, L. and Reid, G. (2003) *Introduction to Dyslexia*. David Fulton, London.

Weedon, C. and Reid, G. (2003) *Special Needs Assessment Profile (SNAP)*. Hodder & Stoughton, London (version 2, pub. 2006, version 3 2009).

Reid, G. and Wearmouth, J. (eds) (2002) *Dyslexia and Literacy: Research and Practice*. Wiley, Chichester.

Peer, L. and Reid, G (eds) (2001) *Dyslexia: Successful Inclusion in the Secondary School*. David Fulton, London.

Reid, G. and Kirk, J. (2000) *Dyslexia in Adults: Education and Employment*. John Wiley and Sons, Chichester, reprinted 2006.

Peer, L. and Reid, G. (eds) (2000) *Multilingualism, Literacy and Dyslexia: A Challenge for Educators*. David Fulton, London.

Came, F. and Reid, G. (2008) *Common Assessment Framework*. Learning Works International, Marlborough.

Green, S. and Reid, G. (2009) *Effective Learning: Ideas into Action*. Continuum, London.

Foreword

By Sir Jackie Stewart

I was very pleased to receive an invitation from Gavin Reid to write the foreword for this fourth edition of his *Dyslexia: A Practitioner's Handbook*.

Gavin has been a great contributor to the entire dyslexia movement and he is now spreading his wings beyond Scotland, the country of his birth, to be involved in the Middle and Far East and North America, and has lectured in many other countries around the world on the subject.

I, for my part, am a dyslexic, who was only identified as such at the age of 41, when both my sons were struggling at school in Switzerland. Although it would have seemed that the school had no great knowledge of anything to do with learning disabilities at the time, they at least recognised that both my sons simply couldn't keep up with the other class members in most of the subjects. They also had the sense to suggest that my sons be assessed and recommended a specialist in London who could undertake that.

This event had an immense impact on my life because on that very day, during the assessment of my son Mark, the professor involved asked if I personally had ever experienced learning difficulties, which of course I had, having failed almost every exam that my school was able to invent. I walked out of his consulting room with great relief; realising for the first time that I was not 'stupid, dumb or thick', but that I was a dyslexic.

I now commit an enormous amount of my life to the dyslexic movement, not just in Scotland (where I am President of Dyslexia Scotland) and in the rest of the UK (where I am a Vice-President of the British Dyslexia Association), but worldwide, trying to enhance the dyslexic movement, working with governments, ministers for education, university chancellors and deans of teacher-training colleges.

It is very apparent that even with the help that is currently being provided to support those children who are suffering with learning difficulties, unless we immediately integrate with the teacher-training colleges (who are prepared to restructure their curriculum) to ensure that every single new teacher that qualifies into the profession has the skills for the early recognition of children with learning disabilities, and knows how to progress them on to more developed specialists in the field, we are not going to fully deal with, or resolve, the problem.

The educational authorities in a great many countries have a lot to answer for, because to a large extent around the world, a great many educators have simply ignored a child or young person who cannot accomplish the simple skills that others find so easy. They cannot read, write or count correctly, they get blamed for being lazy, for not paying attention, and therefore are identified not only by their teachers, but also by their peers, as being 'dumb, stupid and thick', just as I was.

The pain, removal of self-esteem, frustration and humiliation that this brings to a young person can be devastating and can tarnish their lives forever. The problem moves from classroom to playground and they suffer intensely, to a point where they may turn to the abuse of alcohol and drugs to escape from the reality of their inadequacies.

A very large percentage of the existing established teacher body, because they have not been educated on the subject, allow those children to be left on the scrapheap of the educational system. They therefore leave school with little education, which considerably reduces their opportunity to secure a decent job or even gain employment. They are therefore robbed of the chance to reach their true potential, which, in my opinion, is totally unacceptable and indeed a sin.

Many dyslexics are truly creative people and the few that are able to succeed in life turn out to be hugely successful in many cases. For any government or educational authority to ignore those suffering from dyslexia, which amounts to at least 10% of the population of any country, is an unacceptable position.

The loss to a nation of many of them, who end up unemployed or turn to crime and end up in prison, is well documented. Well in excess of 50% of the prison population in most countries are dyslexic, which is simply unacceptable in the world in which we live. It would seem that most governments are still unaware of those statistics and that is why the work that Gavin Reid is doing around the world is so important. Gavin has a wealth of experience, with considerable knowledge, and has a proven track record in this field of dyslexia.

This book will benefit a multitude of people who are capable of assisting the young, and the mature, to overcome the hurdle that dyslexia provides. Those who can be led and informed into providing support for dyslexics will themselves be stimulated and fulfilled, through providing a lifeline to those who in many instances have been left as debris in school classrooms around the world. This is not a territorial problem, it is a unilateral problem.

Few people can communicate as successfully as Gavin Reid on this subject; he reaches out, not just to those who suffer the pains, frustrations and inadequacies that dyslexia provides, but just as importantly, he opens the eyes of the parents to allow them to give better understanding, consideration and support to the children that they have borne. With more knowledge those same parents are able to make greater demands on the schools, the teachers and authorities, who should be responsible for each and every one of the students who pass through their hands.

With many congratulations to Gavin Reid not only for the creation of this book, but also for spreading the news.

SIR JACKIE STEWART

Preface

Throughout the 25 years I have been involved in the field of dyslexia, when I visited schools, talked to teachers and assessed children with dyslexia one point has been reinforced many times—that point is simply that best practice in dyslexia is best practice in teaching! There is no magic cure—no magic programme, but there are many excellent approaches that together with good teaching can make a significant difference to the lives of children and adults with dyslexia and their families.

This book is about the child, and the adult, with dyslexia, but it is also about the school system, the school management, the curriculum, government policy, differentiation, learning styles, teaching approaches and learning strategies. The most effective method of dealing with dyslexia is dependent on good practice in learning and best practice in teaching.

It is heartening to witness the general acceptance of dyslexia among teachers, administrators and governments. Since the start of the twenty-first century we have seen a number of countries actively seeking out expertise in dyslexia, through legislation, working parties and in effect paving the way for changes in school systems to accommodate the needs of students such as those with dyslexia. But as Sir Jackie Stewart indicated in the foreword to this book, there is still much to be done.

One of these areas is in teacher education. Though there has been significant progress in this area, there are still a number of unresolved issues (these are discussed in Chapter 19). In general, however, there has been progress in professional development with the introduction of specialized training courses in the area of dyslexia. This is extremely encouraging as it is readily acknowledged by those working in this field that every teacher in every classroom should have at least an awareness of dyslexia and every school should have at least one teacher who has been on a higher-level training course in dyslexia. There are now dyslexia courses being run at universities and colleges in many countries and these courses, with a mix of theory and practice, can provide teachers with the understanding of what dyslexia is and the practical knowledge to tackle it in the classroom situation. More than that, however, courses should help teachers understand children with dyslexia, their needs, their challenges and their abilities.

This increased interest in training, and keeping up to date with new developments, has in fact prompted this fourth edition of *Dyslexia: A Practitioners Handbook*. When I wrote the first edition in 1994, there were few courses available and very little at university level. It is encouraging to witness how the field has developed since then, but what has provided most satisfaction has been the efforts by education authorities to endorse professional development and support the training of teachers in dyslexia. This has been at a number of levels—short courses, courses for teaching assistants and lengthier post-graduate university courses. It is these levels of training that will ensure that children with dyslexia are understood and their needs met.

It is important also to consider parents—they have much to offer; their experiences, their insights and their support can be invaluable to schools. It is perhaps this collaboration that is the key to eventual success. Research findings can inform, but the real impact can come with effective communication between home and school. The sharing of concerns and the exchange of ideas can prove invaluable. I hope this book can facilitate this in some way and that the information and the reflection provided in this book help to reduce anxieties, raise hopes and foster collaboration.

Finally I would like to acknowledge those who have shared their experiences of dyslexia with me and helped in this way to contribute to the book—the staff at the Red Rose School, the school founders Dr Sionah Lannen and Colin Lannen, Shannon Green from Vancouver, colleagues at the CCET in Kuwait as well as the large number of teachers, psychologists, administrators and parents I have spoken with over the years. I would also like to thank Sir Jackie Stewart for writing the foreword to this book and for the dedication and conviction he has shown to helping develop the cause of dyslexia which has helped a great many parents and teachers to be more equipped and better able to meet the challenges of dyslexia at school and at home.

GAVIN REID
November 2008

Chapter 1

Defining Dyslexia

This chapter will:

- discuss the purpose of a definition for dyslexia;
- provide some pointers to indicate the current breadth of research in the area of dyslexia;
- examine factors influencing a definition;
- provide examples of definitions; and
- highlight the impact of different perspectives and agendas in developing an operational definition for dyslexia.

It is important to be clear when defining dyslexia. Often definitions can be general, vague and serve little real purpose. They can be misinterpreted and misused. Definitions need to be contextualised so that they are relevant to the teaching and learning context. This chapter will seek to provide some clarification on the use of definitions and highlight the need to consider an operational definition for dyslexia.

DEFINING DYSLEXIA

The question one needs to ask is: do we really need to define dyslexia and can we really encapsulate the features and the feelings that accompany dyslexia in a single statement? This point can be considered when one asks people with dyslexia questions such as 'what is dyslexia?' and 'what does it mean to you?' As part of the research for this book I asked some children and adults those questions! There was a considerable range of responses. Some of them are shown below:

'A problem transferring my knowledge into written work'

'For me it is frustration at not being able to complete tasks on time'

'Being different from everyone else'

'Wanting to read books but not getting past the first page'

'Having a bad memory and being so disorganised'

'Feeling different from everyone else'

'Inconsistency in my work—some days I get it right and other days I get the same thing wrong'

'I find it difficult to listen to the teacher for more than a few minutes'

The following comment came from a teacher who is dyslexic:

> *I do not define dyslexia as a bad aspect of my life, I would not be the person I am today if I did not have dyslexia as a part of my genetic and biological makeup. My characteristics of dyslexia have moulded my personality and the experiences and choices I have made in my life, for the good and for the bad. The negative aspects of dyslexia for me is the frustration, confusion and embarrassment I feel when I am involved with tasks which will highlight my difficulties—those which involve memory recall, sequencing, numbers and spelling. I will forget how to do things or misinterpret the instructions, particularly if they were given recently and quickly. The difficulties in being able to remember numbers is real and can cause problems, for example I do not know my parents', partner's or children's telephone numbers. I also find it very difficult to find my way around the alphabet and this affects me on a daily basis. However, it is important to try and keep dyslexia in perspective and see the positive effect it can have on my life. I feel I can empathise with my students and their parents/carers. It helps me to keep working to create accessible teaching resources and approaches; perhaps it feeds my creativity and the speed of ideas, planning and focus which I have. These benefits outweigh the negative aspects because they have enabled me to create effective strategies which help me to carryout the vast majority of tasks and responsibilities I have. Despite the embarrassment dyslexia can and does cause me, I function quite well in this society. But I appreciate that I am fortunate and have opportunities and support which others may not.*

Reading through these statements one feels struck by the emotional feelings attached to them—and that is the problem with a definition of dyslexia: it provides a definitive and descriptive response to what for many can be an area of emotional stress and personal conflict. Yet for education and research purposes a definition is necessary—to assist in developing identification and diagnostic criteria and to inform intervention. Definitions can help to provide a label. For many parents a label is necessary as it can help to kick-start the support process. For adults with dyslexia it can help them develop self-knowledge and eventually coping strategies. For teachers it can provide explanations as to why the child may not be responding to the intervention provided. A definition therefore can be an important catalyst in this process. The problem, however, lies in the lack of a universally accepted definition of dyslexia.

There are many different dimensions to dyslexia—dyslexia is not represented by a single entity, or caused by a single gene. Dyslexia is multifaceted and that can explain why a single universally accepted definition has not yet been achieved. It can be argued, however, that there is some agreement on the constellation of factors that can contribute to dyslexia, but controversy surrounds the respective weighting of these factors. Everatt and Reid (2009) highlight the range of factors that are currently associated with dyslexia:

- Structural and functional brain-related factors (Galaburda and Rosen, 2001; Hynd et al., 1995)
- Genetic factors affecting the developmental migration of magnocells in utero and influencing their subsequent function (Stein, 2008)
- Genetic correlations (Gilger, 2008)
- Procedural timing of sequences in task accomplishment (Fawcett and Nicolson, 2008)
- Processing speed (Wolf and Bowers, 1999)
- Inter-hemisphere transfer (Breznitz, 2008)
- Difficulty in automatising skills (Fawcett and Nicolson, 1992)
- Working memory difficulties (Jeffries and Everatt, 2004)
- Phonological deficit (Snowling, 2000)
- Language features—orthographic transparency (Wimmer, 1993; Share, 2008; Everatt and Elbeheri, 2008)
- Comorbidity between learning disabilities (Bishop and Snowling, 2004; Visser, 2003)
- Literacy achievement levels and the role of IQ in diagnosis (Siegel and Lipka, 2008; Joshi and Aaron, 2008; Wagner, 2008).

These are some of the factors that can influence our understanding of dyslexia, and each can have an impact on how dyslexia is perceived and how assessment and intervention are portrayed.

PURPOSE OF DEFINITIONS

Definitions of dyslexia, particularly those used by education authorities, school districts, voluntary organisations and associations, are abundant and some will be shown here. Often they serve some purpose and it is possible to categorise the type of function they serve:

- *Allocation*—used to allocate resources and develop provision. These would usually focus on discrepancies and provide some discrepancy criteria in order that those who need additional support and special provision could be readily identified.
- *Explanation*—explain to teachers and professionals how they may identify and intervene. These definitions may have a list of statements and characteristics and can merge into operational definitions which provide explanations of the difficulty and how it can impact on practice.
- *Understanding*—help parents and indeed the person with dyslexia understand what it is. It is difficult for a definition to actually do this. Often parents want to know the cause of a difficulty as this helps them more fully understand the extent of the problem and how it might be tackled. It is difficult to do this in a definition.

- *Research*—a research definition can help to provide a discrete and well-defined sample for researchers. This might include set criteria that are easy to measure, such as IQ scores and certain types of discrepancies.
- *Statement definitions*—these are becoming quite common where organisations have their own definition almost as a statement or a mark of status. Increasingly, organisations are seeking to have their own definition of dyslexia. This might be called a statement definition of the organisation, whether voluntary body, parent group or education authority.

HOW SHOULD WE DEFINE DYSLEXIA?

A number of definitions will be shown below—they each have some commonalities but there can also be a difference in the emphasis placed on different characteristics. For example, some will mention neurological factors, others focus on educational characteristics and yet others will make reference to identification criteria.

The definition that has been developed by the author for this book is shown below:

Dyslexia is a processing difference, often characterised by difficulties in literacy acquisition affecting reading, writing and spelling. It can also have an impact on cognitive processes such as memory, speed of processing, time management, co-ordination and automaticity. There may be visual and/or phonological difficulties and there are usually some discrepancies in educational performances.

There will individual differences and individual variation and it is therefore important to consider learning styles and the learning and work context when planning intervention and accommodations.

The main points in this definition are:

- *Processing difference*—this can highlight the differences between individuals and the need to use multi-sensory intervention strategies.
- *Difficulties in literacy acquisition*—without doubt this is one of the key areas as it is usually difficulties with reading that first alert the teacher or the parent. It is important to note that this can be in the form of decoding and encoding and in the production of written output.
- *Cognitive processes*—cognition means learning and processing information and it is this that can be challenging for students with dyslexia. This refers to how information is processed, which affects memory, processing speed, and the ability to retain and transfer information, to utilise prior learning and to develop automaticity. Good teaching can make an impact in relation to cognitive difficulties. First, however, it is necessary to identify the nature of the learning difficulties the child experiences.
- *Discrepancies in educational performances*—this is often one of the most obvious indicators of dyslexia. There can be a difference between the reasoning abilities and the processing performances. This means that students with dyslexia can solve problems and can reason but often they have difficulty in processing the information

and accessing the information to help them solve problems. Discrepancies in different areas of performance can often be noted and often this is very obvious between written and oral work.

- *Individual differences*—it is important to recognise that students with dyslexia are individuals and their individual learning differences need to be respected. Not all students with dyslexia will have the same profile, although they all can meet the criteria for dyslexia.
- *Learning and work context*—some learning and work contexts can highlight the person's dyslexic traits while others can minimise them. For example, if a dyslexic person is attempting to locate information from a library he or she may have difficulty in accessing an index, finding the appropriate book and locating the information in that book. Without guidance this kind of task can be challenging for students with dyslexia. Other tasks such as those that involve some degree of creativity or visual processing may be easier. Getting the task and the environment right for learning is important and highly important for the person with dyslexia.

This type of definition can pave the way for an operational definition. This next step would involve developing some of the points to show the actual characteristics and how these can be acknowledged in the classroom.

DEFINITIONS

What do definitions do?

- Provide some guidance to teachers and researchers.
- Provide information on the nature of reading difficulties.
- Lead to guidance on intervention.
- Develop a general awareness of dyslexia.

Box 1.1 What do definitions do?

But what **might** definitions do?

- Cause confusion because of the variation.
- Generalise a difficulty which in fact can be very individual.
- Mislead the public and practitioners.
- Provide little guidance for assessment or intervention.

Box 1.2 What might definitions do?

Reid-Lyon (1995) suggests that the lack of an appropriate definition has had an impact on research in dyslexia and this has resulted in a reliance on exclusionary criteria and lack of clear selection criteria for the sample being studied. He suggests that a definition must be governed by a theoretical view supported by substantial research and clinical evidence. This should be based on 'constructs' that can be measured directly and consistently, and should provide clear indications of how to identify whether a person is dyslexic. The International Dyslexia Association (IDA) definition was developed from this premise.

The International Dyslexia Association (IDA) definition is as follows:

Dyslexia is a specific learning disability that is neurological in origin. It is characterized by difficulties with accurate and/or fluent word recognition and by poor spelling and decoding abilities. These difficulties typically result from a deficit in the phonological component of language that is often unexpected in relation to other cognitive abilities and the provision of effective classroom instruction. Secondary consequences may include problems in reading comprehension and reduced reading experience that can impede the growth of vocabulary and background knowledge.

Adopted by the Board of Directors: November 12, 2002 www.interdys.org/FactSheets.htm

---

Box 1.3   IDA definition

Dyslexia is a specific learning difficulty which mainly affects the development of literacy and language related skills. It is likely to be present at birth and to be lifelong in its effects. It is characterised by difficulties with phonological processing, rapid naming, working memory, processing speed, and the automatic development of skills that may not match up to an individual's other cognitive abilities. It tends to be resistant to conventional teaching methods, but its effects can be mitigated by appropriately specific intervention, including the application of information technology and supportive counselling.

www.bdadyslexia.org.uk/whatisdyslexia.html, 2008

Box 1.4   BDA definition

Dyslexia is manifested in a continuum of specific learning difficulties related to the acquisition of basic skills in reading, spelling, and/or writing, such difficulties being unexpected in relation to an individual's other abilities and educational experiences.

Dyslexia can be described at the neurological, cognitive and behavioural levels. It is typically characterised by inefficient information processing, including

continued

difficulties in phonological processing, working memory, rapid naming, and automaticity of basic skills. Difficulties in organisation, sequencing and motor skills may also be present.

(Task Force on Dyslexia, 2001, p. 28)

See also Northern Ireland Task Force Report on Dyslexia: www.deni.gov.uk/dyslexia.pdf.

Box 1.5   Task Force on Dyslexia in the Republic of Ireland definition

Four points seem to emerge from the definitions above:

1. a recognition that dyslexia is developmental;
2. an understanding that the central characteristics relate to literacy;
3. an appreciation that different and special teaching and learning approaches are necessary;
4. an acknowledgement that there can be additional secondary factors associated with dyslexia.

Definitions can differ in how they phrase these points and much of that depends on the purpose of the definition. One of the important points, however, is the need to understand that it is crucial for education authorities to develop an operational definition that can be accessed and understood by teachers and parents.

An operational definition should:

1. provide a statement on dyslexia;
2. indicate precisely the identification criteria;
3. indicate how this criteria will be used, and by whom;
4. describe the kind of challenges the students will experience at different stages of schooling and in different areas of the curriculum;
5. indicate the type of supports that will be necessary;
6. provide pointers to resources, books, programs, approaches and technology that can be appropriate;
7. clearly define the roles of teachers, teaching assistants, management and support/resource teachers in carrying out intervention;
8. indicate the role that parents will/can play in the process of identification and support;
9. discuss the implications for preparing the student formal examinations and the types of additional supports and accommodations that can be made available to the student;
10. discuss the implications of curricular choice and curricular access and show how the school can accommodate the student's learning needs;
11. indicate the different levels of training the staff will require and show how these can be achieved;

12. indicate the long-term post-school study and career opportunities and show how the school will ensure that appropriate support and information are provided to student and parents.

It is feasible that these points can be developed and integrated into a policy for dyslexia. Many of these points can be seen in the Northern Ireland and the Republic of Ireland Task Group and Task Force documents (see www.deni.gov.uk).

Reid et al. (2005) found in a study involving all 32 education authorities in Scotland that almost all had some policy in dyslexia—nine had an explicit detailed policy, eight had a detailed policy in the area of specific learning difficulties that included other syndromes in addition to dyslexia and all the others mentioned dyslexia as part of a more generic policy of teaching and learning, e.g., 'Support for Learning Policy', 'Additional Support Needs Policy', 'Inclusive Education Policy'.

But an isolated definition of dyslexia that has not been expanded and contextualised for the learning and teaching context is of minimal value to teachers and perhaps also to parents. Even if education authorities do have a clear definition of dyslexia and have expanded that into an operational policy, there are still barriers that need to be overcome and barriers that can prevent successful implementation.

Crombie (2002a) developed a definition that focuses not on deficits but on accommodations:

> *Dyslexia is a difficulty with literacy which results in a person requiring a set of accommodations to be made to enable them to demonstrate their abilities. Accommodations can be defined as a set of enabling arrangements that are put in place to ensure that the dyslexic person can demonstrate their strengths and abilities and show attainment (cited in Clark (2003), p. 9).*

This type of definition can lead to identifying the barriers to learning in both policy and practice that can have some impact on the need to develop accommodations. The strength of this approach is that it is positive, focuses on teaching and learning and can be set within the classroom context.

BARRIERS TO IMPLEMENTING POLICY

Reid (2004) found that a number of barriers were identified by education authorities that could prevent the policy from being fully implemented. These included:

- concern over numbers of children requiring support;
- the number of requests for additional training;
- reluctance to label too early;
- lack of staff awareness that results in late identification;
- dyslexia is only one of a range of 'inclusion issues';
- lack of clarity of views on dyslexia;
- the 'waiting for an assessment' approach among some teachers is not helpful—they should be able to use their skills and experiences to intervene appropriately even if an assessment has not been conducted.

This latter point is of crucial importance. Teachers are at the front line and they have some responsibility for identification, and early identification in particular, but they can only do this successfully if they have sufficient training and opportunities to follow this up. This is important, as early identification is usually a key factor in an operational definition and overall policy strategy.

ROSE REVIEW AND DYSLEXIA

The area of dyslexia has been the subject of government investigations and initiatives and these have certainly increased during the past decade. The ministerial statement from the UK government in May 2008 (see follow-up to the Rose Review in the UK (July 2008, www.dcsf.gov.uk/jimroseanddyslexia)) indicated that this is because there is now a significant body of scientific research substantiating the various neurological and cognitive components of dyslexia and that this can indicate that special consideration is needed for intervention. This point has not escaped many of the voluntary and professional organisations on dyslexia which collaborated to provide a joint response to the UK government on the Rose Review. The government response indicated that in order to encourage schools' development of best practice in improving outcomes for children with dyslexia, they had provided funding of around £1m over three years to the 'No to Failure' project which, they indicated, is a 'trailblazing' initiative, and additionally they will be evaluating the impact of specialist training for teachers and specialist tuition for children with dyslexia in some schools in three local authority areas. Additionally, they have provided substantial funding to the British Dyslexia Association and Dyslexia Action to run further Partnership for Literacy pilots and develop resources for parents and teachers. These points will be discussed later in this book in the chapters on assessment and intervention, but it is important to note the response to this statement from the voluntary and professional organisations. They indicated that 'our organisations strongly believe that the country should be implementing a simple system where each school would have one teacher trained as a dyslexia/SpLD specialist who can recognise and support children with dyslexia/SpLD. This expertise is already widely available from dyslexia centres, specialist teachers and a number of independent schools who have for many years been providing effective support for dyslexic children in reading, writing, maths, and concentration. Each review and pilot merely adds to the delay in implementing the solution. They have been getting it right for years. We want to see this in all schools in the public sector'. So although there is now more acceptance of the concept of dyslexia, there is still some disagreement and some anxiety that appropriate assessment and intervention procedures are not in place.

EDUCATION FOR LEARNERS WITH DYSLEXIA

'Education for Learners with Dyslexia' is the title of a report published in Scotland (HMIE, 2008) following a lengthy inspection of provision for dyslexia by Her Majesty's Inspectorate of Education (HMIE). Over the period 2007–2008, the

Inspectorate undertook a broad evaluation of provision for children, young people and adults with dyslexia in Scotland. The investigation identified the range and quality of provision in Scotland across all sectors. The Inspectors visited a number of pre-school centres, primary, secondary, independent and special schools, Scotland's colleges and faculties of education in Scottish universities. The key issues raised in the survey of education authorities included:

- the views held and the description of dyslexia used by education authorities;
- the range of provision, including early intervention schemes, specialist units and resources, and specialist teachers;
- teaching approaches, programmes and technological support used across the authority;
- opportunities for staff to undertake training and professional development related to dyslexia; and
- the number of teaching staff with specialist qualifications.

The investigation found that the majority of education authorities adopted a range of approaches which reflected a shared understanding of the way young people learn. The learning and teaching approaches used by most authorities included:

- metacognitive approaches;
- small group and one-to-one teaching;
- reciprocal teaching;
- scaffolding;
- reading recovery;
- synthetic phonics;
- structured phonics programmes.

The report indicated that parents' involvement in their children's review of progress was a particularly strong point of the current practices. Other areas that were considered strengths included:

- the knowledge and approachability of most support for learning staff in linking with parents and providing appropriate curriculum support; and
- learning strategies which helped students to overcome difficulties independently.

The report, however, recognised that there were a number of areas for development. These included:

- involving parents and young people in setting targets in IEPs;
- delays in obtaining an assessment of children who may have dyslexia;
- delays in providing the right support for children with dyslexia;
- raising awareness among parents of difficulties associated with dyslexia and helpful support strategies.

Staff views about how teacher-education institutions could develop their contribution to preparing teachers to meet the needs of students with dyslexia included more time needing to be spent on teaching students how to teach reading. It was interesting to note that most newly qualified teachers reported that they did not have sufficient awareness of the issues relating to dyslexia or a secure grasp of methodology and strategies that could be used to teach literacy and numeracy skills to all children. It is also interesting to appreciate the view expressed in the report that the lack of consensus across universities about what dyslexia is has to be seen as an area for development. It is crucial that there should be uniformity and consensus in this aspect as it is important that new teachers entering the profession have a uniform and consistent induction to dyslexia irrespective of which teacher education establishment they attended. This situation is not confined to Scotland—the same controversies would apply to other areas in the UK and in the USA. Moats (2008) indicated this clearly when she studied how prepared university professors were to teach areas such as dyslexia and reading. Her results indicated that in some cases they had less knowledge than some of their students.

The Scottish report indicated that a mix of views as to what dyslexia actually is prevailed throughout Scotland. Although the majority of authorities found the British Psychological Society's (BPS, 1999a) view helpful, many schools, colleges and universities held a range of perspectives on dyslexia. The report suggests that such 'a mix of views can cause confusion for newly qualified and practising teachers. Teachers and learners should have updated, accessible and practical advice on dyslexia and its impact on young people including co-occurrence with other additional support needs' (p. 34). The recommendation was that the Inspectorate would work with education authorities and the Scottish government to produce examples of best practice in dealing with dyslexia. This is an excellent approach as it ensures dissemination of good practice. There is no doubt that there are some excellent examples of practice in the UK and elsewhere but these need to be identified and disseminated.

DIFFERENT PERSPECTIVES AND AGENDA

There are also differences within the groups of professional practitioners and researchers. Fawcett (2002) suggests that one of the major tensions in dyslexia research has in fact been the range of potentially conflicting viewpoints. These viewpoints have emerged from 'researchers and practitioners; parents and teachers; teachers and educational psychologists; schools and local education authorities; local education authorities and governments—all have different agendas, and much of the time this forces them into opposition'. It is interesting to note that the working party of the BPS that was convened to provide guidance on assessment for psychologists was not able to settle the controversy, although it did make a number of recommendations which have been followed up by psychological services. Also, the definition indicated by the BPS working party is widely used, although it generated some controversy at the time.

Different perspectives can often become an issue when a new intervention is being advocated and may not have wide appeal. This was the case with the controversy over the implementation of, and the research studies examining, an exercise programme—The Dore Programme (see Reynolds and Nicolson, 2007). This became an international issue and the debate centred around issues regarding:

- the debate over mainstream versus alternative interventions;
- the use of commercially directed interventions in schools;
- approaches that use the media to generate evidence of success;
- the extent of the scientific background that has helped to generate the new approach;
- the nature of the trials that have been implemented to examine the implementation and the success of the approach;
- the reference of the approach in peer reviewed journals; and
- the availability of the approach to all who might benefit from it.

Some of the points above are encapsulated in the journal issue indicated above and highlight the anxiety parents and teachers can experience over dyslexia and the need and the responsibility for education authorities to provide information and evaluative comment on the approaches in use and to recognise that new and alternative approaches may have something to offer. The point that any new approach must be scientifically validated is essential before any approach can be used in schools. But at the same time it is important that education authorities are open to new approaches, are able to listen to the wishes of parents, and appreciate that the dynamic nature of the field of dyslexia means that new approaches and different perspectives can emerge and that these need to be considered.

POINTS FOR REFLECTION

- What is the value of a definition of dyslexia? What purpose might it serve?

- The importance of an operational definition.

- The barriers in practice that can prevent policy from being fully and effectively implemented.

- How dyslexia might fit into policy and practice for effective teaching and learning.

- What is the role of teacher education in relation to reading and dyslexia? To what extent is this role being fulfilled?

- The issues that can stem from new and sometimes controversial approaches. Why does dyslexia generate the anxiety and the emotional fervour that can be felt in debates on new approaches?

- How can these issues be resolved to the satisfaction of the different groups which may each have different agendas and priorities?

Chapter 2

Explaining Dyslexia: The Range of Research

There have been significant advances in research in dyslexia over the past 20 years. This has helped to provide explanations of dyslexia and these have resulted in new initiatives in policy and practice. These aspects are covered in a number of chapters in this book and were also referred to in Chapter 1. The impact of the results of research has been far-reaching and a number of new tests, assessments procedures and teaching methodologies have resulted. Yet it can be argued that there is still no clear explanation that is universally accepted of what exactly constitutes dyslexia. Identification is still riddled with controversies despite the emergence of a number of new tests to identify dyslexia, or sub-components of dyslexia. There is still a debate, for example, on how IQ tests can inform a diagnosis—if at all (Siegel and Lipka, 2008). There is also an ongoing debate on the validity of dyslexia as an identifiable syndrome or whether it is a part of the continuum of reading difficulties (Elliott, 2007). Elliott suggests that 'as yet, nobody has been able to demonstrate scientifically that there is this subgroup of poor readers that should be termed dyslexic. There are all sorts of reasons why people don't read well but we can't determine why that is. Dyslexia, as a term, is becoming meaningless' (*The Times*, 27 May 2007; www.timesonline.co.uk/tol/life_and_style/health/features/article1847619.ece).

This chapter will discuss some of the main areas of research on dyslexia from Europe, the United States, Canada, the Middle East, Australia and New Zealand. This research indicates that dyslexia is a global concern and that it is also an area where significant collaborative studies have taken place. Many of these have involved joint initiatives, with researchers from different countries and continents working together. International organisations such as the International Dyslexia Association (www.interdys.org), the Learning Disabilities Association of America (LDA) (www.ldanatl.org), the British Dyslexia Association (www.bdadyslexia.org.uk), research organisations such as International Academy for Research in Learning Disabilities (www.iarld.com) and reading researchers such as those from the Society for the Scientific Study of Reading SSS-R (www.triplesr.org) have all been instrumental in international collaborative initiatives.

Because of the complexities and the significant number of studies focusing on different aspects of dyslexia, it is useful to have some framework for understanding and discussing dyslexia. The causal modelling framework (Morton and Frith, 1995) is seen as a useful guide as it incorporates the neurological dimensions and the cognitive/learning dimensions as well as those related to practice—the educational dimensions—and these areas cover the research dimensions in dyslexia. Additionally, the framework takes into account the need to consider the environment and particularly how the environment can influence the other dimensions. This is especially important as environmental influences (and cultural factors) are extremely important and can have as powerful an effect on learning outcomes as cognitive programmes and reading intervention.

CAUSAL MODELLING FRAMEWORK

The three levels indicated by Frith can also provide a useful guide as they incorporate the perspectives of a range of professionals and each group can have different priorities and interests. For example, the teacher and psychologist will be interested in the behavioural and cognitive dimensions while the neurologist/psychologist will be interested in the neurological and biological factors. Frith (2002) states that 'the important point is that at all three levels interactions with cultural influences occur'. It is important to consider this additional element to this framework, as cultural and environmental factors are influential in today's society and these factors will be discussed elsewhere in this book.

Causal Modelling Framework: an Explanation

Frith (2002) suggests that a causal modelling framework involving three levels of description—behavioural, cognitive and biological—can help to clarify some of the issues relating to the concept of dyslexia. Frith (2002) suggests that dyslexia is a neuro-developmental disorder with a 'biological origin and behavioural signs which extend far beyond problems with written language' (p. 45). The discussion of the research in the remainder of this chapter will broadly follow the causal modeling framework but it needs to be appreciated that one of Frith's points about the framework is that it should be seen as being fluid and flexible and incorporating overlapping dimensions. This means that some aspects such as phonological processing can have an impact on all three—neurological, cognitive and educational dimensions.

GENETIC FACTORS

A considerable amount of research activity has focused on the genetic basis of dyslexia. Gilger et al. (1991) estimate that the risk of a son being dyslexic, if he has a dyslexic father, is about 40%. Much of this work has been focused on the heritability of reading sub-skills and particularly the phonological component. Gilger indicates the complexity of utilising and relying on data derived from genetic studies. This can be noted in the following genetic regions which Gilger suggests are implicated in some way in dyslexia: 1p36, 2p16-p15, 2p11, 6p22.2, 7q32, 11p15.5, 15q21, 13, 16, 2q. He also suggests that these regions can be responsible for different aspects of the reading and writing process such as: reading and verbal ability, single-word reading, spelling, phoneme awareness, phonological decoding, pseudo as well as non-word reading and writing, IQ, language skills, rapid naming and verbal short-term memory.

It can be noted from the above that there is a significant number of factors and studies identifying different areas of the genotype and relating this to different aspects of reading and literacy (the phenotype). Gilger (2008) acknowledges that this broad perspective of the impact of genes on learning and literacy needs to be accounted for and that one needs to be wary of studies that make sweeping generalisations based on genetic evidence. Nevertheless, there is strong evidence that genes do have an impact on dyslexia and there will be children who are 'genetically at risk' of dyslexia. This point is important as it can provide pointers for early identification.

Many of the gene studies do indicate the presence of a possible site for 'dyslexic genes'; many of these are found in Chromosome 6. Significantly, they may be in the same region as the genes implicated in autoimmune diseases that have been reported to show a high level of association with dyslexia (Snowling, 2000). In a longitudinal study Gallagher et al. (2000) found more than half the at-risk group of children aged 6 scored below average compared with a control group on literacy tasks. Castles et al. (1999) found a strong heritability element among 'phonological dyslexics' and Olson et al. (1994; Olson and Byrne 2005) also found a strong heritability component both for phonological decoding and orthographic skills. Familial risk is therefore a useful indicator of dyslexia and is supported by prevalence rates (Molfese et al., 2008) which show how the advances in the field of genetics research highlight the search for the underlying genetic basis of dyslexia.

NEUROBIOLOGICAL FACTORS

The advances in magnetic resonance imaging (MRI) and other forms of brain imagery such as positron emission tomography (PET) are increasingly being used to observe the active processes within the brain as well as brain structure. These have been of great benefit to neuroscientists investigating factors relating to dyslexia. From these studies a number of different factors have emerged focusing on structural and functional brain-related factors. Some of these are discussed below.

VISUAL AND TEMPORAL PROCESSING

Singleton (2009) reports on the concept of visual stress and shows how it can interfere with the ability to read. It can also affect the development of fluent decoding of text and good reading comprehension. He argues that if visual stress is not identified and dealt with early on, children are at risk of remaining unskilled readers, particularly when trying to understand longer and more complex texts. The most widely supported theory of visual stress is that it is the result of a general over-excitation of the visual cortex due to hypersensitivity to contrast or pattern glare. Wilkins's theory (2003) is that the visual cortex functions normally until strong physiological stimulation results in stimulation of neurons that are close together. These neurons share inhibitory neurons and hence normal inhibitory processes will be compromised if they all fire together because the availability of inhibitory neurotransmitters is reduced. The outcome is the triggering of other neurons that signal movement or colours, which are consequently experienced as illusions or hallucinations.

Whiteley and Smith (2001) estimated the prevalence of visual stress in dyslexics to be in the region of 50%. Using ViSS, a computer-based screening tool for visual stress, Singleton and Henderson (2007) found that 41% of dyslexic children in their sample showed high susceptibility to visual stress; the corresponding figure for the non-dyslexic control group was 23%. White et al. (2006) found that 35% of their sample of dyslexic children aged 8–12 years met criteria for visual stress, while only 18% of the non-dyslexic control group matched for non-verbal IQ met criteria for visual stress. These findings raise an important issue on the relationships between dyslexia and visual stress.

MAGNOCELLULAR VISUAL SYSTEM

Singleton (2009) also suggests that the research on the magnocellular visual system can also be related to visual stress. There are two types of cell found in the neural tracts between the retina and the visual cortex: *magnocells* are large cells that code information about contrast and movement; *parvocells* are smaller and code information about detail and colour. (The magnocellular system is also sometimes known as the *transient system*, and the parvocelluar system as the *sustained system*.) Cooperation between these two systems enables us to perceive a stationary image when we move our eyes across a scene or a page of text. When reading, the eyes do not move smoothly across the page but in a series of very quick jumps (saccades) in order to fixate successive portions of the text. During saccades, which typically take about 20–40 milliseconds, vision is suppressed.

Stein (2008) provides evidence that the development of magnocellular neurones is impaired in children with dyslexia. He argues that the visual system provides the main input to both the lexical and the sublexical routes for reading and therefore vision should be seen as the most important sense for reading. One of the main discoveries about the visual system made over the past 25 years, according to Stein, is that the different qualities of visual targets are analysed, not one after the other in series, but by separate, parallel pathways that work simultaneously moving forwards in the visual brain. Stein shows that there are two main kinds of retinal ganglion cell, whose axons project all the visual information back to the brain. Ten per cent of these are known as mangocellular cells because they are noticeably larger than the others and cover a 50 times greater area than those of the much more numerous, but much smaller, parvocells. He therefore suggests that the great variety of visual, phonological, kinaesthetic, sequencing, memory and motor symptoms that are seen in different dyslexics may arise from differences in the particular magnocellular systems that are most affected by the particular mix that each individual dyslexic inherits. These factors, discussed in relation to the magnocellur system and visual stress, can have implications for practice. Stein (2002) has also highlighted convergence difficulties and binocular instability as factors that could affect the stability of the visual stimuli when reading. In terms of intervention, even simple procedures such as the use of coloured overlays can in some cases make a difference. For example, Kriss and Evans (2005) found that 45% of dyslexic children read 5% faster with an overlay, compared with 25% of non-dyslexic control children; when a more conservative criterion of 8% increase in reading speed with an overlay was applied, these figures dropped to 34% and 22%, respectively. Wilkins (1995) has also shown how some dyslexic children and adults may benefit from coloured overlays due to difficulties in some visual processes. Everatt (2002), in a comprehensive review of visual aspects relating to dyslexia, suggests that the visual representation processes, the magnocellular system, factors associated with visual sensitivity and coloured filters, and eye movement coordination can each account for the visual difficulties experienced by people with dyslexia. Everatt suggests that the diversity of the visual deficits that can be identified needs to be clarified, as it may be that the visual-based difficulties derive from the same underlying cause. It should also be noted that not all those diagnosed as dyslexic present visual deficits, and indeed some people who are not dyslexic present evidence of visual deficits.

Furthermore, Stein's (2002) view on the role of the magnocellular system appears to implicate aspects of various complementary theories such as cerebellar immaturity (Fawcett and Nicolson, 2001, 2008) and deficits in essential fatty acids (Richardson, 2002). Other visual intervention strategies are discussed later in this book in the chapters on intervention.

PROCEDURAL TIMING

The lateral zone of the cerebellum is an area that has generated interest over its apparent role in cognitive processes and it has also been implicated in dyslexia (Fawcett and Nicolson, 2008). In terms of its formation, the cerebellum is one of the first brain structures to begin to differentiate, yet it is one of the last to achieve maturity as the cellular organisation of the cerebellum continues to change for many months after birth. According to Fawcett and Nicolson (2008), there is now extensive evidence that the cerebellum is a brain structure particularly susceptible to insult in the case of premature birth, and that such insults can lead to a range of motor, language and cognitive problems subsequently. Fawcett and Nicolson (2008) argue that the cerebellar deficit hypothesis may provide a single coherent explanation of the three criterial difficulties in dyslexia—reading, writing and spelling. They argue that this can place dyslexia research within a meaningful context in terms of the cognitive neuroscience of learning while maintaining its position as a key educational issue. They also suggest that the cerebellar deficit hypothesis provides an explanation for the overlapping factors between dyslexia and the other developmental disorders.

One of the functions of the cerebellum is in the precise timing of procedures (e.g., several motor movements) that accomplish some sort of behavioural response or task performance. This timing of sequences may play a critical role in making task accomplishment or behavioural skills automatic. Indeed, a critical aspect of learning a skill may be to make its accomplishment automatic. This means that the skill can be carried out without the individual giving it too much thought—and resources can be used to undertake other behaviours or processes simultaneously. For most adults and children, the ability to walk, talk and possibly read and write may be partially or completely automatic. Consequently Fawcett and Nicolson (2008) put forward the hypothesis that dyslexic children would have difficulty in automatising any skill (cognitive or motor). They suggest that reading is subject to automaticity, and since all dyslexia hypotheses predict poor reading as a factor in dyslexia then the automatisation deficit hypothesis would be valid in relation to dyslexia. Fawcett (1989) and Fawcett and Nicolson (1992) argue that there is clear support stemming from a set of experiments in which they asked dyslexic children to do two things at once. If a skill is automatic, then the children should have been able to do two or more tasks at the same time. These findings strongly suggested that dyslexic children were not automatic, even at the fundamental skill of balance. For some reason, dyslexic children had difficulty automatising skills, and had therefore to concentrate harder to achieve normal levels of performance. This has clear implications for teaching and learning in that there will be a significant need for over-learning to be utilised with children with dyslexia in the classroom.

HEMISPHERIC SYMMETRY

According to Geschwind and Galaburda (1985), the difficulties in processing information shown by people with dyslexia are due to structural differences between the hemispheres, and this likely develops in the prenatal period. This view has received considerable support from subsequent studies. Knight and Hynd (2002) are of the opinion that the principal findings to emerge from these studies suggest that misplaced cells may be present in some areas of the brain, particularly the outer layer of cortex, which is usually cell-free. According to Galaburda and Rosen (2001), these misplaced cells can be found predominantly in the left hemisphere in areas associated with language. They also note differences in the primary visual and auditory cortex, where differences in neurons and patterns of cellular symmetry can also be noted. This, they suggest, could provide a neural explanation for some of the visual, auditory, sensory and perceptual difficulties that some researchers, such as Fitch et al. (1997) and Zeffiro and Eden (2000), propose are associated with dyslexia.

Brunswick et al. (1999) reported that the PET scans of young dyslexic adults while reading aloud and during word and non-word recognition tasks showed less activation in the left posterior temporal cortex than controls did. These findings suggest that there may be processing differences indicating some deficits in left hemisphere processing among children and adults with dyslexia. Paulesu et al. (1996, 2001) suggest that current theories of dyslexia favour a neuro-cognitive explanation. They suggest that at a neurological level people with dyslexia may have microscopic cortical abnormalities in the form of cortical ectopias and dyslamination of cortical layers.

Reading is a complex activity that involves the interaction of multiple sensory systems and brain networks. Research findings such as those mentioned above can have implications for how the individual accesses print. The implications of this for teaching and learning to read have been the focus of the model proposed by Bakker (1979, 1990). Bakker (1990) and Robertson and Bakker (2002) called this model the 'balance model' of reading. It has been replicated in different countries (Robertson, 2000). Bakker identified different types of reader—'perceptual' and 'linguistic'—each with a different hemispheric preference, and each of these preferences has implications for teaching. The 'perceptual' reader has a right hemisphere processing style and may have good comprehension but poor reading accuracy. On the other hand, the 'linguistic' reader utilises the left hemisphere and reads accurately, but in some cases may be over-reliant on the left hemisphere and may not show the comprehension level of the 'perceptual' reader. Wood (2000) suggests that reading is concerned with translating stimuli across all modalities and that fluency is the key factor in reading acquisition. He cites the role of the visual cortex in reading, which, he asserts, is multimodal as it will accept input from both auditory and visual modalities. The brain, he argues, is high in visual-spatial skills, and this also aids the understanding of information with high phonetic complexity. Since reading is essentially mapping across modalities, according to Wood, then alternative languages such as music and visual graphics are helpful. In short, Wood suggests that our brains are better equipped for reading and more adaptable than we have given them credit for.

PROCESSING SPEED

Breznitz (2008) presents the 'Asynchrony Phenomenon' as a means of explaining dyslexia. This implies that dyslexia is caused by a speed of processing gap within and between the various entities taking part in the word decoding process. Breznitz and colleagues devised a programme that attempted to train the brain to process information at a faster speed. Implementing this programme resulted in a substantial improvement among dyslexic children in the speed at which information was processed (Breznitz and Horowitz, 2007). They also suggested that this improvement was successfully transferred to other material not included in the training programme.

Breznitz (2008) also claims that dyslexic learners exhibit difficulties when transferring information from one hemisphere to another. These differences in inter-hemisphere transfer among dyslexics may stem from information decay in the corpus collosum, or a long non-symmetrical delay in inter-hemisphere transfer time. Shaul and Breznitz (2007) measured information transfer between the left and right hemispheres among dyslexics as compared to regular readers when performing various lexical decision tasks. They found that among dyslexics information arrived in the right hemisphere first, and was then transferred approximately 9–12 ms later to the left hemisphere. Among regular readers, the information arrived in the left hemisphere first and was transferred to the right approximately 4–6 ms later. They also supported these results from source localisation of brain activity in these two reading groups during the word decoding process using low resolution electromagnetic tomography (LORETA). Comparisons between groups revealed greater activation among dyslexic readers between 110 and 140 ms for words, mainly in the right temporal and perisylvian regions, as well as some activation in medial frontal regions. These findings can have significant implications for the classroom, particularly in how information is presented and the pace of lessons in class.

PHONOLOGICAL PROCESSING

There is substantial evidence that the acquisition of phonological skills is crucial for successful reading and that difficulties in acquiring phonological skills are the cause of dyslexia. This perspective has been derived from the substantial evidence that difficulties in phonological processing, particularly when related to phonological decoding, have been a major distinguishing factor between dyslexics and non-dyslexics from early literacy learning to adulthood (Vellutino et al., 2004; Snowling, 2000; Bruck, 1993; Elbro et al., 1994; Rack et al., 1992) and that early phonological training (together with suitable linkage to orthography and literacy experience) improves word literacy and reduces the likelihood of literacy difficulties (Bryant and Bradley, 1985; Elbro et al., 1996). Children who find it difficult to distinguish sounds within verbally presented words would be predicted to have problems learning the alphabetic principle that letters represent sounds, and these would be the children who are most likely to be dyslexic based on the phonological deficit hypothesis.

Hagtvet (1997) and Lundberg (2002), in Norwegian studies, showed that a phonological deficit at age 6 was the strongest predictor of reading difficulties. Other studies have shown speech rate to be a strong predictor of dyslexic difficulties, and this is reflected in the development of the Phonological Abilities Test (Muter et al., 1997; Hatcher and Snowling, 2002).

PHONOLOGICAL AWARENESS AND MULTISENSORY PROGRAMMES

In educational settings there has been considerable activity in the study of phonological awareness in relation to dyslexia. This is reflected in the development of assessment and teaching materials such as the Phonological Abilities Test (Muter et al., 1997), the Phonological Assessment Battery (Frederickson et al., 1997), the Dyslexia Screening Tests (Fawcett and Nicolson, 1996) and the Listening and Literacy Index (Weedon and Reid, 2001). Additionally, there are many phonological teaching approaches, such as Sound Linkage (Hatcher, 1994), the Phonological Awareness Training Programme (Wilson, 1993), the Hickey Multisensory Teaching System (Combley, 2001) and the Multisensory Teaching System for Reading (Johnson et al., 1999).

Wise et al. (1999) conducted a large-scale study using different forms of 'remediation' and found that the actual type of phonological awareness training was less important than the need to embed that training within a well-structured and balanced approach to reading. Adams (1990a, b) argues that combining phonological and 'whole language' approaches to reading should not be seen as incompatible. Indeed, it is now well accepted that poor readers rely on context more than good readers (Nation and Snowling, 1998). Language experience is therefore as vital to the dyslexic child as is a structured phonological awareness programme. This is particularly important in the secondary education sector where it may be inappropriate to provide a phonologically based programme for a dyslexic student. Here the priority may be on language experience, print exposure and comprehension activities.

MORPHOLOGICAL PROCESSING

Deacon et al. (2008) argue that there is extensive evidence of morphological difficulties in dyslexic readers. They provide evidence from Leikin and Zur Hagit (2006) who argued that this interpretation is implicit in the research demonstrating two findings: a deficit in morphological awareness in dyslexics and a contribution of morphological awareness to reading that is independent of phonological awareness. Yet, they indicate that few, if any, researchers would explicitly argue that poor morphological awareness is a causal factor in the development of dyslexia. The probable line is that phonological difficulties are the primary deficit, and that these in turn cause both morphological and reading problems. Deacon et al. also suggest that central deficits, other than phonology, have been nominated as causes of both morphological and some forms of reading difficulties. They argue that one possibility is that dyslexics have deficits in morphological awareness due to general language delays since morphology is considered to be a sensitive indicator of language ability. They therefore indicate that based on this point the vast majority of current views indicate that morphological processing weakness is secondary to primary deficits in some other domain (e.g., general language skills or phonological processing).

It is important to appreciate the role of morphology in reading as the use of morphological information may help to speed access to print. This has implications for reading experience as morphological skills can come from greater reading experience. In fact Abu-Rabia et al.'s (2003) examination of the acquisition of Arabic orthography found that, following phonological awareness, morphological awareness was the most powerful predictor of reading ability. Similar results come from a study of English second-grade poor readers, for whom morphological awareness predicted reading comprehension beyond phonological and orthographic knowledge (Nagy et al., 2003). If phonological awareness is the source of both morphological awareness and reading difficulties for young poor readers, then it would be unlikely for morphological awareness to account for distinctive variance in reading. Deacon et al. suggest that one possibility is that dyslexics' difficulties with morphological processing (at least in comparison to chronological age matches) may originate in their more fundamental phonological difficulties. Yet, according to Deacon et al., phonological difficulties are unlikely to be the sole explanation of difficulties with morphological and reading tasks. The research suggests that morphological awareness as independent, at least to some extent, of phonological abilities needs to be considered. Leikin and Zur Hagit (2006) articulated this when they noted that 'dyslexic readers are forced to resort to morphological decomposition for lexical access since their decoding abilities are not developed and processing the word as a whole is slow and inefficient' (p. 486). Such differences can be viewed as an over-reliance on morphological information in lexical access. This means that morphological processing might be a relative strength in comparison to a phonological weakness.

The implication of taking the role of morphological processing into account is that if the phonological route is not successful then literacy training may at some point need to rely more heavily upon other routes, such as the morphological route to build up word recognition skills. The research conducted by Deacon et al. is important, as it shows that teaching should integrate phonological and morphological instruction for children and adults with dyslexia. It is important to recognise this, as morphological processing is typically characterised as a late-emerging ability that builds on the core foundation of phonological knowledge (Ehri, 2005). It appears, therefore, that morphology may actually provide a compensatory avenue of instruction for dyslexics and, as Deacon et al. suggest, may be the means by which some individuals have overcome dyslexia.

GLUE EAR

Peer (2005, 2009) has developed a strong argument emphasising the need to acknowledge glue ear syndrome as an influential causal factor in dyslexia. She cites evidence from Friel-Palti and Finitzo (1990) which suggests that hearing loss during the first two years of life may result in a delay in emerging receptive or expressive language or both. Additionally, Gravel and Wallace (1995) maintain that although communication skills may appear normal for this group of children on entry to school, other auditory-based deficits may emerge in the classroom situation. They, and others, suggest that there are weaknesses associated with listening comprehension, academic achievement and even attention and behavioural difficulties. Peer argues that 'glue ear' is an ongoing condition for large numbers of children, meaning that they experience significant hearing loss over a lengthy period of time. This may also lead to a lack of concentration as well as an inability to process the fine sounds that are necessary for auditory perception and speed of processing which is a major key to language learning. Furthermore, it does seem to be prevalent. When investigating numbers of children affected by repetitive bouts of the condition, Daly (1997) noted that when investigating school-based incidence, the numbers are as follows: Japan—4–15%; USA—12%; Denmark—16–22%; UK—20–30%; Spain—8%; Kuwait—31%. These figures appear to be significantly higher than would be expected. Peer (2002) recorded that of 1000 people identified as dyslexic, 703 had experienced the condition to such a serious extent that they had undergone surgery. She also indicates that there appears to be a strong link with coexisting allergies, particularly to milk, highlighting a possible weakness in the auto-immune system. Some of the symptoms/characteristics identified by Peer (2009) are shown in Table 2.1.

Peer suggests that glue ear can affect phonological processing and processing speed and cause frustration when learning. She also suggests that this can have considerable implications for bi-lingual learners. Peer strongly supports the view that there is a need to identify and provide for children experiencing dyslexic-type difficulties as early as possible if they are to make the greatest progress in their language and learning, and that the same is necessary for those who have experienced glue ear. It is important that proactive steps should be taken to prepare the child in the prerequisites for learning

Table 2.1 Symptoms/characteristics of glue ear

- Early speech, language or communication difficulties
- Confusion of letters and/or words especially when young
- Mishearing words in speech
- Difficulty in following a conversation/lesson/lecture when background noise is present
- Difficulties learning additional languages
- Spelling difficulties—omission of letters/sounds or phonetically spelled words
- Reading weaknesses—single word, pseudoword, comprehension
- Poor pragmatic language—children missing nuances of language, e.g., question mark
- Poor written expression
- Omission of words
- Incomplete multisyllabic words or sentences
- Confusion of tenses
- Poor use and understanding of words, expressions and terminology
- Delay in understanding subject specific terminology
- Weak general knowledge
- Tiredness and weariness
- Distractibility
- Lack of concentration
- Frustration
- Feelings of insecurity
- Difficulty following instructions
- Social isolation and loneliness
- Lack of understanding of playground rules

Source: Peer, 2009; reproduced with permission

such as phonological skills, development of language and listening and memory skills if glue ear is diagnosed or suspected.

COGNITIVE SKILLS

Dyslexia is essentially a difference in processing information and cognitive factors such as memory and speed of processing difficulties are important at both the cognitive and the education level. These can involve phonological processing as noted above, memory, processing speed and other factors relating to learning. Wolf (1996; Wolf and O'Brien, 2001) highlights the 'double deficit' hypothesis indicating that dyslexic people can have difficulties with both phonological processing and naming speed. It is interesting that speed of processing and semantic fluency are included in some of the popular tests for dyslexic children. Badian (1997) shows evidence for a triple deficit hypothesis, implying that orthographic factors involving visual skills should also be considered.

METACOGNITION

The role of metacognition in learning is also of great importance as this relates to the learner's awareness of thinking and learning and can have considerable implications for how we understand the needs of children with dyslexia (Burden, 2002; Reid, 2001b). Tunmer and Chapman (1996) have shown how dyslexic children have poor metacognitive awareness and how this leads them to adopt inappropriate learning behaviours in reading and spelling. It is important, therefore, to examine the processes that the child used in order to obtain a response. It may be that these processes or steps taken to complete the task were inefficient and ineffective. Chinn (2002) highlights this in relation to mathematics and Wray (2002) in relation to creative writing.

ENVIRONMENTAL FACTORS

The environment is an influential factor in learning. This implies that social and cultural factors can impact on the outcomes of the learning experience. The environment includes the learning context in the classroom, the school and the community and this has an influence on both learning and teaching. It is important, therefore, to consider the individual learning styles and cultural preferences of the learner as well as the policy and ethos of the school. These factors can help to provide a supportive environment that will have a profound influence on the outcome of the learning experience for students with dyslexia.

ADDITIONAL LANGUAGE LEARNING

It is recognised that dyslexic students often suffer from problems reading and writing in a foreign language (Sparks and Ganschow, 1993; Schneider and Crombie, 2003; Dal, 2008; Schneider, 2009). Dal (2008) suggests that one of the major breakthroughs in this field was undoubtedly the discovery of the necessity to relate and analyse the language the learners themselves develop and use during the process of learning. This language, according to Dal, is identified as the interlanguage. The idea of interlanguage is founded upon the assumption that a foreign language learner, at any particular moment in his or her learning sequence, is using a language system which is neither his or her first language, nor the foreign language. It is a third language, with its own grammar, its own lexicon and so on. The rules used by the learner are to be found in neither his or her own mother tongue, nor in the target language. One can define the interlanguage as an emerging linguistic system that has been developed by a learner of a foreign language and who has not yet become fully proficient but is only approximating the target language: preserving some features of the mother tongue in speaking or writing the target language and creating innovations. By recognising the interlanguage, both the research and the teaching of foreign language need to focus more on the learner's needs and ability to communicate a message in the target language. Tal suggests that dyslexic students not only have problems learning grammar and how to write a foreign language but also experience severe difficulties with phonological coding—that is, converting symbols to sounds and sounds to symbols and forming a representation in memory. This is likely to have far-reaching effects on their foreign language learning and their ability to develop an active interlanguage. To help dyslexic students overcome their problems and to develop their interlanguage Dal provides some areas of focus—these include the following:

1. phonological processing (poor grasp of sound, lack of awareness of individual sounds within words);
2. memory (working memory might be limited, there may be inaccurate representations in long-term memory);
3. auditory discrimination (uncertainty of the sound which has been heard, difficulty in discrimination between similar sounds, difficulty in knowing where a spoken word ends and a new word begins);
4. sequencing (getting things in order e.g., letter order in words);
5. speed of processing information (tendency to be slower in responding to incoming information);
6. visual discrimination/recognition (poor ability to differentiate between similar looking words).

In a multinational survey conducted in primary schools in Austria, Denmark and Iceland, Dal et al. aimed to identify what schools could do to help dyslexic students participate in language classes, what language teachers do to help dyslexic students in language classes, what specific tools are used to help dyslexic students and what the language teachers see as the main problems of the dyslexic students learning a foreign language (Dal et al., 2005). The results of the survey indicate that, in general, the schools' policy is to include dyslexic students in foreign language classes but it was noteworthy that there was a huge variation within schools in each country and there was a discrepancy between the countries in the study. According to Dal et al., the results suggest a need to make the problems of dyslexic students in foreign language classes much more transparent in the official policy of the schools.

Dal et al. suggest that the research indicates that the problems dyslexic students experience in learning a foreign language are closely related to written and oral skills in their mother tongue, and that although most language teachers and schools acknowledge that dyslexic students might have difficulties learning a foreign language, the policy of inclusion means that little special provision is made for them in language classes and that many language teachers are unsure how to best teach them.

DYSLEXIA IN DIFFERENT ORTHOGRAPHIES

Everatt and Elbeheri (2008) suggest that the manifestation of dyslexia may vary across different languages and, as such, is not language independent. Languages vary in the way their orthography represents phonology and therefore Everatt and Elbeheri claim that one of the main features that may determine the manifestation of dyslexia across languages is variability in orthography. In some orthographies, this relationship is relatively simple: there is close to a one-to-one correspondence between the written symbol (grapheme) and the basic sound (or phoneme) that it represents. In other orthographies, this correspondence is less transparent. A letter may represent several sounds, and a particular sound may be represented by different letters, depending on the context within which the letter or sound is presented. The English orthography is the best example of this less than transparent relationship between letters and sounds; there are many English words that may be considered irregular or exceptions, based on the typically taught correspondence between graphemes and phonemes. German, in contrast, is relatively transparent for both reading and spelling (see discussions in Wimmer, 1993; Zeigler and Goswami, 2005). Although there are some exceptions (the length of vowel representations may require some more complex rule learning, for example), once the relationships between basic written symbols and sounds have been learnt, German written words should be pronounced with a good degree of accuracy. These cross-transparency differences pose a potential threat to the universality of the phonological deficit viewpoint. At the very least, in order to account for such findings and retain phonological deficits as the main characteristic of dyslexia across languages, the phonological deficit hypothesis may have to incorporate more than phonological awareness weaknesses as a characteristic feature of the deficit.

More regular orthographies may require assessments of literacy skills that test speed of reading rather than accuracy, and measures of speed of reading may be better predicted by measures of speed of processing, such as rapid naming tasks, rather than measures of phonological awareness. Arabic orthography suggests that literacy learning difficulties may be best predicted on the basis of assessment procedures that include measures of phonological processing, including phonological awareness. They suggest that orthography transparency can be a useful predictor of variability across languages in literacy learning.

SELF-DISCLOSURE IN ADULTS

One important consideration is the self-awareness that people with dyslexia have of dyslexia and how this might impact on them in education and in the workplace. One of the key indicators of the level of self-awareness can in fact be gleaned from studies on self-disclosure. Price and Gerber (2008) report on a number of studies in relation to self-disclosure and they themselves have developed a protocol to measure this and to identify reasons why students with dyslexia are reluctant to disclose the nature of their difficulties. Many of the studies in this area relate to adults. Roffman et al. (1990) assessed the effectiveness of a college course for greater disability awareness. They found that greater self-understanding led to willingness to disclose in social and employment settings. On the other hand, Lynch and Gussel (1996) explored disclosure and self-advocacy in post-secondary students with learning disabilities and found that they feared stereotyping and attribution of unfounded characteristics associated with learning disabilities. Vogel and Adelman (2000) investigated former college students 8–15 years past graduation. They discovered that 41% chose not disclose on the job, and if they did it was for the purpose of obtaining job accommodations. Self-disclosure is important because it is a very important element of self-determination. Often people with dyslexia have to be self-advocates and take a lead role in determining the outcomes of workplace accommodations.

Price and Gerber (2008) suggest that the following factors should be considered in the self-disclosure:

- Self-disclosure is driven by context and situation.
- Self-disclosure is the management of personal information.
- Self-disclosure is nestled in the larger concept of self-determination.
- There is risk in self-disclosure.
- Disclosure 'protects' in some contexts.
- Disclosure must include information and not just the label.
- Disclosure is just the beginning.

As Price and Gerber suggest, self-disclosure 'is the "opening gambit" of a process housed under the umbrella of self-determination, but driven by very skilful self-advocacy skills'. Research studies focusing on self-advocacy and self-disclose are important additions to the literature on dyslexia because they directly relate to the individual.

POINTS FOR REFLECTION

- How useful is the research on dyslexia—how might it impact on your practice?

- Consider how the causal modelling framework can fit into your practice—to what extent can it offer an explanation for dyslexia that fits into both policy and practice?

- Given the wide range of areas that can be implicated in understanding dyslexia described in this chapter, consider the importance of perceiving dyslexia within a 'learning' paradigm rather than a 'literacy' one. How appealing is this broader view of dyslexia?

- How important would you consider the environment to be in both identification and intervention for dyslexia? Consider your own learning environment and how suitable it is for learners with dyslexia.

- Consider the importance of examining dyslexia in different orthographies.

- Self-disclosure is an important consideration—how might you help a young person with dyslexia achieve this? Consider how important it might be to spend some time focusing on this aspect.

Chapter 3

Assessment: Issues and Considerations

POINTS TO CONSIDER

Assessment of dyslexia can be a contentious and hotly debated issue. Much of this has to do with the recognition of the syndrome of dyslexia and the characteristics that represent that syndrome. The debate on this was referred to in Chapters 1 and 2, but as there are different views on what constitutes dyslexia this will impinge on the nature and the processes involved in assessment. Additionally, there is the hotly debated issue on the use of IQ tests as a measure for identifying dyslexia. This will also be discussed in this chapter. The use of IQ as a key component of an assessment for dyslexia has been an ongoing issue for a number of years. There is now, in many countries, a quest for teachers and schools to take more ownership for assessment and the identification of needs.

Baroness Mary Warnock, in a foreword to a book (Came and Reid, 2008) on assessment that specifically looks at the role of the teacher in the assessment process, indicated that 'every teacher in every school has the responsibility for noticing a child's problems, assessing precisely what he can and cannot do, and then providing support to help him, or seeing that it is provided by someone else'. She goes on to say that 'if this were done early enough, in many cases the difficulties could be overcome. A child frustrated by an inability to learn, or do something that others seem able to do gets deeper and deeper into trouble. Not only does he fall behind his contemporaries academically, but school becomes a misery. To remedy this sort of disaster for individual children is the avowed purpose of Government, as evidenced in Every Child Matters, and, in Scotland, Getting it Right for Every Child'. These points indicate the importance of teachers taking ownership of assessment as early as possible and that early identification is crucial to prevent the spiral of failure that so often accompanies the school performances of students with literacy difficulties. This chapter and indeed this book takes the view that identifying and meeting needs is a whole school responsibility and that it should not rest in the hands of one individual but essentially be part of a multidisciplinary and collaborative effort to work together for the common good of all children in school.

Ideally an assessment should be able to identify the child's learning needs within the learning context. This means that the assessment should involve more than focusing on the child, but also on the task, the curriculum and the learning and teaching context.

It can be argued that assessment should be dynamic; that is, it should involve more than a description of the child's cognitive abilities and attainments, and provide a full picture to incorporate aspects about the learning situation and the learner as well.

It is important to develop specific aims for an assessment and the process that the assessment should follow. It is important that assessment is not seen as a one-off interaction but as a process that takes place over time. For that reason it is important to develop a framework for the assessment, and this can be adapted depending on the purpose and nature of the assessment. To develop both aims and a framework a number of key questions need to be addressed. These can be categorised as the following—what, why, how, and the effect of assessment.

What is one looking for when conducting an assessment? In relation to dyslexia one may be looking for a specific pattern of cognitive difficulties, such as difficulties in organisation, sequencing, speed of processing, memory and motor difficulties. A pattern of difficulties in attainments in literacy may also be focused on, such as difficulties in phonological awareness, word recognition, spelling rules, visual errors in spelling, letter and word confusion with similar-sounding words and omissions of words, parts of words and individual letters and sounds.

DISCREPANCY CRITERIA

Joshi and Aaron (2008) argue that reading disability (dyslexia) has been traditionally diagnosed on the basis of a discrepancy between IQ scores and reading achievement scores. They, however, advocate a procedure based on the 'discrepancy model'. They suggest that, when implemented, the discrepancy model-based diagnosis of reading disability results in two categories of poor reader, one whose disability is expected because of their low cognitive ability, and the other unexpected. They also believe that despite its long history, the discrepancy-based procedure has recently fallen into disfavour because of its many drawbacks. One of the problems of the discrepancy model is that IQ is not a good predictor of reading scores because the correlation between IQ and reading achievement scores seldom exceeds 0.5. Furthermore, they argue that the relationship between IQ and reading performance is reciprocal rather than unidirectional. One of the most serious problems, they suggest, is that the discrepancy-based diagnosis does not lead to recommendations regarding remedial instruction.

According to Joshi and Aaron (2008), decoding, which is the ability to pronounce the written word, is a skill that is independent of general intelligence (Spearman's 'g' factor), which is what intelligence tests measure. Decoding is described as 'low level processing skill' and comprehension as 'higher level processing skill' by Carver (1998), Catts and Kamhi (2005), and de Jong and van der Leij (2003). Understandably, therefore, the correlation between a skill and general intelligence is low. Despite this, the use of IQ–achievement difference in the diagnosis of reading problems has become deeply entrenched in many educational systems. This policy has also been officially endorsed by the American Psychiatric Association which, in its *Diagnostic and Statistical Manual of Mental Disorders* (DSM-IV; APA, 1994, p. 74), defines reading disability as 'Reading achievement, as measured by individually administered standardized tests of reading accuracy or comprehension, is substantially below what is expected, given the person's chronological age, *measured intelligence*, and age-appropriate education'.

LISTENING COMPREHENSION

Aaron (1991), Savage (2001) and Stanovich (1991) have proposed a measure of listening comprehension in the place of IQ scores for diagnosing dyslexia. Joshi and Aaron argue that, as a diagnostic tool, listening comprehension does not have the many limitations of IQ. The advantage of using listening comprehension is that the diagnostic findings based on listening comprehension can lead to recommendations regarding remedial instruction. It is interesting to note that Wood et al. (1988) obtained an impressive coefficient of correlation of 0.78 between reading and listening comprehension for groups of children with learning disabilities. This can make the listening comprehension measure for children with reading difficulties more attractive. Additionally, Joshi et al. (1998) found that, among a group of fourth-grade children, the coefficient of correlation between IQ and reading comprehension was 0.36, whereas the correlation coefficient between reading comprehension and listening comprehension of these children was 0.69.

COMPONENTIAL MODEL OF READING

Joshi and Aaron therefore propose an alternative model for diagnosing and treating reading disability in the place of that based on IQ–reading score discrepancy. The proposed model for diagnosing and instructing children with reading difficulties is based on the Componential Model of Reading, which focuses on the source of the reading difficulty and targets remedial instruction at the source of the reading problems.

They suggest that the Component Model has an influence on the acquisition of literacy skills in three domains: the cognitive domain, the psychological domain and the ecological domain.

The cognitive domain of the model has two components: word recognition and comprehension. The psychological domain includes components such as motivation and interest, locus of control, learned helplessness, learning styles, teacher expectation, and gender differences. The ecological domain includes the following components: home environment and culture, parental involvement, classroom environment, dialect, and English as a second language.

Decoding skills can be assessed with the aid of a test of non-word reading and a test of spelling. Non-words are also referred to as pseudowords; *daik* and *brane* are examples of non-words.

Listening comprehension can be assessed by more than one test and, consequently, results can vary somewhat depending on the test used (Joshi et al., 1998). One test that has both listening and reading comprehension subtests is the Woodcock Language Proficiency Battery in which both comprehension subtests were normed on the same population and are in the same cloze format. This makes reading and listening comprehension comparable. The Diagnostic Achievement Battery (Newcomer, 1999) and the Wechsler Individual Achievement Test-II (WIAT-II; Wechsler, 2001) also have subtests of listening comprehension. The aim of this model is to identify a discrepancy between decoding and listening comprehension. This model has many attractive features, particularly since the tests that are used are accessible by teachers and do not rely on IQ, and the results can inform teaching.

CURRICULUM FOCUS

At the same time the focus for the assessment can also be on the curriculum, and one may be looking for an explanation as to why a particular child is having difficulty in a specific area of the curriculum and perhaps not another. For example, why may the child be experiencing difficulty in English, but not History or Geography or Science? These are questions that would need to be investigated, and this investigation is as important as individual cognitive and other child-focused assessments. For example, Dargie (2001) suggests that in order to read effectively in History, learners must be able to decode, contextualise and analyse a range of types of text such as diaries, letters, recorded oral testimony, press journalism, posters, leaflets, official documentation such as Acts of Parliament and government reports.

Each textual genre, according to Dargie, can be challenging and may be couched in a specific language format that will not exactly aid comprehension. Moreover, History courses often additionally require learners to be comfortable with this variety of textual types across a range of chronological and cultural contexts. This is an example, therefore, of why it is important to look at the actual demands of the curriculum as well as the abilities of the learner.

The assessment should also identify particular strategies or resources that can help to access the curriculum for a particular child, and for that reason it is important to focus part of the assessment on the actual curriculum. This in fact can be achieved through curriculum-focused teaching approaches that may have strands and targets built into the teaching process.

WHY AN ASSESSMENT?

Why should an assessment be carried out and what purpose does this serve?

Although there may be a number of different reasons why an assessment is required, there are usually some common factors. The assessment may be used for diagnostic purposes in order to provide information that may account for the child's difficulties in learning. At the same time the assessment may be used as a predictive tool in order to obtain some information that can help the teacher predict how the child will cope with particular aspects of the curriculum. Used in this way, however, the information from the assessment may in fact be misused since it may lead to unnecessary curricular restrictions being placed on the child. This, indeed, is one of the misuses of IQ tests since the case may arise where a child assessed as having a low IQ is disadvantaged in terms of curricular access and expectation, and, of course, this should be avoided at all costs.

The assessment may be used in a 'normative' way by comparing the child with his or her peers. Again some caution should be applied, although it may be useful to obtain some kind of data in relation to how the child is progressing in relation to others in the same chronological age range.

If the child has already been assessed, then further assessment can contribute to monitoring and review. This is an important element of any assessment since it assists in measuring the effects of teaching. Assessment should be linked to teaching. There can be a prescriptive element to assessment in that it may offer some suggestions for teaching approaches or programmes.

If there is a suspicion that the child may have dyslexic difficulties and the assessment is being conducted to discover if this is indeed the case, then feeding back this information, particularly to the parents, is essential. If the difficulties are to be effectively tackled then it is important that the school, the parents and the child should be working collaboratively. This is particularly important as research undertaken by Heaton (1996; Riddick, 2009; Reid et al., 2008) indicates the relief that parents often experience following the many months of uncertainty prior to a formal assessment.

HOW—THE ASSESSMENT PROCESS

The issue of how an assessment should be conducted is an important one. It is necessary to access a range of assessment strategies and not simply opt for one particular type of assessment or test. Indeed, although there are a number of tests—'dyslexia tests'—there is actually no single test for dyslexia. In fact, Tunmer (1997) suggests that the best contemporary psychological assessments may draw on 20–30 individual test results. In a Scottish study involving all 32 education authorities, Reid et al. (2005) found that over 50 different tests/assessment strategies were used to assess for dyslexia.

Essentially, assessment to identify dyslexia involves a process, not a test. It is important to ensure that a test, and the manner in which the results are used, is valid. Clearly, how one tackles the assessment depends to a great extent on the purpose of the assessment. For example, standardised tests, although these may be limited in terms of diagnostic information, can provide useful information with which to measure progress.

It is useful to have a battery of strategies prepared, or an assessment framework that can accommodate and be adapted to the school context. Such a framework is provided in some detail in the Report of the Task Force on Dyslexia (2001). In the report there is a Phased Process of Assessment that suggests details of procedures, tests and strategies that can be used by the teacher: Phase 1 (ages 3–5), Phase 2 (ages 5–7), Phase 3 (ages 7–12), Phase 4 (age 12 onwards). In each of the phases, indicators of dyslexia are provided as well as guidance to the teacher on which aspects should be considered and what the tests should be attempting to identify as well as the possible outcomes of reviews. This aspect of the document without doubt represents a clear framework for the identification of dyslexia.

It is essential to link assessment, teaching and the curriculum. Assessment, therefore, should not be conducted in isolation, but within the context of the curriculum, the child's progress within the classroom and his or her particular learning preferences. It is, therefore, important to look at the process of learning—the strategies used by the child—in addition to the product; that is, the actual outcomes or the attainment level.

Many forms of assessment that look at attainments can be described as static, in that they test what the child can do without assistance. Assessment, however, can also be provided with an additional dynamic dimension, thus allowing the assessment process to be used more flexibly. It has been argued (Campione and Brown, 1989) that when conducting an assessment the teacher should not be asking, 'what can the child do?' but 'what do I need to do to help the child successfully complete the assessment?' The help that is necessary to facilitate the correct response from the child should be noted. Thus, the teacher is focusing on the process of the assessment, not the product or the outcome of the assessment.

EFFECT OF AN ASSESSMENT

A consideration throughout the assessment process is the effect of the assessment—the assessment outcome for the child, the family and the school. It is important to ensure that the assessment provides information that can be readily linked to a teaching programme or that can be used to help the child cope more effectively with the curriculum. It is also important to bear in mind that a formal assessment, by necessity, provides a 'spotlight' on a particular child, and the child, understandably, quickly becomes aware of this. The assessment, therefore, should be implemented judiciously in order that the child is not exposed to any feelings of failure additional to those already resulting from his or her particular difficulties. The assessment should uncover data that will help in the development of a teaching programme.

The assessment should, however, also uncover some explanations for the child's difficulties and look for particular patterns, such as errors that may be due to visual, auditory, motor, memory or some other cognitive difficulties. These may be identified as a specific pattern. The unearthing of a pattern of difficulties can help the teacher decide on the nature of the child's difficulty and so can assist in the planning of appropriate programmes of work.

ASSESSMENT—POINTS TO CONSIDER

It can be useful to consider the questions above—the why, what, how, and the effect of the assessment—before deciding what form the assessment process will take. It may be useful to consider the following:

- identification of the learner's strengths and weaknesses;
- indication of the learner's current level of performance in attainments;

- an explanation for lack of progress;
- identification of aspects of the learner's performance in reading, writing and spelling, which may typify a 'pattern of errors';
- identification of specific areas of competence;
- identification of student's learning style;
- understanding of the student's learning strategies;
- an indication of specific aspects of the curriculum and curriculum activities that ma interest and motivate the learner.

SOME OTHER CONSIDERATIONS

Self-concept

The identification and assessment of dyslexia is of crucial importance since a full assessment will facilitate the planning of appropriate intervention that will help to prevent the child from becoming engulfed by a feeling of learned helplessness.

Preventing, or at least minimising, such failure removes the threat that intransigent learning difficulties will become so deeply embedded that they not only penetrate the affective domain and in particular the child's self-concept but also result in inappropriate reading styles embedded within the child's learning pattern.

Clearly, therefore, assessment should consider the child's self-concept. Every effort should be made to ensure that the difficulties displayed by the child and the underlying problems do not detract from the development of skills in learning and in access to the curriculum. At the same time, feedback to the child needs to be handled very carefully.

Hales (2001) discusses the hidden effects of dyslexia and suggests that while much research has gone into developing methods of addressing the obvious effects of dyslexia in relation to reading, writing and spelling, much less has been done with the less visible aspects such as anxiety, loss of confidence and low self-esteem. Hales argues that there is a tendency to address the 'mechanics' of the difficulty because these are more obvious and more directly problematic in day-to-day life. The supposition is that if the practical problems of reading and spelling could be solved then dyslexic people would be in a better position to tackle the way they felt. Yet, Hales argues that this is a false premise and that a number of research studies show that a high level of anxiety and frustration is a consistent factor in relation to dyslexia.

He suggests that the difficulties of dyslexia cannot be addressed in isolation from other factors and that there is a reciprocal relationship between learning and living and in particular how each affects the person's self-concept. Hales suggests that the effect on dyslexic children participating in school produces an almost immediate drop in self-confidence, and that their self-confidence begins to fall almost from the start of formal education and does not return to even approximately its original level until school-days are nearly over. Reid and Kirk (2001) discuss the cycle of 'disaffection, defiance and depression' and provide evidence from a number of studies to suggest that people with dyslexia, and in particular teenagers, are particularly vulnerable and that the whole aspect of self-esteem needs to be carefully considered and managed. This point is also supported by Hales, who suggests that the vulnerable period of transfer from primary to secondary is one that needs careful attention.

Hales (2001) describes various strategies that the dyslexic young person can adopt. These include denial, which can be deliberate or indeed unconscious according to Hales. Children with dyslexia do not want to be different, and this may lead to denial and counterproductive feelings. The result of this is usually a lowering of self-esteem, as the person knows they are not facing the reality of the situation.

Another strategy or reaction, according to Hales, is the denial of responsibility—this can lead to pointing the blame at others or indeed not adjusting to the demands of school and perhaps society. On the other hand, some dyslexic children react by overcompensating, by trying to be 'perfect', and become heavily involved in extracurricular areas and often achieve acceptance and popularity in this way. This, however, may not be possible and some children can become the 'class clown'.

This can, of course, result in difficulties with authority. Eventually, this can become a 'learned behaviour' and an automatic reaction to a situation of stress. This may lead to the cycle of defiance and deviance described by Reid and Kirk (2001) and the lasting situation of the effect of the 'scars of dyslexia' described by Osmond (1994).

According to Hales, the situation can arise when the 'group' rejects the individual and the person realises that he or she is no longer the leader—or even a member of the group. This realisation can also lead to lowering of self-esteem.

This may help to explain why dyslexic children and young people have difficulty in dealing with many of the pressures often associated with learning and the classroom, such as the 'pressure to keep up' and being told to read aloud in front of their peers.

This can result in feelings of inadequacy (Riddick, 1995a, b, 2002). Chapman and Tunmer (1997) found that students aged 5–7, who were having problems with reading, were also developing a 'negative self-concept' where reading was concerned. They suggested that this had a negative influence on the individuals' 'actual attainment' and progress within the academic setting.

The Role of Parents

Reid et al. (2008) suggest that parents value good communication with the school and dialogue with teachers who are knowledgeable on dyslexia. But parents nevertheless can have a number of anxieties relating to the need for their children to reach his or her potential. It is important, therefore, that parents are seen to have a key role in identifying needs and throughout the assessment. This will help to strengthen the communication process between home and school which has been shown to be of significant importance in measured outcomes of progress in literacy (Shaywitz, 2003; Mittler, 2002; Reid, 2004).

Riddick (1996) shows that advice from parents is helpful to decide how best to provide feedback to the child following an assessment.

What role, therefore, can parents play in an assessment? Parents usually know their child very well and can note, for example, the differences in the learning pattern and skills between different children in the same family. They may note that one child, for example, may take longer to master the alphabet, may be more reluctant to read than others, may be more forgetful, maybe even a bit clumsier. Many of these things can be quite normal and merely highlight the normal individual differences between children—even children in the same family.

But if parents are concerned, it is usually for a reason and every professional and individual needs to treat that concern seriously. Parents may be concerned if they know someone with dyslexia, or have read about dyslexia, and see some similarities between these observations and descriptions and their observations of their own child. Communication between home and school is vitally important in both the identification and the support of the young child with dyslexia.

Wearmouth and Reid (2002) suggest that one of the major challenges facing teachers of students with dyslexia is the need to fully appreciate and understand the perspectives and the experiences of the student. Ideally, this should be tackled in a positive and meaningful way. They suggest that students should have more scope for self-advocacy. This, of course, can be uncomfortable and difficult for the teacher to manage. Wearmouth and Reid suggest that self-advocacy in this way can run counter to more traditional models of teaching and learning. Many of these traditional models, in fact, place an emphasis on conformity and 'fitting in' to the established pattern of the school and education system. Students' views are not always sought, but in the case of dyslexic children it can be highly desirable to obtain such views. Self-advocacy, therefore, should not be seen as a threat to classroom control and class discipline, but as a positive and welcome aspect relating to the emotional and social well-being of the child.

It is also important that the child has some awareness of dyslexia, what it is, and how it may affect learning and subject and career choice. Ideally, dyslexia should place no limitations at all on the child, particularly if the school system is an inclusive one. It is, therefore, beneficial and perhaps essential that time is taken to explain to the dyslexic child exactly how he or she can cope with dyslexia and any difficulties that may arise from this. The child may be concerned with any stigma, real or imaginary, that may arise from the label dyslexia. There may well be a need to educate not only some members of staff about what dyslexia is but also some of the child's peer group. Friendship and acceptance by a child's peer group is of high importance to the child, and this should be acknowledged in the assessment and preparation of any individual programme that is developed following the assessment.

ASSESSMENT AND INCLUSION

Peacey (2001) suggests that children with special educational needs do not always require different teaching approaches, but what is crucial is that the school and the teacher utilise the best possible teaching approaches based on what has been seen and known to work. Peacey suggests that the key aspect of inclusion is a vision of 'teamwork within school communities, teamwork within local authorities, and other systems of management and, indeed, teamwork supported by government ministers' (p. 25). The success of an inclusionary system, however, demands more than teamwork and Peacey stresses strongly that the learning environment is vitally important.

The quality of the environment, the way that everybody feels about the place in which they work, has real importance. An assessment, therefore, needs to consider the learning environment and, in particular, aspects of the school and the school climate as well as the need for teamwork. These are key factors in the fully inclusive school. This view is also supported by Wearmouth (2001), who suggests that the learning environment can potentially create barriers to or facilitate literacy development, and one of the complex challenges for those planning programmes to address dyslexic students' learning needs is to focus on this aspect. In relation to the assessment process Wearmouth suggests that this challenge can be met by focusing on the characteristics of the individual student, the perspectives of the parents and the school, and the planning of programmes that take account of all these perspectives, which can then be embedded into the whole school curriculum within an inclusive school.

THE BILINGUAL LEARNER

Landon (2001) suggests that for bilingual learners the problem may lie with the system as well as the lack of sensitive instruments to diagnose dyslexia in this population.

He suggests that inclusion of bilingual learners requires recognition and positive accommodations in relation to both language and culture. He suggests that if schools fail to appreciate this, it will likely lead to poor standards of literacy development. If this is the case, Landon argues, the school need look no further to explain the literacy difficulties that bilingual learners have—by definition, they simply are unable to meet the standards. This would imply that any concern as to whether a child is dyslexic is immaterial. The language and the cultural needs of bilingual learners need to be met within the education system, and this needs to be considered within an assessment. Indeed, the Task Force on Dyslexia (2001) noted that there were no Irish (the language) norms for many of the test instruments in general use and no recently developed, standardised norm-referenced tests of reading in Irish. The report recommended that the Department of Education and Science should seek to remedy this and the cultural appropriateness of testing and intervention materials.

Everatt and Elbeheri (2008) argue that the nature of the assessment can differ for different languages and this needs to be taken into account. They suggest that one of the main features that may determine the manifestation of dyslexia across languages is variability in orthography. Despite commonalities in literacy learning across languages, they maintain that there is evidence that the factors which predict literacy learning, and can distinguish the dyslexic from the non-dyslexic, may vary across languages. For example, a more transparent orthography has been found to lead to increased accuracy in literacy in the early years of acquisition. Assessments of literacy skills within such orthographies, therefore, according to Everatt and Elbeheri, have often focused on rate/speed of reading rather than reading accuracy. They use the Arabic language as an example and the need to take culture- and linguistic-specific criteria into account. Current data, they maintain, suggests that measures of reading accuracy and phonological awareness can be useful in distinguishing ability differences amongst Arabic children, even in the initial grades of formal learning, and that awareness measures may be more predictive of early literacy levels than measures of rapid naming.

POINTS FOR REFLECTION

- Why is it important to consider the learning context when undertaking an assessment? Reflect on how this might be achieved in your work context.

- Consider why assessment for dyslexia can be so controversial

- Consider the role of the teacher in the assessment process.

- What do you understand by the term discrepancy criteria in relation to assessment?

- In what way might the componential approach to assessment be an attractive model to use?

- What might you see as the key points to consider in an assessment?

Chapter 4

Identifying Needs

This chapter will provide an overview of the criteria for the identification and assessment of dyslexia. It was noted in the previous chapter that identifying dyslexia involves more than selecting and administering a test. It should be seen as a dynamic process rather than a static one and the process needs to consider a number of factors, such as an indication of the implications of the learner's profile for the individual, the school or college, the parents and the family, and for subject and career choice. There are therefore wide-ranging implications that can arise from an assessment for dyslexia. It is important to discuss these implications with the parents and, if appropriate, with the learner.

Much of the information that is needed for an assessment cannot be gathered from the administration of a basic checklist, or indeed from a snapshot assessment using a standardised test. Assessment is a dynamic process, and ideally this process should involve a range of strategies and be conducted in the learning context and over a period of time. The use of background information can help to provide a fuller picture, but ideally the person or team conducting the assessment should have information about the curriculum, the teaching approaches and the learning context.

Some of the criteria that need to be considered for an assessment include the following:

- the reasons for the assessment;
- the nature of the assessment;
- what the assessment may reveal;
- age and stage of the child;
- the learning pattern and cognitive style of the child;
- cognitive factors associated with learning and dyslexia;
- previous history;
- information from parents;
- assessment of the curriculum;
- information on attainments;
- metacognitive factors; and
- how the assessment can link with intervention and the curriculum.

Some of this information may vary depending on the child, the school and the country. Different countries can operate different principles in relation to the purposes and processes of an assessment for dyslexia.

Information-processing should be a key focus of an assessment and this is essentially a cognitive activity. This means that how information is presented (input), how the information is understood, memorised and learnt (cognition), and how it is displayed by the learner (output), which of course can be in a written mode, are each important parts of the cognitive processes in learning.

The factors within the information-processing cycle are important in relation to dyslexia because children with dyslexia often have difficulty in actually receiving the information (input), particularly if it is provided verbally. This can have implications for the use of standardised tests, which are often administered verbally, and the child has to process the information using the auditory modality.

Similarly, there is much evidence that children with dyslexia can have difficulties in relation to cognition. Cognition refers to how children think and process information in order to understand it, how they relate the information to previous knowledge and how it is organised and stored in long-term memory. Since these areas can represent difficulties often associated with dyslexia, there is a tendency to focus on these cognitive factors.

The other factor associated with dyslexia and information-processing is the output of information. It is interesting to note that often children with dyslexia do not reveal their full ability in tests because responding to test items involves immediate responses, some of which are in written form and all of which have to be delivered without any help from the examiner. Yet, children with dyslexia often respond well to cues and 'information steps' to help them engage in the line of thinking that will elicit the correct response. But, in standard tests this type of help is not permitted because the norms and conventions of tests are the same for all children; this fact ignores the nature of the difficulties experienced by dyslexic children. It is therefore reasonable to suggest that a one-off, snapshot, cognitive-type assessment will not provide a fully accurate picture. It can, however, provide sufficient information for an experienced and trained teacher, psychologist or other professional to put forward a strong hypothesis relating to the child's processing and attainment pattern, and to make connections between this and the presence of dyslexia.

It is important, therefore, to reiterate at this point that the identification and assessment of dyslexia is a process. This process should be conducted over time and should include curriculum aspects, learning factors and observations made within the teaching and classroom environment as well as information from parents.

FACTORS THAT CAN PROMPT CONCERN

Pre-school

Concern may be raised in a pre-school child if some of the following are present:

- forgetfulness;
- speech difficulty;

- reversal of letters;
- difficulty remembering letters of the alphabet;
- difficulty remembering the sequence of letters of the alphabet;
- there is a history of dyslexia in the family;
- coordination difficulties (e.g., bumping into tables and chairs);
- tasks that require fine-motor skills such as tying shoelaces;
- slow at reacting to some tasks;
- reluctance to concentrate on a task for a reasonable period of time;
- confusing words which sound similar.

School Age

- Reluctance to go to school
- Signs of not enjoying school
- Reluctance to read
- Difficulty learning words and letters
- Difficulty and phonics (sounds)
- Poor memory
- Co-ordination difficulties
- Losing items
- Difficulty forming letters
- Difficulty copying
- Difficulty colouring
- Poor organisation of materials

After Around Two Years at School

- Hesitant at reading
- Poor word-attack skills
- Poor knowledge of the sounds and words continued
- Difficulty recognising where in words particular sounds come from
- Spelling difficulty
- Substitution of words when reading (e.g., bus for car)

Upper Primary

As above but also:

- behaviour difficulties;
- frustration;
- may show abilities in other subjects apart from reading.

Secondary

- As above
- Takes a long time over homework

- Misreads words
- Wants others to tell him or her information
- Poor general knowledge
- Takes longer than others in most written tasks

LINKING ASSESSMENT WITH THE PLANNING OF INTERVENTION

It is vital that the approaches and strategies selected for assessment provide the information needed to facilitate the implementation of appropriate teaching approaches. This means that careful preparation and planning are necessary before embarking on assessment, and the questions relating to what, why, how and effect must be addressed at this planning stage and reviewed throughout the assessment.

In many countries 'individual educational programmes' (IEPs) are drawn up following an assessment. These are important, and it must be emphasised that although dyslexic children share common aspects they are still essentially individuals. Each assessment needs to be discussed and intervention planned to meet the needs of that individual. The actual learning environment and the curriculum experienced by that child also need to be considered.

According to Tod and Fairman (2001), the key aspects of IEPs include:

- the provision for diverse needs embedded in whole-school practice;
- the need for formative reflection and analysis rather than merely summative reporting;
- student and parent involvement;
- the use of a variety of instructions;
- rigorous evaluation of the effectiveness of additional or otherwise extra support;
- the sharing of responsibility for special educational needs' support with other adults;
- peer involvement; and
- collaborative multi-agency planning.

If the above factors are to be products of the assessment then the process of assessment will need to be planned to ensure that it is possible to implement a programme with the information that will be gathered.

COMORBIDITY

Comorbidity is a term often used to describe the overlap that may exist between different specific learning difficulties. It has been suggested (Richardson, 2002) that this term is not a useful one, and that referring to the descriptive features of the different conditions would be more appropriate. This concurs with developmental work (Weedon and Reid, 2002, 2008) that identified 18 specific learning difficulties with specific characteristics. These data have contributed to the development of an assessment tool called

SNAP (Special Needs Assessment Profile). This has not only highlighted the distinctive features of different specific learning difficulties, but also the overlap between them.

ASSESSING PERFORMANCES

An assessment needs to consider the student's performances in the classroom situation. Although valuable data can be gathered from cognitive assessment, this should be accompanied with information on how the individual performs in relation to the different components of the curriculum. Curriculum-focused assessment can be diagnostic and preventative. It does not necessarily focus on the child's deficits, but can identify strengths; and, if noted, these strengths can form the basis of a subsequent teaching programme. Crombie (2002a) suggests what she describes as a 'solution based' approach to assessment. This implies that students' performances within the curriculum should be the measuring tool for assessing for dyslexia, not psychometric tests. Therefore, students who perform measurably better in cases when reading and writing criteria are removed from the task can be described as dyslexic. This suggestion, which focuses on performance and the curriculum, holds much promise in terms of developing education authority policy and, in particular, early identification. According to Crombie, using this premise, 'dyslexia' is not a name for the deficit, but a name for how the deficits manifest themselves in different individuals.

CRITERIA: SUMMARY

Assessment for dyslexia should consider three aspects—difficulties, discrepancies and differences. The central difficulty is usually related to the decoding or the encoding of print, and this may be the result of different contributory factors. For example, some difficulties may include phonological processing, visual-processing difficulties, memory factors, organisational and sequencing difficulties, motor and coordination difficulties, language problems or perceptual difficulties of an auditory or visual nature.

Discrepancies become apparent when we make comparisons between decoding and reading/listening comprehension, between oral and written responses and between performances within the different subject areas of the curriculum.

It is also important to acknowledge the differences between individual learners. This particularly applies to dyslexic children. An assessment, therefore, should also consider learning and cognitive styles as well as the learning and teaching environment. An appreciation of this can help to link assessment and effective teaching. This also helps to take the child's preferences for learning into account; these, in fact, should be a key factor in an assessment.

A wide range of assessment strategies and criteria can be used to help recognise the difficulties, discrepancies and differences displayed by learners. Some of these are described and discussed in this and the next chapter. The criteria listed in Table 4.1 can be used as a guide for this.

The purpose of the assessment must be the first question to be asked. This is crucial for the selection of the assessment approaches to be used and the type of outcome

Table 4.1 The assessment: criteria to consider

- *Purpose*—what is the context for the assessment?
- *Reason*—why is the assessment being carried out?
- *Profiles*—obtain information on the child's strengths and weaknesses
- *Attainment profile*—pattern of reading and spelling errors, performances in writing and comprehension
- *Cognitive profile*—what are the strengths and weaknesses—working memory, processing speed, long-term memory, phonological memory?
- *Performances*—how is learning carried out?
- *The process*—learning behaviours—frequency of on-task/off-task, work in groups/on own/short task preference/able to persist with task
- *Provision*—the context—The curriculum—degree of differentiation, pace of learning, expectations
- *The classroom*—environment, colour, noise level, wall displays, rules, degree of freedom to move around
- *The community*—culture, background information
- *Concerns*—reason for initial concern
- *Home/school links*—1 Level of communication, ease of communication

expected from the assessment. Similarly, the profiles give an indication of the child's strengths and weaknesses, and it is important that this should include an indication of cognitive functioning as well as attainments. This is particularly important as there is much evidence regarding the cognitive/information-processing aspects related to dyslexia.

Although the information from the profiles can be used comparatively to note discrepancies in the performances of cognitive and attainment tasks, this is not the only use to which this information can be put. It should be used diagnostically to help provide some information about the learner's strategies, the nature of the difficulties and, indeed, the type of tasks that may present difficulty and some possible reasons for this difficulty.

For example, in a cognitive, working memory task involving digits that are reversed, one should be interested in how the learner achieved the correct or incorrect response. Identifying the strategies the learner used can be an important piece of information as these can have an impact on learning.

Whatever the motivation for undertaking an assessment, it is important to have clear aims and objectives, and these should be relayed to the parents well before the assessment commences. It is also important to view assessment from the curriculum and learning perspectives as opposed to within-child factors. Wearmouth et al. (2002; Reid and Came, 2009) discuss barriers to literacy, and these need to be investigated to assess why the child is not acquiring literacy skills. Reid and Came (2009) suggest that when identifying the barriers to learning it is important to include: cognitive (learning skills), environmental (learning experience) and progress in basic attainments (literacy acquisition) (see Table 4.2). This highlights the need not to focus solely on the child, but to look at the task that is being presented, the expectations being placed on the learner and the learner's readiness for the task.

Table 4.2   A holistic view of the barriers to learning

Cognitive factors

- Differences in information processing:
  - visual-orthographic processing phonological processing;
  - limited capacity working memory;
  - poor sequencing;
  - weak spatial awareness;
  - lacking coordination/dexterity.

Educational factors

- Challenges that derive from cognitive differences:
  - reading;
  - spelling;
  - writing;
  - proofreading;
  - numeracy;
  - organisation;
  - inappropriate labelling;
  - social communication;
  - on-task behaviour;
  - planning;
  - time keeping.
- Family history and context

Social/Emotional factors that give rise to:

- lack of confidence;
- low self-esteem;
- isolation;
- anxiety;
- stress;
- lack of understanding from peers and adults;
- lack of hope due to history of failure.
- Family history and context

Environmental factors

- Mismatch with learning needs:
  - literacy demands;
  - aural demands;
  - restrictions in movement;
  - lack of visual aids/prompts;
  - undue time pressures;
  - peer and social expectations;
  - limited access to technology;
  - too much stimulation and lack of structure to information;
  - noise levels;
  - formal learning situations create discomfort, stress, poor concentration.

Source: adapted from Reid and Came, 2009

In developing criteria for an assessment it is important therefore to incorporate all those aspects that relate to the curriculum and to attempt to identify the barriers to learning and literacy that might be experienced by the learner with dyslexia. These barriers can be identified by observing and discussing with the child, and the parents, the difficulties encountered by the learner and how these are currently being tackled. Just as there is no 'magic' formula for overcoming the difficulties associated with dyslexia, there is no 'magic' tool for identifying these difficulties. Certainly the range of tests that are discussed in the next chapter can be of considerable assistance, and many of these tests have strong predictive validity. Essentially, however, identifying dyslexia involves more than administering a test—it involves a process, and that process needs to include the learning environment, the curriculum and the student's learning opportunities, as well as the cognitive factors associated with dyslexia. That is why it is crucial to identify and develop a rationale for assessment and, specifically, the 'next step' after the assessment. It is important that assessment is linked to intervention, and by identifying 'barriers to learning' the link between assessment and intervention can be strengthened. For that reason it is also important that the teacher adopts a leading role in the assessment.

WHOSE RESPONSIBILITY

Historically, in the UK and in most other countries, assessment for dyslexia has been the responsibility of a specialist teacher or an educational psychologist. This is understandable as the specialist teacher has an appreciation of how dyslexia can affect the progress of the student in the classroom situation and the educational psychologist can provide refined quantitative and qualitative insights relating to the cognitive abilities and difficulties experienced by the student. Ideally, both the information that can be obtained from cognitive measures and that which can be obtained from classroom and curriculum assessment are needed. It is interesting to note that one of the recommendations of the BPS Working Party Report on Dyslexia (BPS, 1999a) was that 'educational psychologists work more closely with schools to develop effective school-based assessment, intervention and monitoring and, within that context, also carry out detailed psychological assessment and programme planning...' (p. 69). It is therefore clear that no one individual, nor one test, holds the key to identifying dyslexia, but that this can best be achieved with reference to a range of strategies and the involvement of a number of key personnel. The following two chapters, therefore, will look in detail at these barriers to literacy and learning, by focusing on how existing tests can be used and how a range of assessment strategies can be utilised.

EARLY IDENTIFICATION

One of the key issues in the assessment process is that of early identification. How such identification should take place and when it can most effectively and most sensitively be conducted are matters of some debate. This is clearly an important aspect of the assessment process, and it is important that schools have procedures in place to meet the needs of early identification. Other aspects also need to be considered, such as whole-school policy, role of other professionals, linkage with teaching, role of parents, and professional development and training. Knight et al. (2009) suggest that it may not be desirable to diagnose and label a young child who may not be reading as dyslexic, but as early as three years of age some young children display behaviours that indicate that they are not developing oral language, phonological awareness and motor skills as one would expect. They argue that some of these children will be diagnosed with dyslexia, while others need intervention to allow them to have the necessary experiences to become readers. The point is that the children in both groups are at risk for developing reading difficulties. This is the essence of early identification—not to label but to identify those who are at risk of developing difficulties in acquiring literacy. There is no doubt that early identification is crucial and can make a significant difference to the achievement outcome of children who are at risk. Knight et al. (2009) provide evidence of early identification of reading difficulty along with targeted, research-based interventions improving children's chances of becoming more effective readers (Henry, 2003; Lynch, 2007; Southern Education Foundation, 2007, 2008). This begs the questions below:

- When should early identification take place, how should it be conducted and by whom?
- What criteria should be used at this early stage for a diagnosis?

If someone asks the first of these questions (when should this take place?), then I would suggest that they have misunderstood the whole concept of early identification.

Certainly, as the term implies, 'early identification' does mean some form of 'intervention' in order to note the difficulties that some young children may be experiencing. But we need to be careful that early identification does not focus exclusively on 'within-child' deficits that can be sometimes be apparent before the child has had an opportunity to benefit from the learning opportunities in nursery or school. The term 'early identification' would therefore be more accurate if it were extended to 'early identification of learning needs'.

Many systems currently used to identify these learning needs at an early stage utilise a combination of both the 'needs model' and the 'child deficit model'. It is possible to merge these two in a complementary manner.

It is also important to focus on 'curriculum access' rather than 'child deficits'. An example of a document that does include 'curriculum access' as an integral part of the identification procedures for dyslexia is the Report of Task Force on Dyslexia for the Republic of Ireland (Task Force on Dyslexia, 2001). This document highlights the phrase 'Continuum of Identification and Provision'. This is a policy-led identification and support model. The model involves the identification of students who are at risk, review of guidance and advice, differentiated responses, regular assessment by class or learning support teachers, curriculum development to take profile into account and implementation of the individual learning programme and the monitoring of outcomes.

MODELS OF IDENTIFICATION

In 1990 Pumfrey suggested that the concept of diagnosis and treatment is based on a medical model and is not therefore appropriate to the education context. Teachers, Pumfrey (1990) asserted, ought to be wary of moving down the classification escalator, which he described as moving from individual differences to deviations, difficulties, disabilities, deficits and eventually to defects.

Yet, while this 'classification escalator' is clearly something that ought to be avoided and something that underlines the inherent dangers of hasty diagnosis or perceiving lack of attainments as a within-child difficulty that requires diagnosis and perhaps a label, it is still beneficial to implement some form of early identification procedures, despite these risks.

It is argued that the intricacies of the reading process result in significant numbers of children adopting ineffective reading strategies, which need to be identified and modified by the teacher otherwise the error behaviour can become too entrenched. To ensure, that a medical diagnosis–treatment model is not perceived as the principal assessment strategy, it is important that assessment is undertaken by the class teacher, using a range of strategies, and that this assessment is linked to teaching and the curriculum.

Some other models currently in use are described below. It is often the case that countries/education authorities use a combination of the key elements in the models below, but some identifiable overriding principles can be noted from, on the one hand, a child deficit/medical perspective to, on the other, a full curriculum-directed approach that focuses on 'curriculum access' rather than 'specific deficits'.

EXPERT/INTERVENTION—ATTAINMENT

Discrepancy Model

This model is essentially a child deficit model and usually focuses on concerns that may arise from parents and teachers relating to lack of expected progress in attainments.

It usually operates through the intervention of another professional such as an educational psychologist or speech and language therapist. This often happens when some concern is expressed, and usually the diagnosis is based on cognitive and clinical evidence as well as background information and case history. While this model can be used as a basis for resource allocation, it is not without critics. One of the main points of contention stems from the lack of agreement of 'experts' as to exactly which criteria, and to what extent, various factors can contribute to a dyslexia diagnosis. For example, Tunmer (1997) suggests that a 'dyslexia index' can be observed from various calculations using at least six core or ability tests, four diagnostic tests and three achievement tests. The result is a comprehensive accumulation of data on the child and his or her academic achievement. Turner suggests that a dyslexia index comprising six levels can be detected from this information. This index would range from 'no dyslexia signs' at 0.0 standard deviation to 'very severe dyslexia' at above 2.0 standard deviation. Turner provides comprehensive and convincing examples to support the value of such an index, and its major achievement lies in the attempt by Turner to quantify what has been described as 'a variable syndrome' (Pumfrey, 1995). In view of this variability it is perhaps desirable to obtain some measurable data to quantify the degree of severity, or the presence of dyslexia. Pumfrey (2001, 2002) applauds the explicit rationale and methodology of the Dyslexia Index and suggests that this constitutes a challenging contribution to professional practice in assessment. At the same time, of course, it rests on the diagnostic assumptions made by these tests, and whether they are sufficiently robust and sufficiently wide-ranging to incorporate all the variables that can contribute to the presence of dyslexia. This point is also noted by Pumfrey (2001) when he suggests that 'whether his seven point scale of dyslexia severity will be seen as fair depends on the validity of the assumptions on which the diagnostic procedures are based' (p. 151).

Similarly, cognitive criteria that have a long-established history of use in the identification of dyslexia are often termed the ACID profile, because of their use of the Arithmetic, Coding, Information and Digit span profile from the Wechsler Intelligence Scale (WISC). Indeed, these criteria were used in the Hillingdon judgement (Garland, 1997) when it was suggested in the report that 'individuals with a pattern of dyslexic difficulties typically do rather badly on ACID compared with the remainder' (p. 3). Yet, Frederickson (1999) draws together evidence from several studies (Ward et al., 1995; Watkins et al., 1997; Prifitera and Dersch, 1993) to suggest that the 'statements on the ACID profile contained in the Hillingdon judgement are not supported by the research evidence...(and that) educational psychologists cannot legitimately be criticised if they do not use an ACID profile to identify children with special learning difficulties, but can be criticised if they place strong reliance on its use for this purpose' (p. 7). The evidence that supports Frederickson's assertion is based on the view from the research studies noted above. These studies suggest that although the incidence of the presence of an ACID profile in children with special learning difficulties may have been greater, it did not reach any level of statistical significance. Ward et al. (1995) suggest that this low incidence renders it 'clinically meaningless'. This point can also be seen as an implication of the BPS working party report (BPS, 1999a), which noted that in relation to approaches to assessment and models of responses, some of the responses indicated 'what is distinctive about Educational Psychologist assessment as opposed to specialist teacher assessment?' (p. 91). Another response indicated that 'it would be helpful to have an assessment model which can be used by teachers in consultation with E.P.s' (p. 92). Similar conclusions can be made about the SCAD profile—this profile refers to a calculation of the sum of the picture completion, picture arrangement, block design and object assembly minus the sum of the scaled scores for symbol search, coding, arithmetic and digit span of the WISC. If the result of this calculation leads to a score greater than 9 then this represents a statistically significant difference. While the SCAD profile may have been found to be higher in a population with special learning difficulties than in a random sample, Frederickson (1999) suggests that the differences are significant enough to make them useful in a diagnosis. This view is supported by Kaufman (1994), who suggests that any differences noted as a result of using a SCAD formula would not necessarily distinguish children with learning disabilities from other exceptional children.

It is not too surprising, therefore, in view of these comments that one of the conclusions to the working report published by the BPS on dyslexia and psychological Assessment indicated that 'assessment of and intervention in relation to dyslexia/specific learning difficulties is seen largely to be the responsibility of mainstream schools with educational psychologists supporting schools in identifying and meeting needs' (p. 93). These statements and certainly the conclusion to this report seem to cast some doubt over the expert/intervention model expressed above and, indeed, places the responsibility in the hands of the school and, in particular, trained and experienced school staff. Clearly, this has implications for training and resourcing. Such training has been the focus of a number of university and other courses, and to date the British Dyslexia Association has accredited over 35 courses at a level that would permit successful course participants to undertake informed assessment of dyslexia in some way. Additionally, there is now a trend for other countries to develop high quality courses in dyslexia and disseminate these to teachers who up until then had little or no access to such courses other than in distance learning (see www.ccetkuwait.org).

Stage/Process/Policy Model

This is a popular model and can often be integral to an education authority's 'policy' for identification and intervention. It can be child focused, which rests on the assumptions that the child should reach certain 'benchmarks' by a certain age or stage. This is essentially a child deficit model, but uses curriculum features to assist in the diagnosis.

It is interesting to note that the SEN Code of Practice (DfES, 2001), although it is a stage model, does appear to be more rooted within the school and the curriculum. This is apparent from descriptions such as 'school action' and 'school action plus' replacing the earlier 'stages' of the 1994 Code of Practice. The code states that 'assessment should not be regarded as a single event but rather as a continuing process' (para 5.11 of the SEN Code of Practice, DfES, 2001). The Code of Practice is a stage process model because it does have distinct stages. 'Initial concern' is the stage when the class teacher registers concern because the child is not learning as effectively as he or she could—this knowledge clearly results from the teacher observing the child in the class situation over a period of time. The next stage, 'school action', occurs when the child makes little or no progress, even when teaching approaches are targeted at dealing with the child's identified weaknesses. At this stage the school SENCO (Statement of Educational Needs Coordinator) will make further assessments and consult with colleagues, parents and other relevant professionals, although the class teacher will remain responsible for working with the student on a daily basis and for planning and implementing an IEP. The next stage would be 'school action plus', which is when the school accesses additional specialists who might in fact have a whole-school role as well as being able to provide advice on individual students. 'School action plus' occurs when the child makes little or no progress over a long period and is working at a level well below his or her age.

In England, the Common Assessment Framework (CAF) is increasingly being used and became a statutory requirement from April 2008 for a child or young person with multiple additional needs requiring support from two or more agencies. This framework provides a degree of uniformity but also can empower teachers to be more involved in the assessment process.

Came and Reid (2008) provide materials that can be used in conjunction with the Common Assessment Framework and also with the principles and practices advocated in Every Child Matters (England and Wales, HMSO, 2004) and Getting it Right for Every Child (Scotland, Scottish Executive, 2008).

Came and Reid suggest that informal teacher assessment can provide supporting documentation for the integrated assessment, planning and recording framework advocated in the 2008 legislation.

Curriculum-focused Model

This model essentially operates in the classroom, and the key person is the class teacher. Irrespective of a diagnosis, the teacher tackles the child's learning from a problem-solving perspective using curriculum access as the target and often differentiation as the means. Many teaching approaches based on behavioural principles also follow the principles of this model. This model is consistent with the practice as well as the principles of inclusion and requires clear curriculum objectives to pinpoint the student's progress.

BARRIERS TO LEARNING

It is useful, therefore, to view early identification and, indeed, the assessment process in terms of overcoming barriers to learning rather than through a child-deficit focus. In reality, however, information on both the child and the curriculum is needed. Essentially, the overcoming barriers to learning approach requires that all children undertake the same curriculum, irrespective of the perceived abilities and difficulties. An example of this can be the way in which curriculum objectives are identified and assessing the extent to which the child has met them and what action may be needed to help him or her meet the objectives more fully. This action can take the form of some assistance for the child, but equally it can be in terms of reassessing the objectives or refining them in some way to make them more accessible.

A key aspect of this is the monitoring process, which must be based on actual curriculum attainments. The process can be extended to include details of the nature of the work within the curriculum that the child is finding challenging; for example, which letters does the child know and not know and which books can the child read fluently and why should this be the case? Such an approach needs to view the child's class work in a comprehensive and detailed manner, otherwise it can become merely another type of checklist. Additionally, a degree of precision is needed to assist the teacher to see whether the child is achieving the targets. In order to do this, a sample of work is necessary and should be taken from the actual work of the class.

The importance of this type of perspective is that the emphasis is on the barriers that prevent the child from meeting these targets rather than identifying what the child cannot do. This is essentially a whole-staff and therefore a whole-school responsibility as it is important that attitudes relating to progress and curriculum access are consistent throughout the school. Children who do have some difficulties and find aspects of the curriculum challenging are usually very sensitive and can detect a change of attitude with a change of teacher. It is important, therefore, that there is a consistent view throughout the school on the notion of dyslexia and the role of teachers and the curriculum in making effective learning a reality for all children, including those with dyslexia, through the medium of the curriculum.

WHOLE-SCHOOL INVOLVEMENT

It is the view of many involved in this area that dyslexia identification and how to teach dyslexic children are the responsibility of specialists, and such specialists should therefore be identified within schools and undertake the responsibility of identifying and meeting the needs of children with dyslexia. This, however, should not be the case. Ideally, responsibility should be on a whole-school basis and all teachers should have some knowledge of dyslexia; in particular, the literacy and learning needs of children with dyslexia.

One of the key questions relating to this is how whole-school involvement can be successfully and effectively implemented. Some of the factors below can be used as a guide to this, as each will have some role in the development and implementing of whole-school policies on dyslexia.

This model can be viewed as one that is interactive and involves the whole school, because it emphasises the need for staff training, awareness of the curriculum and teaching implications, and regular consultancy. Key aspects include initial early warning signs, assessment and consultancy, and monitoring and review. These are described below from the perspective of the class teacher.

Early Warning Signs

The class teacher may identify coordination difficulties, difficulties with pencil grip, immature use of language, sequencing or organisational difficulties prior to the teaching of reading skills. These difficulties can be highlighted through classroom observation, discussions with parents and diagnostic assessment.

Assessment/Consultancy with Management Team

The discussion of difficulties and possible materials and resources that can be used is an important aspect, and time should be specifically allocated for this. Close monitoring of progress is needed when reading skills are taught, looking out for:

- auditory discrimination in recognising and repeating sounds;
- visual difficulties, such as failure to recognise letters, comparison between visually similar letters, missing lines when reading confusing picture cues;
- sequencing difficulties, such as confusing the order of letters, words or digits;

- organisational difficulties, such as directional confusion, laterality problems and sequencing difficulties;
- memory—inability to follow instructions, particularly when more than one item is to be remembered;
- motor difficulties—for example, poor pencil grip, awkward gait, poor coordination;
- difficulty doing two simple tasks simultaneously.

Monitoring/Review Meeting

This meeting would probably be with the school management and nursery staff to discuss the necessity of a fuller assessment and how this should proceed. Some suggestions about revision of the teaching methods, to support the teacher, need to be made at this stage. Discussions with parents are also important here. Such suggested revisions to teaching should then be carried out, during which time the teacher records progress and difficulties.

School management would then call a meeting with parents to review and discuss progress and determine any further action if necessary; for instance, the involvement of other professionals, such as educational psychologists and speech therapists.

POINTS FOR REFLECTION

- Consider what is meant by dynamic assessment. How might this fit into the framework for assessment in your school?

- Consider the importance of linking the assessment with intervention—reflect on the type of information that would be important for this.

- Consider the purposes and aims of an assessment—how might you view these in your school?

- Consider the importance of early identification—how might this be planned for within the assessment process?

- Reflect on models of assessment in relation to your own teaching context. Consider the model used in your school. How does this fit into the following:

  - the identification of the barriers to learning,

  - the need to provide a curriculum focus,

  - the need to obtain information that will inform IEPs, and

  - the extent with which it links assessment with intervention?

Chapter 5

Assessment: Approaches and Resources

Although there are a number of tests that include the term 'dyslexia' in the title there is, in fact, no dyslexia test—the identification of dyslexia is a process, and that process includes more than the administration of a solitary test. The tests that are available will be discussed in this chapter, and further examples can be found in Appendix 1. This chapter will look at the specific practices and the processes involved in an assessment. This process includes the gathering of data from a wide range of sources because it is necessary to investigate the influence of factors other than those relating to the individual student.

It can be suggested that dyslexia is contextual. This means that the extent of dyslexic difficulties will be more obvious in some environments and contexts than in others. It is important to observe and gather information on the learning environment and the learning or work context, as these factors may be influential in assessing the performance of the person with dyslexia. Environmental, classroom, curricular or workplace considerations may in fact be sufficient to minimise the effects of dyslexia, but in order to ascertain the role of these factors, part of the assessment has to be conducted in that environment—classroom or workplace. An assessment, therefore, is not only about the individual but about the learning opportunities, the environment, the individual's learning preferences, and the biological and cognitive factors associated with dyslexia as well.

This chapter will also describe the environmental and learning factors that can be influential in the outcome of an assessment for dyslexia.

THE USE OF TESTS—POINTS TO PONDER

Assessment is a powerful educational tool for promoting learning. However, assessment activities should be appropriate to the aims of the assessment, the objectives of the curriculum, and the individual student. Dyslexia is a difficulty with information processing. This means that when carrying out an assessment it is important to identify the processing skills of the child. Often the reasoning and understanding are unaffected, but the actual processing of information can be challenging. Areas such as accessing print, decoding and encoding print, processing speed and memory as well as written output are all involved in the processing activities necessary for literacy acquisition.

In the previous chapter it was suggested that assessment for dyslexia should consider three aspects—discrepancies, difficulties and differences. Discrepancies become apparent when we make comparisons between decoding and reading/listening comprehension, between oral and written responses and between performances within the different subject areas of the curriculum. The central difficulty is usually related to the decoding or the encoding of print, and this may be the result of different contributory factors. For example, some difficulties may include phonological processing, visual-processing difficulties, memory factors, organisational and sequencing difficulties, motor and coordination difficulties, language problems or perceptual difficulties of an auditory or visual nature. It is also important to acknowledge the differences between individual learners. This particularly applies to dyslexic children. An assessment, therefore, should also consider learning and cognitive styles as well as the learning and teaching environment. This also helps to take the child's preferences for learning into account, which, in fact, should be one of the aims of an assessment.

COGNITIVE MEASURES

One of the most well-used practices in the assessment procedures for dyslexia is to obtain a measure of intellectual functioning as part of the investigation into discrepancies. Often the WISC is used as an ability measure as it is well standardised and translated into a number of languages (WISC-IV; Wechsler, 2004). The use of ability measures such as the WISC, however, according to Siegel (1989, 1992), rests on all or some of the following assumptions:

- that tests of ability or IQ are valid and reliable measures, so that there is some virtue in examining discrepancies between ability and achievement;
- that particular subtests are valid instruments in the assessment of specific cognitive subskills;
- that distinctive patterns may emerge that can be reliably correlated with learning difficulties; and
- that IQ and reading share a causal dependency, with IQ factors influencing reading ability.

Siegel (1989) argues that the evidence in relation to these points is inconsistent. IQ tests do not necessarily measure intelligence, but in fact measure factual knowledge, expressive language ability, short-term memory and other skills related to learning. The stages within the information-processing cycle are important in relation to dyslexia. Often children with dyslexia have difficulty in actually receiving the information—input—particularly if it is provided verbally. This can have implications for the use of standardised tests, which are often administered verbally, and the child has to process the information using the auditory modality such as the IQ test.

Siegel and Lipka (2008) show that there is a decreasing trend in the use of IQ as part of the 'Learning Disabilities' (LD) definition over the four decades from the 1970s.

It is accepted, however, that children with dyslexia can have difficulties in relation to cognition (Singleton, 2002). Cognition involves how children think and process information in order to understand it, to relate it to previous knowledge and to store it in long-term memory. Since these cognitive factors can represent difficulties often associated with dyslexia, there is a tendency to focus an assessment principally on these cognitive factors. The other factor associated with dyslexia and information-processing is the output of information. As was mentioned in the previous chapter, children with dyslexia often do not perform to their best in tests because responding to test items involves immediate and sometimes written responses without any help from the examiner. Yet, children with dyslexia more often than not respond well to cues and with assisted assessment can often reveal skills and aptitudes that are concealed in traditionally administered psychometric tests. Siegel and Lipka (2008), in addition to showing that recent studies have demonstrated the limitation of IQ in assessing students with learning disabilities, also suggest that IQ is irrelevant to a definition of LD, except possibly to 'define the border between learning disabilities and retardation'.

ASSESSMENT OF PROCESSING SKILLS

It is widely accepted, however, that the principal tool used in an assessment for dyslexia is in fact instruments that measure intellectual functioning, such as the Wechsler Intelligence Scale (WISC-IV). A significant breakthrough in terms of process assessment has emerged from the revision of the Process Assessment of the Learner (PAL-11) Diagnostic Assessment for Reading and Writing (Berninger, 2007). Berninger suggests that intelligence tests such as the WISC-IV may offer correlation data with measures of academic achievement, but do not explain why a child is experiencing poor learning outcomes or how to intervene to improve learning outcomes. It may indicate that a child needs intervention but it does not tell us precisely what kind of intervention would be the most effective. The Process Assessment (PAL 11) materials developed by Berninger provide informative data on why a child may be underachieving in reading or writing and give guidance on how such difficulties can be tackled.

The subtests of the PAL-11 target those neuro-developmental processes most relevant to reading and writing. These include: orthographic skills, phonological skills, morphological and syntactic skills, rapid automatic naming, silent reading fluency, word-specific spellings and narrative compositional fluency. The test is very specific and extremely well conceptualised. The reading-related subtests are in the form of domains such as orthographic coding, phonological coding, morphological/syntactic coding, verbal working memory and rapid automatic naming. For each of these domains there are at least two to four specific subtests. For example, orthographic coding contains subtests on receptive coding and expressive coding. The receptive coding subtest is used to measure the processes involved in coding written words into memory and analysing units of the written word without having the child writing or pronouncing them. This suite of tests can provide an alternative, or at least reduce the dependency on the use of measures of intellectual functioning.

Similarly, the Wechsler Individual Achievement Test (WIAT-11) provides comprehensive insights into literacy acquisition and the scores can be correlated with the measures on the WISC. While there is a range of skills taken into account in the WIAT-11, it is still up to the examiner to attempt to use the data diagnostically. Essentially the results inform us on the extent of the child's difficulties but do not provide guidance on the areas within the reading process that can precisely account for these difficulties. The WIAT-11 does provide composite measures on key aspects such as reading, mathematics, written language and oral language and although, for example, the reading composite includes a test on pseudoword decoding, it does not inform us of the reasons for the child's difficulties. For example, difficulties in pseudoword reading can suggest difficulties in applying phonetic decoding skills but it does not tell us what kind of phonological difficulty the child experiences.

This emphasises the need to used tests selectively and purposefully. It is important to obtain measures of the extent of the difficulty but equally it is important to obtain evidence of the nature of the difficulties experienced and reasons for these difficulties. This information is necessary if appropriate and effective intervention is to be put in place.

COMPREHENSIVE TEST OF PHONOLOGICAL PROCESSING (CTOPP)

There are more specific tests that can accompany some of those mentioned above and can provide diagnostic criteria as well as age/grade-related measures. One such example is the Comprehensive Test of Phonological Processing (CTOPP; Wagner et al., 1999). The authors have placed the test within a theoretical framework that pinpoints three types of phonological processing relevant for mastery of written language—phonological awareness, phonological memory and rapid naming. Phonological awareness refers to an individual's awareness of and access to the sound structure of oral language. It is important to assess phonological awareness as this is often seen as one of the principal difficulties in dyslexia and, furthermore, studies show that children who are weak in phonological awareness show improved reading performance after being given intervention designed to improve their phonological awareness (Torgeson et al., 1992; Torgeson et al., 1997).

The other areas in the CTOPP theoretical model are phonological memory and rapid naming. Phonological memory refers to coding information phonologically for temporary storage in working or short-term memory. This is often referred to as the 'phonological loop' (Baddeley, 1986; Torgeson, 1996). Difficulties in this area can restrict a child's abilities to learn new material. Phonological coding in working memory, according to Wagner et al. (1999), plays an important role in decoding new words, particularly multi-syllabic words.

The third aspect of the model underpinning the CTOPP is rapid naming. This relates to the efficiency with which young readers are able to retrieve phonological codes associated with individual phonemes, word segments and entire words. This is important, as it has been shown that individuals who have difficulty in rapid naming usually have difficulty in reading fluency and that individuals who have difficulty in both rapid naming and phonological awareness (double deficit) will have greater difficulty in learning to read than individuals with deficits in either rapid naming or phonological awareness (Bowers and Wolf, 1993).

This type of test not only provides precise diagnostic information but can also be used as a means of monitoring and evaluating a child's progress with the intervention that is being used.

WOODCOCK READING MASTERY TESTS

A similar process is used in the Woodcock Reading Mastery Tests—Revised (Woodcock, 1998). There are three main areas to the model used in this test battery: reading readiness, basic skills and reading comprehension. For readiness, therefore, visual/auditory learning and letter identification are included; for basic skills, word identification and word attack; and for reading comprehension, word comprehension and passage comprehension. This provides a comprehensive model using dimensions of reading that can lead to a diagnostic understanding of the child's difficulties. Additionally, there is a word attack error inventory which records the child's errors on target sounds and target syllables. This type of reading inventory is formal and structured.

GRAY ORAL READING TESTS (GORT-4)

There is some benefit in using more informal measures to record precise reading errors, such as the system of recording miscues. The Gray Oral Reading Tests (GORT-4) does precisely that. This particular test looks at both bottom-up and top-down processes. It includes the recording of errors in graded passages to obtain accuracy scores and timed reading for fluency as well as questions on the passage for the reading comprehension component. Additionally, however, it includes a miscue analysis system to record miscues. The miscues are divided into five types: meaning similarity—word error in relation to the meaning of the story; function similarity—word error in regard to the grammatical correctness of the word substituted in the sentence; graphic/phonemic similarity—the appropriateness of the word error as to its similarity to the look and sound of the printed word; multiple sources—this refers to the word error that has a combined meaning, function and graphic-phonemic similarity to the word; and self-correction, which refers to the occasions when a word error is immediately corrected by the student (Wiederholt and Bryant, 2001). This system can provide useful diagnostic information that in itself can inform planning.

STANDARDISED/PSYCHOMETRIC CRITERIA

Standardised or norm-referenced tests provide some form of score or measure, which is compared with the average scores of a standardised sample. From this type of test one can obtain, for example, a reading age or IQ score. As well as providing an indication of the student's progress in relation to his or her peers, these tests can also provide information that can be used diagnostically. Important factors in standardised tests relate to test construction and, particularly, aspects relating to validity and reliability. Standardised tests must have high validity and reliability, and this is usually indicated in the test manual. This means that the tests are well constructed and thus the teacher can use the data from the test with some confidence. There are, however, some potential pitfalls in the use of standardised tests, and they are described in this chapter. If a standardised test is to be used, for whatever purpose, it is important to check that it has been constructed soundly and has high content validity and high reliability.

STANDARDISATION

If one is attempting to standardise a test that can be used nationally across different populations of children or, indeed, selecting a standardised test for use, it is important to note a number of important points:

- *The sample*—it is important that the sample is a representative one. Factors that should be considered include urban/rural locations, cultural background, age and sex, first language, and size and selection of sample. It is important, therefore, for users of tests of any type to check the standardisation procedures that were used in the construction of the test. It is also important to check the nature of the piloting that was carried out before the standardisation data were gathered.
- *Reliability*—this refers to the reliability in obtaining the same responses from the test if repeated under similar conditions. Reliability can be called 'replicability' or 'stability'. It essentially refers to the extent to which a child would obtain the same score in a test if he or she had done the test on a different day. It can be measured by determining how far the score on one question can be predicted from the same student's score on other questions in the test. The reliability can be calculated using the Kuder–Richardson formula 20 (KR20).
- *Validity*—this refers to the design of the test and whether the test actually measures what it was designed to measure, such as IQ, decoding, verbal comprehension, spelling. This is not the same as reliability. A test may well be reliable and give consistent results over time, and this would mean something: very likely that the test is a good measure of something, but not necessarily the item it is intended to measure. Sometimes, the term 'content' or 'face validity' is used to describe validity. This refers to the extent to which the questions in the test conform to expert opinion of what good questions for that test should be. This may refer to the language used, the age appropriateness of the test material and whether cultural and social factors have been considered in the development of the test items.
- *Confidence interval*—this refers to whether the student, if he or she took the test repeatedly, would obtain approximately the same score.
- *Homogeneity*—This means that if the different items in the test actually measure the same skill or attainment then it should be expected that, over a group of students, test items should show high levels of inter-correlation. At the same time, if items are accessing different skills or attainments they would likely show lower levels of inter-correlation.

PSYCHOMETRIC

The term 'psychometric' refers to measurement and the use of standardised instruments to measure some ability or attainment. It is understandable, given the different aspects described above that are essential in the development of a standardised test, that such tests need to be treated with some caution. Sometimes, tests such as these can be misinterpreted and misused.

Psychometric or standardised tests attempt to establish what would be the norm for children of a specific age. Such norm-referenced tests typically produce measures in terms of ranks (e.g., standardised reading scores), but they may fall short of highlighting appropriate intervention strategies because the scores do not provide any information on the child, apart from a score. It says little or nothing of the child's strategies for providing a response, nor of the process of thought that was utilised by the child to obtain a response.

An example of a psychometric and widely used standardised test is the Wechsler Intelligence Scales (WISC). Although the concept of IQ is a controversial one, this is still a good example of a standardised test because it has been well constructed and standardised. The Wechsler Intelligence Scale for Children was originally devised as an assessment tool for psychologists and psychometricians. It provides both an IQ and subtest profile. It was revised and re-standardised in 1974 and an updated version with more modern and appropriate test materials was produced in 1992 (WISC-III) and a further revised version in 2005—the WISC-IV. This test has four scales:

- verbal comprehension, which assesses the development of a child's language skills and includes tests of expressive vocabulary, comprehension, reasoning, and general knowledge;
- perceptual reasoning, which assesses the development of a child's visual perceptual skills which includes tests of spatial analysis, visual perceptual reasoning and observation;
- working memory, which assesses the student's working memory and attention; and
- processing speed, which assesses motor (manual) skills and speed of information processing.

Cooper (1995) suggests that the WISC series of tests are probably the best validated and most widely accepted measures of children's intellectual functioning in the world. However, their use is not without controversy (Siegel, 1992; Stanovich, 1991, p. 96). Miles (1996) argues that the concept of global IQ for dyslexic children is a misleading one because it will not provide a valid reflection of their real abilities. This assertion undermines the view that the subtests and even subtest patterns can reveal useful information in the assessment of dyslexia.

WECHSLER INDIVIDUAL ACHIEVEMENT TEST (WIAT)

The WIAT can be used alongside the WISC as the WIAT-11 is correlated with the WISC-IV. The WIAT comprises four sub-sections—reading, mathematics, written language (including spelling) and oral language (including listening comprehension).

The listening comprehension comprises receptive and expressive vocabulary and sentence comprehension. Together the subtests in the WIAT can provide a reliable indicator of the child's literacy and mathematical dimensions.

COMMENT

The use of an intelligence test to identify children who have essentially a reading difficulty has accumulated some controversy. There is strong evidence to dispute the assertion that IQ and reading ability share a causal dependency. Stanovich (1992) argues that the key to reading disability is related to the problem of phonological processing. This notion indeed has widespread support (Tunmer and Greaney, 2008; Wagner, 2008). Stanovich further argues that phonological processes are independent of intelligence and are not measured or directly taken account of in IQ tests.

The difficulty known as hyperlexia (Aaron, 1989; Healy, 1982, 1991; Joshi and Aaron, 2008) can be used as evidence to dispute any valid association between IQ and reading attainment. Hyperlexia has been described as affecting those children with good decoding skills but poor comprehension, indicating a low general IQ. It has been argued that listening comprehension correlates more highly with reading ability than IQ. The evidence from studies of hyperlexia (Aram and Healy, 1988; Joshi and Aaron, 2008) suggests that children with low IQ scores can be good mechanical readers. This raises doubt about the existence of a causal relationship between IQ and reading ability.

It is important that tests such as the WISC are used diagnostically, particularly in the assessment of children with dyslexia. In addition to obtaining a score, one can observe how the child/adult responds to specific test items, which ones appear to motivate him or her more than others, and how sustained his or her attention is throughout the assessment. It is important that administration of these tests is not a means to an end—and if they are used, it should be acknowledged that they constitute only part of the assessment process.

PHONOLOGICAL REPRESENTATION AND ASSESSMENT

Hatcher and Snowling (2002) suggest that the status of a child's representation of spoken words determines the ease or difficulty with which they learn to read and that it is important to assess the quality of the phonological representations, to discover whether they are well developed or 'fuzzy'. It is necessary to attempt to identify the various aspects that make up phonological representations. Hatcher and Snowling suggest that some of the easier phonological tasks can be completed by children before they have started reading, while others are only attainable by children once they have started the process of learning to read, and that these tasks test different underlying abilities. It is important to have an understanding of the phonological level of the tasks in order to present them appropriately and interpret them correctly.

Adams (1990b) reviewed various phonological tasks and was able to identify at least five levels of difficulty:

- knowledge of nursery rhymes, which involves only an ear for the sounds of words;
- awareness of rhyme and alliteration, which requires both sensitivity to the sounds and an ability to focus on certain sounds;
- blending of phonemes and splitting of syllables to identify phonemes—this demands an awareness that words can be subdivided into smaller sounds;
- phoneme segmentation, which requires a thorough understanding that words can be analysed into a series of phonemes;
- phoneme manipulation, which requires a child not only to understand and produce phonemes but also to be able to manipulate them by addition, deletion or transposition.

It is important that assessment of phonological representations should identify the specific aspects of the different types of phonological tasks that contribute to the reading process. Hatcher and Snowling suggest that the following should be used for phonological awareness tasks.

- rhyme recognition and detection tests;
- rhyme oddity tasks that present the child with a set of three or four spoken words and require the child to identify which one does not belong to a group; and
- alliteration tasks that assess the ability to isolate initial sounds in words.

Phonological production tasks are those that include:

- rhyme production;
- syllable blending;
- phoneme-blending; and
- phoneme segmentation, which assess a child's ability to segment words into separate sounds.

Phonological manipulation can be identified by adding, deleting or transposing sounds. A phoneme deletion task assesses the child's ability to isolate a single phoneme, remove it from a word and thereby produce a new word. A Spoonerisms test is also useful as it assesses a child's ability to segment words and to synthesise the segments to produce a new word. For example, exchanging the beginning sounds of the words 'bold–coat' would become 'cold–boat'. Hatcher and Snowling (2002) also suggest that naming speed and fluency tests are useful as they assess the speed of phonological production. If an item is weakly represented, it may be irretrievable, retrieved incorrectly or remain on the tip of the tongue. Short-term memory tasks are also sensitive to the accessibility of phonological representations.

In order to read, children need to be able to combine the ability to segment words into sounds with their knowledge of letter names and sounds. Hatcher and Snowling therefore argue that it is fundamental that letter knowledge is assessed and monitored. A number of commercially produced assessment batteries are now available to do this. They include a range of phonological awareness and phonological processing tests.

SCREENING

The screening of children at virtually any stage in education is an issue that has aroused considerable debate and controversy. Three main questions can be raised in relation to screening:

- What is the most desirable age (or ages) for children to be screened?
- Which skills, abilities and attainments in performances should children be screened for?
- How should the results of any screening procedures be used?

Additionally, the benefits of screening need to be weighed against the costs in terms of staff and resources that are necessary to implement effective screening procedures.

This raises the issue as to whether screening should be for all children, or only for those who do not appear to be making satisfactory progress. Crombie (2002c) has developed a curriculum and multidisciplinary approach to screening to identify children in the nursery and early years who are at risk of dyslexia, throughout one education authority. She suggests that some generic principles should be taken into account when considering how to identify the learning needs of dyslexic students at an early stage. She argues that teachers are often hesitant to label a child dyslexic, but suggests that good communication with parents and an understanding of dyslexia will enable teachers to discuss with parents the reasons for their reluctance to label.

Again, the message of early identification is the same, whether the purpose is to label or not—that is, to identify appropriate intervention strategies for struggling readers. Crombie's nursery screening procedure is intended for use during the pre-school years. The purpose of this procedure, according to Crombie, is that the screening should also flag up any children who show signs of specific problems. This may indicate that such children are slightly slower to develop certain specific skills or are less mature than the rest of the group. When considering children's profiles, account needs to be taken of children who may be up to a year younger than the rest of the pre-school year group. At this stage some apparent problems may only be due to immaturity, so it is important not to read too much into this information at this stage. The key aspect is that specific intervention rather than a label is the prime objective of these screening procedures.

Crombie's screening focuses on the following main areas of learning:

- Emotional, personal and social development. This looks at home background and culture as these factors are likely to have a strong influence on emotional, personal and social development.
- Communication and language. Children who have poor phonological skills at this stage and a lack of awareness of rhyme and rhythm may have later difficulties in learning to read and write. It is important to acknowledge this, as the pre-school year is generally a period of rapid growth in language, with increasing awareness of sounds and words.
- Difficulty in listening to stories at this stage can also be identified, and this may indicate later attention problems. Memory is also important in language and communication skills, and children who are unable to remember more than two

items of information, for instance, may appear to be disobedient when, in fact, they are unable to remember what it is they were told to do.

- Information can also be gathered on whether they are able to remember the sequence of events in a story or may be unable to repeat the syllables that make up a poly-syllabic word. Speech too can be informally observed to ensure that the child has sufficient control of the tongue and lips to reproduce sounds in the desired way. This can be assessed when the child is telling or retelling a story

- Polysyllabic words and nonsense words can be repeated as part of a game. The teacher can also note any problems with pronunciation.

- Knowledge and understanding of the world. From this the child's interest and motivation to learn can be recognised. One can note the extent to which the child needs adult direction to explore and investigate an appreciation of the learning environment. The skills the student uses in some activities, such as categorisation, naming, ordering and sequencing, can be noted. One can also note the extent of integration of the senses and the extent to which the child can take advantage of multi-sensory learning—hearing, seeing, touching, saying, acting out, singing and the sense of smell, where this is appropriate.

- Expressive and aesthetic development. An awareness of rhythm will facilitate language-learning and will help in music. Provide opportunities for children who are weak in tapping out a rhythm or keeping reasonable time to music to gain expertise in these areas. Activity-singing games and simple dance sequences will identify those children whose short-term memory is likely to inhibit their learning. They will also identify those children who seem likely to be able to develop a high level of expertise in these areas.

- Physical development and movement. Movement can be assessed by the teacher as part of the routine observations made within the classroom situation.

- Coordination skills can be assessed at this early stage through observation in physical activities and in writing. Balance has been found to be an important ability for learning: children who are poor at balance tasks while doing something else are likely to encounter other learning problems. This can be done by asking the child to balance on one foot while at the same time reciting a rhyme.

Crombie's 'Nursery Screening' assesses characteristics associated with the individual learner in the learning environment. This is important, as it not only provides pointers to those children who may be at risk of literacy failure but also promotes multidisciplinary collaboration between professions and with parents. This type of screening, because it utilises the context of the learning environment, can be seen as a preventative approach and one that provides a link between assessment and teaching.

CURRICULUM ASSESSMENT

While standardised assessment can provide some important information that can be used diagnostically, it is vital that the assessment should also include an analysis of the task/curriculum that the child is working on. It is important to note how the child tackles specific tasks, the type of tasks that prove difficult and how aspects of the task can be adapted to enable the learner to succeed. This form of assessment can be very instrumental in the development of individual educational programmes.

Holloway (2000), focusing on secondary-age students with dyslexia, suggests curriculum assessment procedures, which she has termed 'realistic assessment procedures' (RAP), whose aim is to assess language-based learning needs in the curriculum context. This procedure includes the following:

- *Cloze procedure*—this involves the student completing sentences and passages where words have been deleted. This helps to encourage skimming and scanning as well as reading for meaning.
- *Silent reading fluency*—this is a timed two-minute reading exercise. At the end of that time the reader has to mark how far he or she has read—Holloway suggests that if the reader has read less than 100 words a minute it is likely that he or she is using a mechanical approach. The reader also has to write a sentence about the passage that has just been read.
- *Individual assessment through reading aloud*—while this may be difficult and stressful for students with dyslexia, it can provide useful information on the student's reading behaviour, such as finger-pointing at words, mispronunciation and fluency.
- *Timed free-writing/free-writing assessment*—this involves a five-minute exercise that can reveal a number of aspects about the student's performance, such as the quality of the actual content of the piece, the writing style, spelling errors, use of sentences and paragraphs, and if there is a mismatch between the student's oral and written performance. This can also be used to assess the spelling needs of the student.
- *Spelling test*—the response to this can be analysed diagnostically, and inconsistencies in the spelling pattern and the type of spelling errors (visual/phonological) can be identified. For example, some of the error types suggested by Holloway include: contraction errors such as 'volve' for 'involve'; kinaesthetic errors that relate to poorly formed letters such as 'mdrket' for 'market'; sequencing errors such as getting the order of words mixed; transposition errors that are frequently noted in dyslexic children when parts of words are in the wrong order, such as 'canibet' for 'cabinet'; and phonological errors such as 'brot' for 'brought'.

Holloway also suggests curriculum assessment to include note-taking and dictation skills that would be particularly challenging for most students with dyslexia, and, therefore, this would have to be administered judiciously. This example is typical of a structured, curriculum-based assessment for literacy skills focusing on literacy performances.

The key point is that the assessment is based on the student's own performances in a natural environment using work activities that are meaningful to the student at that time. Furthermore, it also offers a structured framework based on curriculum assessment. It is important that diagnostic information is obtained on the student's performances, and this must be done in as natural a way as possible.

MISCUE ANALYSIS

The system known as miscue analysis can also offer a structure to investigate reading behaviours in a natural manner using curriculum-related text. This strategy is based on the 'top-down' approach to reading that has developed from the work of Goodman (1976). Goodman argued that the reader initially has to make predictions as to the most likely meaning of the text. Such predictions were based on how the reader perceived the graphic, syntactic and semantic information contained in the text. The reader, therefore, according to Goodman, engages in hypothesis-testing to either confirm or disprove the prediction—this he named the 'psycholinguistic guessing game'.

It was therefore assumed that miscues occur systematically and irrespective of whether reading is silent or aloud and that the degree of sense the child makes of the material reflects his or her use of prior knowledge.

The marking system that is usually adopted in miscue analysis is indicated below, although some specific tests such as the GORT-4, discussed earlier in this chapter, uses different marking criteria from those listed here:

- *Omissions*—these may occur in relation to reading speed (e.g., when the child's normal silent reading speed is used when reading orally). As the child progresses in reading ability and reading speed increases, omissions may still be noted as they tend to increase as reading speed increases.
- *Additions*—these may reflect superficial reading with perhaps an over-dependence on context clues.
- *Substitutions*—these can be visual or semantic substitutions. In younger readers substitutions would tend to be visual, and in older readers contextual. In the latter case they may reflect an over-dependence on context clues.
- *Repetitions*—these may indicate poor directional attack and perhaps some anticipatory uncertainty on the part of the reader about a word to be read.
- *Reversals*—these may reflect the lack of left–right orientation. Reversals may also indicate some visual difficulty and perhaps a lack of reading for meaning.
- *Hesitations*—these can occur when the reader is unsure of the text and perhaps lacking in confidence in reading. For the same reason that repetitions may occur, the reader may also be anticipating a different word later in the sentence.
- *Self-corrections*—these would occur when the reader becomes more aware of meaning and less dependent on simple word recognition.

It is important to observe whether the miscue produces syntactically or semantically acceptable text and whether the child is able to self-correct. It is, therefore, possible to obtain useful data on the child's reading pattern by observing the reading errors and noting the significance of these oral errors.

Arnold (1992) produced a diagnostic reading record. This also contains case studies that highlight assessment through the use of miscue analysis. In addition, it includes a teacher's handbook and student profile sheets and focuses on observations of reading behaviour and an examination of oral reading through discussion in order to obtain the child's level of understanding of the passage.

ASSESSMENT IN CONTEXT

Dargie (2001) provides examples of how dyslexic learners can be assessed in a range of skills within the context of the History curriculum. An instance of this is the examination of primary sources of historical information and assessment of how the dyslexic learner deals with tasks associated with this. One example is for students to contrast the facts about Macbeth known to modern historians with the key elements of the fictional representation offered by Shakespeare (Dargie, 1995). Dargie (2001) also suggests that examples of writing by dyslexic students on historical matters frequently exhibit aspects of the following organisational symptoms:

• difficulty in appreciating the relative importance and relevance of information/ideas;
• difficulty in sorting and arranging historical information into an appropriate textual format; and
• difficulty in distinguishing between general and particular pieces of evidence and judging their relative importance.

Additionally, students with dyslexia usually possess a relatively restricted vocabulary, and this is also a factor that can restrict evaluative comment on historical evidence.

Dargie suggests that internal school-based assessment in History should take account of the cognitive and emotional difficulties that the dyslexic student can face when being tested. He cites the example of one model that was designed to provide students with a range of assessment activities in order to structure the amount of reading and writing required of students in a suitably progressive way. The test consisted of six short tasks that focused upon the previous month's work on the topic of early peoples. As this was the first History test experienced by these Term 1 students (new arrivals in the secondary school), bolstering the self-esteem of less confident learners was a key principle underlying the design of the test. Learners who had been previously identified by primary teachers as experiencing difficulties in reading, writing and information-processing were provided with a differentiated degree of support in three of the activities.

The first section of the test consisted of four relatively simple tasks that required little writing and that were intended to remind students of the work covered throughout the unit:

• Completing a simple cloze passage with an answer box provided.
• Matching a table of names to pictures of specific artefacts used by early people.
• Listing things from the prehistoric period found by archaeologists in the school's local area. The test papers contained a memory trigger in the form of a local map used by the teacher in the lesson on this aspect of the topic.
• Completing five sentence stems such as 'We know the Skara Brae people in Orkney were shepherds because...' This fourth exercise required students to apply recalled subject knowledge to complete the sentence appropriately.

However, three of the five sentence conclusions had been clued up by triggers in the first exercise to provide assistance for students with memory difficulties. Line indicators were used in the test paper to encourage students to write as fully as possible. The fourth task also acted as a bridge from the deliberately simple initial tasks requiring a short response to the second section of the test, which consisted of two extended writing activities in which dyslexic learners were assisted by a five-stem writing frame. This form of assessment is also metacognitive as it provides an opportunity for scaffolding to other more complex tasks and concepts and helps students to be aware of how they achieved certain tasks. Importantly, however, this example provides a link between assessment and practice within a meaningful context.

In Biology, Howlett (2001) suggests that the following list can present difficulties and can therefore be used as a means of helping to identify the nature of the difficulties experienced by dyslexic students in this subject:

- remembering and recalling 'names' accurately, for text and diagrams;
- spelling of technical words;
- learning of many factual details;
- assimilating abstract concepts;
- drawing and labelling of diagrams;
- practical work—remembering and following instructions accurately and fully, and recording observations/data accurately, in orderly manner and fast enough; having confidence to ask about anything not understood or to come up with original questions and comments.

METACOGNITIVE ASSESSMENT

Metacognition refers to the child's self-knowledge of learning. It examines the quality of the learning process: the structure and organisation of the learner's knowledge base, of mental models (schemata) and efficiency of student self-monitoring. Metacognitive knowledge therefore involves both content and process knowledge. Most traditional forms of assessment look only at the content base, and what the child can and cannot do becomes the product of the assessment. It is important to consider, however, that a preoccupation with identifying the nature of the dyslexic difficulties should not prevent an assessment of the child's learning processes. This has considerable linkage with appropriate teaching and how materials should be presented.

There are a number of ways of assessing the metacognitive strategies of dyslexic children. Some of these are described below.

Assisted Assessment

Campione and Brown (1989), dissatisfied with the limited information that can be obtained from normative procedures, have developed a soundly researched model for assisted or dynamic assessment, focusing on the task and the process of learning. They have also linked this form of assessment with the intervention model known as Reciprocal Teaching (Palincsar and Klenk, 1992).

The focus of Campione and Brown's work relates to aspects of learning and transfer; the information obtained provides an indication of the nature and amount of help needed by the child, rather than the child's level of attainment or improvement. This can be revealed through 'prompts', memory tasks and help with developing learning strategies.

Campione and Brown argue that there should be a link between assessment and instruction. They argue that traditional tests are intended to be predictive and prescriptive, but fail on both counts. Their argument rests on the assertions that children can be too readily mis-classified and that traditional tests do not really provide a clear indication of what is really required for instruction.

Campione and Brown (1989) argue that the context of assessment is important and divide assessment into two aspects.

Static Tests

In these the child works unaided on sets of items and is given but a single chance to demonstrate his or her proficiency. Thus:

- no aid is provided;
- social interaction between the tester and the child is minimised;
- objective scoring systems can be readily implemented;
- norms can be available.

Although such tests may fulfil a purpose, they have considerable shortcomings as they say nothing about the processes involved in the acquisition of the responses. For example:

- some children may get the right answer for the wrong reason;
- students may be mis-classified because they have not yet acquired the competence, but are in the process of acquiring it.

Dynamic Tests

Dynamic-type tests emphasise the individual's potential for change. Such tests do not attempt to assess how much improvement has taken place, but rather how much help children need to reach a specified criterion and how much help they will need to transfer this to novel situations. Such tests are therefore metacognitive in that they can provide information on how the child is learning. By noting the cues necessary to facilitate the correct response from the child, the teacher can obtain some information on how the child thinks and learns. Such information can be relayed back to the child to illustrate how he or she managed to obtain the correct response. Thus, assessment is a learning experience, not a testing one.

There are a number of different forms of dynamic assessment models, such as Feuerstein's Learning Potential Assessment Device (LPAD), which is inextricably linked to the Intervention Model—Instrumental Enrichment (Feuerstein, 1979), which is an intervention programme that aims to develop an individual's thinking skills and overall cognitive ability. The programme consists of 14 sets of cognitive activities that can be utilised in a classroom situation as part of the curriculum activities or as an individual programme (Burden, 2002). The LPAD battery includes both verbal and non-verbal tasks, analogical reasoning, numerical reasoning, memory strategies and conceptual categorisations; it also utilises Raven's Progressive Matrices (Raven, 1992, 1993), which is a measure of non-verbal reasoning, as one of the measures.

Extensive training is required to develop proficiency in the administration of the LPAD, although it has been described as the 'most comprehensive and theoretically grounded expression of dynamic assessment' (Lidz, 1991).

MULTIPLE INTELLIGENCES APPROACHES

Lazear (1994, 1999), utilising Gardner's theory of multiple intelligences (Gardner, 1985), has contributed greatly to a new assessment paradigm consisting of multiple intelligences approaches. Though the author quite rightly argues that a multiple intelligences assessment should grow out of a multiple intelligences curriculum, some significant insights can be gained for assessment in general by utilising the approach advocated by Lazear.

The multiple intelligences model suggests that assessment should be comprehensive and consider a number of different elements. Lazear contends that assessment should be used to enhance students' learning and, particularly, to experience their ability to transfer learning to other areas and, indeed, beyond formal schooling. Lazear further contends that, because there are no standard students, instruction of testing should be individualised and varied. Lazear's model lends itself to curriculum-based assessment.

Assessment, therefore, should be occurring simultaneously with learning and should be an inbuilt factor within the curriculum. Curriculum-based assessment, particularly using a multiple intelligences approach, ensures that the assessment process is relevant to the actual curricular work with which the student is involved.

A COMPONENTS APPROACH

The limitations of discrepancy models of assessment such as intellectual/attainment discrepancies have led to the development of alternative criteria and procedures to assist in the differential diagnosis of reading difficulties.

One such approach, known as the 'components approach' (Aaron, 1989, 1994; Aaron and Joshi, 1992; Joshi and Aaron, 2008), examines the components of the reading process. The main aims of the components approach to assessment are:

- to distinguish the dyslexic child from the 'slow learner' child who displays reading difficulties;
- to distinguish the dyslexic child from the child who has a comprehension deficit in reading;
- to adapt the assessment for classroom use, to make it available for the teacher and psychologist;
- to allow for a complete diagnostic procedure that would be comprehensive enough to include quantitative as well as qualitative information that is relevant to the reading process.

The main strands of the components approach are:

- the identification of the factors that determine performance;
- a description of the components of reading;
- an evaluation of the child's functioning in relation to these components.

Aaron (1989) describes four main components of reading:

- verbal comprehension;
- phonological awareness;
- decoding speed; and
- listening comprehension.

It can be argued that decoding and comprehension are the two most important components of reading, representing visual and auditory processing skills together with meaningful comprehension. (This simultaneous processing involving decoding and comprehension may require hemispheric integration and justify the claim that reading is a holistic activity.)

In most readers, decoding and comprehension are consistent and complementary. Therefore, as a child reads (decodes the print) meaning is simultaneously expressed. It can be suggested that:

- comprehension is a controlled process (i.e., is attention-demanding) with limited capacity;
- decoding is an automatised process (i.e., is not attention-demanding) and does not require reader's conscious control.

It is known that for dyslexic children decoding does not readily become automatised (Fawcett, 1989; Fawcett and Nicolson, 2008) and therefore requires:

- attention-demanding operations;
- conscious control from the reader.

These are also factors in comprehension, and hence it is argued that dyslexic readers, when decoding, draw on some of the capacities that should be focusing on comprehension and thereby weaken their potential for comprehension while reading. This suggestion is supported by work on visual imagery in reading (Bell, 1991; www.psllcnj.com/visualizing_and_verbalizing.htm, accessed November 2008), which claims that the decoding process weakens the dyslexic child's gestalt (right hemisphere) and consequently this affects comprehension.

Joshi and Aaron (2008) suggest that differences in reading achievement are due to factors associated with either decoding or comprehension or a combination of both. To differentiate between these two abilities, it is necessary to assess them independently. Thus, reading comprehension has to be assessed without involving the decoding of print. A components approach to assessment that can be readily carried out by the teacher can include the following:

- decoding test (non-word-reading test);
- word-reading test;
- phonological awareness test;
- listening comprehension test;
- reading comprehension test.

Aaron (1989; Joshi and Aaron, 2008) has indicated three different categories of reading disorders: dyslexic readers, hyperlexic readers and non-specific-reading disabled readers. Dyslexic readers have poor decoding, but relatively good comprehension, while non-specific-reading disabled readers show poor comprehension and poor decoding skills. The hyperlexic reader has good decoding skills, but poor comprehension.

An interesting difference can be noted between hyperlexic readers and dyslexic readers. Hyperlexic readers are those who can decode and are therefore good at reading mechanically, while dyslexic readers are poor at decoding and read inaccurately, but can perform better in reading comprehension tasks.

This emphasises that the key components of the reading process that are to be assessed are:

- decoding;
- listening/reading comprehension.

The components approach is a diagnostic procedure that does not rely solely on norm-referenced, standardised tests, but can be applied with locally developed assessment materials from which programmes can be developed in the context of the curriculum and the classroom activities.

Joshi and Aaron (2008) contend that a measure of listening comprehension is more appropriate in diagnosing reading difficulties than, for example, an IQ measure. Listening comprehension tests do not possess the same drawbacks as IQ measures and the diagnostic findings can link directly to teaching procedures. The components approach, therefore, gains support from the view that reading comprehension and listening comprehension are highly correlated and that reading is made up of two components: comprehension and decoding.

OBSERVATIONAL ASSESSMENT

The essence of this chapter is that while there are a number of assessment tools dedicated to identifying dyslexia, these should be used in conjunction with other curriculum-based forms of assessment. One method of accumulating this type of data is through observation. This form of assessment can also yield informative data that can inform teaching. Observational assessment is contextualised and can be used flexibly to ensure that the data obtained are the type of information required.

It is important, however, that the observer recognises the drawbacks of observational assessment in that often it provides only a snapshot of the child unless it is implemented in different contexts over time. Nevertheless, this type of assessment can be particularly useful for children with dyslexic difficulties as some standardised tests may not provide the kind of diagnostic information that is needed in order to develop a teaching programme. There are a number of different forms of observational assessment. These can provide important data and offer some pointers as to appropriate teaching strategies as well.

An observation schedule or framework should be constructed prior to the assessment.

A number of benefits of observation schedules can be identified; for example, they can be flexible, adaptable to different situations and can be used within the context of the learning situation. Hopefully, a 'natural' response will then be recorded free from the influence of 'test contamination' factors. Throughout the observation it is important to record not only what the student does or can do, but how the response is achieved—the cues required, and the level and extent of the assistance needed at the stages the student needs to go through to solve a problem or obtain a response.

With increased importance being placed on early identification and metacognitive aspects of learning, procedures such as observational criteria can have an important role to play in the assessment process.

OBSERVATIONAL FRAMEWORK

In this framework one is looking at a broad range of areas that can relate to some of the difficulties experienced by children with specific learning difficulties or dyslexia.

It is important to gather information that relates to the child, the learning situation and context. The aim is not just to find out how or why the child is having difficulty, but to gain some insight and understanding into the strategies and processes of learning for that child.

A framework for observational assessment for specific learning difficulties can therefore include the areas listed below.

Attention

- What is the length of attention span?
- Under what conditions is attention enhanced?
- What are the factors contributing to distractibility?
- What is the level of attention or distractibility under different learning conditions?

Organisation

- What are the organisational preferences?
- What degree of structure is required?
- How good is the organisation of work, desk, self?
- What are the reactions to imposed organisation?

Sequencing

- Is there the ability to follow sequences without aid?
- Is there a general difficulty with sequencing (e.g., with work, carrying out instructions, words when reading, individual letters in written work)?

Interaction

- What degree of interaction is there with peers, adults?
- What is the preferred interaction: one-to-one, small groups or whole class?
- How is the interaction sustained?

Language

- Is language expressive?
- Is the meaning accurately conveyed?
- Is language spontaneous or prompted?
- Is there appropriate use of natural breaks in speech?
- Is there expressive language in different contexts (e.g., one-to-one, small group or class group)?
- Are there errors, omissions and difficulties in conversation and responses (e.g., mispronunciations, questions have to be repeated or clarified)?

Comprehension

- How does the child comprehend information?
- What type of cues most readily facilitate comprehension?
- Are schemas used?
- What type of instructions are most easily understood: written, oral or visual?
- How readily can knowledge be transferred to other areas?

Reading

- What are the reading preferences: aloud, silent?
- What type of errors crop up?

Visual

- Is there the ability to discriminate between letters that look the same?
- Is there inability to appreciate that the same letter may look different (e.g., 'G' or 'g')?
- Does omission or transposition of parts of a word occur (this could indicate a visual segmentation difficulty)?

Auditory

- Are there difficulties in auditory discrimination?
- Is there inability to hear consonant sounds in initial, medial or final position?
- Is there auditory sequencing?

- Is there auditory blending?
- Is there an auditory segmentation?

Motivation/Initiative

- What is the interest level of the child?
- How is motivation increased, what kind of prompting and cueing is necessary?
- To what extent does the child take responsibility for his or her own learning?
- What kind of help is required?

Self-concept

- What tasks are more likely to be tackled with confidence?
- When is confidence low?
- What is the level of self-concept and confidence in different contexts?

Relaxation

- Is the child relaxed when learning?
- Is there evidence of tension or relaxation?

Learning Preferences

The following learning preferences need to be ascertained:

- auditory;
- visual;
- oral;
- kinaesthetic;
- tactile;
- global;
- analytic.

It is important, therefore, to note in observational assessment the preferred mode of learning. Many children will, of course, show preferences and skills in a number of modes of learning. Multi-sensory teaching, therefore, is crucial in order to accommodate as many modes as possible.

Learning Context

When assessing the nature and degree of the difficulty experienced by the child, it is important to take into account the learning context. This context, depending on the learner's preferred style, can either exacerbate the difficulty or minimise the problem

(Reid, 1992, 1994a; Given and Reid, 1999). The contextual factors below should there-fore be considered:

- classroom;
- role of teacher;
- task;
- materials and resources.

Observation and assessment need to adopt a holistic perspective:

- observing components within a framework for learning;
- observing some factors within that framework associated with specific learning difficulties or dyslexia;
- observing preferred styles of learning;
- acknowledging the importance of the learning context.

SYSTEMATIC OBSERVATION

Structured systematic observation can yield some important information in relation to the student's strengths, difficulties and actual performances in the classroom context. Perhaps the most sophisticated of the systematic observation strategies are those devised for the Reading Recovery Programme. Clay (1993) provides a detailed analysis of systematic observation. This analysis is called the 'running record' and the observation tasks are designed to help the teacher focus on precisely what happens when the child is reading. Although the Clay observation tasks were designed to develop a running record for use with the Reading Recovery Programme, some of the general principles can be utilised for use with dyslexic children. Clay suggests that, to observe systematically, one must:

- observe precisely what children are saying and doing;
- use tasks that are closely related to the learning tasks of the classroom;
- observe what children have been able to learn;
- identify from this the reading behaviour they should now be taught;
- focus the child's general reading behaviour to training on reading tasks rather than on specific sub-skills such as visual perception or auditory discrimination.

In order to achieve the above, Clay has developed a 'diagnostic survey' (the Running Record), which looks at directional movement, motor coordination, reading fluency, error behaviour, oral language skills, letter identification skills, concepts about print and writing skills.

This latter aspect is particularly important as writing skills may provide some indi-cation of any reading problems (e.g., a poor writing vocabulary may indicate that the child is taking very little notice of visual differences in print). The weakness in visual discrimination may be because the hand and eye are not complementing each other, and this is an important aspect of early writing. Additionally, other factors in writing such as language level and message quality are also important to note. In writing, children are required to pay attention to details of letters, letter sequences, sound sequences and the links between messages in oral language and messages in printed language.

Other useful aspects of Clay's model involve the 'concepts of print test', which addresses vital aspects relating to the child's knowledge of print and familiarity with books. Questions about whether the child can distinguish the front from the back of the book, left from right, recognise errors in print, distinguish between capital and lower case and locate first and last letters are all addressed. This provides crucial information at this early stage of reading—information that certainly should be gathered for children who are at risk of failing in literacy.

Clay's observation approach also focuses on strategies for decoding. The teacher should therefore record the different strategies the child uses in relation to location and movement, language, how the child deals with difficulties (e.g., seeking help, searching for further cues and the extent of self-correction). Self-correction, according to Clay, is an important aspect of reading progress and needs to be accurately recorded.

SUMMARY

A range of approaches have been described in this chapter. To recap, these include standardised, diagnostic, phonological assessment, curriculum, components of reading assessment, metacognitive, screening and observational approaches.

No one approach can provide both sufficient data to identify and assess dyslexia and provide a sufficient and effective linkage with teaching. Different factors need to be taken into account and all assessment procedures discussed in this chapter have considerable merits. The factors that determine what approach or approaches should be used relate to the reasons for the assessment and the purposes to which the information is to be put. It is, however, important to bear in mind that different children may well display different profiles and still be identified as dyslexic. Ideally, the assessment should link with teaching, and if this is a successful outcome of the assessment then it will have been put to a valid and worthwhile use.

POINTS FOR REFLECTION

- Consider the tests you use for identifying dyslexia. What do the tests attempt to find out? How have the tests been developed?

- Consider the role of IQ in assessment. How helpful do you find the information relating to IQ? What use can you put this information to?

- Consider three factors that are discussed in this chapter—the assessment of processing skills, reasoning skills and attainments (performances). How might you incorporate these factors into an assessment process for dyslexia?

continued

- Reflect on the factors that might account for the difficulties children experience in reading. How might you obtain more information on this from the assessment process?

- Reflect on the use of screening tests—what might be the advantages and disadvantages of using such tests? How might these fit into an early identification model? What other factors might you need to incorporate into this type of model?

- Reflect on the use of curriculum and observational assessment. How useful might you find this sort of information?

- Consider the differences between 'static' tests and 'dynamic assessment'—weigh up the advantages and disadvantages of each.

- Consider how you might develop your own observational framework for identifying children at risk of dyslexia. Reflect on how useful you might find this.

Chapter 6

Reading—Social, Cultural and Government Perspectives

THE SOCIAL CONTEXT FOR LITERACY

Reading can be seen as the extraction of meaning from print. Yet this is doing a great disservice to reading and to literacy. Reading needs to be seen as much wider than just obtaining meaning from print. It is a dynamic and crucial aspect of learning, and reading can be a catalyst for the acquisition of language skills, social skills, critical thinking skills and social and cultural awareness.

LITERACY AND CULTURE

Reading helps to provide an appreciation of culture, the conventions of society and the social convention seen in the purposes placed on the use of literacy by society. Reading is therefore an integral component of social and cultural development in most societies today. The culture of a society can be shaped through the use of books and the conventions of print. Berryman and Wearmouth (2009) describe the concept of culture as one that is often used by various groups to identify and define themselves and to differentiate themselves from others. In this regard, culture may therefore be defined by the relationships, interactions and icons within which specific groups of people engage over a period of time. Culture therefore provides a platform for the literate society and a fundamental foundation for the books that are produced. Bruner (1990) argues that 'it is culture, not biology, that shapes human life and the human mind,... by imposing the patterns inherent in the culture's symbolic systems—its language and discourse modes, the forms of logical and narrative explication...' (p. 34).

This underlines the importance of culture for today's literate societies. One of the key points in relation to culture and education is that, as Harker (2007) suggests, it is important for the family and the community culture of the students to be understood and supported by schools, and crucially so in multicultural societies. It is also important that this becomes a two-way transmission of information facilitating a mutual cultural understanding and that it commences as early as possible in the child's school career. An excellent example of this is in East Renfrewshire in Scotland where a system of home/community teachers who engage with families at the pre-school stage in the family's own home has been developed. These teachers were able to identify children at risk of failing in literacy development and then implement early intervention approaches at the pre-school stage, taking the child's social and cultural situation into account (Wearmouth et al., 2003).

It is important that teachers have an awareness of the student's cultural background. In fact, Berryman and Wearmouth (2009) suggest that when teachers give students' home cultures a central position within the pedagogy of the classroom, student learning is more effective. They suggest that one of the reasons for this is that the learning of new concepts is linked to prior knowledge stemming from outside the classroom. Alton-Lee (2006) argues that a 'substantial amount of classroom time is wasted because the instructional experiences do not match children's memory processes' (p. 618). It seems therefore that the greater the distance between the world of the teacher and that of the child, the greater importance culturally responsive pedagogies can potentially have. Bishop (2003) suggests that when there is a cultural mismatch between the teacher and the student it must be the teacher who makes the cognitive adjustment. This has implications for the teaching of reading and language skills and particularly the selection of reading material.

DEFINING LITERACY

One of the key aspects relating to literacy levels and to illiteracy definitions is the question how we define literacy. According to Eames (2002), literacy educators have faced a number of challenges relating to defining literacy and attempting to incorpo-rate the prevailing views and fashions by addressing the question 'what is literacy' and translating this into effective teaching approaches with measurable outcomes. This has been particularly challenging because often disparate views have been put forward about what constitutes literacy and how literacy should be taught. Eames (2002) sug-gests that the responses to these challenges have often resulted in a polarisation of the teaching community about the benefits of some approaches over others. Definitions of 'literacy' are many and various and have been defined as the ability to read and write or extended to include the ability to calculate numbers or having a basic knowledge of mathematics and calculation. In line with these definitions, a child or adult who has difficulties with literacy might be described as a child or adult who has difficulties with basic reading and writing. While this can include being competent in mathematics, many people might agree that they would see difficulties in reading and writing as the main barrier to being a literate citizen (Wearmouth et al., 2003).

This definition of what constitutes literacy leads us to see literacy as a set of technical skills involving the decoding of written text and the ability to write and produce written text. Moreover, it tends to focus on reading and writing as separate skills which can be evaluated and measured. While this may seem a straightforward and uncomplicated view of literacy, if we look more closely we see that even this apparently simple view of literacy implies that there different levels of literacy and different expectations of what being literate might entail. Within this view of literacy it is possible to define being literate as achieving 'basic literacy' or 'functional literacy' and having difficulties with literacy as 'functional illiteracy'.

Au and Raphael (2000) suggest that as definitions of literacy have changed, so have the curriculum, instruction and assessments associated with them. They cite the example of Michigan state in the 1980s, when, following a redefinition of reading from fluent print decoding to an interactive process emphasising comprehension, major changes followed in English language arts' standards that tested higher levels of comprehension and writing in response to text. The dilemmas and the challenges associated with reading appear to surround the need to provide a balanced literacy curriculum where 'children are exposed both to direct instruction in reading skills together with the experiences that encourage social collaboration and constructive problem solving associated with an integrated language arts approach' (Morrow et al., 1999, p. 474). This highlights the challenge to teachers and management who need to define literacy and evaluate the effects of different approaches.

This also explains government influence and concern over literacy standards in the community. Essentially, literacy should reflect the pluralistic contexts in which children live. This view is very apparent in the work of Glynn and colleagues in New Zealand and also Soler and Smith (2000) who found that the privileging of certain 'literacies' and literary traditions over others can lead to a systematised exclusion of 'literacies' in different cultures and languages.

This has implications for teaching methodologies, teaching resources and measures of assessment, all of which can support the different views, the conflicts and the challenges to which educators need to respond in relation to defining literacy. In general, this emphasizes the need for a broad definition of literacy that can reflect and embrace the cultural and linguistic diversities we increasingly meet in the classroom among readers of all abilities, including children with dyslexia.

CRITICAL LITERACY

The points made above in relation to what one means by literacy and the use of literacy is encapsulated in the term 'critical literacy'. Hall (1998) terms critical literacy as coming to understand what are one's own literacy practices and one's responses to texts at an individual, personal and social level. According to Eames (2002), critical literacy can be placed at the highest stage of the literacy hierarchy, the overarching concept transforming multiple literacy concepts and contexts. She suggests that critical literacy involves constructing meaning from text and that such meanings are achieved during interaction of reader and text, during discussion of text and when listening and responding to others. This has important implications for children with dyslexia and particularly young adults who may not have efficient decoding skills, but nevertheless should not be deprived of the spin-off social and cognitive benefits of literacy seen in this way. Wray (2006) acknowledges that critical literacy is not a new concept and can be recognized as critical language awareness, critical social literacy and critically aware literacy. He argues, however, that there are some common threads running through the different approaches to critical literacy. One of the crucial factors rests on the assumption that being literate is not sufficient. He argues that teachers who engage in critical literacy 'will encourage students to investigate, question and challenge relationships between language and social practices that advantage some groups over others' (p. 21). He also argues that critical literacy often challenges the racial and class tensions that can characterise some societies. Wray therefore suggests that critical literacy is 'about transforming taken for granted social and language practices or assumptions for the good of as many people as possible' (p. 21).

Rassool (1999) suggests that the multidimensional view of literacy is one that is integrally linked with ideology, culture, knowledge and power. This view of literacy counters the traditional functional view of literacy as an autonomous set of technical skills and shifts the emphasis away from concerns about process, or individual behaviours during reading, to that of active involvement within a defined learning context. Rassool also draws attention to the ongoing debate of the ways in which different disciplinary frameworks draw upon social psychology, sociolinguistics, social anthropology and critical theory and that this has resulted in the conceptualisation of literacy as a multidimensional culturally related process.

This is particularly evident for educators working in multicultural and multilingual contexts. Diniz (2002) reflects on his own personal experience of multicultural contexts. He himself is multilingual, from a multi-ethnic background; he was born in Africa to a Portuguese father, his mother was of Indian origin and he is married to a Brazilian. Diniz draws upon his own experiences as a practising educational psychologist and academic researcher working in areas related to special needs; he has identified some of the major socio-cultural factors that contribute to barriers to literacy acquisition and points out their importance for teachers. He comments that

> *one of the things I've learned from research is that the connections (between race, ethnicity, culture, family and literacy) are not acknowledged. That is key (point for Practitioners) to understand that there are connections. If one believes in child centeredness of learning and if we believe that we start from where the children are, then we're starting from the home, the home in the sense of the child's environment. So the first thing one wants to know about that is what is the cultural context within which the child is learning. Those might be articulated in terms of the language, or languages very often, that are used in the home. (Diniz, 2002)*

Diniz agrees that barriers can arise and that cognitive literacy difficulties such as dyslexia may be masked by teachers' assumptions about culture. He argues that teachers need to be able to differentiate between cognitive and cultural issues in relation to difficulties in literacy development at the classroom level in order to support students' literacy learning in the most appropriate ways. One of the key aspects of the above is that literacy should engage the reader and in order to do this the content and the context must be culturally familiar, or at least a pre-reading activity takes place to help to engage the reader in the cultural and social context.

Table 6.1   Structure to engage in critical literacy

Information	Background
	Country
	Town
	Area
	Author
	Author's background
	Other information about author
Purpose of book	Why did the author write the book?
	Key message of book
Content/style	Genre of book
	The role of author
	Tense of prose
	Pace of book
	Story line
Inferences made in book	Is there a hidden message in the book?
	What is the meaning of the book from your perspective?
Impact of book	Was/is the book popular?
	Did it serve its purpose?
	Readership of book? Children, adults?
	Did the book change the way you think about the issues?
	How powerful was it as an agent of change?

Engaging the Reader through Critical Literacy

It is suggested therefore that one of the other key points about critical literacy, particularly in relation to children with dyslexia, is that critical literacy can help to engage the reader, particularly if the reading activity is structured around the ideas relating to critical literacy. Some suggestions for this structure are shown in Table 6.1.

Baker et al. (2000) suggest that engaged readers tend to be achieving readers. It is particularly important to engage children with dyslexia fully in the reading activity in order to provide some appreciation of the text. They may not get this from unstructured reading as they may well omit some of the key words or misread the text.

CHALLENGING ASSUMPTIONS

According to Hunt (2002), however, 'critical literacy' challenges assumptions that texts can ever convey 'objective meanings' or that literacy is an ideologically neutral tool. It asserts that both readers and writers approach texts in ways that are conditioned by such factors as purpose, power relations, gender and historical period. These factors are expressed through a variety of rhetorical devices (such as vocabulary and grammatical structure choices) and by the writer's selection of which voices and positions to express and which to omit. He suggests that this can be seen in some forms of newspaper reporting and advertising that select information that favours one view at the expense of another. The implication for teachers of this, according to Hunt, is that they need to do more than simply train students to become skilled decoders. He suggests that decoding is an essential part of the reading process, but it is only one aspect of a set of socio-cultural practices that also encompasses working out what the text means, knowing how to use the text in context and how the text has been constructed to produce specific effects on the reader. This implies that in order to become independent readers children with dyslexia need to be aware of these dimensions, questioning the choices and assumptions that underlie the writer's words.

Taking these points into consideration, the goal of literacy teaching is therefore the empowerment of the reader. Critical literacy teachers, according to Hunt, approach this goal in various ways and need to encourage multiple interpretations rather than a quest for definitive meaning. Hunt cites the following framework (from Luke et al., 2001, p. 16) of questions that can structure critical investigations:

- What is the topic?
- How is it being presented?
- What themes and discourses are being used? Who is writing to whom? Whose voices and positions are being expressed?
- Whose voices and positions are not being expressed?
- What is the text trying to do for you?
- What other ways are there of writing about the topic?
- What wasn't said about the topic?
- Why?

Berryman and Wearmouth (2009) discuss the Australian programme Reading to Learn (Rose et al., 1999), which focuses on scaffolding students' literacy learning by modelling the correct answers and rewarding students when they respond in kind. In this way, new language and literacy learning is part of the social and cultural contexts in which students engage (Vygotsky, 1978). Through strategic guidance and scaffolding by their teachers, high levels of initial support can be gradually reduced as students develop new skills and are able to complete increasingly challenging tasks with greater levels on independence.

Koop and Rose (2008), using data from the Murdi Paaki region of New South Wales, Australia, showed that providing indigenous students with literacy skills helped to engage them successfully at all levels of schooling. In their study, teacher expectations were made explicit to the learners, who were supported, through the scaffolding process, through interactive teaching and learning support. Teachers indicated that students developed confidence and competence in literacy and developed literacy skills that were far broader than being able to read, write and spell. Students developed an educational platform that enabled them to access 'the academic "ways of speaking and thinking" that are necessary for educational success' (Koop and Rose, 2008, p. 43). In this way their learning is accelerated and students are able to catch up with their more advanced peers.

This study also highlights the importance of developing critical and engaging literacy approaches for dyslexic children that are much broader than the technical skills of reading.

GOVERNMENT INITIATIVES

Given the importance of culture for developing literacy and language skills, it is not surprising that governments around the world have engaged in efforts to enhance the literacy skills of children. In New Zealand, for example, in 2001 the government reported on the findings of the Education and Science Committee inquiry into teaching of reading in New Zealand. The report conceded that 'for most of the past decade...schools have received little assistance from the ministry in achieving national literacy goals. We are pleased this is now changing.' The report, however, did acknowledge that current literacy strategies are effective for most of the students in New Zealand, but 'there is compelling evidence that these strategies do not work for certain groups of poor performers, which may together number up to 20 per cent of students'. The key point about this is that it indicates a government concern with reading standards, and with how the government can influence, support and evaluate these standards and achieve national goals in literacy. This implies that the government is interested not only in standards but also in how these standards are achieved. The teaching of reading and the support necessary to develop quality teaching programmes and materials are seen as a concern of the New Zealand government in the same way as the introduction of the National Literacy strategy in England and Wales indicates a greater government involvement with the teaching in the class as well as the outcomes of education. Government is now concerned with how reading is taught.

In the UK Sir Jim Rose's review of the primary curriculum to include recommendations on the identification and teaching of children with dyslexia was profiled in May 2008. The review indicated that a great deal had been done and was under way to support dyslexic children and their families. The aim of the ministerial statement (May 2008) was to highlight how the government had encouraged best practice in schools by improving outcomes for children with dyslexia. This included additional funding for projects such as the 'No to Failure' project. The government indicated that the 'No to Failure' project is 'trailblazing and [involved] evaluating the impact of specialist training for teachers and specialist tuition for children with dyslexia in some schools in 3 local authority areas'. Much of this response emanated from submissions from dyslexia organisations against the Rose Review which came down heavily in support of the synthetic phonic approach.

The dyslexia organisations responded to this in the following way (May 2008):

It is important to note, however, that the evidence base for teaching of dyslexic students has been well established through longitudinal international research. We know how to support these children effectively. Our organisations strongly believe that the country should be implementing a simple system where each school would have one teacher trained as a dyslexia/SpLD specialist who can recognise and support children with dyslexia/SpLD. This expertise is already widely available from dyslexia centres, specialist teachers and a number of independent schools who have for many years been providing effective support for dyslexic children in reading, writing, maths, and concentration. Each review and pilot merely adds to the delay in implementing the solution. They have been getting it right for years. We want to see this in all schools in the public sector.

There are a number of issues stemming from this relating to the teaching of reading: the methodology used and the mode of teaching—small group, one on one or whole class. These have implications for students with dyslexia and will be dealt with in more depth in the chapter on teaching. For this chapter the key point is that the government has involved itself to a great extent and taken significant responsibility for the teaching of reading!

LITERACY STANDARDS AND INTERNATIONAL COMPARISONS

There has been increasing interest in national reading levels and international comparisons. Much of this has been fuelled by concern over literacy standards. Curtis (2008) draws attention to the fact that, in England, around 20% of children emerge from their primary school experience without the basic levels of attainment in literacy expected of them. This is in spite of a 10-year intensive focus on literacy teaching by the UK government. The CBI's 2008 Education and Skills Survey, 'Taking Stock' (CBI, 2008), found that 41% of employers surveyed were concerned about employees' basic literacy. For firms with basic skills concerns, the quality of written English—constructing properly spelt sentences with accurate grammar—was the major literacy concern (72%).

The report suggested that poor basic skills among the workforce have significant consequences for business. Low levels of literacy (and numeracy) result in poor customer service (40%) and lower productivity (34%)—seriously affecting business performance. Shiel (2002) argues that many countries wish to participate in surveys because the results provide policy-makers with information that can be used to monitor standards or implement reforms. For example, in 1991 the International Association for the Evaluation of Educational Achievement (IEA) and the Reading Literacy Study (RLS) assessed the achievement of 9–14-year-olds in 32 countries (20 at the lower age level and 31 at the higher age level). Participating countries at both age levels included Finland, Canada, Ireland and the USA. Although England did not participate in the original study, the IEA test was administered by the National Foundation for Educational Research in England and Wales to a representative sample of English and Welsh 9-year-olds in 1996, so the performance of English/Welsh students can be compared with that of 9-year-olds in other countries in 1991 (see Brooks et al., 1996).

In the IEA/RLS, 'reading literacy' was defined as 'the ability to understand and use those written language forms required by society and/or valued by the individual' (Elley, 1992, p. 3). The national samples of students who participated in the assessment were presented with three types of text: narrative texts (continuous texts in which the writer's aim is to tell a story, whether fact or fiction); expository texts (continuous prose designed to describe, explain or convey factual information); and document texts (structured texts presented in the form of charts, tables, maps and sets of directions). The vast majority of comprehension questions based on these texts were of the multiple-choice variety; the remainder were of the short-answer type. Test questions tapped five levels of text processing that were assumed to be in roughly hierarchical order: literal response (verbatim match), paraphrase, main idea, inference, and locate and process information. As with other international studies, care was taken to ensure that both passages and questions represented the reading curricula in participating countries and that strict guidelines were adhered to in translating test materials, in order to ensure comparability of outcomes across countries.

The outcomes of the IEA/RLS were reported in a variety of ways, including mean (average) overall reading literacy scores by country as well as mean country scores for understanding of narrative, expository and document texts. Finland achieved the highest mean score at ages 9 and 14. In a ranking of countries at age 9, Ireland and England/Wales were ranked 12th and 21st, respectively, out of 28 countries. However, because of measurement error, their respective mean scores were found not to be statistically significantly different from one another (Brooks et al., 1996). At age 14, Ireland was ranked 20th of 31 countries, suggesting a decline in achievement between 9- and 14-year-olds. However, Ireland's mean score at age 14 was not significantly different from the mean scores of nine other countries, or from the international country average (Elley, 1992). Differences were observed in the performance of students on the three text types used in the study. Nine-year-olds in both Ireland and England/Wales did best on narrative texts, next best on expository texts and poorest on documents. This has implications for the question 'what is reading', since it covers not only different facets of literacy but can also be utilised for different functions. This is important because of governments' preoccupation with literacy standards and the implications of the apparent results of assessment of these standards for groups such as dyslexic children.

PISA STUDY

In the PISA 2000 study (Shiel et al., 2001), 28 OECD countries and four non-OECD countries (Brazil, Latvia, Liechtenstein and the Russian Federation) participated and only one country, Finland, achieved a significantly higher mean. The USA ranked 15th for combined reading literacy with a mean slightly above the average, while Canada ranked 2nd with a score significantly higher than the mean, but Canadian students scored the highest in the subscale that measured the ability to 'reflect on and evaluate texts'. It is interesting to note that in the rankings of mathematical and scientific literacy measures, Japan and the Republic of Korea achieved the top two ratings—Japan for mathematical literacy and Korea for scientific literacy.

This emphasizes the different literacy priorities of different countries and underlines the functional use of literacy as a social, cultural and economic medium. There are usually a number of reasons that one country should fare better than others in literacy attainment measures, and, as mentioned above, these can include social and environmental as well as educational reasons. It is important, therefore, that dyslexia should also be seen in that wider social and environmental context and not confined to the educational domain. This is implied in the definition of reading literacy in the PISA study. In this study, reading literacy is defined as 'understanding, using and reflecting on written texts, in order to achieve one's goals, to develop one's knowledge and potential, and to participate in society' (OECD, 2000, p. 20).

LITERACY INITIATIVES

There have also been a great number of literacy initiatives, such as the Literacy Commission in Scotland (2008). This commission was launched in June 2008 with the aim of eradicating illiteracy in Scotland. This followed on from an example in an area of Scotland—West Dunbartonshire—which has experienced significant success with reducing illiteracy levels (Mackay, personal correspondence, 2008). The West Dumbarton initiative was based on a paper called *A Vision for Transforming the Reading Achievement of All Children* (Mackay, 1997). The aim of the paper was not only to raise significantly the attainment levels of every child, including the highest achievers, but also to eradicate illiteracy. The result of the initiative was that in 10 years, i.e., by June 2007, only three students in mainstream schools had not achieved the literacy target compared to over 20% in 1997 who were below functional literacy levels.

The points made in this chapter will be placed in context in the next chapter, which looks at the process of learning to read and then the need to consider the influence of different orthographies from linguistic and cultural perspectives.

POINTS FOR REFLECTION

- Consider how you might define literacy—reflect on how this definition matches the materials and resources you have available.

- Consider what is meant by critical literacy—reflect on the implications of this for students with dyslexia.

- Consider the role of governments in dealing with literacy initiatives. Is this a valid role? Reflect on the current initiatives in your country that have taken place. How helpful do you think these are?

- Reflect on the need to be cautious when considering literacy standards and international comparisons.

Chapter 7

The Acquisition of Literacy

WHAT IS READING?

What is reading? This question, despite its apparent simplicity, can raise a number of issues. Eames highlights the concepts of literacy promoted by the English Language Curriculum in the Republic of Ireland (NCCA, 1999). This proposes that reading involves both 'learning to read' and 'reading to learn'. This counters the view of reading as a narrow mastering of the technical skills relating to print. Reading is much broader than this, and this broader view has implications for studies that report on literacy levels among different populations of children and adults. It is important when interpreting these studies to ascertain the perspective held by the researchers and the criteria used to measure reading levels.

Wray (2009) argues that it is precisely an over-emphasis on initial skills which might actually create some of the literacy problems that teachers later have to deal with. He suggests that for many children the problem they have with literacy is related more to their engagement with it (or lack of) than it is to their potential to learn the requisite skills. In our answer to this question 'what is reading?', therefore, we need to be sure that it incorporates the technical mastering of reading as well as factors such as comprehension and engagement with the narrative. Learning to read requires a number of skills. Many of these are considered pre-reading skills and some develop as a result of reading itself. Being deprived of reading fluency, for example, can affect the development of many of the necessary sub-skills of reading.

FACTORS TO CONSIDER

Some specific factors that are important in the acquisition of literacy include word attack skills (such as letter recognition, segmentation, blending, phonemic awareness, analogy strategies and grapheme–phoneme correspondence) and word recognition skills (such as recognition of word patterns and the use of visual memory skills). There is substantial evidence that phonological awareness is crucial to the acquisition of print (Lindamood and Lindamood, 1998; Vellutino et al., 2004; Mahfoudi and Haynes, 2009). Phonological awareness is an umbrella term that includes awareness and manipulation of speech at the word, syllable and phoneme levels. Mahfoudi and Haynes (2009), quoting the National Reading Panel (2000) in the USA, argues that explicit, structured phonics instruction—teaching of rules that link speech information with letters and letter patterns—improves word recognition skills and contributes to spelling, decoding fluency, and reading comprehension in typically developing children as well as children with dyslexia and related language learning difficulties (National Reading Panel, 2000).

Other factors (such as environmental considerations, development of the concepts of print, development of language concepts and how the whole concept of reading is viewed by the learner) are also important. According to Wray (2009), there is a great deal of research (Keene and Zimmerman, 2007) which indicates the importance of children's prior knowledge in their understanding of new knowledge as a key factor in literacy development. He also argues that it is important that this prior knowledge needs to be brought to the forefront of the learner's mind, that is, made explicit, if it is to be utilised effectively.

Ehri (2002) suggests that, initially, to become skilled readers children need to acquire knowledge of the alphabetic system and that this process presents some difficulty to struggling readers. It is important that teachers understand the processes involved in reading. Ehri suggests that learning to read involves two basic processes. One involves learning to decipher the print (i.e., learning to transform letter sequences into familiar words). The other involves comprehending the meaning of the print. When children attain reading skills, they learn to perform both these processes in a way that allows their attention to focus on the meaning of the text while the mechanics of reading, including deciphering, operate unobtrusively and out of awareness.

Ehri suggests that children acquire listening comprehension skills in the course of learning to speak. She also argues that decoding print is not a natural process in the same way as speech. The brain is specialised for processing spoken language, but not written language (Liberman, 1992). In order for reading and writing skills to develop, Ehri suggests that written language must penetrate and gain a foothold in the mechanisms used by the brain to process speech.

READING AS A PROCESS

These factors underline the view that reading is an interactive and reciprocal process. In other words, the more skills the child has access to, the more competent he or she will become, not only in reading as an activity but also in the development of the sub-skills of reading. The flip side of this also applies—that is, those children who lack competence in reading sub-skills will not have ready access to print and are consequently deprived of an opportunity to develop these skills. which can have an adverse affect on comprehension and other cognitive benefits derived from reading.

This is described as the Matthew effect (Stanovich, 1986), which means the 'rich' get 'richer' and the 'poor' get 'poorer'. Therefore, those children who have reading skills will have greater opportunity to develop other linguistic, comprehension and cognitive skills through the practice of reading. Reading is therefore interactive and reciprocal and this is highlighted in the model suggested by Adams (1990a). Adam's model of the reading system highlights the interactions between context, meaning, orthography (print) and phonology (speech).

The orthographic processor is responsible for sequencing the letters in a word, the phonological processor for matching those letters to the letter sound, the meaning processor relates to the reader's knowledge of word meaning and the context processor provides an overview of the meaning of the text. These processors work together and receive feedback from each other.

Ehri (2002) suggests that children can use at least two different methods to read words as they process text. These are:

- *decoding words*—this involves transforming letters into sounds and blending the sounds to form recognisable words;
- *analogising to known words*—using this method, readers may read a new word by recognising how its spelling is similar to a word they already know as a sight word; for example, reading beak by analogy to peak.

Goswami (1990) showed that beginning readers can use their knowledge of rhyming words to read words by analogy, especially if the rhyming clue words are in view. However, Ehri suggests that having some decoding skills appears to be required for beginners to analogise using sight words in memory (Ehri and Robbins, 1992). She also indicates that predicting words from graphophonemic and context cues, such as pictures, the preceding text or beginning letters, can help readers predict the identity of an unfamiliar word through using the syntactic context.

Ehri also suggests that children can read by 'sight'. This involves reading words by memory, which requires children to access information stored in memory from previous experiences of reading the words. This means that the child must have previously read the word. Ehri suggests that in each of the above—the use of context, beginning letters, or graphophonemic cues—the processes differ. As readers attain literacy skills they learn to read words in all four ways. It is important to recognize, therefore, that for children with dyslexia who may have difficulty in utilising one particular approach it is important to attempt another method. This highlights the fact that there is no one single approach to teaching and acquiring literacy.

READING SKILLS

The skills used in reading are little different from many of the skills used in other aspects of learning. For example, linguistic, visual and auditory skills are all essential for access to reading. These skills are also used in other learning activities such as in speech, listening and creative and visual work. These skills develop independently of reading because they are used in learning activities other than reading.

READING PRACTICE

The research does indicate, however, that reading can help to further develop the skills noted above. This highlights the importance of being an able and motivated reader. The view that the actual practice of reading fosters reading and learning skills is quite prevalent (Stanovich, 1988; Wray and Lewis, 1997; Wray, 2009). This means that reading practice is essential to develop skills as a reader and for children with dyslexia it is essential that this practice should be structured and guided by the teacher. Reading practice also helps to develop automaticity. This is important for reading fluency.

DEVELOPING READING SKILLS

Adams (1990b) suggests that activities designed to develop young children's awareness of words, syllables and phonemes significantly increase their later success in learning to read and write. The impact of phonemic training on reading acquisition, Adams suggests, is especially strong when phonemes are taught together with the letters by which they are represented. This suggests an important role for the teacher in the fostering of reading skills.

Adams (1990a) also suggests that independent writing activities can help foster an appreciation of text and its comprehension. She also promotes phonic instruction to help with both the sounds of words and the spellings of words. Reading aloud to children, according to Adams, is perhaps the single most important activity for building the knowledge and skills eventually required for reading.

KEY FACTORS

Many of the visual and auditory aspects of reading do not develop spontaneously in children with dyslexia. These skills need to be taught, and usually in an explicit, sensitive and structured manner. Some of the skills that are required in reading include automatic rapid word and letter recognition, phonological and visual skills, and knowledge of the concepts of print.

These include:

- auditory factors:
  - recognition of letter sounds;
  - recognition of sounds and letter groups or patterns;
  - sequencing of sounds;
  - discriminating sounds from other sounds;
  - discriminating sounds within words;

- linguistic factors:
  - the flow of oral language does not always make the break between words clear;
  - retaining the sounds in memory;
  - articulating sounds;
  - recognising the sounds in written form;
- visual factors:
  - recognise the visual cues of letters and words;
  - familiarity with left–right orientation;
  - recognising word patterns;
  - recognising letter and word shapes;
- contextual factors:
  - acquiring vocabulary knowledge;
  - acquiring general knowledge;
  - using context as an aid to word recognition, comprehension and analogy skills.

How one decides to prioritise the teaching of these skills within a programme or approach depends to a great extent on the strengths and difficulties of the child. This interaction of skills underlines the multifaceted nature of reading and the long-standing notion that no one method, medium, approach or even philosophy holds the key to the process of learning to read (DES, 1975).

Hunt (2002) suggests that there are dangers in using findings about what skilled readers do in order to draw direct implications about teaching practices for non-readers. He quotes an example from the work of Goodman (1976) that used the evidence from miscue analyses conducted on competent readers to argue that effective and efficient reading is driven more by cognition than grapho-phonemic processes. He speculated that the fluent reader 'samples the print', using just enough visual information to confirm hypotheses derived from context. This 'top down model' of reading persuaded many to adopt the strategy, which became known as the 'psycholinguistic guessing game' (Goodman, 1976). Thus, inexperienced readers confronted with an unfamiliar word were discouraged from sounding the word out and, instead, persuaded to guess what would make sense in the context.

However, it has now been suggested that readers actually fixate on each word, and, in fact, good readers do not need to use context because they have efficient decoding skills. In fact, the reliance on context is more characteristic of poor readers who use guess-work to compensate for inefficient word recognition (Stanovich and Stanovich, 1995). According to Hunt (2002), these developments in knowledge about skilled reading behaviour have been used as arguments against teaching children to focus on the meaning of what they read until the alphabetic principle is firmly in place and children are able to recognise a number of regular words in isolation (McGuinness, 1998).

There are dangers in exclusively depending on either the 'bottom-up' skills approach or the use of text experience and context (top-down). Both are necessary for effective reading. According to Hunt, the teaching implications of emphasising context through the use of natural language books, discussion of stories and their links to real life, and encouragement of active comprehension strategies provides learners and teachers with a vision of literacy much richer than that offered in code-based reading schemes. This in fact highlights the long-standing debate described by Soler and Smith (2000; Chall, 1967) as the 'reading wars'.

Luke et al. (2001) describes today's young readers as surfers on an ocean of signs: 'post-modern childhood involves the navigation of an endless sea of texts'. Whether or not children can recognise the actual words of these texts rapidly and automatically, they will be affected by the social and commercial pressures that they exert. Hunt (2002) suggests, therefore, that when developing a reading programme for children with dyslexia, word recognition teaching approaches should be accompanied by a critical literacy approach to enable texts that shape children's lives to have a more direct impact. Hunt actually suggests that the types of text that critical literacy involves could provide supportive, motivating contexts for these learners to begin to acquire access to the lexicon. This point will be developed in the following chapter in which key aspects of critical literacy will be discussed.

THE DEVELOPMENT OF READING

Developing Print Awareness

There are a number of important sub-skills that contribute to the reading process. These skills do not all appear at once, but are developing skills relating to a number of factors. Harrison (1994) cites research evidence suggesting that a child's background such as intelligence, prior learning and home background contribute approximately 85% to what is achieved in school; the other 15% attributed to schooling includes teacher input and teaching methods. From this it follows that the reading skills acquired at an early stage are extremely important—specifically these are skills in language, comprehension and vocabulary.

Visual Aspects

Adams (1990a) discusses the importance of the visual aspects of print and how this relates to the different types of print young children come across—the sources range from instructions for toys to comic books. She asserts that this visual awareness of print does not develop in isolation, but becomes a component of the developing child's environment. This leads to the child developing concepts of print such as left and right, words, sentences, the back of the book and the front. It is important, therefore, to ensure that the child has a grasp of these basic concepts of print, a point highlighted by Clay (1985) in the Reading Recovery Programme. Tunmer et al. (1988) found that the performances of children on tests designed to measure concepts about print have been found to predict future reading achievement. Adams suggests that basic knowledge about print is essentially the foundation upon which the orthographic and phonological skills are built.

There is evidence that visual difficulties can have a key role to play in the barriers experienced by children with dyslexia (Everatt, 2002; Singleton, 2009). Singleton shows how visual stress that may be experienced by children with dyslexia can affect reading fluency and other reading skills. Adams (1990a) suggests that recognising the visual identities of letters is an important stage in reading development and that this skill takes time and practice and necessitates a degree of visual attention. Adams suggests that the cause of poor readers displaying errors in letter orientation may reflect insufficient knowledge of letter shapes. It seems, therefore, that the reading process is underpinned by the visual recognition of individual letters and then transposing these letters into their phonological correspondences.

Role of Phonological Information

Tunmer and Greaney (2008) highlight the importance of utilising phonological information to identify unfamiliar words. They suggest that it is crucial to recognise phonological skills and strategies in beginning literacy development. Research has established that making use of letter–sound relationships to identify unknown words is the basic mechanism for acquiring sight word knowledge (Ehri, 2005; Tunmer and Chapman, 1998, 2006). Tunmer and Greaney suggest that the formation of visuo-phonological connections between printed words and their spoken counterparts in memory provides the basis for fast, efficient recognition of words, which in turn frees up cognitive resources for allocation to sentence comprehension and text integration processes. They indicate that for children encountering difficulty in making connections between speech and print, explicit instruction in phonemic awareness and alphabetic coding skills is critical.

Phonological Representations and Dyslexia

There is a considerable body of evidence to show that dyslexic children have difficulties that primarily affect the phonological domain of language processing. Hatcher and Snowling (2002) suggest an extremely influential hypothesis which in recent years has indicated that the difficulties associated with dyslexia and reading can be traced to problems at the level of phonological representations. Dyslexia, they suggest, is considered a specific disorder of development because phonological processing is selectively impaired in dyslexic people while other aspects of their language, for instance their vocabulary and grammatical skills, are normal. Snowling and Hulme (1994) argued that children create phonological representations by mapping the speech they hear on to the speech they produce, and vice versa. Gradually over development, the specification of spoken words built up through this process becomes more and more detailed as the child's proficiency with speech increases. This would imply that phonological representations have a key role to play in the development of reading as well as speech.

Hatcher and Snowling (2002) report that the most consistently reported phonological difficulties found in dyslexia are limitations of verbal short-term memory. These can be noted in difficulties in following instructions, memorising lists, carrying numbers and in keeping up with dictation. They report that the evidence from brain-imaging studies indicates that the brain regions that are usually highly active in normal readers during short-term memory tasks show lower levels of functional activation even in highly literate dyslexic readers (Paulesu et al., 1996).

STAGES OF READING DEVELOPMENT

The reading process can also be monitored through a series of stages. Frith (1985) identifies the following developmental stages in the acquisition of reading skills.

Logographic Stage

The child makes use of visual recognition of overall word patterns—thus, he or she is able to recognise words as units. This may not necessarily mean that the child can reproduce these words accurately (this would be an alphabetic skill), and as a result the child can easily misspell words he or she is able to read.

Alphabetic Stage

The child tackles the sound/symbol correspondence, and one can identify if children possess this one-to-one correspondence between the letter and the sound. Ehri suggests that the alphabetic stage can be divided into four phases that capture the changes that occur in the development of sight word reading: pre-alphabetic, partial alphabetic, full alphabetic and consolidated alphabetic (Ehri, 1995a, 1999; Ehri and McCormick, 1998). Each phase is labelled to reflect the predominant type of connection that links the written forms of sight words to their pronunciations and meanings in memory. Therefore, during the pre-alphabetic phase beginners remember how to read sight words by forming connections between selected visual attributes of words and their pronunciations or meanings. This phase is called pre-alphabetic because letter–sound relations are not involved in the connections.

When pre-alphabetic readers read print in their environment, such as stop signs and fast food restaurant signs, they do this, according to Ehri, by remembering visual cues accompanying the print rather than the written words themselves.

The next phase is the partial alphabetic phase. Here beginners remember how to read sight words by forming partial alphabetic connections between only some of the letters in written words and sounds detected in their pronunciations. Because first and final letters are especially salient, these are often the cues that are remembered.

To remember sight words in this way, partial alphabetic readers need to know some letter–sound correspondences and have some phonemic segmentation. During the next phase, the full alphabetic phase, beginners remember how to read sight words by forming complete grapho-phonemic connections. This is possible because readers know how the major graphemes symbolise phonemes in the conventional spelling system (Venezky, 1970, 1999). In applying this knowledge to form connections for sight words, spellings become fully bonded to pronunciations in memory (Ehri, 1992; Perfetti, 1992).

The final phase, according to Ehri, is the full alphabetic phase when readers are able to decode words by transforming graphemes into phonemes, and they are able to retain sight words in memory by connecting graphemes to phonemes. These processes acquaint them with the pronunciations of syllabic and sub-syllabic spelling patterns that recur in different words. The letters in these patterns become consolidated into larger spelling–sound units that can be used to decode words and to retain sight words in memory.

Orthographic Stage

The child possesses and comprehends knowledge of the letter–sound relationship as well as structure and meaning. Thus, as well as being aware of rules the child can use cues and context.

It has been argued that children with dyslexia can find the alphabetic stage difficult because the sound–symbol correspondence rests to a great extent on skills in phonics. Before children, therefore, acquire a competent understanding of the relationship between letter units (graphemes) and sound units (phonemes) they need a degree of phonological awareness (Snowling, 2000).

Frith (2002) puts forward the view that writing and the desire to write helps to enhance the alphabetic stage of reading because spelling is linked more directly to the alphabetic principle and letter–sound relationships. This view is also supported by the work of Bradley and Bryant (1991), who found that beginner readers in the process of acquiring the skills of the alphabetic stage use visual strategies for reading, but phonological strategies for spelling. In their study children read correctly words that were visually distinctive such as 'school' and 'light', but failed to read simpler words like 'bun' and 'sit'. Yet these children tended to spell correctly words they had failed to read such as 'bun' and 'sit' and spell incorrectly words they had read by focusing on the visual patterns (school, light).

The alphabetic reader, according to Snowling (2000), may also find difficulty reading words that have inconsistent orthographic patterns, but that are pronounced in the same way. Similarly, irregular words are mispronounced (e.g., 'island' would be pronounced 'is-land').

This developmental aspect of reading serves to illustrate the importance of the procedure of error analysis and identifying the type and pattern of errors made by children with difficulties in reading.

LIMITATIONS OF THE STAGE MODEL OF READING

Snowling (2000) suggests some limitations of the staged models of reading. She suggests that the mechanisms involved in the transitions between stages are unclear. She also suggests that the stage model of reading implies an ordered sequence of stages or phases, yet it is acknowledged that the course of reading development is not the same for all children and, indeed, the actual reading strategies used by children may be influenced to a great extent by the teaching regime to which they are exposed. Additionally, in some situations some children omit one of the stages. Snowling (2000) cites the example of the German language where children quickly reach a high level of competence in the alphabetic stage, and therefore a logographic stage is not easily observed (Wimmer, 1996). Similarly, Snowling cites a number of studies that claim that dyslexic readers can reach the orthographic phase without passing through the alphabetic phase.

Vellutino et al. (2004) argue that the evidence suggests that inadequate facility in word identification, due, in most cases, to more basic deficits in alphabetic coding, is the basic cause of difficulties in learning to read.

The evidence suggests, they argue, that, in most cases, phonological skills deficiencies associated with phonological coding deficits are the probable causes of the reading difficulties rather than visual, semantic or syntactic deficits. They do acknowledge, though, that in some children reading difficulties may be associated with general language deficits. Vellutino et al. argue that skilled reading involves comprehension of meaning from running text and this is a complex process that depends on adequate development of two component processes: word identification and language comprehension. Word identification is a lexical retrieval process that involves visual recognition of a uniquely ordered array of letters as a familiar word and implicit (or explicit) retrieval of the name and meaning of that word from memory.

Language comprehension involves integration of the meanings of spoken or written words in ways that facilitate understanding and integration of sentences in spoken or written text in the interest of understanding the broader concepts and ideas represented by those sentences. They argue that children who have difficulty in acquiring phonological awareness and learning to map alphabetic symbols to sound will also have difficulty acquiring orthographic awareness and general orthographic knowledge. There is abundant evidence, they assert, that the child who has limited phonological awareness and limited alphabetic mapping skills also has limited orthographic awareness and limited orthographic knowledge.

Although they acknowledge that there is considerable evidence that limited knowledge of print concepts and conventions and limited pragmatic knowledge have often been observed in children who also experience early reading difficulties and can certainly contribute to early reading and language difficulties, limitations in such knowledge are probably not basic causes of specific reading disability.

They argue that there is now strong and highly accepted evidence in support of weak phonological coding as an underlying cause of the disorder. They define phonological coding as the ability to use speech codes to represent information in the form of words and parts of words. Their evidence for this comes from training and intervention studies which have documented that direct instruction designed to facilitate phonological awareness and letter–sound mapping has a positive effect on word identification, spelling, and reading ability in general.

This has implications for intervention and the approaches used to teach reading to children with dyslexia.

READING AND MEMORY

There is also evidence that dyslexic children's reading development can be affected by long-term memory factors. This can account for many difficulties, such as problems memorising the days of the week or the months of the year, mastering multiplication tables and learning a foreign language. Dal (2008) suggests that memory difficulties, for example difficulties associated with storing and subsequently accessing new vocabulary, can be challenging for learners with dyslexia. He suggests that foreign language learning makes intensive use of memorisation. In order for words and phrases to be memorised, they-first have to enter short-term working memory, so that they can be transferred to long-term memory. At a later stage they must then be recalled into working memory to be assembled into coherent messages, an important cognitive ability which is seen as a necessity for developing the learner's schema for language learning. He argues that dyslexic students are likely to have difficulty at all stages and that each stage will require consolidation. Hatcher and Snowling (2002) suggest that this long-term learning problem can be related to the retrieval of phonological information from long-term memory and can account for the word-finding difficulties often experienced by children with dyslexia.

RELATIONSHIP BETWEEN PHONOLOGY AND ORTHOGRAPHY

It can be argued that the persistent difficulties with phonological awareness associated with dyslexia are not universal, but appear to be specific to children learning to read in irregular or 'deep' orthographies, such as English (Everatt and Elbeheri, 2008). The task of learning to read in an alphabetic system requires the child to associate letters with their sounds, and then appreciate how sounds can be blended together to make words. At a basic level, therefore, learning to read requires the child to establish a set of connections between the letters (graphemes) of printed words and the speech sounds (phonemes) of spoken words. This relationship between 'orthography' and 'phonology' needs to be made at a 'fine-grained level'—the phoneme level—to ensure that new words that have not been seen before can be decoded, otherwise the dyslexic child will be faced with a considerable challenge at each new word, as she or he will not have the bank of phonological knowledge to decode new words.

Hatcher and Snowling (2002) argue that the relationships between orthography and phonology are important both in the early stages of learning to read and in the development of automatic reading skills that subsequently account for reading fluency. They suggest that in English these relationships also provide a scaffold for learning multi-letter (e.g., -ough, -igh), morphemic (-tion, -cian) and inconsistent (-ea) spelling–sound correspondences. They hypothesise that, although dyslexic children can learn to read words they have been taught, they code the correspondences between the letters of these words and their pronunciations at a 'coarse-grained level'—chunks rather than phonemes. A consequence is that dyslexic children have difficulty generalising this knowledge, and therefore one of the most robust signs of dyslexia is poor non-word reading. It can be observed that some dyslexic children can circumvent decoding difficulties to some extent by relying or over-relying on the semantic and syntactic context (Nation and Snowling, 1998). But this is usually not totally successful, especially in the early years as the child will not have accumulated sufficient language knowledge to use this strategy successfully. Even if this strategy is utilised, Hatcher and Snowling (2002) show that reading often remains slow and that use of global reading strategies may not be conducive to spelling, which usually remains poor across the lifespan. Essentially, learning to read is an interactive process to which children bring all their language skills and knowledge of phonological processing, and a deficit in phonological representation is the most likely source of most of the reading (and spelling) difficulties experienced by dyslexic children.

It is widely accepted (Hatcher and Snowling, 2002) that all children do not learn to read in the same way. Children have different combinations of cognitive skills and have individual styles of processing information. For example, one child may have severe phonological deficits, but good visual memory skills, while another child may have weak phonological skills and slow speed of processing. Additionally, children will very likely have experienced different methods of being taught how to read. Teaching programmes on reading should therefore recognise this and the difficulties that will confront dyslexic children if these correspondences are taught in isolation. It is important that a teaching programme integrates the visual, phonic and context aspects of reading simultaneously at all stages in reading, from early development through to competence.

DYSLEXIA AND DIFFERENT ORTHOGRAPHIES

There is convincing evidence that the manifestation of dyslexia can vary across different languages (Everatt and Elbeheri, 2008). One of the key factors that can account for this variability is the differences in the orthographic features of different languages. Everatt and Elbeheri indicate that in some orthographies there is close to a one-to-one correspondence between the written symbol (grapheme) and the basic sound (or phoneme). In other orthographies, this correspondence is less transparent. A letter may represent several sounds, and a particular sound may be represented by different letters, depending on the context within which the letter or sound is presented. They indicate that the English orthography is the best example of a less than transparent relationship between letters and sounds; there are many English words that may be considered irregular or exceptions because there is not a direct relationship between the grapheme and phoneme.

German, in contrast, is relatively transparent for both reading and spelling (Wimmer, 1993; Zeigler and Goswami, 2005). Similarly, Hungarian has a highly transparent orthography (Smythe et al., 2004), which means that the Hungarian child should be able to pronounce written words relatively accurately simply from sounding-out the individual letters or letter combinations within a word. For the Hungarian child, a new word can be sounded-out with relative ease, leading to good word-decoding accuracy levels and potentially increasing written-word learning.

The difference in how dyslexia can be noted in different languages can have implications for assessment. Much of the assessment procedures for dyslexia are based on identifying difficulties in phonological awareness and phonological processing. The work based on Arabic orthography suggests that literacy learning difficulties may be best predicted on the basis of assessment procedures that include measures of phonological processing, including phonological awareness (Elbeheri and

Everatt, 2008). Irrespective of the orthography, it seems that measures of phonological processing seem to present the best tools for predicting literacy weaknesses and identifying the underlying problems associated with dyslexia.

POINTS FOR REFLECTION

- Consider the key factors required for the development of reading skills and reflect on how you might prioritise these skills in a teaching programme.

- Consider the role of the phonological representation hypothesis in relation to the acquisition of literacy for students with dyslexia.

- Reflect on the relationship between phonology and orthography and particularly the influence of different orthographies. Consider the impact this may have on intervention for students with dyslexia.

Chapter 8

Reading Models and Methods

The previous chapter looked at the acquisition of literacy and particularly the skills needed for developing literacy. This chapter will look specifically at models of literacy and strategies that can accompany those models. It is important also to consider the debate and the controversy associated with teaching reading and to consider the experience of learning to read from the perspectives of students with dyslexia. It is important to have this in mind as you consider the different theoretical and practical approaches.

BOTTOM-UP AND TOP DOWN MODELS

There are two general models of the reading process. These have come to be known as 'bottom-up' (i.e., data-driven) and 'top-down' (i.e., concept-driven) models (Box 8.1).

The 'bottom-up' model suggests that, first, we look at the stimulus (i.e., the components of the letters) and then move to the meaning.

'Bottom-up' theorists argue that the brain attends to every bit of available information, thus we read letter-by-letter so quickly that it becomes automatic. The 'top-down' model is concept-driven. The reader attempts to absorb the meaning of the text from the cues that are available. These cues can include:

- the context of the passage being read—this relates to the syntactic context (i.e., the structure of the sentence) and semantic context (i.e., the anticipated meaning of the passage);
- the graphic information available (i.e., what the word looks like)—the reader anticipates the word or sentence from these descriptive cues.

Goodman's (1976) model, known as the psycholinguistic guessing game, strongly advocated a top-down approach to reading. This model asserts that good readers make efficient use of hypothesis formation and prediction in reading and thus make good use of the contextual cues available to the reader. Additionally, the efficiency in prediction of text means that good readers, according to Goodman, will have less need to rely on graphic cues and therefore do not have to process every visual characteristic of text.

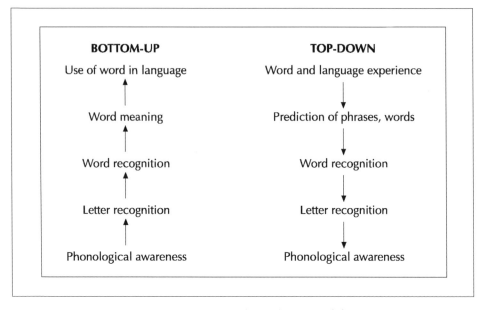

Box 8.1 Bottom-up and top-down models

Goodman's model of the reading process has, however, been subject to powerful criticism. The main exponents of this criticism are Tunmer (1994), Stanovich (1988), Adams (1990a) and Liberman and Liberman (1992). Essentially, the counterarguments to Goodman's model suggest that the central tenet of the model, that good readers are dependent on context for word recognition, is inaccurate. It is suggested, in fact, that it is poor readers who are dependent on context; good readers do not need to rely on context as they possess efficient word recognition skills, can recognise words effortlessly and can utilise maximum cognitive capacity for comprehension. The effort required for poor readers to recognise words reduces their cognitive capacity for comprehension.

Additionally, there is now considerable evidence (Adams, 1990b) that good readers actually fixate nearly every word as they read. This process is achieved rapidly in efficient readers; therefore, less cognitive effort is required than, for example, with poor readers. So, even when the word is highly predictable, good readers actually process every word visually.

Lovegrove (1993) shows that poor readers have a weak transient visual system and a normal sustained one. This results in interference between the two systems and has implications for the processing of visual stimuli in reading, since reading involves the synchronisation of both transient and sustained systems. This may have implications for masking parts of a page that are not being focused on at that time. It certainly has implications for allowing sufficient processing time for poor readers: eye movement studies reveal that they fixate on practically every word in a text, sometimes more than once (Ehri, 2002).

Although there may be flaws in the detail of Goodman's model, many of the messages contained within it require consideration, such as the view that skilled readers have the ability and the opportunity to make efficient use of context. Additionally,

Goodman's (1976) emphasis on reading for meaning should not be lost, but must be balanced with other reading skills within a teaching programme.

Both 'top-down' and 'bottom-up' models have limitations in terms of an understanding of the reading process, because clearly readers draw on both these processes when reading. The Interactive Compensatory Model attempts to explain how these dual processes work. This model acknowledges that reading involves recognising words based on information provided simultaneously from both the text and the reader, and, as proposed by Stanovich (1988), focuses on the following assumptions:

• Readers use information simultaneously from different levels and do not necessarily begin at either the graphic (bottom-up) or the contextual (top-down) level.
• During their development of reading skills, readers may rely more heavily on some levels of processing than on others (e.g., they may use context to greater or lesser extents).
• The reader's weaknesses are compensated for by his or her strengths.

Stanovich casts doubt on the view that good readers use the top-down model more than poor readers. Indeed, as indicated above, good readers pay more attention to graphic detail and poor readers rely more on context. Thus, higher-level processing of text does not necessarily need the completion of all lower levels of processing.

Stanovich's model, therefore, takes account of the fact that many poor readers have developed strategies for compensating for their information processing difficulties. Most models of reading are derivations from the 'top-down' or 'bottom-up' processes.

CONNECTIONIST MODELS

The dual route model (Coltheart, 1978) has for many years predominated in relation to the development of reading. It assumes that readers have two strategies at their disposal—a direct/visual strategy that is used for reading familiar words and an indirect route that involves the use of phonological strategies, which are used for reading unfamiliar words that are not within the child's sight vocabulary. There are now a number of alternatives to this view. These alternatives can be referred to as connectionist approaches or parallel distributed processing (PDP) models. These models offer a framework that can be applied to a range of cognitive processing activities, such as language acquisition and memory as well as reading (McClelland, 1988).

The connectionist model applied to the reading process suggests that children learn to read through the reciprocal association between knowledge of letter strings and phonemes and the development of the ability to map letters and strings of letters to the phonemes that make up the sound units in language. This model would suggest that children access all the cognitive capacities at their disposal to do this. Ehri (1995a), in fact, suggests that children develop a single orthographic system over time rather than utilise a dual route model. The connectionist approach also implies that regular words will be accessed more easily than irregular words, as the former will conform to a pattern that the child will learn over time and exposure to print.

The English language, unlike some other languages such as German, Spanish and Italian, contains a considerable number of irregular patterns that contradict a pattern that the child may have learnt. For this reason, regular words are more easily learnt than irregular words, and, because knowledge of irregular patterns places cognitive demands on memory and familiarity with phonological representations, these can be quite challenging for dyslexic children. One of the difficulties with models such as the connectionist model is that they may explain the processes involved in reading, but they do not inform us about the conscious reading strategies that readers may adopt. Nevertheless, this model does place some importance on over-learning as it implies that the connections become stronger with associations, and the more associations that are made then the stronger the connections will be.

According to Snowling (2000), these connections form a knowledge base that can be drawn upon when the child is faced with a new word. Snowling (2000) discusses adaptations of these models, and one in particular that is attractive is the adaptation by Plaut et al. (1996) which provides a role for semantic representation as well as phonological representation in the development of connections within the reading process.

BALANCE MODEL OF READING

Robertson and Bakker (2002) acknowledge in the balance model of reading that the reading process can be complex. In order to achieve fluency in reading the beginning reader first has to understand the perceptual features of text, and this has to become an automatic activity that the child can do without consciously thinking about it. Second, the child eventually becomes more familiar with syntactical rules, and this is accompanied by an increase in the number of known words that the child can read automatically. This means that the child will be able to process large parts of a sentence as one chunk rather than reading individual letters and syllables. According to Robertson and Bakker, the balance model of reading implies that reading is guided by syntactical rules and linguistic experience and is predominantly mediated by the left cerebral hemisphere. This means that reading develops through mediation, initially of the right hemisphere when the child automatises the perceptual features of the letter and then through the left hemisphere as the syntactic and lexical features of reading develop.

Bakker (1979, 1990) suggested when he first introduced the balance model that it was possible that some children may not be able to shift from right to left in the hemispheric mediation of reading. This means that these children remain beginning readers in that they will lack the reading fluency that accompanies advancement in reading and they will continue to read slowly and in a fragmented fashion. Bakker classified these children as P-type dyslexic children (P for perceptual), as it was hypothesised that they very likely stick to the perceptual features of text.

Similarly, it was also thought possible that some other children shift to left hemispheric processing of text too early. These children read quickly, but as they tend to overlook the perceptual features they make many errors. Bakker classified these children as L-type (linguistic) dyslexic readers in view of their efforts to use linguistic strategies.

The implication of this for teaching has been the subject of a great deal of research, and techniques such as hemisphere-specific stimulation (HSS) have been applied. Such programmes provide for the flashing of words in the right (for P-types) or left (for L-types) visual field, in order to stimulate the left and right cerebral hemisphere. Words are spoken to the right ear of P-dyslexics (left hemisphere stimulation) while the other ear is listening to non-vocal music, and to the left ear of L-dyslexics (right hemisphere stimulation) while the other ear is listening to non-vocal music.

Hemisphere-alluding stimulation (HAS) is a technique that provides the reader with phonetically and syntactically demanding text for P-types in order to stimulate left hemispheric processing, and the reading of perceptually demanding text in order to stimulate right hemispheric processing. This model has been applied in a number of research studies and in practice in many countries (Robertson, 2000; Robertson and Bakker, 2002).

METHOD OF TEACHING READING

The most popular methods used by teachers in the teaching of reading include the following:

- phonic or phonically based;
- look and say—reading through sight word recognition;
- language experience—using context, background knowledge and language under-standing.

Phonic Model

The phonic method highlights the importance of phonology and the sounds of letters and letter combinations (Figure 8.1).

There are a number of structured phonic programmes in existence that teach children to distinguish the 44 phonemes or sound units of English, by using a variety of strategies. These strategies may include colour-coding and marks to indicate short or long sounds.

Although phonic programmes are structured, and structure is beneficial for children with specific learning difficulties, there are also difficulties associated with such programmes. The most important of these include the possibility that:

- they may increase the burden on children's short- and long-term memories by increasing what the child needs to remember;
- there are still words that need to be taught as sight vocabulary because they do not fall into the 'sound blending' category, such as 'one' and 'many'.

Phonic methods can help children who have an obvious difficulty in mastering and remembering sound blends and vowel digraphs and have difficulty in synthesising them to make a word. At the same time they present learning that may seem to be

Phonics Checklist

Consonants

	Initial	Final
s		
m		
r		
t		
b		
f		
n		
p		
d		
h		
c /k/		
g /g/		
j		
l		
k		
v		
w		
z		
c /s/		
g /j/		
qu		
y		

	Final Only
ck	
x	
ss	
ll	
tt	
ff	
bb	
dd	
pp	

Short Vowels

CVC words	
a	
e	
i	
o	
u	

Blends

	Initial
bl	
cl	
ft	
pl	
br	
dr	
gr	
tr	
cr	
fr	
pr	
gl	
sl	
sn	
sp	
st	
sw	
sc	
sk	

	Final
ft	
lp	
mp	
nd	
nk	
nt	
pt	
sk	
sp	
st	

Consonant Diagraps

sh	
ch	
th	
wh	
ph	

Long Vowels

CVCe words	
a	
e	
i	
o	
u	

Y as a Vowel

/e/ (bunny)	
/i/ (by)	

Vowels followed by r

ar	
or	
er	
ir	
ur	

Silent Letters

Initial		Final	
kn		-tch	
wr		-dge	
gh		-gh	
sc		-lk	
gn			

Vowel Digraphs

ai (paid)	
ay (pay)	
oa (boat)	
ee (tree)	
oe (toe)	
oi (join)	
oy (joy)	
ew (chew)	
ou (cloud)	
ou (soup)	
au (haul)	
aw (saw)	
ea (preach)	
ea (deaf)	

Vowel digraphs. cont.

ow (crow)	
ow (crow)	
oo (boot)	
oo (hook)	
ie (pie)	
ie (thief)	
ey (they)	
ey (valley)	
ei (ceiling)	
ui (build)	
ui (fruit)	

Prefixes

dis	
un	
re	
im	
in	
mis	
pre	

Suffixes

-ful	
-ly	
-less	
-ness	
-able	
-lble	
-lon	
-ment	
-er	
-or	
-en	

Vowels in Spelling Patterns

ind (bind)	
ild (wild)	
igh (high)	
old (cold)	
oit (colt)	
ost (host)	
ost (cost)	

Figure 8.1 Phonic checklist (reproduced by permission of Educators Publishing Service (31 Smith Place, Cambridge, MA (800) 225-5750, www.epsbooks.com); from Chall and Popp, (1996)).

out of context. Some difficulty may be identified in merging the two components (i.e., knowledge of sound and knowledge of language) to facilitate a meaningful reading experience.

Chall and Popp (1996) emphasise the need to teach phonics and argue that if taught well it is highly meaningful—through phonics children can get close to the sound of a word and through that to the meaning of the word. They suggest a systematic phonics approach from pre-school, with related activities set within a total reading programme.

Frith (1995) emphasises the nature of the phonological 'core variable' in literacy learning and particularly how it is associated with dyslexia. The Causal Model Framework (Frith, 2002) highlights the distinctiveness of phonological competence by focusing on three levels for assessing phonological difficulties: biological observations about brain functioning, at the cognitical level in relation to the hypothetical constructs of intellectual ability and phonological processing ability, and at the behavioural level in relation to performance in assessments such as phonological awareness tests, naming speed tests, and non-word, reading and spelling tests.

Support for the phonological core variable model as an explanation of the difficulties associated with dyslexia has led to illuminative research activity and the development of phonological skills training programmes (Reason and Frederickson, 1996; Henry, 2003; Sawyer and Bernstein, 2008).

Look-and-say Model

Look-and-say methods emphasise exposure to print on the grounds that children will become familiar with words and build up a sight vocabulary with increased exposure. The emphasis is therefore on meaningful units of language rather than sounds of speech (Figure 8.2). This type of method therefore requires attractive books that can become progressively more demanding. The use of flashcards and pictures can be used in the initial stages. The method, however, assumes a good memory for shapes of letters and words as well as the ability to master many of the irregularities of spelling and sound—symbol correspondence. This, of course, may be difficult for children with dyslexic difficulties, particularly since their memory may be weak and can rapidly become overloaded. Some elements of the phonic approaches can accompany most look-and-say methods.

Indeed, Chall and Popp (1996) suggest that a good phonics programme needs to pay attention to sight recognition and that fluent reading depends on both automatic sight recognition and the application of phonic knowledge.

Language Experience Models

Language experience methods focus on the use of language, both oral and written, as an aid to learning to read through various modes of language enrichment. This helps the reader develop important language concepts and schemata, which in turn help to bring meaning to print. Although the child may have a decoding problem, the experience gained in language can help to compensate for this and bring some meaning to the text. This model engages the child in the process of going from thought to speech and then to encoding in print and from print to reading.

Ehri (1999), however, suggests that there are three essential interrelated ingredients in the knowledge base for teachers that help to inform them in making decisions on reading instruction. These are (1) knowledge about the reading process, (2) knowledge about teaching methods and how these facilitate the reading process and (3) knowledge

```
┌─────────────────────────────────────────────────────────────────┐
│              THE PHONEMES OF THE ENGLISH LANGUAGE                 │
│                                                                   │
│         Vowels (20)                    Consonants (24)            │
│     Symbol   Sound (or value)      Symbol   Sound (or value)      │
└─────────────────────────────────────────────────────────────────┘
```

Symbol	Sound (or value)	Symbol	Sound (or value)
aɪ	try - write	b	back - rubber
aʊ	noun - now	d	day - rudder
ɑ	father	dʒ	judge - George - raj
ɒ	wash - odd	ð	this - other
æ	cat - trap	f	few - puff
eɪ	day - steak - face	g	got - bigger
əʊ	go - goat	h	hot
ɛ	get	j	yet
ɛə	fair - square	k	car - key - clock - trekked - quay
ɜ	her - stir - word - nurse	l	lip
i	he - see	m	much - hammer
ɪ	ship	n	now - runner
ɪə	hear - here	ŋ	sing
o	force	p	Pen - pepper
ɔ	north - war	r	round - sorry
ɔɪ	noise - toy	s	see - missed
u	lunar - pool	ʃ	ship - mission
ʊ	foot - put	t	ten
ʊə	pure	tʃ	church - latch
ʌ	bud - blood - love	θ	three - heath
		v	very
		w	will
		z	zeal
		ʒ	decision - treasure

(Total = 44)

Figure 8.2 The phonemes of the English language (reproduced by permission of Whurr Publications; from Doyle, 1996).

about observational procedures to identify the processes that readers are facilitating and the processes they have difficulty with. Therefore, knowledge of the reading process is important, but it is equally important to relate this knowledge to classroom practices and particularly to observing how children relate to the reading process in the class. Clay (1985) has devoted a considerable part of the assessment component of the reading recovery programme to analysing children's reading behaviours.

DEVELOPING READING SKILLS

There is considerable evidence to suggest that pre-reading activities can significantly assist the development of the reading process. Such activities, as well as developing pre-reading skills, help to develop essential skills in reading comprehension. Reading is interactive, as it combines the reader's background experience and previous knowledge with the 'new' text to be read. This interaction provides the reader with meaning and interpretation. Reading, therefore, is an interaction of previous knowledge involving the use of semantic and syntactic cues and accuracy in the decoding of print. It is important that in teaching reading these aspects are considered. It is likely that the child with dyslexia will find this interactive process difficult as his or her efforts and cognitive capacities are directed to either mechanically decoding the print or obtaining the meaning from print—the simultaneous interaction of these processes is not easily accomplished.

Two key elements of reading are the understanding of print and the message (purpose) of the print (Box 8.2). They both have to be carefully considered in the selection and development of reading programmes and strategies for children dyslexia.

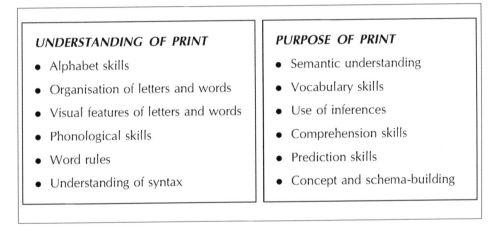

UNDERSTANDING OF PRINT	*PURPOSE OF PRINT*
• Alphabet skills	• Semantic understanding
• Organisation of letters and words	• Vocabulary skills
• Visual features of letters and words	• Use of inferences
• Phonological skills	• Comprehension skills
• Word rules	• Prediction skills
• Understanding of syntax	• Concept and schema-building

Box 8.2   Reading skills

TEACHING READING—THE DEBATE

The teaching of reading and the field of literacy has been subject to long-standing debate. Theories and methods have been reviewed, revised and recycled. Literacy is one of the areas that appear vulnerable to political initiatives and educational trends. It can become a heated subject of debate, particularly following revelations of dismal and disappointing attainment scores in national and international surveys. The issue of reading standards can be a national concern and lead to national debate. This has been evident in the UK regarding the follow-up debate to the Rose Report (see Chapter 6).

Soler (2002) suggests that the literacy debate has been a consequence of the increase in scientific procedures to measure progress and the increasing interest in international comparisons in literacy levels, which in some cases show a decline. Many have argued that the decline is due to a trend towards the whole-language model of reading. Wray, however, challenges this view by arguing that the evidence for suggesting that a decline in reading standards is due to the move toward a whole-language approach is not strong. He suggests that the whole-language movement is not practised widely enough to account for such a decline in reading standards. He further suggests that the criteria for assessing reading attainment need to be questioned since they raise the fundamental point, 'What is reading?'

At the same time it might be argued, 'What is whole-language?' Bergeron (1990) attempted to obtain a consensual definition of whole-language from the literature and found that it was defined as an approach, a philosophy, an orientation, a theory, a theoretical orientation, a programme, a curriculum, a perspective on education and an attitude of mind. It is difficult either to promote or to criticise a movement when it is so loosely defined.

To attempt to find the positive aspects of this loose interpretation called 'whole-language', one can look for some common factors in Bergeron's responses. Adams (1990a) argues that some commonalities include:

- construction of meaning from text;
- developing and explaining the functional dimensions of text;
- student-centred classrooms;
- integration of language arts.

The long-standing view that emerged from the work of Goodman (1976; Smith, 1971) suggests that skilful readers do not process individual letters, spelling–sound translations are irrelevant for reading and it is therefore not necessary to teach spellings and sounds. This view suggests that the teaching of phonics should not be emphasised, because children have to learn phonic rules by themselves and can only do this through experience in reading. Phonics teaching, therefore, according to this view, can result in an overemphasis on the technical decoding skills and as a result the meaning of the text will be lost.

There are considerable arguments against this (Adams, 1990a; Turner, 1991; Rose, 2006). These centre on the need for children to read words and acquire automaticity in the technical sub-skills of reading before they can obtain meaning from a text. Adams (1990a), in fact, argues that automaticity develops from actually reading words and not by ignoring or guessing them.

This view is supported by researchers and educationalists in other countries. Adamik-Jászò (1995) describes the Hungarian experience as based on reading programmes focusing on the oral language development of the child. This indicates that phonemic awareness is an essential prerequisite of reading instruction. Studies by Johnston et al. (1995), comparing the book experience approach in New Zealand with a systematic phonics approach in Scotland, showed that children in the phonics programme were significantly better at reading non-words and had significantly superior reading comprehension.

Ehri (1995a, 2002) suggests that for sight word reading to develop, learners must acquire and apply knowledge of the alphabetic system. She asserts that a weakness in the whole-language approach is the absence of systematic phonics instruction at the early stages. Attention is not paid to the need for young children to master the alphabetic system through learning letter shapes and names, sounds and letter correspondences, and blending sounds into words. Many children do not acquire these skills merely through exposure to print.

Tunmer and Greaney (2008) from a New Zealand perspective argue that providing struggling readers with explicit and systematic instruction in word analysis skills outside the context of reading text is crucial. They suggest that this would ensure that children with reading difficulties recognise the importance of focusing on word-level cues as the most useful source of information in identifying words. They also maintain that this helps them overcome a tendency to rely on sentence context cues to identify unfamiliar words in text rather than using context to supplement word-level information. Pressley (2006) argues that one of the major distinguishing characteristics of struggling readers is their tendency to rely heavily on sentence context cues to compensate for their deficient alphabetic coding skills.

This view, however, is not without counterargument. For example, Stainthorp (1995) reports on a study that suggests that top-down, context-driven strategies can modify performance in reading. She accepts, however, that the beneficial effects of context are partly dependent upon children having developed some decoding skills, and the skills required for decoding should not be left to chance. This view is reiterated by Turner (1995), who suggests that children learn to read by being taught, although he suggests that the component skills of reading are initially learnt independently.

Bryant (1994) contends that both forms of linguistic knowledge, constituent sounds and language experience, play an important part in children's acquisition and development of reading and writing skills. He reports on a longitudinal study in which children's scores in phonological tasks predicted the progress they made in learning about letter–sound associations, and that scores in semantic and syntactic tasks were good predictors of children's ability to use context and decipher difficult words within a meaningful context. Bryant concludes that each form of linguistic knowledge makes an independent and specific contribution to the reading process, particularly since the children's scores in the phonological task did not predict the children's success in the use of context and, similarly, scores in the semantic and syntactic tasks were not significant in predicting phonological skills.

Clearly, a balanced approach is necessary when looking at the teaching of reading. Both the phonic method and the whole-language movement have many commendable aspects—both should be utilised in relation to the needs of the individual reader.

Welch and Freebody (2002) suggest that psychology, human development and educational measurement have been the disciplines that have traditionally informed our understanding of how to teach reading, and this has assumed that the teaching of reading is politically neutral and objectively quantifiable. However, according to Wearmouth et al. (2003), this view has been countered. They suggest drawing on the work of Welch (1991) on cross-disciplinary studies, which itself draws upon history, politics, linguistics and economics. These studies counter this traditional view of the teaching and evaluation of literacy and link them to differing dominant visions of what literacy is for and how we must teach it. The implication is that reading and literacy practices not only meet cultural and social needs but also actually shape how cultures develop.

Welch and Freebody (2002) suggest that there are some general aspects to reading debates across national and international contexts. These include concern about literacy standards and particularly declining standards (slide hypothesis). Also, the increase in demands for literacy competencies for effective civil, social and cultural functioning in our society have perhaps created the misleading impression of a decline in literacy standards. It should, however, be noted that children with dyslexic difficulties usually have considerable difficulty in phonological awareness and, as a result, in acquiring alphabetic and phonic knowledge. This therefore needs to be considered in the development of a balanced programme for dyslexic children.

READING INTERVENTIONS

Vadasy and Sanders (2008) argue that most reading interventions have been designed and evaluated for use by teachers. They suggest, however, that some progammes have been designed for teaching assistants (paraeducators). These include the popular US programmes:

Phono-Graphix (www.readamerica.net; Fill et al., 1998; McGuinness et al., 1996);

Spell Read P.A.T. (www.kaplank12.com; Rashotte et al., 2001);

Read Naturally (Hasbrouck et al., 1999);

Great Leaps (Mercer et al., 2000) fluency building programs; and

REWARDS: Reading Excellence: Word Attack and Rate Development Strategies (Archer et al., 2000; Archer, 1981; Vachon, 1998).

In the UK, teaching assistants are often assigned to teach reading from a prescribed approach. Reid and Green (2007b) suggest that teaching assistants have considerable potential to offer support to staff and students and can be seen as a major contributor within the school. One of the key features of this is the management commitment to training teaching assistants and management recognition of the potential of teaching assistants who have enhanced levels of training. In the case of students with dyslexia it is critically important that teaching assistants have at least some training as they can then support the teacher in implementing literacy programmes.

Vadasy and Sanders (2008) designed a study using approaches that could be used by trained teaching assistants. This study specifically targeted four areas of instruction recommended by the National Reading Panel (National Reading Panel, 2000). These are:

- phonemic awareness;
- phonics;
- fluency; and
- motivation.

The interventions in this study provided students with explicit and systematic instruction in letter–sound relationships, decoding strategies and carefully coordinated spelling instruction. Students had daily opportunities to practise accurate and fluent reading in decodable stories that feature the letters and sounds they are learning. Letter–sound relationships are introduced at a reasonable pace, with extensive practice opportunities and cumulative review of previously taught relationships. Decoding instruction was explicit, with guided practice, scaffolding and modelling. The outcome of these studies was highly encouraging, with the students showing gains in most areas.

Vadasy et al. (2006) implemented a kindergarten intervention which was evaluated in three studies, two randomised and one quasi-randomised. In the first randomised study, the teaching assistants (paraeducator/tutors) provided 18 weeks of individual instruction in phonemic and alphabetic skills to kindergarten students who averaged in the 10th–25th percentile at pre-test in receptive vocabulary, phonological awareness and reading accuracy. The instructional components were:

1. *Letter–sound correspondence*—letter names and sounds were introduced at a rate of about one new letter name/sound every two lessons. Students practised pointing to the letters, saying the sounds, and writing the letters that matched the sounds provided by the instructor.
2. *Phoneme segmenting*—students practised segmenting consonant–vowel–consonant (cvc) words into three phonemes. Students were instructed to repeat the word, point to each box as they spoke a phoneme, and then sweep their finger under the boxes and say the word fast.
3. *Word reading and spelling*—this involved phoneme blending, pointing to an example word in each lesson, stretching out the sounds without stopping between phonemes, and then saying the word fast. Students then practised blending orally 6–9 words per lesson, with scaffolding and assistance. There was explicit instruction in how to map letters to phonemes.
4. *Irregular word instruction*—the lessons featured high-frequency irregular words that appeared in the decodable texts. The tutor supplied the word, and the student pointed to the word, spelt it aloud, and read the word again.
5. *Phoneme blending*—to add practice in recognising orally blended words, the tutor asked the student to guess the word (say it fast) that the tutor said in a slow, stretched-out way (without stopping between phonemes, just as the student was learning to do in the word reading activity).
6. *Alphabet naming practice*—depending upon the student's progress in alphabetic skills, the tutor implemented one of these activities: (a) say the alphabet (letter names) while pointing to the letters on the letter-sound card; (b) say the alphabet (letter names) without looking at the letters/chart; (c) point to the letters that the tutor names; or (d) name the letters that the tutor points to.
7. *Assisted oral reading practice*—students practised reading aloud in decodable storybooks for the last 10 minutes of each instructional session.

They found that tutored students maintained higher levels of performance across reading outcomes through the end of first grade. The phonics-based interventions described include features associated with the sustained use of reading interventions: high student acceptance; practical, concrete and accessible materials; high degree of specificity; professional development that includes modelling of strategies and ongoing problem solving; attention to implementation in typical schools; and perceived benefits for students. Vadasy and Sanders (2008) argued that trained teaching assistants (para-professionals) can be responsible for implementing this type of programme and that students who fail to respond to this first line of instruction in the early years can then be evaluated before it is too late and more intense and more skilled intervention implemented.

Sawyer and Bernstein (2008) tested the assumption that more rapid mastery of phonological awareness skills would offer an advantage to those children with dyslexia with a core phonological deficit. They suggested that it appeared that those who had mastered phonological awareness skills earlier also demonstrated greater gains in decoding overall.

Their study substantiates the supportive role of phonological awareness in the acquisition and development of literacy skills. Sawyer and Bernstein also argued that because dyslexia is the most common learning disability in the United States, accounting for 80% of all learning disabilities (Katusic et al., 2001), it is imperative that all teachers be educated to understand the nature of dyslexia and the specific difficulties these students encounter in their progress towards literacy. They argue that an integrated approach to literacy instruction with dyslexia is necessary.

METHODOLOGICAL ISSUES IN READING INTERVENTION RESEARCH

Several factors need to be considered in interpreting and in designing and evaluating reading intervention programmes. One important factor is the characteristics of the sample and whether or not the sample is a discrete group. Tunmer and Greaney (2008) suggest that poor readers with comorbid disorders such as attentional or behavioural problems may respond differently to particular interventions compared to children without these disorders.

The setting, or combination of settings, under which the teacher–student interactions are carried out can also be influential, as well as the period of time and for how long, and for what reasons (Tunmer and Greaney, 2008). In the case of dyslexia, conceptual factors are also important. For example, Tunmer and Greaney argue that the conceptualisation of what skilled reading is and how it is acquired will greatly influence how we define reading disability or dyslexia. Therefore, factors such as the causes of the problems in learning to read, and what we believe are the most effective intervention strategies for helping students to overcome persistent literacy learning difficulties, will influence research studies. This can have implications for the selection of the sample as well as the selection of the reading programme.

The nature of the reading approaches used in research on reading intervention needs to be considered alongside the current level and the current characteristics of the participant in the study. Torgeson (2005) suggests that the stage of reading development at which the difficulty occurred, and the type and severity of the processing deficit responsible for the difficulty, are influential and will affect the outcome of the study.

For example, Tunmer and Chapman (2004) argued that, as a consequence of developmentally limiting deficits in phonological awareness and knowledge of print at the outset of learning to read, many struggling readers take longer than usual to acquire the self-improving alphabetic coding skills necessary for achieving progress in reading. To support their view, Tunmer and Greaney cite Vellutino et al. (1996), who pointed out that 'any given level of reading achievement is a by-product of a complex interaction between one's endowment and the quality of one's literacy experience and instruction...the optimally endowed child may be able to profit from less than optimal experience and instruction, whereas the inadequately endowed child may have difficulty profiting from even optimal experience and instruction' (p. 62).

FACTORS TO CONSIDER IN DEVELOPING AND USING READING APPROACHES

Ehri (2002) suggests that teachers need to monitor beginning readers' progress in acquiring letter knowledge and phonemic awareness to make sure that it is occurring for each child. This is particularly important in the early stages because there is considerable variability among children in the rate of development of reading skills. Ehri suggests that even at this early stage, extra teaching time is required for children who enter school without letter knowledge and phonemic awareness or for those children who experience some difficulty acquiring these skills. She suggests teaching the major grapheme–phoneme correspondences, vowel correspondences, how to segment pronunciations into the full array of phonemes and how to match these up to graphemes in the spellings of words to fully analyse words.

There are many activities that can be utilised to support a structured phonics programme. Among the most appropriate of these is the use of games and structured activities to reinforce a particular teaching point. Many of these games and activities can be developed by the teacher, although there are some excellent examples available commercially. See www.smartkids.co.uk and www.crossboweducation.com.

Activities can include syllable segmentation games such as clapping out the sound of children's names; rhyming skills games such as nursery rhymes and alliteration games such as games using pairs of objects with the same sound.

Other strategies that can be used are those that rely on the use of context. Readers can utilise two principal types of context:

- syntactic context—the grammatical structure of sentences and clues from prefixes, punctuation, word endings and word order;
- semantic context—the meaning of words and the meaningful relations between words.

Syntactic context helps the reader predict the written word. If the child is reading only key words he or she will not be able to draw on syntactic context for meaning. Snowling (2000, 2002) refers to the triangle model of reading (Seidenberg and

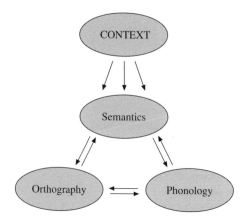

Figure 8.3   The triangle model of reading (reproduced by permission of BPS; from Snowling, 2002).

McClelland, 1989) and the connectionist model (Plaut et al., 1996), which highlight the connections between orthography and phonology, and the connections between these aspects and semantics stemming from the context (Figure 8.3). Snowling (2002) suggests that the semantic pathway of dyslexic readers operates normally and although dyslexic children tend not to be fluent readers, they can show extensive use of comprehension-monitoring strategies and self-correction to ensure they have understood what they have read. The study by Nation and Snowling (1998), which compared the ability of dyslexic readers and poor comprehenders, showed that in the context condition the dyslexic children fared best, which highlighted the view that dyslexic children benefited more from context than both a younger control group matched for reading age and poor comprehenders. Nation and Snowling therefore suggest that dyslexic readers who have decoding difficulties may be able to compensate by relying on contextual cues to support the decoding process. Semantic or contextual context relates to the meaning of words and how they convey messages. This acts as a powerful aid to reading, and many readers with poor decoding skills can rely, perhaps too much, on the use of semantic context. Using inferences and even accurate guessing can be a powerful aid to dealing with the written word. It is important, therefore, that learners develop skills in using inferences and identifying the main theme and points in a particular story.

Context, therefore, as a reading strategy can be important and is evident in the following ways:

- within the sentence—before and after the word being read;
- within the text—before and after the sentence being read;
- within the reader—entire store of knowledge and experience.

To utilise fully the benefits of contextual reading it is also important for the reader to have a stock of sight words in order that the context can be accurately obtained. For example, it has been argued by the proponents of the language experience approach that, instead of helping children build up a stock of sight words in order to read, perhaps teaching should be directed to help children read in order to build up a stock of sight words. This would mean that sight words can be built up gradually within the context of reading itself.

It is interesting to note that the 220 words on the Dolch list—that is, the most commonly used words—make up around 75% of the words in primary reading materials (Chall and Popp, 1996).

A classic dilemma is exemplified here between encouraging, indeed insisting on, reading accuracy of all the words and accepting the accurate reading of key words that should be sufficient through the use of semantic cues for comprehension acquisition.

The reading of every word, although it may help the reader obtain the full use of the benefits of syntactic cues, can restrict the reader's use of prediction and inferences because attention and concentration are absorbed in accurate decoding.

Contextual strategies can be effective because

- words are easier to identify in context than in isolation;
- beginning readers can often identify words in context that they cannot identify in isolation;
- they can be used to predict what might come next; and
- the syntactic and semantic context can help to confirm or correct these identifications.

THE LITERACY EXPERIENCE

Au and Raphael (2000) make a strong case for supporting the literacy development of a diverse range of students with both age-appropriate and reading-level-appropriate materials. They suggest that 'teaching reading carries with it two obligations. On the one hand, we must make sure that all students are taught at an instructional level, within their zone of proximal development so that they make appropriate progress each year. On the other hand regardless of reading level, we must engage students of every age in critical thinking using age-appropriate materials' (p. 152). This has implications for dyslexic children and for motivation and positive attitudes towards the nature of literacy. Eames (2002) reports on successes despite dyslexic students' difficulties with written language—the children in the study reported motivation in reading about their own interests, which included car magazines, sport, history and warfare.

There is now a considered opinion that literacy can be an agent of change, and the thrust of this chapter has indicated that literacy is much broader than reading alone.

Literacy has been presented in terms of a socially constructed phenomenon embedded within the cultural context (Eames, 2002; Wray, 2002; Vygotsky, 1978; Bruner, 1986). It therefore stands to reason that the teaching of literacy should consider both the diversity of the children being taught and the cultural and social implications of literacy. Moreover, the cognitive and critical thinking aspects of literacy should also be considered.

The experience of language and of learning is vital for a critical appreciation of literacy, and it is therefore vital that groups such as dyslexic children should not be overlooked as they need to obtain the broader perspectives offered by literacy to appreciate different societies and cultures. Ideally, this should be received through reading and careful provision of age-appropriate reading material. But if this is not feasible, the social, cultural and cognitive implications of literacy should be achieved through some other medium—discussion, film or through listening. Similarly, assessment needs to reflect and capture this broad view of literacy and measure appropriate outcomes. Eames (2002) suggests that these factors give rise to a number of key implications for practice. These include:

- the notion of a broad definition of literacy that stresses higher-order functions and critical thinking;
- the recognition that literacy is not simply a single ability or process, but rather the symbiotic interaction of abilities and learning processes;
- the need for well-thought-out teaching programmes that reflect a broad definition of literacy and that are responsive to dyslexic children's interests and preferred learning styles;
- teaching materials and literature should reflect philosophies of teaching and need to be both age- and reading-level appropriate.

A balanced view, therefore, of the teaching of literacy needs to include constructivist approaches to learning and literacy where the teacher is the key agent. Teaching programmes should therefore emphasise a range of interactive and reflective teaching methods that engage the learner in metacognitive processes to promote critical thinking as well as the social and cultural factors that enrich the learning and the life of readers.

FRAMEWORK FOR TEACHING

An example of a framework for teaching literacy followed on from the release of the National Literacy Strategy in England (The Framework for Teaching, DfEE, 1998). This document set out the teaching objectives in literacy for students from reception to Year 6. It was this document that set out the format of a Literacy Hour as a daily period of time throughout the school that would be dedicated to 'literacy teaching time for all students' (DfEE, 1998, p. 8). The Hour was intended to cover both reading and writing and was to take the form of an introduction of 30 minutes, 20 minutes of independent work and a 10-minute plenary. It essentially comprises the whole class, with a balance of reading and writing (15 minutes approximately), focusing on shared text work; another whole-class 15 minutes on word work; group and independent work for 20 minutes, such as independent reading; and whole-class reviewing for the final 10 minutes, reflecting and consolidating teaching points.

Although it is generally accepted that dyslexia is more than a reading difficulty (Fawcett, 2002), there is still little doubt that literacy is a crucial element of dyslexia and indeed in success at school. The school curriculum is dominated by the need to acquire literacy skills, and without these skills children can be placed at a marked disadvantage throughout school. Additionally, it has been shown that literacy can have significant socio-cultural as well as cognitive implications (Wearmouth et al., 2003). The acquisition of literacy, therefore, is necessary for the development of learning and life skills.

The importance of literacy is highlighted by Welch and Freebody (2002), who argue that, 'literacy education is at the centre of debates about society and instruction, in and out of school...and is a site from which to view the shifting fortunes of contesting interests; public and private...host communities and ethnic minorities and increasingly school, work-place and market-place. Further these contests often target the issue of standards of literacy, rather than, say, the methods or the materials of literacy education' (p. 62). It is precisely this situation that can disadvantage the child with dyslexia. Governments' demands for higher overall levels of literacy achievement, while on the surface commendable, can be sought at the expense of failing to acknowledge the specific methods needed for children with specific literacy difficulties. As this chapter has shown, there is more to literacy development than an increase in reading age. Eames (2002) pinpoints this when she reports that governments are essentially responding to the rising demands for literacy and not to the declining absolute standards of literacy. She argues that, 'the educational community needs to be aware that these higher demands may be unrealistic at certain developmental stages...(we need to) be reasonable in our expectations of students' literacy performances and not overdriven by market forces' (pp. 336–337). It is important, therefore, to ensure that children with dyslexia who may require specific teaching approaches are not casualties of such market forces. The implications of this are that literacy is more than a single ability or process and should be viewed from a broader perspective. The perspective should include critical thinking skills and metacognitive processes as well as the family and socio-cultural needs. Teaching programmes for literacy therefore need to reflect this broader conceptualisation and need to consider the individual student's cognitive, social and cultural needs as well as the need to achieve higher attainment levels as might be measured by conventional tests. But the importance of the cognitive, social and cultural factors that can be associated with literacy development should not be lost in the increasing desire, particularly among politicians and policy-makers, for quantitative data on literacy levels.

SUMMARY

This chapter has looked at some principles in the acquisition of literacy by focusing on reading and has examined a variety of approaches by discussing some of the problems children with dyslexia may display in relation to reading. Since the concept of dyslexia is essentially a multifaceted one with neurological, psychological and educational perspectives, it follows that the teaching of reading should be flexible and should consider the child's learning difficulties and preferences in the educational context. Clearly, no one approach can be singled out and a combination of methods involving the teaching of sight words, phonics and context is preferable.

At the same time, one must also look at what the child brings to the situation and have some knowledge of the child's background knowledge and preferred learning styles and strategies. All of these aspects are important to facilitate the acquisition of literacy.

POINTS FOR REFLECTION

- Consider the bottom-up and top-down models of reading. Reflect on the strategies and approaches you may use for each of these models.

- Consider the implications for teaching reading for the models mentioned in this chapter. Reflect on the model(s) you use in your teaching. What are the advantages and disadvantages of these models?

- Reflect on the debate on the teaching of reading. How might you achieve a balanced approach to the arguments and the debate?

- Consider how you might evaluate your practice in the teaching of reading. Reflect on some of the methodological issues discussed in the chapter.

- Consider the factors you need to take into account when developing materials to assist in the teaching of literacy. Consider phonological awareness approaches, literacy frameworks and the literacy experience.

Chapter 9

The Acquisition of Literacy: Spelling

WHY IS SPELLING DIFFICULT?

Many children with dyslexia find spelling more difficult than reading, and this can often persist well into adulthood. To find the reason for this we need to look at the theoretical background to spelling and from that identify the reasons why children with dyslexia can find spelling quite challenging. There is little doubt that the spoken language system, how aware the child is of language and the components of language influence the development of spelling. There is also considerable evidence that children with dyslexia have difficulty with the language system, particularly phonological awareness, and the relationship between sound and symbol.

Snowling (2000) suggests that there is less likelihood that children with dyslexia can utilise compensatory strategies with spelling as successfully as they can with reading. This would indicate that the teaching of spelling, particularly the language aspects of sounds, and the components of words are extremely important to successful spelling.

Snowling also suggests that the evidence on the development of spelling through exposure to written language in reading shows that this in itself is not enough for efficient spelling. Factors such as phonological awareness, knowledge of syntax and the syntactic function of words as well as meaning all have a role to play in the development of spelling skills. It is not surprising, therefore, that children with dyslexia consistently have difficulty with spelling, particularly as they often learn to read through the use of contextual strategies rather than phonological systems and because they cannot utilise context as successfully in spelling as in reading. This can cause some difficulty as they have to rely on their knowledge of phonic rules, letter strings and word rules. Additionally, they have to be aware of the initial sounds of the word from memory, and this can also cause some difficulty.

Spelling, therefore, can be a difficult processing operation for many—it is more difficult to use context, and it requires the need to be familiar with phonological representations and the correspondence between phoneme and grapheme. Spelling places demands on the memory and because it is a written activity it can also place demands on mental operations involved in the kinaesthetic factors associated with integrating writing with a mental activity such as spelling. Many of these factors are challenging for dyslexic children, and it is not unusual for children with dyslexia to be more advanced in reading than in spelling.

SYSTEMS INVOLVED IN SPELLING

Phonological Systems

Bradley and Bryant (1991) indicated that there is a strong relationship between children's phonological awareness at age 4 and their spelling (and reading) achievement at age 8. Snowling (2000, 1994) highlighted the nature of dyslexic children's spelling errors and showed that there was a significant difference in the nature of the spelling errors in dyslexic children compared with a control group. The dyslexic children showed more 'phonetically unacceptable' errors than the control group. In other words, the errors of the dyslexic group may not have been recognisable as the word because of a lack of phonetic similarity. This implies that the dyslexic children in this group did not have developed phonological representation, but were using letter naming strategies to spell phonologically regular words.

Spelling and Speech

Snowling et al. (1992) analysed in detail the spelling errors of a dyslexic child in relation to the connections between spelling and speech and found that difficulties were experienced with distinguishing between the voiced/voiceless sounds such as 'b' and 'p' and 'g' and 'k' in his spelling. Snowling (2000), therefore, suggests that the absence of a sound pattern of spoken words results in a lack of a framework on which to hang information needed for accurate spelling.

Visual Systems

Visual difficulties can also contribute to the spelling pattern of dyslexic children, particularly visual sequences. This has been shown by Romani et al. (1999), who found that it is possible even for spellers who have a good 'holistic' reading strategy, and therefore a good memory for visual configurations, to have a poor visual sequential memory. This means that these children would have difficulty learning letter sequences, and this can account for spelling errors. Ehri (2002) suggests that it may be important to enhance children's interest in the spellings of new words and in discovering how letters connect to sounds systematically. Children are taught to count the phonemes in words, then to look at spellings and match up graphemes to phonemes by placing letters in Elkonin boxes that provide one space for each letter that symbolises a separate sound. Also, teaching children to spell words by analysing and remembering how letters represent sounds in the words helps children fully analyse the graphophonemic relations needed to store words in memory.

Ehri (2002) suggests that there is normally a close correlation between reading and spelling and that often the first step in adding a new sight word to memory is successfully decoding the word or reading it by analogy to a known word. She therefore argues that children need to be taught these two strategies for reading unfamiliar words. These particular strategies, Ehri believes, are easier to acquire once children reach the full alphabetic phase and once they begin to accumulate a growing number of sight words whose spellings have been fully connected to pronunciations and meanings in memory.

SPELLING SKILLS

There are many skills involved in spelling and many of these skills are those that can be difficult for the dyslexic child to acquire. It is possible to examine these skills through the initial prerequisites of recognising rhymes and rhyming words. This is usually quite challenging for dyslexic children and further emphasises the need for early intervention using an effective phonics programme with over-learning and practice at development of rhyming skills. Achievement in spelling and phonics is closely associated in the early years. Chall and Popp (1996) suggest that children who are good in phonics are usually good in spelling, and those who are good in phonics and spelling are usually good in word recognition, oral reading accuracy and silent reading comprehension.

This further illustrates the cumulative and associative effect of different strands of literacy acquisition and also underlines why spelling is important for the acquisition of literacy and in the learning process. The next skill for spelling is blending spoken words into sounds. This again emphasizes the need for children to experiment with writing at an early stage as this provides practice in sounding out words as they write them and blending the sounds into words before moving on to making representations of the phonic structures in writing the beginning of words. This can be done visually as well as auditorily and again underlines the importance of multi-sensory principles, particularly in the early stages. All the skills in this initial stage of learning to spell—which all involve some competence in the early acquisition of phonological skills—are challenging for dyslexic children. Of course, what presents a greater threat is that the dyslexic difficulties at this stage may not have been identified and the child may already have feelings of failure and often a reluctance to write.

To spell, children also need to recognise the individual sounds and regular word patterns, which would involve knowledge of consonant and vowel digraphs and consonant blends. Children with dyslexic difficulties can find this challenging because of the difficulty with sound–symbol correspondence. But additionally, they find irregular words particularly challenging as these have often to be learnt visually and may not conform to the rules they are attempting to learn for conventional spellings.

Reason and Boote (1994) suggest the following stages in spelling:

- Stage one—recognition of rhymes and rhyming words; blending spoken word into sounds; making some representations of phonic structures in writing words;
- Stage two—writing single sounds and some common harder words such as 'have' and 'went';
- Stage three—consonant digraphs (ch, sh, th); consonant blends (sl, fr, sk, nd); vowel digraphs (ea, au, ow); magic e (came, mine);
- Stage four—able to spell most words and able to use a dictionary.

There is also a transition stage—the stage when children move from the reliance on phonemes to a recognition of the importance of graphemic (visual) patterns. This can also be challenging for dyslexic children. At this stage the spelling errors of children are often through the misuse of phonic equivalents—for example, they may put 'gait' for 'gate' because they have attempted to learn the vowel sound 'ai'. According to Marsh et al. (1980), the transitional stages of spelling can be fairly lengthy—they compared the spelling pattern of children of different ages and found that there seemed to be a ceiling for a dependency on phonological strategies at an early age—but the strategy of using analogy seemed to come later, after age 7. According to Smith et al. (1998), at the transitional stage the teacher should prioritise work on silent letters, suffixes and prefixes, and activities to encourage visual skills such as looking for small words within longer words and variations of the 'look, say, cover, write and check' method, which is discussed below.

One of the difficulties with spelling in the English language is the irregularity of many of the words. This means that children need to be aware of the phonology of the language (i.e., how the letters and sounds link together) and the orthography (i.e., the pattern of the letter strings). Because the orthography is irregular, spelling can present a difficulty to many children. Children have to understand very early on that for some words sounding out is successful, but for others they need to remember the pattern of the letter strings because the words are phonologically irregular.

SPELLING DEVELOPMENT

One of the influential studies on the development of spelling was the study conducted by Treiman (1993). This suggests that children at the very outset rely heavily on phonology. Treiman also suggests that children are aware of orthographic conventions even at an early stage. They seem to be aware of any two letters that are always grouped together; for example, 'ed' at the end of a word. This view conflicts with the stage model of spelling, which suggests that the orthographic rules are not acquired until a later stage.

The developmental stages of spelling, according to Smith (1994), suggest that dyslexic children will have difficulty with the phonetic stages and with the transitional stages of spelling and this will require considerable teacher support and awareness. Usually, this transitional stage would occur around the second year in school, and it would be at this stage that those children with dyslexic difficulties, whether recognised or not, will begin to be aware of their own difficulties with spelling and may begin to show a reluctance to write. A clear difference can exist between good and poor spellers in the performance in phonological tasks. This means that successful spelling is related to children's awareness of the underlying phonological structure of words. This is supported by Rohl and Tunmer (1988), who found that good spellers were better at phonemic segmentation tasks than older children matched for spelling age.

Furthermore, Bradley and Bryant (1991; Snowling, 2000; Joshi and Carreker, 2009) showed that measures of rhyme judgement and letter knowledge in pre-school children were a good predictor of subsequent performance in spelling. Thus, children who can recognise words that sound and look alike would tend to have a good memory for spelling patterns. Indeed, Bradley and Huxford (1994) show that sound categorisation in particular plays an important role in developing memory patterns for spelling.

SPELLING POLICY

It is important that schools have policies in spelling, and ideally this policy should be seen as a whole-school one—that is, not just a policy for poor spellers, but an overarching policy for all that has the mechanisms to meet the needs of all, including those with severe spelling difficulties such as the children with dyslexia. Such a policy should include some basic aims and overall rationale for the policy. In the case of spelling this is not too difficult to justify. It is indicated in the National Literacy Strategy (England and Wales) that students must understand the spelling system and that spelling does have a high profile in literacy or any literacy strategy—the debate, in fact, relates to how high a profile it should have and how spelling should be taught. As well as indicating the aims and rationale of a spelling policy, one must also highlight the processes involved in assessment, teaching and monitoring.

SPELLING STRATEGIES

Word Lists

The use of word lists can be a successful strategy for many with some form of spelling difficulties. Word lists can be a general list composed from words commonly used by children at certain ages. Word lists can also be in the form of specific lists that focus on the child's own particular spelling difficulties. One of the difficulties with using this strategy with dyslexic children is that often the spelling pattern of dyslexic children is inconsistent, and therefore words not included in a list because they have been able to spell them may still be spelt wrongly in some situations, such as in examinations where it may be necessary to write at speed.

It may also be useful to construct a specific word list of subject-specific words and those that have similar sounds, or look similar. These can be confusing for dyslexic learners; for example, 'cerebrum' and 'cerebellum'. Taking an instance in biology, Howlett (2001) suggests that it is useful to compile an alphabetically arranged biology spelling book for each year group. She suggests that such a spelling checklist can include other useful information such as definitions—'respiration', 'ecosystem', 'osmosis' and 'immunisation'. Additionally, the spelling book can contain a table showing singular and plural endings such as 'vertebra' and 'vertebrae' and irregular endings such as 'stoma' and 'stomata'—these can be problematic for dyslexic children. It is usually easier for children to learn words in context, so it would be useful to have a sentence next to the word to provide a clue to its meaning as well as its spelling properties. In relation to the spelling properties, the parts of the word that are usually misspelt by the student can also be highlighted. The benefit of this type of strategy is that it can be individualised for each child.

There are many different customised and commercial strategies that can be used to help with spelling, but ideally one needs to utilise a range of approaches and strategies, as the same approach may not be effective for all. The general principles, however, of good teaching—that is, multi-sensory strategies such as visual, auditory, kinaesthetic and tactile—should not be overlooked as these help with over-learning and automaticity. The most effective way to achieve automaticity is through using the word that is being learnt in as many different forms as possible, in different subjects and different contexts. Other spelling strategies are given in the following subsections.

For spelling, just as in reading, phonological awareness programmes implemented at an early stage can be very cost-effective and can prevent the onset of serious spelling difficulties. This can also include work on onset and rime, vowel and consonant recognition as well as rhyming games, matching pictures, and sound and visual discrimination.

Visual Strategies

There are a number of visual strategies that can be used in spelling. In fact, Peters (1970) suggests that spelling is essentially a visual–motor activity. Some of the predominantly visual approaches are described below.

Look, Cover, Write, Check

This is a well-established strategy for spelling, and was the outcome of longitudinal research conducted by Peters (1985). The stages include:

- *Look*—this involves active engagement of the writer looking closely at the word with the intention of reproducing it. Finger-tracing the word at this stage, which utilises kinaesthetic memory, can result in a stronger memory trace and enhance the chances of the child with specific difficulties remembering the visual features of the word. Bradley (personal communication, 1994; Bradley, 1990) suggests in her 'simultaneous oral spelling' strategy that saying the letters at this initial stage can also help to reinforce the memory trace for the word. It is also important that the look stage is not skipped or rushed through before the child has had an opportunity to develop visual strategies to help memorise the visual features. Such strategies can include making visual analogies of the word by recognising the visual features and similarities of the letters and the word to other words, or acknowledging the distinctive features. For example, in the word 'window' there are a number of visual aspects that could help with memory, such as the first and last letter being the same and the distinctiveness of the letter 'w'. At this stage it is also possible to draw attention to words within words, such as the word 'tent' in 'attention' and 'ask' in 'basket'.

- *Cover*—this involves visual memory and takes practice. Some children can adapt to this better than others. This type of activity lends itself very well to a game, and this can be motivating for children. Visual memory can of course be practised with a range of visual games and with games and activities involving visual discrimination. For example, Crossbow Educational (www.crossboweducation.com) produce a wide range of games, such as 'Rummyword', 'Breakdown' and 'Funfish', all of which can help provide practice in visual activities that can have a spin-off for spelling. Additionally, mnemonics as well as game-type activities can be used as an aid for visual memory.

- *Write*—this is an important stage as it provides the kinaesthetic practice. Many practitioners suggest that at this stage cursive handwriting should be encouraged. In fact, Peters (1985) suggests that there is a link between clear cursive writing and good spelling.

- *Check*—this provides the learner with some responsibility for his or her own spelling. It is important to reduce dependency on the teacher as soon as possible and to promote the activity of self-correction. While 'look, cover, write, check' as a strategy can be very successful for many children, it does place demands on memory and particularly visual memory. It is important, therefore, to ensure that it is suitable for the individual child and that other strategies are also considered.

Simultaneous Oral Spelling

Bradley (1989, 1990) has shown that rhyming is a particularly useful form of categorisation for developing spelling skills and that practice in sound categorisation through nursery rhymes and rhyming word games in early language play helps spelling (Box 9.1). Many children have problems remembering 'chunks', such as 'igh' in 'sight' and 'fight'. If children cannot do this, then every word will be unique. Irregular words can also be learnt using multi-sensory techniques. It has been shown in this chapter that phonological aspects are important in the development of reading and spelling skills. This seems to have considerable importance, particularly for dyslexic children who do not automatically relate the sounds.

- Have the word written correctly, or made with the letters.

- Say the word.

- Write the word, spelling out each letter as it is written, using cursive script.

- The child needs to see each letter, hear its name and receive kinaesthetic feedback through the movement of the arm and throat muscles.

continued

- Check to see if the word is correct.

- Cover up the word and repeat the process. Continue to practise the word in this way, three times a day, for one week. By this time the word should be committed to memory. However, only one word will have been learned.

- This final step involves the categorisation of the word with other words that sound and look a like. So, if the word that has been learned is round the student is then shown that she or he can also spell 'ground', 'pound', 'found', 'mound', 'sound', 'around', 'bound', 'grounded', 'pounding', etc. That is, she or he has learned six, eight or more words for the effort of one.

Box 9.1   Bradley's procedure for Simultaneous Oral Spelling (reproduced by permission of Lynette Bradley, pers. commun.)

Language Experience Approaches

Smith (1994) suggests that there is a great deal of scope for encouraging expressive writing using an adult helper to facilitate the development of language experience and spelling. She suggests that writing for communication and spelling need to be kept separate, otherwise the expressive output of the writing may become inhibited through constantly checking and correcting the spelling. She suggests that when children are identifying spelling errors they should first identify the mistakes and then proceed to underline them or use some other 'code'. Topping (2001), in fact, suggests actually drawing a line through the misspelling as it helps to visually reinforce the wrong spelling. Smith suggests that after finding out the correct spelling the child should then proceed through the 'look, cover, write, check' process. She also suggests that support for the inexperienced writer can include scribed writing, group scribed writing, an initial scribed start, collaborative writing with a more experienced writer, use of a word processor and spellchecker, and using redrafting of class work as homework, rather than writing completely new material at home. Many of these strategies would be useful for children with dyslexia, particularly if the writing process is seen as separate from the need for accurate spelling.

Although children do make progress with practice, this can only really effectively occur in spelling if the child has the opportunity to correct and note the correct spelling before proceeding with further work, otherwise the spelling error pattern is reinforced. It therefore requires a degree of judgement by the teacher to help the child self-correct, indicate spelling errors not noted by the child and motivate the child to write freely irrespective of the errors. All are important and each needs to be carefully handled.

Cued Spelling

The Cued Spelling technique shares the same principles as paired reading and other peer-tutoring developments (Croft and Topping, 1992). The technique comprises 10 steps for learning and spelling, four points to remember and two reviews

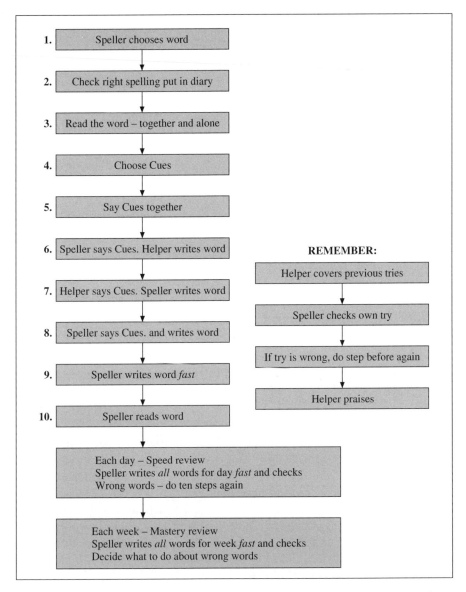

1. Speller chooses word
2. Check right spelling put in diary
3. Read the word – together and alone
4. Choose Cues
5. Say Cues together
6. Speller says Cues. Helper writes word
7. Helper says Cues. Speller writes word
8. Speller says Cues. and writes word
9. Speller writes word *fast*
10. Speller reads word

Each day – Speed review
Speller writes *all* words for day *fast* and checks
Wrong words – do ten steps again

Each week – Mastery review
Speller writes *all* words for week *fast* and checks
Decide what to do about wrong words

REMEMBER:
Helper covers previous tries
Speller checks own try
If try is wrong, do step before again
Helper praises

Figure 9.1 Cued Spelling: the 10 steps (reproduced by permission of Topping, 1992d, 2001, 2001; © Kirklees Metropolitan Council; accessed November 2008 from www.dundee.ac.uk/ eswce/research/projects/trwresources/menu/downloads/flowchart.pdf).

(see Figure 9.1). The points to remember help to consolidate the learning and the two reviews involve a daily and a weekly review. In the daily review the speller writes all the words for the day and checks them—the wrong words are then noted and the learner goes through the 10 steps again for these words.

The speller adopts the same procedure for the weekly review and identifies the wrong words. Discussion would then take place on the best approach for the learner to tackle the wrongly spelt words. If the learner writes a word inaccurately he or she is encouraged to delete the word from memory by erasing it or boldly scoring it out. This can be particularly useful if the learner has a strong visual memory and the image of the incorrect word may remain and be recalled at some future point. The Cued Spelling technique is highly interactive, but aims to encourage 'self-managed' learning. The technique attempts to eliminate the fear of failure through the use of prompt correction procedures. As in paired reading, modelling and praise are integral to the application of Cued Spelling. According to Topping and Watt (1992), 7-year-old children have been successfully trained in its use in about one hour, substantial progress can be made on norm-referenced spelling tests and improvements have been found in error rate and qualitative indicators in continuous free writing.

A number of studies support Topping and Watt's assertion regarding the merits of the technique. Scoble (1988) describes how the technique is also used with adult literacy and provides some examples of the application of Cued Spelling in the home with spouses, parents and friends as tutors. Oxley and Topping (1990) report on a peer-tutoring project using Cued Spelling in which eight 7-and 8-year-old students were tutored by eight 9-year-olds. The self-concept as a speller of both tutees and tutors showed a significant positive shift compared with a control group. The Cued Spelling technique is relatively simple to apply and the pack includes a demonstration video.

SPELLING MATERIALS

The ACE Spelling Dictionary

The *ACE Spelling Dictionary* (Moseley and Nicol, 1995) is specifically aimed at dyslexic children and can provide them with an easy and independent means of finding words at speed. Initially, students have to be taught how to use the dictionary, but there are many examples where teachers have indicated that this can be done in around three lessons (Turner, 1991). Additionally, there are activities that accompany the dictionary—ACE Spelling Activities. These consist of photocopiable worksheets with spelling activities based on the use of syllables, discriminating between different parts of speech, and other activities linked to the *ACE Spelling Dictionary*. It also includes advice on the use of common word lists.

Catchwords

This set of books can be useful for observing the progression from the semi-phonetic to phonetic to the transition stage in spelling. The first book provides examples of rhyming activities, and subsequent books in the series highlight word-building and common letter patterns. The series also contains suggestions on developing a whole-school spelling policy, a comprehensive word bank and guidance for involving parents.

Photocopiable Resources

There are a number of photocopiable resources for spelling, usually in ring-bound files, which can be easily accessed by the teacher:

- *Exercise Your Spelling* (Hodder & Stoughton).
- *Early Steps to Literacy* (Kickstart Publications).
- *Folens Spelling File* (Folens).
- *High Frequency Spelling Fun* (Timesavers).
- *Limericks, Laughs and Vowel Digraphs* (Crossbow Educational).
- *Rime Time* (Crossbow Educational).
- *Sound Beginnings* (LDA).
- *Spell It Out* (Hilda King Educational Services).
- *Spelling Rules OK* (Chalkface Publications).
- *Thrass Spelling Book* (Collins Educational).
- *Wordsnakes* (Crossbow Educational).
- *Crackerspell* (Jordanhill Publications).

These photocopiable activities would be useful for children with dyslexia as they can be used and developed in a multi-sensory way. Additionally, because they are photocopiable they can be used repetitively and interspersed with other activities. This can promote over-learning and, as will be seen in some of the following chapters, over-learning is essential for students with dyslexia.

POINTS FOR REFLECTION

- Consider the skills needed for spelling. Reflect on why students with dyslexia may find it difficult to acquire these skills.

- Consider some spelling strategies and approaches and reflect on the skills that students will be acquiring when using these strategies.

- Study some resources for spelling—try to evaluate how these may be useful in the light of the information in this chapter. Try to justify why a particular resource is being used.

Chapter 10

Expressive Writing

THE IMPORTANCE OF WRITING

It can be suggested that writing plays a key role in the school curriculum. This is because writing can be the means of assessing competence in class work, but more importantly writing can promote higher-order thinking skills, reflection and other language and literacy skills. These skills may not be readily accessed by dyslexic children and this can often place the young person with dyslexia at a disadvantage, particularly since writing has a high academic status and a high impact on achieving curriculum objectives. Yet dyslexic learners can be creative in their thinking and imagination and can have the potential to write some exceptionally creative pieces of work.

This, however, is not straightforward as creative writing is not an isolated activity. Creative writing involves many other skills, particularly skills associated with sequencing, focusing on a story line, grammar, spelling and directing the responses to meet the needs of the task that has been set—in other words, ensuring that the written piece is both relevant and coherent. During an interview with a dyslexic adult who is now an established author, Reid and Kirk (2001) found that one of the key difficulties was self-esteem and confidence. Supports are necessary to help minimise the impact of this. The person interviewed indicated the type of supports she found useful:

Becoming a writer was a real challenge for me. My friends were helpful with proof reading, but now my word processor does so much of that for me, it has been a great help. I like a challenge which is probably why I became a writer and I am also creative. The plot for the novel I have written came to me in a dream. This started me off in my career as a writer. I am now also a freelance travel writer. Looking back I suppose I would have had an easier passage at school if I had received some of the allowances which dyslexic people now get such as extra time in the exams. This would have been ideal for me because I usually have to read my work several times to pick out the errors. I suppose determination, support and good coping strategies have seen me through. I have been fortunate in the support from my family and friends.

One can view Susan's (*not her real name*) story as inspirational, I am sure some of her teachers would have advised her against becoming a writer. Nevertheless, this emphasises the value of support at the right time from the right type of person. Throughout the interview she was full of praise for her English teacher and attaches much of her success at school to that teacher. It also underlines the need for people with dyslexia to be determined and usually they are! In a similar fashion to Susan they often tackle an activity to prove to themselves that they can actually do it. Through determination they can become very good at some tasks.

Susan's story also highlights the need for dyslexic people, irrespective of the support offered, to accept the challenge, devise their own strategies and use their strengths. But it does indicate the value of support and the right type of support being available at the right time. This chapter will discuss the challenges of writing but also indicate some of the supports that can help the person with dyslexia deal with these challenges.

RELATIONSHIP BETWEEN WRITING AND SPELLING

There is a wealth of research to indicate that there is a strong relationship between spelling and writing (Read, 1971; Chomsky, 1986; Moseley, 1989). Joshi and Carreker (2009) describe spelling as the greatest ornament in writing. It follows that lack of confidence in spelling can have a considerable detrimental effect on children's written expression.

According to Chall and Popp (1996), the practice of writing and sounding out words that have been written is an excellent preparation for learning conventional spelling and phonics. Additionally, they suggest that early writing also illustrates the important principle that learning is cumulative—which means that the children need to know the alphabet letters in order to use them in writing. This in turn helps to provide children with the opportunity to practise using these letters in writing, together with the sounds of the letters. Additionally, being aware of a spelling difficulty can restrict the child's enthusiasm for writing. For that reason it is preferable to insist that spelling will not be taken into account in a written piece. It is important to grade a piece of work not on spelling but purely on content. Berninger et al. (1998; Berninger, 2004) argues that children with spelling problems write fewer words than children who do not have such a problem. She also presents a view that handwriting and spelling account for 66% of the variance in primary-grade writing fluency. This highlights the point that the student should be aware that spelling will not impact on the overall grade but it also highlights the need to encourage students with dyslexia to use a word processor as early as possible in the writing process.

EXPRESSIVE WRITING: THE PROCESS

There are many stages involved in the writing process. Children come to writing with a range of prior experiences and preconceived ideas, and many, particularly dyslexic children, view writing as hard work. Despite the potential to write creatively, they can still see it as a challenge and a chore. It almost goes without saying that it is important for students to associate writing with enjoyment and success. Yet writing is important, as it not only presents the writer's thoughts on paper but can help to develop other key cognitive skills.

COGNITIVE SKILLS ASSOCIATED WITH WRITING

Some of the cognitive skills associated with writing can include the following:

- *Organisation*—the writer has to organise the information in order to ensure that the reader has full and clear comprehension. This includes logical connections among ideas. There are implications here for the importance of planning, as this will help the writer organise the written work. At the same time it needs to be appreciated that planning may not come easily for students with dyslexia and they need to be shown how to plan.
- *Sequencing*—it is important that the writing piece flows. The content needs to be in the appropriate sequence and again this might be a difficulty for the student with dyslexia. It may be useful to provide a structure which will help the student follow a plan.
- *Identifying key points*—One of the crucial points about writing is that it should be relevant. Therefore it is important that the key points are recognised and highlighted in the written piece. It is a common mistake for learners with dyslexia to highlight those points which in fact are not that important and this can usually be at the expense of more important points.
- *Developing a story line*—this requires a degree of imagination but it also requires a working vocabulary. This can be problematic for students with dyslexia. It is therefore a good idea to provide the key vocabulary for students, ensuring that the meanings are provided for words that sound the same or are visually similar.
- *Imagination*—students with dyslexia can often have a vivid imagination. But it is important to harness this and to translate it into a written form. This can be challenging, and to overcome this they may have to discuss it first. Discussion can be a powerful tool for students with dyslexia and this can help them develop their ideas and plan how to put these into the written piece.
- *Grammar/syntax*—students with dyslexia often have difficulty with syntax and it can be demoralising for them to receive a piece of writing back from the teacher with red scores regarding grammatical errors. There are ways of overcoming this, such as discussing with the student different ways of expressing information and then indicating which is the most grammatically correct. Avoid using red pens as this can be visually disempowering for the student. Specific word processing programs such as Text help© can be very useful as this program can be tailored for the dyslexic student and help with syntax, organisation and spelling.
- *Memory*—usually the writer has to recall information and remember what they have previously said to avoid repetition. Writing therefore can help develop and consolidate memory skills.

WRITING IN THE CURRICULUM

Moats (2005a, 2005b) provides a strong case for the importance of writing in the curriculum. She indicates that writing is not one of the 'critical components' of reading listed in the Reading Excellence initiatives, and the National Reading Panel report (2000) does not include a section on writing, but nevertheless writing is an essential component of a comprehensive literacy programme. She argues that reading comprehension is enhanced when students write a response to their reading. She suggests that writing facilitates phonological awareness, spelling knowledge, vocabulary, and familiarity with the language, structures and, very importantly, with thinking itself.

Moats believes that writing is a difficult skill for students with dyslexia to master. It takes longer to write proficiently because writing uses the four processors essential for word recognition—phonological, orthographic, meaning and context—but also draws on other skills such as language skills, motor, memory, attention and cognitive functions such as organisation and sustained attention. She argues that it is dependent on high and low levels of cognitive skills. According to Moats (2005a, 2005b), high-level skills are logical connections, connecting ideas, maintaining a writing goal and taking the reader's perspective. Lower-level skills are letter formation, sound–spelling links, recall of sight words and use of punctuation.

Moats suggests that writing involves three distinct sub-processes: generating ideas, setting goals and organising information. These factors need to be discussed and dealt with at the planning stage. This is particularly important for children with dyslexia.

DEVELOPING METACOGNITIVE SKILLS THROUGH WRITING

Wray (2009) suggests that of all the processes of literacy and language, writing is the most self-evidently metacognitive. He proposes that by expressing these thoughts in a visible way, students can subsequently rethink, revise and redraft, and are allowed to reflect upon their own thinking. Wray suggests, therefore, that writing is metacognitive and that metacognitive knowledge consists of dimensions of personal, task and strategy knowledge. This implies that self-knowledge is important at both the pre-writing and writing stages. The writer's ideas, sequences, and starting and finishing points are reflected on, as well as the information to be covered and the ideas the writer wants to incorporate in the writing piece. Wray suggests that the actual task is important and that the writer reflects on the different genres, the structure and accessibility of the writing for the reader, and how the reader may be guided through the writing piece.

Knowledge of the process is also important for metacognition and reflection. Students need to reflect on the processes they go through as they write in order to reassure themselves that the processes they use are entirely normal and will, in the end, produce the right results. Being aware of how they as individuals learn, the task and the processes help the writer to control the writing process, allow them to check on their own progress, choose alternative strategies, change direction and make an evaluation of the emerging and completed product.

It is important that teachers ensure that children are given adequate opportunities to acquire the requisite knowledge about themselves as writers, about the writing process and about the demands of particular writing tasks, including textual structures. They also need to ensure that this knowledge develops beyond simply knowing that certain things can be done in writing to knowing how they can be done, and why they should be done. Therefore the focus is on the process involved in the emerging and finished product rather than on the product itself.

METACOGNITIVE STRATEGIES FOR WRITING

Some strategies to help integrate metacognitive skills in the writing process include:

- Thinking aloud while writing.
- Critically examining and revising writing decisions, for example asking themselves 'why did you write this?', or 'why did you explain something in this manner?'
- Anticipating potential difficulties and making judgements and reconciliations between competing ideas as well as showing an alertness to the needs of their potential and actual readership.

These all promote learner independence and reflection. Wray suggests that expert writers are more likely to have in mind several alternative ways of handling their writing task and that their writing consists not only of expressing what they wish to say, but of actually working this out as they write. This 'knowledge transforming' has been described by a variety of professional writers.

On the other hand, students with learning difficulties tend to lack the metacognitive control that would enable them to implement and regulate a range of learning strategies. They are also less successful in regulating their textual understanding and fail to monitor or correct potential confusions as they read others' texts and produce texts themselves for others to read. This lack of ability can prevent them from successfully rereading, monitoring and revising their texts. Wray argues, therefore, that younger and less experienced writers are less able to operate metacognitively in their writing than expert writers, and moreover that the actual level of metacognitive awareness may be a major factor which differentiates between skilled and poor writers.

Graham and Harris (1993) note that the metacognitive approaches to writing emphasise the different processes of writing and these can be separated out and focused upon individually. They go on to indicate that the area researched most thoroughly in relation to students with difficulties in literacy development is the use of strategies intended to highlight planning processes. Wray (2009) provides examples of these, including: self-directed techniques for generating words relevant to the content of the script, the use of writing frames to generate and organise ideas, and articulating process goals for establishing the way in which the end product is to be achieved. Writing frames are well established and can help to form a structure for the writer. For example, a writing frame can follow the pattern shown in Box 10.1.

I like to read this because ....

But that means I am not able to consider ....

Yet at the same time this means that ....

This is an informative book because ....

But I would have a better understanding if ....

But I have learnt .... from the book.

Box 10.1   A pattern for a writing frame

Eames (2002) studied the writing pattern of dyslexic children and indicated that the sample of dyslexic children she studied made little use of metacognitive strategies. She reports that in mainstream classes the boys frequently displayed lack of interest, opted out and used diversion tactics. Yet, in one-to-one review/revision exercises with these students about their written drafts, there was increased evidence that they knew a lot about writing. They were able to comment on the application of self-correction strategies, to evaluate their own writing and to make suggestions for improvement. Eames suggests that the important aspect related to this example is that the students have the ability to monitor their own work and develop their writing style, but need some initial impetus from the teacher in order to activate these skills.

The more students monitor their own work and utilise metacognitive strategies, the more likely they are to take responsibility for their own learning. This is important, and vital for children with dyslexia, who need to reflect on their own learning and be aware of how they carried out a particular piece of work and how they could utilise similar strategies in a different piece of work.

Eames (2002) suggests that this has considerable implications for teachers and for teacher education. She suggests that teachers need to:

- talk to students before designing and implementing programmes of work to establish students' interests and preferred learning styles and learning environment;
- know how to facilitate writers on the journey from initial to final draft;
- understand that the writing task will not be completed in one sitting;
- facilitate interim sessions, mid-process, where writers have an opportunity to reflect on what they have written, to discuss it, to share it and to self-monitor their work in progress; and
- engage in these practices habitually until they become part of students' normal practice.

Writing is a vehicle for expression, and this can influence thought and the development of concepts. Children learn through the exercise of writing, and it is therefore important that this opportunity for cognitive and metacognitive development should not be minimised for children with dyslexia. Often they may avoid writing, but writing, like any other learning task, can be made dyslexia-friendly.

STRATEGIES FOR WRITING

There are many strategies that can be utilised to make writing more meaningful and fulfilling for the dyslexic child. These include:

- the use of themes related to the particular interest of the dyslexic child;
- examining the purpose of writing and introducing different reasons for developing a piece of writing;
- using writing to experience poetry, drama and script-writing;
- linking the writing task to the interests of the child; and
- introducing the writing task in a manner consistent with the student's learning style.

Reid and Green (2007a) suggest that writing can be embellished through the use of themes. They suggest, for example, the following activity:

1. Get the student to list 10 favourite things. Then have them number the list from 1 to 10, with number 1 being their absolute favourite.
2. Ask the students to draw a cloud in the centre of the page. Inside write 'My Favourite Things'. Next they will write their three top favourite things coming out of the web and then sketch a small drawing of those three things.
3. The next step is getting the student to expand on each of their favourite things with details and descriptive words; this will be the 'what' and 'why' of their favourite things.
4. They should also continue on with visuals, adding little drawings that represent what they are writing. Adding colour will help with the detail and the description when they move to the paragraph-writing stage.

An example of this can be seen below:

My Favourite Things

1. **Rain**
   - Feels good on my skin
     - Tingly
     - Cold
     - Wet
     - Taste (catching raindrops on my tongue)
   - Smell
     - Fresh
     - Damp

- Sound
  - ♦ Loud thunder
  - ♦ Rain on rooftops

MOTIVATION AND WRITING

Motivation is an important factor in writing and one of the key aspects of motivation is having a sense of purpose (Reid, 2007a). For many the sight, or indeed the thought, of certain types of tasks can be sufficient to de-motivate them. It is important, therefore, that when the writing task is set it is seen by the student as an achievable task. This in fact can be the first major barrier that has to be overcome in order to maintain motivation. Some learners with dyslexia, if they have experienced repeated failure, will become totally de-motivated and will not want to engage in writing in any way at all. It is important that children can experience success before they become de-motivated.

It is for that reason that great care must be taken when developing writing tasks to ensure that they are motivating and, importantly, that the learner believes the task is achievable. It is important that the writing task is broken down into small steps and that every step represents an achievable outcome for the learner. It is important, therefore, to see writing as a series of steps. This can be achieved by identifying the stages in writing such as those shown in Box 10.2.

Brain storming—ideas, themes, topics.

Background knowledge—what is already known about a topic, what has still to be found out.

Research—finding out, making notes, writing a mind map of the story.

Planning—firming up ideas and organising how the writing pierce will be subdivided.

Writing introduction—write introduction, review and revise.

Drafting—words to be used, paragraph sequencing, paragraph themes.

Revise and review—how is it to be presented.

Box 10.2   Example of a writing task

Motivation by reward can also be a useful method of developing the student's enthusiasm for writing. This should be seen as a short-term strategy—a step towards self-motivation. Rewards are normally only successful in the short term and can help children who need a boost, particularly if they are finding the task challenging, and often this is the case with children with dyslexia. Rewards must also be achievable and the learner must value the reward. It is best if the reward is negotiated with the learner, but the best reward is for the student to see a successful outcome to the writing process. For that reason it is necessary to identify a purpose for the writing and indicate how it will be used—perhaps as part of a wall display or class magazine.

PLANNING

Planning to a great extent requires:

- *The generation of ideas*—this means that the student may have to be provided with a list of possible ideas that can stem from topics. Another way of generating ideas is through discussion. This can inspire the student but also help him or her reflect on what he or she may want to say.
- *Decide on a context*—where is the narrative taking place? There may need to be some pre-writing discussion on this to ensure that the student has a detailed picture of the context and the background to the written work. It is also a good idea to ask the student why this place was chosen. Again this will encourage pre-writing reflection.
- *Decide on the audience/goals*—who is it to be written for? The age of the readership? Is it to be descriptive or fast moving? Encourage the student to reflect on what is to be communicated—what does he or she really want to say?
- *Organisation of the written piece*—what should come first? How much detail will the opening paragraph provide? What will each paragraph cover?

PRE-WRITING FRAMEWORK

It is a good idea to provide a framework for children's writing. The North West Educational Laboratory in Portland, Oregon (NWREL) (www.nwrel.org) highlighted some of the stages of the writing process and the skills required for this. The stages they identified are:

- ideas;
- organisation;
- voice;
- word choice;
- sentence fluency;
- conventions;
- presentation.

These stages developed by the NWREL are discussed below.

Ideas/Detail

They suggest that ideas are the heart of the written work. The content of the piece, the main theme, together with all the details that enrich and develop that theme, rest on the ideas. It is important that time is spent on developing ideas and that the ideas are strong and well thought through. They suggest that successful writers do not tell readers things they already know; e.g., 'It was a sunny day, and the sky was blue, the clouds were fluffy white...' They notice what others overlook, seek out the extraordinary, the unusual, the bits and pieces of life that others might not see.

Organisation

It is suggested that organisation is the internal structure of a piece of writing. Organisational structure can be based on comparison–contrast, deductive logic, point-by-point analysis, development of a central theme, chronological history of an event, or any other identifiable pattern. When the organisation is clear, the piece becomes meaningful. Events proceed logically; information is given to the reader in the right doses at the right times so that the reader never loses interest. Connections are strong, which is another way of saying that bridges from one idea to the next hold up.

Voice

The voice is the writer and the writer's views come across though the piece of writing. They suggest that voice is the heart and soul of the writing. When the writer is engaged personally with the topic, he or she imparts a personal tone and flavour to the piece that is unmistakably his or hers alone. This is an individual factor—different from the mark of all other writers; this is what the NWREL call the voice.

Word Choice

Word choice is the use of rich, colourful language that communicates not just in a functional way, but in a way that moves and enlightens the reader. In good descriptive writing, strong word choice clarifies and expands ideas. In persuasive writing, careful word choice moves the reader to a new vision of things. Strong word choice is characterised not so much by an exceptional vocabulary that impresses the reader, but more by the skill to use everyday words well.

Sentence Fluency

Sentence fluency is the rhythm and flow of the language, the sound of word patterns, the way in which the writing plays to the ear, not just to the eye. How does it sound when read aloud? This can provide an indication of the fluency and the meaning of the writing piece.

Conventions

Conventions are the mechanical correctness of the piece—spelling, grammar and usage, paragraphing (indenting at the appropriate spots), use of capitals, and punctuation. Writing that is strong in conventions has been proofread and edited with care.

Presentation

Presentation combines both visual and verbal elements. It is the way we 'exhibit' our message on paper. Even if our ideas, words and sentences are vivid, precise and well constructed, the piece will not be inviting to read unless the guidelines of presentation are present. One of the important aspects of presentation is knowing the audience. This needs to be established at the outset as it can have an impact on how the materials will be presented.

The NWREL have conducted a number of research studies on this model—one such study was a five-year, multi-site experimental study examining the impact of a writing intervention on the performance of fifth-grade students. The results indicated that using the Traits© writing model, the writing was more focused and it aided planning and the revision of student writing.

Another study conducted was in a Saudi Aramco school (NWREL, 2000, www. nwrel.org). This involved a single school study of fourth-grade students, showing the percentage of students at each level of performance pre- and post-trait implementation. The study showed an increase of 7% in the number of students meeting or exceeding the district writing standard through using the Traits model.

The above use of a traits model can be extremely beneficial for students with dyslexia because it is highly structured. Students with dyslexia need a structure and clear steps such as those indicated in this model.

DEVELOPING IDEAS

It is important that time is spent on the developing of ideas. Reid and Green (2007a) show how brainstorming can be an excellent way to collect ideas and to help students to develop vocabulary. During this activity it is a good idea to get the students to make as long a list as possible to begin with and then narrow it down later.

Practice at brainstorming is important and this can be done by giving the students a list of topics to brainstorm. Reid and Green (2007a) suggest the following because they may be of interest to the student:

- Skateboard Brand Names
- Vacation Destinations
- Things that are Green
- Sports Equipment
- Things to take to the Beach
- Cars
- Types of Dogs
- Musicians
- Favourite Snack Foods

Students with dyslexia often freeze up when they are asked to write, as it can be such a daunting task for them. Yet if they are provided with a structure and an opportunity to be creative, the writing exercise can be successful. Reid and Green

(2007a) suggest getting the students to draw images to help them develop their writing skills. For example, in a piece of writing about a forest they suggest that the students draw in the details from the following prompts:

- Are there hills or mountains?
- Is there a shoreline; are there beaches or is your forest at the edge of a steep cliff? Do the beaches have sand or rocks?
- Are there streams and rivers? Are they wide and lazy or dangerous with white-water rapids?
- What about lakes, swamps or marshes?
- Is it sunny or does it rain all the time?
- What kind of trees are in your forest?
- What sort of insects, reptiles, birds or mammals lives in your forest?
- What do you smell?
- How does the air feel?

They are also encouraged to add colour to their forest as well detail.

When the students have completed their drawing they can organise their ideas and write several paragraphs describing their forest (adapted from Reid and Green, 2007a).

It is important to look for as many different ways as possible to generate a piece of writing. This could mean providing the opening paragraph for the student or providing a list of structure or key words. This latter suggestion is included in the programme Visualising and Verbalising (Bell, 1992), where the student receives structure words such as background, colour, mood, people, time of day, weather and action to help the student extract and imagine details from a picture to help with the writing process.

HANDWRITING

It can be the case that children are reluctant to write because they have a handwriting difficulty. The use of computers and specialised computer software can help to overcome any de-motivation that might arise from handwriting difficulties.

It is important that children with dyslexia are encouraged to become proficient in the use of the keyboard at as young an age as possible, especially for those with handwriting difficulties.

Nevertheless, there is a considerable amount of materials on handwriting that can help in the development of a programme for children with difficulties in forming letters.

Many handwriting programmes have been customised and developed by teachers, and these can be very successful. Alston (1993, 1996) has developed a number of programmes and some key principles in the teaching of handwriting. One key factor is that the handwriting programme should be used consistently each day, even if only for a short time.

SUMMARY

It is important to view the writing process for children with dyslexia as being of paramount importance. Spelling, handwriting and the generation of vocabulary have all been made more easily accessible with word processing and the appropriate software.

It is important to recognise that successful writing can lead to more positive self-esteem and this will have a spin-off to other areas of learning. It is also important to appreciate that children with dyslexia will require a structure and 'cues' to lead them into the writing process. They should not necessarily start with a blank sheet of paper. The use of visuals, for example, as cues can be helpful, and structure words can provide the essential vocabulary components as well as acting as a trigger to extend writing. Pre-task discussion is also essential, as it can facilitate reflection on the part of the student and allow him or her to think through the various paragraphs and the purposes of the piece of writing. This highlights the importance of planning, and time should be taken to ensure that the student takes this seriously as it will be essential for organisation as well as sequencing of the written piece. It is important to bear in mind that students with dyslexia can be highly proficient writers.

POINTS FOR REFLECTION

- Consider how you may develop creativity in students with dyslexia. What kind of supports can help to facilitate this?

- Reflect on the importance of writing as a 'spin-off' for other activities and skills.

- Reflect on some strategies for motivating learners with dyslexia to write.

- Consider how you may assist the learner with dyslexia to plan and implement a piece of creative writing. Consider the following: frameworks, ideas, detail, organisation, structure, vocabulary, language expression and presentation.

Chapter 11

Teaching Approaches: Points to Consider

This chapter will discuss some of the most appropriate teaching approaches used for children with dyslexia. The debate about what constitutes appropriate intervention for children with dyslexia will also be discussed. It has been argued (Norwich, 2009) that provision for dyslexia should be seen as a continuum of mainstream provision and that there is not a sufficiently strong case for qualitatively different approaches for children with dyslexia. Brooks (2002, 2007) suggests that the evidence highlights the importance of early intervention schemes but that, in general, ordinary teaching does not enable children with literacy difficulties to catch up. Research evidence on the effectiveness of literacy interventions with differing theoretical bases and various implementation characteristics has produced mixed conclusions, but Burroughs-Lange (2008) suggests that generally short-term gains can be demonstrated. This is supported by the views expressed by Vellutino et al. (2004).

It is important, therefore, that schools accumulate reliable evidence of gains that can be expected in order to evaluate what will be most successful for the particular learning needs of children. This will help teacher selection of programmes and enhance parental confidence in the intervention being carried out.

Teaching approaches for children with dyslexia can basically be divided into four broad areas: individualised approaches, support approaches, assisted learning and whole-school approaches (Reid, 2004). In determining the most appropriate programmes and strategies for children with dyslexia, a number of factors must be considered, including:

- *The context*—what is the nature of the learning and teaching provision, the class size, opportunities for withdrawal, classroom environment and the age and stage of the individual student?
- *The identification of needs*—in what way does the assessment and analysis of needs inform teaching? Have the needs been appropriately identified? Can the individual's strengths and difficulties be identified from the results of the assessment?

- *The curriculum*—how can the teaching approaches be related to the curriculum? Are any gains made by these approaches readily transferable to other aspects of the curriculum?
- *The learner*—what are the individual factors that can help the learner make appropriate gains from the teaching approach? Is the approach suitable for the individual's learning style? Are there opportunities for extended learning?

It is important to view teaching approaches and programmes in relation to the individual and not in relation to the syndrome or label. A label can be misleading—it can be more of a general term and may not provide the descriptive and learning characteristics needed to develop appropriate approaches. Some programmes may be highly evaluated by teachers and have established a reputation as a successful multi-sensory programme, but this does not necessarily mean that the programme will be effective with all dyslexic children. Each child has to be viewed individually. If an established programme is to be used then it is wise to check out the views of colleagues who have used this particular programme. Many national and international organisations associated with dyslexia and effective learning now have internet-based forums where practitioners can exchange ideas (see, for example, www.learning-works.org.uk).

THE CONTEXT

The context relates to the classroom environment, the type of provision and the teaching situation as well as whole-school factors such as school ethos and degree of culture and dyslexia-friendliness. One of the issues often prevalent in looking at the teaching and learning context is that of one-to-one tuition, withdrawal and within-class support for children with dyslexia. This has been an ongoing debate and there are many pros and cons to each type of provision. Elbaum et al. (2000) argue that there is a strong case for the success of one-to-one instruction and that classroom teachers would generally describe it as the ideal teaching practice. Elbaum et al. suggest that the effectiveness of one-to-one provision has been validated by empirical research, particularly in relation to children with reading difficulties. Yet the reality, according to Elbaum et al., is that in mainstream classrooms it is seldom implemented, and even in special education classes one-to-one instruction may occur in only a limited way.

This underlines the importance of recognising that not all dyslexic children will respond to the same type of provision and support to the same extent. Specialist teachers who work cooperatively with class teachers, withdrawal of children for individual tuition and specific provision outwith the mainstream school can all be effective in some way. To ascertain the most appropriate method and approach it is important to identify the student's needs and to be aware that despite the label these needs may differ from child to child.

Each of these approaches can be effective. It is important that the teacher uses the teaching and learning context and the knowledge obtained on the child to the child's maximum benefit. This can be done through the development of contextualised teaching materials and accessing teaching and learning programmes for children with dyslexia that can be effectively adapted to different teaching situations and contexts.

One of the crucial aspects of the different approaches that can be used in different contexts is that of communication, particularly when the child is withdrawn or receives provision out with school. Green (2008) undertook a study looking at this aspect and particularly the role of teachers and parents in developing effective communication to support the child's literacy development. She found that very few of the teachers in the study, who taught students who were receiving additional tuition out with school, were knowledgeable about the approach being utilised. Her findings suggested the need for a detailed and contextualised communication protocol between teachers, parents and the tutors carrying out the additional tutoring.

ASSESSMENT AND THE CURRICULUM

One of the objectives, perhaps the principal objective, of an assessment is to provide some guidance to help in the development of teaching programmes. To do this it is crucial to identify the child's learning needs. Came and Reid (2008) show how this can be done by using informal assessment. They suggest that informal assessment can provide more useful information than formal standardised assessments. Information about the children and their learning habits and preferences can be obtained from informal assessment, although they stress that informal assessment needs to be used appropriately. But the strength of informal observation or self-report assessment is that it provides a picture of the learner in the learning context. It is also flexible and can be used to analyse different aspects of the learning situation. It can say much about the learner's self-perception and self-esteem and can be used in the development of an individual programme.

It is also important to find out which teaching programmes and strategies have already been used and how successful they have been—and to attempt to find out why particular approaches have or, indeed, have not been successful. This will help to determine which teaching approaches should be implemented for that student and help to match the learner with the approach, based on both this knowledge and the knowledge gained from identifying needs through the informal assessment.

It is important, therefore, to examine the assessment findings in a holistic manner by looking at all aspects of the assessment, such as strengths, weaknesses, self-concept, interest, motivation and the learning preferences of the student, and to link these factors to an appropriate teaching programme.

THE LEARNER

It is important to adopt a holistic perspective, looking not only at the learner's strengths and weaknesses, but also the preferred learning style. Under what conditions would the child be most likely to learn? Which approaches may be preferred by the learner? In what way would these approaches help to maintain the learner's interest and motivation as well as enhancing self-esteem? These questions and issues must be considered before deciding on appropriate intervention and teaching programmes.

In the main, students with dyslexia usually have a right hemisphere processing style. This means that they will prefer to process information visually and holistically. In relation to teaching, this would mean that they will prefer an overview of the information, or the task to be tackled first, before setting about tackling the individual components of the task. In terms of teaching reading, this would mean that first they would need an overview of the story line, the main characters and the general context before embarking on reading the book. Other suggestions from a cognitive perspective include:

- providing one task at a time to ensure that it has been understood and consolidated before embarking on the next task;
- allowing additional time to complete tasks;
- helping the student develop effective long-term memory strategies for retaining and recalling information; this may be through using a visual approach.

Although children with dyslexia have some common core difficulties, they do not represent an identical discrete entity with identical profiles. Therefore, intervention and teaching programmes will be tailored to the needs profile of the individual learner, and this will vary depending on the preferred learning style and cognitive profile of each dyslexic child. This knowledge of the learner, which can be most readily recorded by the class teacher, is, therefore, of extreme importance. It will help to successfully match the needs and learning style of the child with the teaching and the requirements of the curriculum.

PROGRAMMES AND APPROACHES—SOME CONSIDERATIONS

It is important to link programmes and approaches together because, while there are a considerable number of well-evaluated and effective commercially produced programmes for dyslexia, it is very seldom that a programme can be used without specific training. Even if a programme has clear instructions, there is some skill attached to implementing such programmes and often the context will determine whether the programme can be used; for example, many programmes are specifically geared to a one-to-one approach. Therefore, the teacher needs to be aware that it may be more productive to view intervention through a series of approaches rather than a discrete programme.

Automaticity, Over-learning and Structure

There is a considerable body of evidence that intervention strategies for teaching reading and spelling skills to dyslexic children should be both multi-sensory and phonic and that this type of teaching can benefit most children in any class at most stages (Crombie, 2002b). Additionally, it is a well-established view that dyslexic children require considerable over-learning to achieve automaticity. Automaticity is important for the learning of any skill, but it is particularly important for children with dyslexia as there is evidence (Fawcett, 1989, 2002; Fawcett and Nicolson, 2001, 2008) that dyslexic children have a dyslexia automatisation deficit—the 'DAD hypothesis' (Nicolson and Fawcett, 1990). This means that children with dyslexia will require additional time to develop automaticity in any skill, but particularly in literacy, and this factor needs to be considered in a teaching programme.

Nicolson and Fawcett proposed that dyslexic children have difficulties making skills automatic (so that one no longer needs to think how to do the skill). Automaticity develops from long practice under consistent conditions, and underpins almost all of our highly practised skills, from speech to walking to arithmetic. Nicolson and Fawcett (1990) noted that, unlike language, reading is not a 'special' skill for humans. They argue that humans are not evolutionarily adapted to read—few people could read at all until the last two or three hundred years. One of the critical aspects of learning a skill is to make it automatic, so that one can do it fluently without thinking about it. By adulthood, most skills—walking, talking, reading—are so deeply over-learned that we no longer have any insight into how we acquired them.

Fawcett and Nicolson (2008) suggest that there is no theoretical reason to expect that automatisation of the processes in reading is qualitatively different from the general processes of automatising any other complex skill. Automatisation is a key requirement for reading, and Fawcett and Nicolson suggest that there is extensive evidence that dyslexic children, even when reading well, are less fluent, requiring more time and effort to read than would a non-dyslexic child of the same reading age. The automatisation deficit hypothesis was supported by a set of experiments in which dyslexic children were asked to do two things at once. If a skill is automatic, then one ought to be able to do something else at the same time (assuming it does not directly interfere with the first skill) with little or no loss of performance. A theoretically significant finding was for balance—a highly automatic skill with no language component. Nicolson and Fawcett (1990; Fawcett and Nicolson, 1992) found that that although a group of dyslexic adolescents were normally able to balance as well as 'controls' (non-dyslexic children matched for age and IQ), their balance deteriorated very significantly when they had to do something else at the same time, whereas the controls' balance was not affected at all. The deficit obtained for a range of secondary tasks, including concurrent counting, concurrent reaction time tasks, and blindfold balance. Fawcett and Nicolson (2008) suggest that these findings strongly suggest that dyslexic children were not automatic even at the fundamental skill of balance and they argue, therefore, that dyslexic children have to concentrate harder to achieve normal levels of performance in most tasks.

Structure

As well as the additional time factors needed to acquire automaticity, it is also important to develop a carefully planned structure for a teaching programme that takes automaticity into account. Crombie (2002b) suggests that 'structure' requires much more than detailing the teaching order of the points that children must learn, but should also involve the learning experiences provided to the student. For example, Crombie suggests that if a child requires to spell a word, but is unaware of the order of the sounds being heard, jumbling of letters will be likely to occur unless visual memory can compensate for this weakness. Teaching the child to repeat words to herself or himself, while listening to the order of the sounds, is, according to Crombie (2002b), time well spent. This is particularly important as, often, children with dyslexic difficulties do not automatically pick up the order of sounds. This means that the interaction between teacher and student is important, and some children need to be taught before they can learn a particular skill or sequence.

It is important to develop a framework to help provide a structure. An example of this is shown in Box 11.1.

Student criteria	Comment
Learning style	Seems to be a visual learner, likes working in groups
Organisation	Forgets equipment, needs a lot of reminders
Attention	Attends well when discussing and making something—difficulty in listening for more than two or three minutes
Reading accuracy	Has difficulty in blending, tends to read visually and confuses words that sound alike
Reading fluency	Hesitates a lot when reading—reads slowly
Spelling single words	Has difficulty with words with double consonants
Spelling in context	Confuses 'their' and 'there' and similar words—makes more spelling mistakes in written work
Expressive writing	Does not write a lot—knows more than he or she is able to write. Does not organise written work very well
Memory	Good long-term memory but forgets instructions readily
Comprehension	Needs a lot of explanation—often needs one-to-one explanation and has to be shown what to do with examples.

(*Source*: Reid and Green, 2007b)

Box 11.1   Framework for planning: information obtained from observation and interaction with the student

It is crucial that all teachers are aware of how to develop a structure or a framework for teaching dyslexic children. It is important because children with dyslexia can learn in a different way and it is crucial that they are allowed to do this and that school staff are aware of some general guidelines that can help recognise the differences in learning shown by dyslexic students. Reid and Green (2007a) indicate that the following general points should be considered:

- Use charts and diagrams to highlight the bigger picture of what is being taught.
- Use mime and gesture to help the kinaesthetic learner, that is, the learner who prefers to learn through active involvement and experience. For example, drama is a good type of kinaesthetic activity.
- Add pictures to text.
- Use colour to highlight key words.

- Label diagrams and charts.
- Use games to consolidate vocabulary.
- Make packs of pocket size cards of important words.
- Use different colours for different purposes.
- Combine listening and reading by providing text and tape.
- Use mind maps®, spidergrams.
- Present information in small amounts with frequent opportunities for repetition and revision.

(*Source*: Reid and Green, 2007a)

In order to provide an effective structure when developing worksheets and pro-grammes of work to take the student's dyslexic difficulties into account, Reid and Green (2007a) suggest that the following specific points should be considered:

- Is the font used large enough and clear enough for the student?
- Is the vocabulary at the right level for the student?
- Is the structure learner-friendly—are there opportunities for revising and recapping on what has been learnt and opportunities for summing up?
- Is it sufficiently interesting to hold the child's attention?
- Are there enough visuals to assist the learner follow the information?
- Is the task achievable? Will the student succeed with it or will it be too challenging?
- Is it possible for the learner to investigate and find out more information without assistance?
- Are the instructions clear?
- Will the learner realise what the outcome of the task is supposed to look like?
- Is there a reward at the end of the task or is there some progression that the student is able to appreciate?
- Are there opportunities for the student to self-monitor and self-correct?

OVER-LEARNING

Automaticity can also be acquired through over-learning, but it is important that this is not seen as rote repetition of the material to be learned. Over-learning provides a good opportunity to utilise a range of materials and a variety of techniques. There are a considerable number of games and 'fun-type' activities available that can help to vary the learning experiences and promote automaticity.

For example, games where children have to find picture cards beginning or ending with specific sounds or where children have to think of as many words as possible ending in that particular letter sound can be fun and can also help to develop automatic-ity. There are also games available (see resources in Appendix 2) such as homophone games that are designed to improve spelling and recognition of keywords, and a vowel discrimination game that helps to increase auditory awareness and improve word attack skills. Many types of word games and activities also include memory games, sequenc-ing activities, mnemonics, free-writing games and rhyme songs.

These game activities can be used by the class teacher as they do not require any specialist training. It is important, however, that class teachers have some awareness of dyslexia so that these activities can be used appropriately in a teaching programme. Crombie (2002b), in fact, argues that one of the main challenges facing teachers is the need to find varied approaches to learning that will motivate children and will provide the key elements that the child requires as well. If the child does not respond to a structured programme, the teaching programme should be re-evaluated.

This would help to decide whether it is the most appropriate programme to use. It is also important to consider other factors, as the child may not be responding because he or she needs a longer period to achieve the objective of the programme. It is important that objectives should not be seen only as short-term attainment gains—in fact, it is often the case that children with dyslexia require sustained and persistent support. Sometimes this support can be, in fact, more of the same. This is why it is important to vary the learning experiences, otherwise the child can become bored and de-motivated.

According to Crombie, therefore, teachers need to have or be able to access a range of knowledge about technology, hardware and software that is available to support individual needs, as well as having a knowledge of how the appropriate materials can be accessed. This is a challenge because structured, multi-sensory, phonic work may well benefit many children at the early stages, but the provision of support within the classroom becomes more difficult for the teacher as the child becomes older, and this can be a particular challenge to teachers at the secondary stage.

PRINCIPLES

While it is important to individualise and contextualise approaches and programmes for students with dyslexia, it is important to consider some of the overriding principles.

Townend (2000) suggests that the principles of a specialist teaching programme for children with dyslexia should include:

- *Structure*—this includes a progression which should be logical and in small steps and, importantly, the links between the steps should be explicit.
- A *multi-sensory element*—this should be active and interactive as well as incorporating elements of all the modalities—visual, auditory, kinaesthetic and tactile.
- *Reinforcement*—skills that are learnt need to be practised, learnt and preserved in long-term memory. This can be achieved through reinforcement and is, in fact, necessary for automatic access of the word or skill that has been learnt.
- *Skill teaching*—teaching is not only about providing information, but about accessing useful and transferable skills as well—for example, phonological awareness skills can be later transferred and utilised in writing skills.
- *Metacognitive aspects*—this should be seen as an integral component of all programmes and helps with bridging and transferring knowledge, understanding and skills. Essentially, it involves thinking about thinking and the learners self-questioning how a particular response was arrived at.

ISSUES

There are a number of issues to consider when developing or selecting an approach for children with dyslexia. According to Townend (2000), an effective teaching programme for dyslexic children should include, apart from phonological aspects, other factors such as the promotion of attention and listening, the development of spoken language, development of fine motor skills and handwriting, sequencing and directionality, and the development of short- and long-term memory skills. It has been well documented that the principles of a teaching programme for dyslexic children include multi-sensory, structured, cumulative and sequential aspects (Reid, 1996). Additionally, it is likely that the programme will also have a phonic emphasis, although a number of dyslexic children may present with more pronounced visual difficulties, rather than those of a phonic nature (Everatt, 2002). It is important, as indicated earlier, that each dyslexic child should be viewed as an individual, and therefore any programme formula should not be too prescriptive.

Walker (2000), however, discusses an evaluation study using the structured, cumulative, multi-sensory teaching formula (Rack and Walker, 1994) and shows that the students who were taught in this way for one to two hours a week for just over two years doubled their rate of progress in spelling and did even better in reading. According to Walker (2000), this emphasises some key factors in developing a programme: such as the view that the student with dyslexia may need more input and a different structure of teaching from other children; the teacher should be aware of the factors associated with the acquisition of literacy and the particular difficulties in literacy that can be noted in dyslexic children; the principles of multi-sensory teaching; the importance of selecting clear and coherent teaching aims; and an awareness of the important role played by pre-reading strategies and proofreading as a post-writing strategy in the teaching of students with dyslexia. It is important, therefore, that the principles of constructing a teaching programme for dyslexic children and the factors that should be recognised in implementing such as programme are acknowledged. It is also important, however, that programmes should not be used too prescriptively and that commercially produced programmes fit into the aims of the school. The teacher should be ready to discard or adapt a particular programme for a child if it does not seem to be making real headway. This point is emphasised by Lannen (2008, personal communication), head teacher of a day school for children with dyslexia and other specific learning difficulties. Lannen indicates that any programme needs to fit into the overall context of the classroom environment. She suggests that the role of the school ethos and the holistic nature of the intervention required for children with dyslexia cannot be underestimated. One of the issues alluded to earlier was that relating to one-to-one intervention as opposed to whole-class teaching. Elbaum et al. (2000) conducted a meta-analysis of intervention research to investigate the effectiveness of one-on-one tutoring programmes. Thirty-one studies from 1977–1998 were analysed. Control groups were used in most of the studies and this mainly consisted of regular classroom instruction. In the one-to-one group they also considered intervention duration and intensity. They found that on average 'students who received one to one instruction performed at a level 2/5 of a standard deviation higher than the average level of the comparison group' (p. 616). The authors argued that this degree of shift would be sufficient to allow these students to keep up with classroom instruction and to avoid academic failure. The results also concurred with Swanson's (1999) findings that intervention duration was not significantly associated with outcomes. An interesting finding from the Elbaum et al. meta-analysis was that relating to comparisons between one-to-one intervention and small group intervention. They discuss the comparison between Reading Recovery (one-to-one) and small group (2–5 students) using the Project READ approach (Acalin, 1995) and found no significant difference in outcomes. This also concurred with the findings of Evans (1996) who undertook a similar study. At least 10 of the studies reported by Elbaum et al. used Reading Recovery as the one-to-one intervention approach. They point out, however, that many of the studies did not distinguish between continued and discontinued students and often do not report data on discontinued students. The implication is that a number of students dropped out of the programme owing to failure to make adequate progress and this data was not taken into account. For example, in a study by Ramaswami (1994), 18 out of 30 students were dropped. Elbaum et al. argue that studies that compare selectively reduced treatment groups with control groups that remain intact are extremely suspect. Additionally, Chapman et al. (1999) raise concern regarding the psychometric properties of some of the measures used to assess Reading Recovery outcomes.

Elbaum et al. suggest that the meta-analysis does not provide support for the superiority of Reading Recovery over other forms of one-to-one intervention. They suggest that about 30% of the students who started the Reading Recovery programme did not complete it and do not perform better than the control group. Elbaum et al. raise concern that despite this data there are still 'sweeping endorsements of Reading Recovery . . . in the literature' (p. 617). On a final note, Elbaum et al. suggest that 'well designed, reliably implemented, one to one interventions can make a significant contribution to improved reading outcomes for many students whose poor reading skills place them at risk of academic failure' (p. 617).

In summary, Reid (2007b) suggests that the following factors should be considered as key components of a teaching programme or an approach for students with dyslexia:

- Balance between bottom-up emphasis on phonics and top-down focus on meaning.
- An emphasis on developing listening skills.
- Ample opportunities for oral work.
- Appreciates the importance of discussion to develop language and thinking skills.
- Recognises that phonic skills need to be the key focus.
- Recognises the need to build up a sight vocabulary through whole word recognition.
- Appreciates the need to develop sentence and paragraph awareness as this is essential for creative writing as well as reading for meaning.
- Clear focus on comprehension-building activities.
- Attempts to highlight reading and spelling connections.
- Opportunities for developing skills in creative writing.
- Provides opportunities to develop imagination and creativity.
- Ensures practice in the use of syntactic and semantic cues.
- Places an emphasis on learning the 44 phonemes of the English language and a knowledge of the 17 vowel sounds and the 27 consonant sounds.

- Includes development of pre-reading skills, such as visual and auditory perception.
- Provides opportunities to practise visual and auditory discrimination.
- Facilitates practice in fine motor skills.
- Acknowledges the need to develop knowledge of colour, number, orientation and directions.
- Includes game activities to stimulate interest and over-learning.
- Develops syllable segmentation to build up word attack skills.
- Practice at using rhymes and rhyme judgement, rhyme production.
- Recognises the importance of alliteration and word activities to develop familiarity with words and their meaning.
- Uses strategies such as onset and rime to build up a word bank.

Irrespective of the issues and the debate on what constitutes appropriate intervention for students with dyslexia, it is crucial to identify individual needs. The 'differences' between students with dyslexia need to be acknowledged. Therefore a programme or approach that may work for one student may not be effective for others. It is important to observe the approaches and strategies used by students when they are in a learning situation. We can learn from them and this can guide us in our planning and in our intervention. Students need to be as much a part of the planning of intervention as teachers. It is important that we can cultivate independence in learning and reduce the students' need to be dependent on a teacher or support teacher. Ensuring that they are part of the planning process can help to achieve this.

POINTS FOR REFLECTION

- Consider what might constitute an appropriate teaching approach for students with dyslexia. Reflect on why there might be some controversy regarding this.

- Consider the importance of planning intervention for students with dyslexia. Use the framework for planning in this chapter as a guide and develop an intervention plan for a learner with dyslexia.

- Consider the following statement: Intervention is *not* about remediation but about reconstruction, i.e., providing the learner with the skills, abilities and confidence to 'reconstruct' the child's learning potential that has often been eroded by early school failure. Reflect on this statement in the light of your plan and the intervention for students with dyslexia.

Chapter 12

Supporting Literacy:
Individualised Programmes

We are fortunate in the area of dyslexia in that there is a vast range of programmes and approaches to choose from. At the same time this can be confusing for teachers and parents, particularly since many of the commercialised programmes have similarities and many claim that they will almost work miracles! The previous chapter does provide some guidance on selecting an approach or programme and this should be considered when selecting an approach, particularly since many schools are working within strict budgetary constraints.

Basically there are four types of approach. These are:

- *Individualised programmes*—these are usually programmes that are highly structured. They can be seen as essentially free-standing and can form a central element of the overall strategy for teaching children with dyslexia.
- *Support approaches and strategies*—these may utilise the same principles as some of the individual programmes, but can be used more selectively by the teacher, thus making it possible to integrate them more easily within the normal activities of the curriculum.
- *Assisted learning techniques*—these techniques can utilise many different methods, but a central, essential component is the aspect of learning from others. These programmes could therefore involve either peer or adult support and interaction and utilise some of the principles of modelling.
- *Whole-class approaches*—these approaches recognise that dyslexia is a whole-class and whole-school concern, and not just the responsibility of individual teachers. Such approaches require an established and accessible policy framework for consultancy, whole-school screening and monitoring of children's progress. Early identification is a further key aspect of a whole-school approach.

CRITERIA FOR SELECTION

It is important to consider the rationale for using particular programmes and approaches. Within the categories described here: individualised learning, support approaches and strategies, assisted learning and whole-class approaches, there are many different ways of using the resources to support the student with dyslexia. The criteria for selecting programmes and approaches therefore need to be carefully considered. Reports investigating the most effective reading approaches can provide guidance. We are fortunate to have access to detailed government-commissioned reports on reading from the USA (National Reading Panel, 2000), the UK (the Independent Review of the Teaching of Early Reading (Rose Report), DfES, 2006) and from New Zealand when the government reported on the findings of the Education and Science Committee inquiry into teaching of reading in New Zealand in 2001, as well as numerous local and national initiatives such as the Northern Ireland and Republic of Ireland Task Force Reports and local education initiatives throughout the UK (for example, City of Edinburgh Guidelines on Dyslexia (Primary) (Houston, 2002) and Secondary (Thomson, 2007).

Individualised Programmes

Most individualised programmes incorporate some or all of the following principles and approaches:

- multi-sensory;
- over-learning and automaticity;
- highly structured and usually phonically based;
- sequential and cumulative.

Multi-sensory methods utilise all available senses simultaneously. This can be summed up in the phrase 'hear it, say it, see it and write it'. These methods have been used for many years and have been further refined in the UK (Hornsby and Shear, 1980; Augur and Briggs; 1992) in phonic structured programmes that incorporate multi-sensory techniques. Similarly, in North America, Henry (2003) has shown the benefits of the Orton–Gillingham (OG) approach and this is confirmed in the website of the Canadian Academy of Therapeutic Tutors (CATT) (www.ogtutors.com/aboutog.php).

The view expressed here is that studies by the National Institute of Child Health and Human Development (NICHD) in the United States have concluded that the best strategy for preventing and correcting reading problems is explicit, systematic instruction that emphasises:

- early letter knowledge and phonemic awareness;
- instruction in letter–sound correspondence and spelling generalisations;
- opportunity and encouragement to use spelling–sound knowledge in reading and writing;
- daily sessions for supported and independent reading with attention to fluency and comprehension;
- active exploration of concepts provided in written text.

The Canadian Academy indicates that the Orton–Gillingham approach meets all of these criteria.

Over-learning is deemed necessary for children with dyslexic difficulties. The short- and long-term memory difficulties experienced by dyslexic children mean that considerable reinforcement and repetition are necessary. The structured approaches evident in programmes of work for dyslexic children usually provide a linear progression, thus enabling the learner to complete and master a particular skill in the reading or learning process before advancing to a subsequent skill. This implies that learning occurs in a linear developmental manner. Although there is evidence from learning theory to suggest that this may be the case, there is still some doubt in the case of reading that mastery of the component sub-skills results in skilled reading. In reading, a number of cognitive skills, such as memory and visual, auditory and oral skills, interact (Snowling, 2000; Fawcett and Nicolson, 2008). This interaction is the key feature; so, it is important that the skills are taught together and purposefully with the practice of reading as the focus.

Sequential approaches are usually appropriate for children with dyslexia because it may be necessary for them to master sub-skills before moving to more advanced materials. Hence a sequential and cumulative approach may not only provide a structure to their learning but help to make learning more meaningful and effective as well.

Many of the individual programmes, however, have been evaluated positively. For example, Hornsby and Miles (1980) conducted a series of investigations examining 'dyslexia-centred teaching' programmes with the aim of evaluating how effective these programmes were in alleviating dyslexia. This study and a follow-up study (Hornsby and Farmer, 1990) indicate that the programmes did result in an improvement in terms of students' reading and spelling ages. Additionally, other programme providers have published reports on the effectiveness of particular programmes as well as the publication of independent evaluations. For example, Johnson et al. (1999) reported on the Multisensory Teaching Scheme for Reading, and Moss (2000) on Units of Sound and other programmes such as the Bangor Dyslexia Teaching System and Teaching Reading through Spelling (Turner, 2002).

Some examples of individual programmes popular in the United States are shown in Box 12.1.

IDA Matrix of Programs

The International Dyslexia Association (IDA) have produced a short matrix of multi-sensory structured language programs indicating the type of programme delivery, the level of phonic instruction, how each program deals with fluency, comprehension, written expression and text construction and the level of training needed for the program.

The programs included in the matrix are:

OG (www.OrtonAcademy.org)

Alphabetic Phonics (www.ALTAread.org)

continued

Association Method (www.usm.edu/dubard)

Language! (www.SoprisWest.com)

Lexia-Herman Method (see Appendix 2)

Lindamood–Bell (www.Lindamoodbell.com)

Project Read (www.Projectread.com)

Slingerland (www.Slingerland.org)

Sonday System (www.SondaySystem.com)

Sounds in Syllables, Spalding Method (www.Spalding.org)

Starting Over: A Combined Teaching Manual and Student Workbook for Reading, Writing, Spelling, Vocabulary, and Handwriting by Joan Knight (www.epsbooks.com/dynamic/catalog/series.asp?seriesonly=1655M)

Wilson Fundations and Wilson Reading (www.wilsonlanguage.com).

(*Source*: IDA www.inter-dys.org)

Box 12.1   Programmes in practice—some examples

Categories of Approaches

Individual Programmes

- Alphabetic Phonics   www.epsbooks.com/downloads/samplers/S-alphabetic_phonics.pdf
- Alpha to Omega   www.amazon.co.uk/Alpha-Omega-Teaching-Reading-Spelling/dp/0435104233
  www.crossboweducation.com/Alpha_to_Omega_phonics%20games.htm
- Bangor Dyslexia Teaching System   eu.wiley.com/WileyCDA/WileyTitle/productCd-1861560559.html
- Hickey Language Course   www.amazon.co.uk/Hickey-Multisensory-Language-Course/dp/1861561784
- Reading Recovery   www.readingrecovery.org
- Orton–Gillingham   www.ortonacademy.org/approach.html
  www.ogtutors.com/aboutog.php
- Slingerland   www.slingerland.org/administration/testimonials.html
- Sound Linkage   eu.wiley.com/WileyCDA/WileyTitle/productCd-1861561768.html
- Toe by Toe   www.toebytoe.co.uk
- Units of Sound   www.dyslexiaaction.org.uk
- THRASS   www.thrass.co.uk
- Letterland   www.letterland.com

It should be noted that some of the above programmes can be used in small group and whole-class teaching

Support Approaches

These include the following:

- Simultaneous Oral Spelling
- PhonicCodecracker/Crackerspell (Sylvia Russell)
- Neuro-motor programmes
- Visual acuity activities
- Multi-sensory Teaching System for Reading

Assisted Learning

- Word Games
- Paired Reading
- Cued Spelling
- Peer Tutoring

Whole-Class Approaches

- Circle time
- Study skills
- Computer programmes
- Educational kinesiology
- Literacy projects
- Thinking skills
- Study skills approaches
- Reciprocal teaching

This chapter will discuss some of the individualised programmes and the other approaches will be discussed in the following chapter.

ALPHA TO OMEGA

Alpha to Omega is a phonetic, linguistic approach to the teaching of reading and can be used as a programme or as resource material. It is highly structured and follows a logical pattern of steps that promotes the acquisition of phonological and language skills. There is an emphasis on learning the 44 phonemes from which all English words are composed. These consist of the 17 vowel sounds and the 27 consonant sounds. There is also an emphasis on the acquisition of language structure, focusing on content words (nouns, verbs, adjectives) and finite words (prepositions and participles). There is, therefore, an emphasis on using words in the context of a sentence.

The programme provides a highly structured format for the teaching of sentences and for grammatical structure. There are also three accompanying and very useful activity packs designed for different stages. These packs provide appropriate back-up exercises to reinforce the teaching programme. There is also an extremely useful programme of learning games—before Alpha—that can be used with children under five. These games are in a series of structured stages, are multi-sensory and aim to foster language development and other pre-reading skills such as visual and auditory perception and discrimination, fine-motor control, spatial relationships and knowledge of colour, number and directions.

ORTON–GILLINGHAM

Programmes based on this approach have become a central focus for multi-sensory teaching for children with dyslexia. The programmes offer a structured, phonic-based approach that incorporates the total language experience and focuses on the letter sounds and the blending of these sounds into syllables and words. The approach rests heavily on the interaction of visual, auditory and kinaesthetic aspects of language.

Recent studies by the National Institute of Child Health and Human Development (NICHD) in the United States have concluded that the best strategy for preventing and correcting reading problems is explicit, systematic phonic instruction.

According to the Canadian Academy of Therapeutic Tutors, the Orton–Gillingham approach meets all of these criteria (www.ogtutors.com) (accessed September 2008).

Orton–Gillingham lessons, according to Henry (1996, 2003), always incorporate card drills, spelling and reading and usually include activities such as:

- Card drills—this involves the use of commercial or teacher-made cards containing the common letter patterns to strengthen the visual modality: phonemes (sounds) for auditory and kinaesthetic reinforcement and syllables and whole words to help develop blending skills.
- Word lists and phrases.
- Oral reading selection—this involves the teacher first reading the passage, then the student.
- Spelling of phonetic and non-phonetic words.
- Handwriting—with attention being placed on pencil grip, writing posture and letter formation. This would also include tracing, copying and practice and making cursive connections such as *br, bl*.
- Composition—encouragement to develop writing sentences, paragraphs and short stories.

Henry (2003) also maintains that lessons take place as a 'dynamic discussion session with the teacher acting as facilitator as well as instructor' (p. xiv).

PROCEDURE

- To begin with, ten letters are taught—two vowels (a,i) and eight consonants (f,l,b, j,h,m,p,t).

- Each of the letters is introduced with a key word.
- The difference between vowels and consonants is taught together with the position of the mouth in the pronunciation of the sounds (different coloured cards are used for vowels and consonant).
- Once the child has mastered the letter name and sound, the programme then advances to introduction of blending the letters and sounds.
- This begins with simple three-letter words and the child repeats the sounds until the word is spoken without pauses between the constituent sounds.
- The visual–kinaesthetic and auditory–kinaesthetic associations are formed by the student tracing, saying, copying and writing each word.
- Reading of text begins after the student has mastered the consonant–vowel–consonant words to a higher automatic level, i.e., when the student can recognise and use these words.

The OG approach is more suited to one-to-one teaching but the key principles of over-learning, automaticity and multi-sensory approaches are very apparent in OG and these principles can be utilised within the classroom curriculum.

There is also considerable scope in this approach for building metacognitive skills and developing comprehension-building exercises (Green, 2006). The dynamic aspect is important and interactive games can complement, expand and clarify many of the language skills in OG lessons.

In the USA, Morgan Dynamic Phonics (www.dynamicphonics.com) have produced a series of phonic programmes that focus on user-friendly approaches using the principles of Orton–Gillingham, which include the use of humour and interaction. Ott (1997, 2007) suggests that the following UK programmes are based on the Orton–Gillingham method:

- *Alpha to Omega* (Hornsby and Shear, 1980);
- *The Bangor Dyslexia Teaching System* (Miles, 1989);
- *The Hickey Multisensory Language Course* (Augur and Briggs, 1992);
- *Dyslexia: A Teaching Handbook* (Thomson and Watkins, 1990);
- *Units of Sound* (Bramley, 1996).

THE HICKEY MULTISENSORY LANGUAGE COURSE

The Hickey Multisensory Language Course (Augur and Briggs, 1992; third edition revised by Combley, 2001) recognises the importance of the need to learn sequentially the letters of the alphabet. The dyslexic child, however, will usually have some difficulty in learning and remembering the names and sequence of the alphabetic letters as well as understanding that the letters represent speech sounds that make up words.

The programme is based on multi-sensory principles and the alphabet is introduced using wooden or plastic letters; the child can look at the letter, pick it up, feel it with eyes open or closed and say its sound. Therefore, the visual, auditory and tactile–kinaesthetic channels of learning are all being utilised with a common goal.

The programme also suggests some activities to help the child become familiar with the alphabet:

- learning the letters sequentially;
- positioning of each letter of the alphabet;
- naming and recognising the shape of the letters.

These programmes involve games and the use of dictionaries to help the child become familiar with the order of the letters and the direction to go (e.g., he or she needs to know that 'I' comes before 'K'), the letters in the first half of the alphabet and those letters in the second half. The alphabet can be further divided into sections, thus making it easier for the child to remember the section of the alphabet in which a letter appears, for example:

A B C D

E F G H I J K L M

N O P Q R

S T U V W X Y Z

The Hickey language course includes: activities related to sorting and matching the capital, lower case, printed and written forms of the letters; practising sequencing skills with cut-out letters and shapes; and practising positioning each letter in the alphabet in relation to the other letters (this involves finding missing letters and going backwards and forwards in the alphabet).

The course also indicates the importance of recognising where the accent falls in a word, since this clearly affects the spelling and rhythm. Rhyming games can be developed to encourage the use of accent by placing it on different letters of the alphabet. This helps to train children's hearing to recognise when a letter has an accent or is stressed in a word.

The course includes reading and spelling packs that focus on securing a relationship between sounds and symbols. This process begins with single letters and progresses to consonant blends, vowel continuations and then to complex letter groupings.

The reading packs consist of a set of cards; on one side, the lower case letter is displayed in bold with an upper case (capital) letter shown in the bottom right-hand corner in order to establish the link between the two letters. The reverse side of the card indicates a key word that contains the sound of the letter with the actual sound combination in brackets. Rather than providing a visual image of the key word, a space is left for the child to draw the image. This helps to make the image more meaningful to the child and also utilises and reinforces visual and kinaesthetic skills.

The spelling pack is similar in structure to the reading pack. On the front of the card the sound made by the letter is displayed in brackets, while the back contains both the sound and the actual letter(s). Sounds for which there is a choice of spellings will in time show all the possible ways in which the sound can be made. Cue words are also given on the back as a prompt, in case the child forgets one of the choices.

Spelling is seen as being of prime importance by the authors of the programme since they view it as an 'all round perceptual experience'. The multi-sensory method used involves the following process:

- the child repeats the sound heard;
- feels the shape the sound makes in the mouth;
- makes the sound and listens;
- writes the letter(s).

This process involves over-learning and multi-sensory strategies.

BANGOR DYSLEXIA TEACHING SYSTEM

The Bangor Dyslexia Teaching System (Miles, 1989) is a structured, sequential teaching programme developed for teachers and speech and language therapists involved in supporting children with dyslexia.

A useful aspect of this programme is the division between primary and secondary students. Although it is acknowledged that some secondary students are still 'beginning' readers and need to go through the same initial stages of acquiring literacy as 'beginning readers' in the primary school, the programme makes some special provision and adaptations for secondary students. This helps to make the secondary material more age appropriate.

The basic philosophy of the programme is not unlike that of other structured, phonic programmes for dyslexic children. It focuses on phonological difficulties and the problems dyslexic children have in mastering the alphabetic code. The programme attempts to provide children with some competence, at the earliest stage possible, in recognising and categorising speech sounds. Miles (1989) argues that it is not possible for children to benefit from 'top down' language experience approaches to reading if they have not mastered the basic principles of literacy. Some of these principles, which the programme for primary-aged children focuses on, include: the teaching of basic letter sounds and the structure of words, long vowels, common word patterns, irregular words, alphabet and dictionary skills, grammatical rules and silent letters.

The programme attempts to acknowledge that dyslexic children may have difficulties with both visual and auditory processing. The issue of auditory processing, particularly relating to the acquisition of phonic skills, is well documented (Stanovich, 1991; Rack, 1994; Snowling, 2000; Lundberg, 2002; Torgeson, 2004). Additionally, reports by Stein et al. (Stein, 2008; Everatt, 2002; Singleton, 2009) helped to sustain the debate on visual aspects of reading and the difficulties some dyslexic children may have in picking out visual letter patterns.

The programme shares the same principles as those utilised by other similar programmes for dyslexic children. It is highly structured and the teacher has to proceed systematically through the programme. The aspect of over-learning is acknowledged to be important, and therefore revision of material already learnt occupies an important place in the implementation of the programme.

One of the difficulties inherent in following the principle of over-learning is the aspect of boredom, which may result from repetitive revision of material already learnt. This programme acknowledges that pitfall and suggests ways of overcoming it through the use of games and other adapted materials.

The multi-sensory teaching element is also crucial in this programme. Some of the exercises attempt to engage all the available senses simultaneously, thus acknowledging the accepted view that dyslexic children benefit from multi-sensory learning.

The programme also utilises the particular benefits of mnemonics for dyslexic children as well as the notion of reading and spelling as an integrated activity. Some emphasis is also placed on encouraging dyslexic children to use oral language to plan their work. It is felt that such verbalisations help children clarify their thoughts and planning before embarking on a course of action. There is also a useful appendix containing guidance on handwriting, alphabet and dictionary skills.

The secondary component of the programme provides useful advice on dealing with the problem of teaching basic literacy to older students. Miles (1989) suggests that the material for older students should include words of more than one syllable, even though the student is at the early stages of literacy. Some effort is made to ensure that the student is familiar with polysyllabic words in order that the potential for creative writing is not unduly restricted. At the secondary stage the aspect of reading for meaning is of great importance in order to ensure sustained motivation.

The Bangor Dyslexia Teaching System acknowledges this and suggests a range of techniques that can help to support the student through the decoding difficulty in order that maximum meaning and pleasure can be derived from the text. Such suggestions include: supplying difficult words; introducing the story and the book's background and characters; pointing out clues such as capital letters and titles; encouraging fluency by reading from one full stop to the next; omitting words that are difficult, thus encouraging the use of context to obtain meaning; practice; and reading rhymes and limericks that aid sound and syllable awareness.

The programme for secondary students, although less structured than that for primary students, includes sections on syllabification and stress, plurals, short and long vowel patterns, silent letters, prefixes and suffixes.

The Bangor Dyslexia Teaching System clearly attempts to teach the dyslexic child the basic rules of literacy and the English language. Although the programme can stand on its own, it would be advisable for the teacher to attempt to integrate and relate the programme within the child's class work. This can be possible by selecting those aspects of the programme that are most useful and would be particularly appropriate for secondary students, whose learning priorities, Miles acknowledges, the teacher would need to take into account.

TACKLING DYSLEXIA

Cooke (2002) has developed a different version of the above and incorporates new approaches to teaching phonics. She also indicates that the nature of the task is important, and the programme she has developed takes this into account as well as literacy and numeracy skills. Cooke's programme also considers the role of parents, estimating the reading level of books, computer technology and factors relating to the National Literacy strategy and the Literacy Hour in England and Wales.

ALPHABETIC PHONICS

The key principles found in the majority of individualised programmes for dyslexic children—multi-sensory techniques, automaticity and over-learning—are all found in the Alphabetic Phonics programme (www.epsbooks.com/downloads/samplers/ S-alphabetic_phonics.pdf). Additionally, the programme recognises the importance of discovery learning. Opportunities for discovery learning are found throughout this highly structured programme. The programme, which stems from the Orton–Gillingham multi-sensory approach, was developed in Dallas, Texas, by Aylett Cox. She has described Alphabetic Phonics as a structured system of teaching students the coding patterns of the English language (Cox, 1985).

Cox asserts that such a phonic-based programme is necessary because around 85% of the 30 000 most commonly used English words can be considered phonetically regular and therefore predictable. Thus, learning phonetic rules can allow the child to access the majority of commonly used words. Alphabetic Phonics provides training in the development of automaticity through the use of flash cards and over-learning through repetitive practice in reading and spelling until 95% mastery is achieved.

The programme also incorporates opportunities to develop creativity in expression and in the sequencing of ideas.

The programme is highly structured, with daily lessons of around one hour. Lessons incorporate a variety of tasks that help to keep the child's attention directed at the activities and prevent tedium or boredom. In this programme, reading comprehension instruction does not begin until the student has reached a minimal level of accuracy in relation to decoding skills. Cox, however, does recognise that children will learn and retain new vocabulary more effectively and efficiently through experiential learning and that this is particularly applicable to dyslexic children.

Although a number of studies have claimed impressive results using the Alphabetic Phonics Programme (Ray, 1986; Frankiewicz, 1985), it has been asserted that the research methodology used and the lack of effective control groups somewhat diminish the impressive results of these studies (Clark, 1988). Additionally, in order to teach the programme effectively, it has been maintained that 480 hours of teacher training is required, based on knowledge of the structure of the English language, knowledge of phonetic rules and patterns in spelling, and integration of these activities into a structured, hierarchical curriculum. An accompanying text, *Foundations for Literacy* (Cox, 1992), does, however, provide an easy-to-follow lesson guide for the teacher.

In the programme Cox suggests a number of linkages between multi-sensory activities and the letter, such as association of cursive shape, speech sound, graphic symbol and kinaesthetic memory. The principles and practices of this programme, such as structure, multi-sensory technique, emphasis on automaticity, emphasis on building comprehension skills, experiential learning and listening skills, and in particular recognition of letter sounds, can have desirable outcomes. These can readily be adapted and implemented into teaching programmes devised for different needs and contexts.

THE SLINGERLAND PROGRAMME

The Slingerland Programme is an adaptation of the Orton–Gillingham Programme. Essentially, the programme was developed as a screening approach to help minimise the difficulties experienced by children in language and literacy. The Slingerland Screening Tests accompany the programme and are usually administered in the early stages of education.

The programme shares similar features with other programmes. Multi-sensory teaching permeates the programme, which begins by introducing letters of the alphabet.

The programme follows the format below.

Writing

This is the first step and usually the following order is adopted:

- tracing;
- copying;
- writing in the air;
- simultaneously writing from memory and saying the letter.

Letter Sounds

This involves naming the letter, then the key word associated with the letter and then the letter sound.

Blending

This is introduced with oral activities and may involve repetitive use and blends with kinaesthetic support to reinforce the material being learnt.

Decoding

In decoding, students begin with three letters—consonant–vowel–consonant (e.g., words such as 'bay' and 'way'). They are required to:

- pronounce the initial consonant;
- then the vowel;
- then blend the two;
- and pronounce the final consonant;
- and say the whole word.

Vowel digraphs and vowel–consonant digraphs are taught as units, although Slingerland maintains that consonant blends are usually learnt more easily.

Reading for Meaning

Once decoding has been sufficiently mastered, a whole-word approach is encouraged in the reading of text. Initially, students undergo a 'preparation for reading' lesson when some time is spent producing, recognising and reading words and the students become familiar with the image of the word. There is also some emphasis on teacher modelling by reading aloud. To foster reading comprehension skills, the teacher cues in appropriate clues into the questioning technique (e.g., which seven words tell us where the house was?—'it was built on a high hill'). The Slingerland Programme is highly specific and highly structured and contains some useful strategies and ideas.

Research into the effectiveness of the Slingerland Programme indicates that it can produce significant gains in a number of language aspects, such as listening comprehension, punctuation, grammar, syntax, spelling and study skills. Gains have also been noted in vocabulary and the use of inference in reading (Wolf, 1985; McCulloch, 1985).

In terms of research to support the approach, M. J. Palmer (2001) found significant results with a study of 90 students in groups enrolled in Slingerland classrooms located in California, Alaska, Washington, Texas, and Oregon, and 90 in a control group from mainstreamed fourth- and fifth-grade classrooms located in Washington. Significant results were obtained in the study. The control group preformed better in spelling using manuscript and cursive handwriting than the experimental group using manuscript. Further examination of the experimental groups indicated that students who were more familiar with manuscript than with cursive handwriting had better spelling scores using manuscript writing. However, those students who used cursive exclusively during the school day showed stronger abilities in spelling with cursive handwriting. Direct instruction of handwriting is important, and automaticity of handwriting style does have an effect on spelling ability (www.slingerland.org/administration/research.html, accessed September 2008). The Slingerland Institute also provide evidence that they meet the criteria set by the National Institute of Child Health and Human Development (NICHD) (Reid Lyon and Kameenui, www.ed.gov/inits/americareads/nichd.html, accessed September 2008) that when teaching children who have a difficult time learning to read, explicit, systematic instruction is most effective in teaching reading. This instruction should:

- teach phonemic awareness (e.g., tell me the sounds in the word 'sat') at an early age (kindergarten);
- teach the common sound–spelling relationships in words;
- teach children how to say the sounds in the words;
- use text that is composed of words that use sound–spelling correspondences that children have learnt;
- use interesting stories to develop vocabulary and language comprehension.

The most effective classroom method for early reading instruction involves a combination of explicit instruction in word recognition skills and reading comprehension strategies with opportunities to apply and practise these skills in literature.

LETTERLAND

Letterland, developed by Lyn Wendon, consists of many different elements. The materials are extremely useful for teaching reading, spelling and writing, and for developing and sustaining motivation. The programmes are internationally renowned, as well over 50% of all primary schools in England and Ireland rely on this programme (Letterland International, 1997). Letterland encompasses a number of teaching elements based on recognised and essential components of the teaching of reading. The major elements are: language, with an emphasis on listening, speaking and communicating; phonic skills; whole-word recognition skills; sentence awareness; comprehension; reading and spelling connections; and preliminary skills in creative writing. The materials consist of teachers' guides, wall-charts, code cards, flashcards, wordbooks, cassettes and song-books, photocopiable material, workbooks, games and resources, software, videos, and materials specifically designed for use at home.

The programme may also be seen as a preventative approach, since it is appropriate for early intervention and may also facilitate the reinforcement of important developmental concepts in learning, such as object constancy.

The Letterland system essentially grew out of close observations of failing readers, and the materials reinforce the importance of a reading-for-meaning orientation to print. The system encourages motivation and exploration of written language and results in schools. Wendon (1993) suggests that Letterland can account for a measurable decrease in the number of children in schools requiring extra help with reading and spelling.

Letterland focuses on letters and sounds, and by using pictograms encourages children to appreciate letter stages and sounds, thereby reinforcing both the shape and the sound of letters and words. Integrated within this, however, are the programmes and exercises on whole-word recognition, reading for meaning, spelling and creative writing. Spelling is not presented as a series of rules, but instead through a story approach, focusing on the Letterland characters.

Progress through the Letterland programme is by a series of steps. These steps can provide the teacher with choice and flexibility, and the programme can be implemented to the whole class, in small groups or individually. There are a number of aspects about Letterland that make it useful for some children with dyslexia. These include the use of pictograms—which can be particularly beneficial to the learner with difficulties in phonological awareness and auditory skills. The use of the story approach to reading and spelling that encourages the processing of information using long-term memory is particularly beneficial to dyslexic children whose short-term memory is generally weak. The range of activities incorporating different approaches allows the learner to develop imagination and creativity in the use of letters and words. Other useful aspects include the focus on the context aspects of reading and the use of syntactic and semantic cues.

Letterland have produced mnemonic phonics (2008) and the authors suggest that it meets the critieria as 'high-quality phonic work' as defined by the Rose Review. This includes a well-established multi-sensory synthetic phonics programme that satisfies all the core criteria; a programme that covers all the major letter–sound correspondences, with structured daily lesson plans and support materials for each of them that follow a clear, incremental teaching order that facilitates blending, segmenting and word-building from early on. The Letterland lesson plans are short and simple, making it easier to move quickly from basic alphabet knowledge and skills to more complex words, spellings and independent reading. (www.standards.dfes.gov.uk/phonics/programmes/publishers/letterland; www.letterland.com/news/2008-04-12-mnemonic-phonics-makes-the-grade; accessed September 2008)

READING RECOVERY

Reading Recovery is an early reading and writing intervention programme, developed by Marie Clay (1985, 1992), that focuses on children who, after one year at school, have lagged significantly behind their peers in reading and writing. Marie Clay originally introduced the programme in New Zealand, but it has now been shown that the programme can be successfully transferred to other countries and contexts (Pinnell et al., 1988a, b, 1991; Wright, 1992; Cazden, 1999).

The programme aims to boost the reading attainments of the selected children over a relatively short period, around 12 to 20 weeks, with specially trained teachers carrying out the programme, seeing children on an individual basis for 30 minutes daily. The programme centres around the individual child's strengths and weaknesses as assessed by the actual reading programme. It is not, therefore, structured around a set of principles and practices to which the child has to be accommodated, but rather the programme adapts itself to the child's specific requirements and needs.

It utilises both bottom-up and top-down reading approaches and, therefore, encourages the use of decoding strategies through the use of phonics and awareness of meaning through an awareness of the context and language of the text.

The programme aims to produce 'independent readers whose reading improves whenever they read' (Clay, 1985). There is an emphasis, therefore, on strategies that the reader can apply to other texts and situations, and there is evidence that gains made in the Reading Recovery programme will be maintained over time.

For some children the Reading Recovery programme may need to be supplemented by additional sessions, which could include:

- re-reading familiar books;
- taking a running record;
- reinforcing letter identification;
- writing a story, thus learning sounds in words;
- comprehension of story;
- introducing a new book.

It is also important that the child is helped to develop a self-improving system. This would encourage the child to:

- be aware of his or her own learning;
- take control and responsibility for his or her own learning.

The goal of teaching reading is to assist the child to produce effective strategies for working on text, and, according to Clay, this can be done through focusing on the practices of self-correcting and self-monitoring. The main components of the programme include:

- learning about direction;
- locating and focusing on aspects of print;
- spatial layout of books;
- writing stories;
- learning sounds in words;
- comprehension;
- reading books;
- using print as a cue;
- sound and letter sequence;
- word analysis;
- fluency.

A typical Reading Recovery lesson would include analysis of the child's decoding strategies, the encouragement of fluent reading through the provision of opportunities to link sounds and letters, the reading of familiar texts and the introduction of new books.

Identification

Since the programme provides an intensive input to those children lagging in reading, it is vitally important that the identification procedures are sound in order to ensure that the children who receive the benefits of this programme are those who would not otherwise make satisfactory progress. The lowest-achieving children in a class group, after a year at school at around 6 years of age, are admitted into the programme. Clay believes that by the end of the first year at primary school it is possible to identify children who are failing. She suggests that this can be achieved through systematic observation of children's learning behaviour, together with a diagnostic survey.

The systematic observation takes the form of noting precisely what children are saying and doing in relation to reading, so the focus is on reading tasks rather than specific sub-skills such as visual perception or auditory dissemination. In order to identify the child's reading behaviour, Marie Clay has developed a diagnostic survey that involves taking a 'Running Record' of precisely how the child is performing in relation to reading. This type of analysis of children's errors in reading can provide clues in relation to children's strengths and weaknesses in reading.

The diagnostic survey includes directional movement (which looks at general directional concepts, including motor coordination, impulsivity and hesitancy), error behaviour (focusing on oral language skills, speed of responding and the use of semantic and syntactic context), the use of visual and memory cues, the rate of self-correction, and the child's preferred mode of identifying letters (alphabetic, sound or cueing from words). The survey also includes details of the child's writing skills. This is particularly important since it may provide some indication of any reading problems as well as language level and message quality.

Evaluation of Reading Recovery

Much of the research evidence that examines the effectiveness of this programme is impressive. The participating children appear to display gains that allow them to reach average levels of performance in reading within a relatively short period (Wright, 1992). There are, however, a number of studies that are critical of the programme.

Meek (1985) argues that the programme is rather restrictive in that it does not allow for children's reading preferences in relation to choice of material, and Adams (1990a) observes that the phonics element in Reading Recovery is not systematic and does not emphasise structures such as 'word families'. The programme, according to Topping and Wolfendale (1985), does not make adequate allowance for the effective role that parents can play in enhancing literacy skills, and Glynn et al. (1989) argue that many of the gains made by children who have participated in the Reading Recovery Programme have disappeared after a year. Johnston (1992) feels that programmes such as Reading Recovery are only necessary because of the trend from phonics-focused programmes, and she concludes that 'rather than wait until children fail in a non-phonics programme, it would be very much better for them either to be taught routines in a reading programme which emphasises phonics as well as reading for memory, or for the class teacher to have such a scheme available for those who are making very slow progress'.

Dombey (1992), arguing on behalf of the National Association for the Teaching of English, puts forward some doubts about the efficacy of Reading Recovery because it focuses on one particular age group—6-year-olds—and because it requires intensive training of a few specialists with little opportunity for dissemination of the skills of these specialists so that the effects of the programme do not fully percolate into mainstream classes. Dombey further argues that it could be more cost-effective to study the existing provision for the teaching of reading and to identify ways in which this could be improved; for example, by ensuring that all teachers of young children have the time needed to teach reading thoroughly and by providing those teachers with adequate training in the teaching of reading for all children.

Cazden (1999) comments on the demonstrated success of Reading Recovery, but suggests that despite this, it continues to be controversial. This is because some children who have not progressed sufficiently after a time on Reading Recovery continue with the programme, and this can mean that they do not fully participate in the language teaching in the class. This has been a particular criticism of those proponents of the 'whole language' movement. Clay and Cazden (1990), however, argue that Reading

Recovery is neither 'whole language' nor 'phonics', but takes what they describe as 'instructional detours'. These instructional detours are the part of the programme that focuses on the reading skills the child requires in order to make sense of 'whole language'. The phonics element of Reading Recovery is conceptually different from the usual implications of phonics teaching because Reading Recovery sees phonological awareness as an outcome of reading and writing, rather than as a prerequisite. Cazden (1999) suggests that it is this mix between the invisible pedagogy of whole language and the visible pedagogy of systemic phonics that has contributed to the success of Reading Recovery. It is this mix, she suggests, which is consistent with Bernstein's classification of invisible and visible pedagogy (Atkinson et al., 1994), that should be seen as an example of programme effectiveness in literacy education. This, she suggests, has also succeeded in weakening the relationship, suggested by Bernstein, between social class and literacy education.

The University of London Institute of Education in the UK conducted a reading recovery study focusing on Comparisons of Literacy Progress of Young Children in London Schools (Burroughs-Lange, 2008) The children, aged around 6 years, who received Reading Recovery in their schools were compared with those in schools which provided them with a range of other interventions. At the start of the study the children had literacy levels below those of a 5-year-old. The study was a follow-up to a study (2005–2006) which investigated the impact of Reading Recovery. In the 2005–2006 study the children participating in the Reading Recovery programme achieved significant gains in all assessments compared with those who did not. At the end of the year the literacy achievement of children who had received Reading Recovery (RR) was in line with their chronological age. The comparison group was 14 months behind with an average reading age of 5 years 5 months. In July 2007 the literacy achievement of those same children remaining in the same 42 schools was again compared. The phonic and word reading, and writing measures, were repeated along with a new reading comprehension measure. At the end of Year 2 the children who had received RR in Year 1 were achieving within or above their chronological age band on all measures and were still around a year ahead of the comparison children in schools where RR was not available. The RR children had an average word reading age of 7y 9m, compared to 6yr 9 m for the comparison children. At the end of Year 2, the children who had received RR were able to write twice as many correctly spelt words as those children who were in the comparison group.

Burroughs-Lange (2008) suggests that the consequences of failure to learn literacy efficiently and at an appropriate time make it imperative that effective early intervention is available for those at risk. This study, she argues, provides strong evidence that schools could enable almost every child to read and write appropriately for their age, if those who were failing were given access to expert teaching in Reading Recovery. The follow-up study she conducted shows that the children's progress was sustained at average levels a year or more after having initially accessed Reading Recovery intervention. There are, however, criticisms of the Reading Recovery programme and its effectiveness. Elbaum et al. (2000) raise concerns about many of the studies that have supported Reading Recovery (see previous chapter).

TOE BY TOE: MULTISENSORY MANUAL FOR TEACHERS AND PARENTS

Toe by Toe (Cowling and Cowling, 1998) is a multi-sensory teaching method highly recommended for teachers and parents, with clear and precise instructions that can be used by a teacher who is new, a classroom assistant, a parent. The programme has a multi-sensory element, a phonic element that places some demands on the student's memory through the planning and the timing of each of the lessons in the book. It can be readily used by parents and the instructions are very clear. The same author has also published a programme called Stride Ahead—An Aid to Comprehension, which can be a useful follow-up to Toe by Toe. Essentially, Stride Ahead has been written for children who can read, but may have difficulty in understanding what they are reading.

The toe by toe website (www.toebytoe.co.uk/school-letters.htm) contains a number of commendations from schools that have used the programme. One example is shown here: 'I am continually impressed with the program. Recent testing is showing substantial gains. Reluctant readers really enjoy using the program' (Resource Teacher, Santa Fe, New Mexico, USA; accessed September 2008). The Toe by Toe website also shows impressive data from schools in New Zealand, the UK and South Africa.

COMMENT—ISSUES TO CONSIDER

The range of individualised programmes for children with dyslexia is impressive, and this chapter has provided summaries of some of the main approaches.

Some of the principles of the programmes and the approaches advocated by their authors, such as 'multi-sensory', 'structured' and 'cumulative' approaches, can provide useful pointers in the development of support materials for dyslexic children. It is also worth considering the comments made by the National Reading Panel in the USA in their report 'Teaching Children to Read: An evidence based assessment of the scientific research literature on reading and its implications for reading instruction' (National Reading Panel, 2000). Of particular interest is the Panel's insistence on using evidence-based criteria to evaluation interventions. They believe that the highest standard of evidence for claims of success of a reading programme is the experimental study, in which it is shown that treatment can make such changes and effect such outcomes. They suggested that when it is not feasible to do a randomised experiment, a quasi-experimental study should be conducted, as this type of study provides a standard of evidence that, while not as high, is acceptable, depending on the study design.

To sustain a claim of effectiveness of a programme the Panel focused on the research design, indicating that the study should be experimental or quasi-experimental, of sufficient size or number and scope (in terms of population served), and that there is substantial correlational or descriptive studies that concur with the findings if any claim of success is to be sustained. They suggested that no claim could be determined on the basis of descriptive or correlational research alone. In the congressional testimony (www.nationalreadingpanel.org/Press/press_rel_langenberg.htm; 26 September 2000), the chairman of the Panel, Donald Langenberg, reported on some of the key points of the report. He suggested that certain instructional methods are better than others, and that many of the more effective methods are ready for implementation in the classroom. He said that there was overwhelming evidence that systematic phonics instruction enhances children's success in learning to read and that such instruction is significantly more effective than instruction that teaches little or no phonics. He also indicated that to become good readers, children must develop phonemic awareness, phonics skills, the ability to read words in text in an accurate and fluent manner, and the ability to apply comprehension strategies consciously and deliberately as they read. Children at risk of reading failure particularly require direct and systematic instruction in these skills, and such instruction should be provided as early as possible. Such instruction should be integrated with the entire kindergarten experience in order to optimise the students' social and emotional development. Langenberg also reported that research on this critical subject of reading effectiveness must stand up to critical, scientific scrutiny.

Similarly, in the UK the Independent Review of the Teaching of Early Reading (Rose Report, DfES, 2006) strongly advocated high quality, systematic phonic work that should be taught discretely. The knowledge, skills and understanding that constitute high quality phonic work should be taught as the prime approach in learning to decode (to read) and encode (to write/spell) print.

Phonic work, the report suggested, should be set within a broad and rich language curriculum that takes full account of developing the four interdependent strands of language: speaking, listening, reading and writing, and enlarging children's stock of words.

Ideally, for a programme or an approach to be of maximum benefit to teachers, it should be easily understood and implemented, but also flexible and adaptable to different contexts and types of dyslexic difficulties. The next chapter, 'Supporting Literacy: Approaches and Strategies', emphasises the benefits of such flexibility and adaptability.

POINTS FOR REFLECTION

- Consider the four approaches discussed in this chapter: individualised, support approaches, assisted learning techniques and whole-class approaches. Reflect on how you may use these different approaches with your students.

- Consider the common elements of the individual approaches outlined in the chapter—identify any similarities in relation to the principles, sequence and materials used for the different approaches.

- Consider the advantages and disadvantages of using an individual approach. Reflect on the factors you may want to consider when selecting a programme.

Chapter 13

Supporting Literacy: Approaches and Strategies

Many of the individualised programmes have conceptually much in common, but there is also a common link in the way they emphasise aspects such as a sequential structure, multi-sensory teaching, over-learning and the development of automaticity.

Support approaches, however, do not necessarily provide an individual programme, but rather can be used by the teacher to help the child develop competencies to allow access to the full range of curriculum activities. They provide a degree of flexibility and choice on the part of the teacher and often do not need any specialist training.

Some of these support materials and approaches are discussed below.

PHONICS INSTRUCTIONAL APPROACHES

- *Analogy phonics*—teaching students unfamiliar words by analogy to known words (e.g., recognising that the rime segment of an unfamiliar word is identical to that of a familiar word, and then blending the known rime with the new word onset, such as reading brick by recognising that -ick is contained in the known word kick, or reading stump by analogy to jump).
- *Analytic phonics*—teaching students to analyse letter–sound relations in previously learnt words to avoid pronouncing sounds in isolation.
- *Embedded phonics*—teaching students phonics skills by embedding phonics instruction in text reading, a more implicit approach that relies to some extent on incidental learning.
- *Phonics through spelling*—teaching students to segment words into phonemes and to select letters for those phonemes (i.e., teaching students to spell words phonemically).
- *Synthetic phonics*—teaching students explicitly to convert letters into sounds (phonemes) and then blend the sounds to form recognizable words.

A number of studies (Johnston et al., 1995) have indicated the merits of synthetic phonics. The Rose Review into the teaching of reading in the UK (Rose Report, 2006) also indicated the merits of this approach. The report discusses the differences between synthetic phonics and analytic phonics. Synthetic phonics refers to an approach to the teaching of reading in which the phonemes [sounds] associated with particular graphemes [letters] are pronounced in isolation and blended together (synthesised). For example, children are taught to take a single-syllable word such as *cat* apart into its three letters, pronounce a phoneme for each letter in turn /k, æ, t/, and blend the phonemes together to form a word. Synthetic phonics for writing reverses the sequence: children are taught to say the word they wish to write, segment it into its phonemes and say them in turn, for example /d, ɔ, g/, and write a grapheme for each phoneme in turn to produce the written word, *dog*.

Analytic phonics, on the other hand, refers to an approach to the teaching of reading in which the phonemes associated with particular graphemes are not pronounced in isolation. Children identify (analyse) the common phoneme in a set of words in which each word contains the phoneme under study. For example, teacher and students discuss how the following words are alike: *pat, park, push*, and *pen*.

Studies suggested that the synthetic phonics programme is an effective method of teaching reading. Many of the approaches suggested for teaching reading to children with dyslexia utilise a synthetic phonics approach. One such approach is discussed below.

Jolly Phonics

Many of the approaches discussed in this chapter and indeed in the previous chapter will include some elements of the above. Some approaches, such as Jolly Phonics (www.jollylearning.co.uk), seem to lean heavily towards synthetic phonics. There is, however, a vast array of stimulating and structured materials available on their website. Jolly Phonics is an example of a thorough foundation for reading and writing. It teaches the letter sounds in a multi-sensory way. Jolly Phonics includes learning the irregular or 'tricky words' such as 'said', 'was' and 'the'. There are also related storybooks. The five basic skills for reading and writing are:

1. learning the letter sounds;
2. learning letter formation;
3. blending;
4. identifying sounds in words;
5. spelling the tricky words.

In Jolly Phonics the 42 main sounds of English are taught, not just the alphabet. The sounds are in seven groups. Some sounds are written with two letters, such as ee and or. These are called digraphs. oo and th can each make two different sounds, as in book and moon, that and three. To distinguish between these two sounds, the digraph is represented in two forms.

This is shown below:

1. s a t i p n
2. c k e h r m d

3. g o u l f b
4. ai j oa ie ee or
5. z w ng v oo oo
6. y x ch sh th th
7. qu ou oi ue er ar

Each sound has an action which helps children remember the letter(s) that represent it. As a child progresses, you can point to the letters and see how quickly they can do the action and say the sound. One letter sound can be taught each day. As a child becomes more confident, the actions are no longer necessary. Children should learn each letter by its sound, not its name.

Jolly Phonics have a considerable range of support materials such as 'Jolly Stories', 'Jolly Phonics' CD-ROM and DVD, 'Finger Phonics Books', 'Jolly Phonics Workbooks' and 'Jolly Songs'.

Ann Arbor Publications

Ann Arbor Publications (www.annarbor.co.uk) provide a considerable number of resources, most of which focus directly on literacy skills. For example, in relation to written expression, the resource Teaching Written Expression may be useful. This programme offers a theoretical framework and a practical step-by-step guide to developing sentences, constructing paragraphs, editing and developing a 'sense of audience'. They have also materials on reading fluency, phonic remedial lessons, sound out listening skills, visual activities and letter, word and sentence tracking. There is also a book on Music tracking by Roy Hardman (ISBN 1 900 506 00 9). In this book the top line on every page gives the sequence for tracking. Subsequent lines each contain one note corresponding to the relevant note on the top line, taking each note in turn.

Interactive Literacy Games

Games and interactive activities can be highly stimulating and motivating for children with dyslexia. Crossbow Education (www.crossboweducation.com) specialise in games for children with dyslexia and produce activities on literacy, numeracy and study skills. These include 'Spingoes', a spinner bingo that comprises a total of 120 games using onset and rime; and 'Funics', a practical handbook of activities to help children to recognise and use rhyming words, blend and segment syllables, identify initial phonemes and link sounds to symbols. 'Funics' is produced by Maggie Ford and Anne Tottman and available from Crossbow Education. Crossbow also produce literacy games including: Alphabet Lotto, which focuses on early phonics; 'Bing-Bang-Bong' and 'CVC Spring', which help develop competence in short vowel sounds; and 'Deebees', which is a stick-and-circle board game to deal with b–d confusion.

They also have board games called: 'Magic-E Spinit and Hotwords', a five-board set for teaching and reinforcing 'h' sounds such as 'wh', 'sh', 'ch', 'th', 'ph', 'gh' and silent 'h'; 'Oh No', a times table photocopiable game book; and 'Tens n' Units', which consists of spinning board games, designed to help children of all ages practise the basics of place value in addition and subtraction. Crossbow also produce a phonic games box (by Joanna Jeffery) called TRUGS (teaching reading through games). This consists of a progressive and phonically structured card game for beginner readers of any age. There are four different styles of educational card game—which ensures variety and over-learning, and creates choice with a progressive phonic structure. The box contains 20 card games (five decks, four reading games per deck), a reading booklet, monitoring booklet and instruction booklet. For synthetic phonics Crossbow retail a 44 sounds desktop chart (six pack) produced by Smart kids (see below). These individual desktop charts enable children to quickly access the various spelling patterns of the 44 phoneme sounds.

Smart Kids

Smart Kids (www.smartkids.co.uk) produce a host of exciting and creative resources. They have expertise in the area of reading difficulties (Milne, 2006) and have some innovative resources. These include smart chute, smart phonics, cluster word-building games, CVC board games, alphabet practice cards, sentence builder and blend magnets. They have a series of self-checking verbs which consist of language cards that represent a common verb which corresponds to the name card of the photographic image. Colour-coding supports the use of these language cards as a self-correcting activity. The pack contains 108 photograph cards and 108 word cards and this type of resource can be excellent for children with dyslexia.

LANGUAGE EXPERIENCE

It is also important that top-down approaches to reading are considered, in order that dyslexic children receive enriched language experience. This can be achieved through discussion and activities such as paired reading, described above. It is important that even if the child cannot access the print content of some books, the language, concepts and narratives should be discussed. This helps to make literacy motivating and emphasises the view that literacy is more than just reading. Literacy embraces many of the social conventions in society and is a powerful tool for social awareness, essential for young people when they leave school. Literacy also has a powerful cognitive component and can help to develop thinking skills in young children as long as reading is seen as much more than accuracy. That is one of the reasons why the experience of extended language and language concepts is important even though the child may not have that level of reading accuracy.

The 5- and 10-minute thrillers from LDA, Cambridge (www.ldalearning.com) consist of high-interest books and CDs that are ideal for the young person with dyslexia. They have also '4 U to read' books with an interest level of 8–12 years but a reading age of under 8 years. Examples of these titles are 'Game Boy', 'Fox Friend', 'Problems with a Python' and 'Hostage'.

The materials from Barrington Stoke Ltd (www.barringtonstoke.co.uk) can be highly beneficial in relation to motivation. The books have been written with the reluctant reader in mind, and they can help children with dyslexia with reading fluency and help to develop reading comprehension and reading speed. They have also included adult titles in their range, which will be very helpful for the adult with dyslexia who finds reading discouraging because of the length of time it takes to read a book. They also produce special primary and secondary introduction packs which each include 12 books.

OTHER SUPPORT APPROACHES

THRASS

THRASS (www.thrass.co.uk) is an acronym for Teaching Handwriting Reading And Spelling Skills. It is a whole-school phonics programme for teaching learners, of any age, about the building blocks of reading and spelling, that is, the 44 phonemes (speech sounds) of spoken English and the graphemes (spelling choices) of written English. The programme teaches learners that, basically, when spelling we change phonemes to graphemes and when reading we change graphemes to phonemes.

The programme is very comprehensive and has an excellent user-friendly website with free downloads. The components include speaking and listening skills, phonemes and key graphemes and letter names and it is suitable for all ages.

The THRASS pack consists of four resources for teaching essential speaking, listening, reading and spelling skills. The THRASS Picture Book, THRASS Picture Cards, THRASS Workbook and THRASS Spelling Tiles can be used in classes by teachers and assistants. The resources can also be used by parents, at home, to support the introduction, revision and assessment of the THRASS key words and base words.

If, when using the Workbook and Spelling Tiles, additional help is required in identifying the phonemes (speech sounds) of English, then the first section of the THRASS Phoneme Machine, the 'Phoneme Grid', can be used. It is downloadable, without charge, from the THRASS website. There is also a THRASS singalong early reading programme. Additionally there is This, is an excellent resource that produces the sounds of each phoneme simply by clicking on the lips of the symbol.

There is a dedicated website for parents with materials (www.thrass.co.uk/phonics4parents.htm). This website has 3D animations, computer graphics, music and sound effects, animation software, streamed Windows Media Video (including features, interviews, demonstration lessons and a video diary, following teachers and parents, this school year, as they implement THRASS).

Units of Sound

This programme (http://www.unitsofsound.net) developed by Dyslexia Action is a realistic solution to teaching reading and spelling for hard-to-reach students. It is a structured, cumulative and multisensory programme to teach reading and spelling that involves a high level of independent work by the student. Each 'unit of sound' (or phonic code) is introduced separately, then used in word blocks, then sentences. It has a very informative website.

TextHelp

The programme known as TextHelp is particularly useful for assisting with essay writing.

TextHelp has a read-back facility and a spellchecker that includes a dyslexic spell check option that searches for common dyslexic errors. Additionally, TextHelp has a word prediction feature that can predict a word from the context of the sentence, giving up to 10 options from a drop-down menu. Often, dyslexic students have a word-finding difficulty, and this feature can therefore be very useful. This software also has a 'word wizard' which provides the user with a definition of any word; options regarding homophones; an outline of a phonic map; and a talking help file.

Inspiration

Inspiration is a software program to help the student develop ideas and organise thinking. Through the use of diagrams it helps the student comprehend concepts and information. Essentially, the use of diagrams can help to make creating and modifying concept maps and ideas easier. The user can also prioritise and rearrange ideas, helping with essay-writing. Inspiration can therefore be used for brainstorming, organising, pre-writing, concept mapping, planning and outlining. There are 35 inbuilt templates, and these can be used for a range of subjects, including English, History and Science. Dyslexic people often think in pictures, rather than words. This technique can be used for note-taking, for remembering information and organising ideas for written work. The Inspiration programme converts this image into a linear outline.

PHONOLOGICAL APPROACHES

There is strong evidence to suggest that phonological factors are of considerable importance in reading (Ellis and Large, 1981; Stanovich, 1991; Rack, 1994; Wilson and Frederickson, 1995). Children with decoding problems appear to be considerably hampered in reading because they are unable to generalise from one word to another. This means that every word they read is unique, indicating that there is a difficulty in learning and applying phonological rules in reading. It therefore emphasises the importance of teaching sounds—phonemes—and ensuring that the child has an awareness of the sound–letter correspondence. Learning words by sight can enable some children to reach a certain standard in reading, but prevents them from adequately tackling new words and extending their vocabulary.

If children have a phonological awareness difficulty, they are more likely to guess the word from the first letter cue and not the first sound (i.e., the word 'KITE' will be tackled from the starting point of the letter 'K' and not the sound 'ki' so the dyslexic reader may well read something like 'KEPT'). It is important, therefore, that beginning readers receive some structured training in the grapheme–phoneme correspondence; this is particularly necessary for dyslexic children who would not automatically, or readily, appreciate the importance of phonic rules in reading.

Descriptions of some structured programmes are given below.

Sound Linkage

Sound Linkage (2nd edition; Hatcher, 2001) is an integrated phonological programme for overcoming reading difficulties. There are materials each dealing with a specific aspect of phonological processing; for example, phoneme blending, identification and discrimination of phonemes, phoneme segmentation, phoneme deletion, phoneme substitution, phoneme transposition and phonological linkage activities.

Although Sound Linkage can be used as an individual structured programme, each section contains a series of activities that can be used to support mainstream curriculum work with dyslexic children. The activities are clearly presented and no complex instructions are necessary. Many of the activities are not new, and many teachers will be aware of the importance of them. To have all these activities in a methodical package, linked to assessment, with a clear overall rationale is an appealing feature of the programme. It is also possible to link the activities to more general curriculum classroom work.

Sound Linkage is a comprehensive programme of activities, linking assessment and teaching, and can be a useful addition to the support materials available to enhance the phonological skills of dyslexic children.

Phonological Awareness Procedure

The useful and easily accessible series of activities to promote phonological awareness (Gorrie and Parkinson, 1995) also begins with an assessment section. Following this, the remainder of the programme is in the form of game activities designed to develop specific areas of phonological development. For example, there are game activities on syllable segmentation, rhyme judgement, rhyme production, alliteration, onset and rime, and phoneme segmentation games. These games provide an excellent resource for the teacher and are suitable for children at different stages of phonological development.

Phonic Code Cracker

Phonic Code Cracker (www.strath.ac.uk/qie/publications.html) has been fully revised and contains a set of materials subdivided into 12 units, each unit covering a different aspect of teaching literacy; for example, Unit 3 deals with initial and final consonant blends, Unit 5 deals with common word endings and Unit 9 deals with common silent letters.

Phonic Code Cracker (Russell, 1993, revised 2000) is a very comprehensive and teacher-friendly set of materials. The scheme has been devised to provide intensive phonic practice for children who have been having difficulty acquiring basic literacy skills. It has been successfully used with children with specific reading difficulties in mainstream primary and secondary schools. There are also accompanying materials such as Phonic Codecracker Board Game, Crackerspell and Time Cracker.

Precision teaching methods are used, but no timescale is recommended as the author acknowledges that each child will have a different rate of learning. Assessment of the student's progress is measured through the use of student record skills. There are also fluency tests, time targets, accompanying computer software and, very important for building self-esteem, a mastery certificate that the child can retain as a record of his or her achievement.

HIGH-INTEREST BOOKS—HISTORY

The BBC Education Scotland Series, published by Wayland (now Hodder-Wayland), of History books for primary-aged children written by Richard Dargie provides an excellent and stimulating source for reluctant readers. The books are on popular topics such as the Vikings and the Romans and include colourful illustrations. They are written in clear text with added features such as date timelines and glossaries, both of which are useful for children with dyslexia.

START TO FINISH BOOKS

The Start to Finish Books series (www.donjohnston.com/products/start_to_finish/library/index.html) can be beneficial as the series, designed to boost reading and comprehension skills, provides a reader profile, a computer book, audiocassette and paperback book. Designed to engage children in reading real literature, the series can help with fluency and motivation. Some of the topics included in the series are: history, famous people, sports, original mysteries and retellings of classic literature. There are over ninety titles in this series of books. The books help the child with dyslexia practice reading fluently together with comprehension. There are also electronic supports that can be used.

Don Johnston also produces some excellent software for children with literacy difficulties. This includes Write:OutLoud3, a programme that supports each step of the writing process, including:

- generating ideas—helps with brainstorming and researching topics;
- expressing ideas—this allows children to hear their words as they write;
- editing work—using a spellchecker that is designed to check for phonetic misspellings;
- revising for meaning—helps with word-finding and improves written expression.

In a small-scale study, MacArthur (1998) found that the experimental group increased their percentage of both legible and correctly spelt words into the 90–100% range from a baseline of 55–85% legible words and 42–75% correctly spelt words.

Fennema-Jansen (2001) sounds a note of caution relating to the use of specialised software. She suggests that simply providing a student with a piece of software, even if it is effective for that student, is generally not sufficient. She argues that students with learning disabilities frequently struggle with multiple aspects of the writing task, and technology rarely addresses all of the student's writing needs. The student therefore needs strategy instruction combined with instruction in the use of technology in order to more fully meet his or her needs.

Fennema-Jansen (2001) does suggest that word prediction software may be more helpful for some tasks than for others. Matching the demands of the task to the word prediction program's dictionary size is an important consideration when selecting a program. When the required vocabulary is more advanced, she claims that the use of customised dictionaries may well result in greater gains in spelling and legibility. Students therefore may benefit from some features of a program more than from other features and this, according to Fennema-Jansen, may vary with the task. It is important, therefore, to take the learning context and the task into consideration when using technology to support the student.

DIFFERENTIATED TEXTS

An example of this is the series of differentiated texts by Hodder Wayland (www. hoddereducation.co.uk/SchoolsandColleges), a series of books with two books on each of the themes covered. These texts cover History topics (such as the Second World War), Geography topics (such as floods and the world's continents) and other diverse topics from energy to cultural festivals. The differentiated texts differ in that they have a reduced text length, more open page layout, bullet points to help with accessing information, clear type face and captions in different print from the main text. There are separate glossaries and indices for the differentiated and non-differentiated texts.

VISUAL FACTORS

It may be useful for the teacher to consider the influence of visual aspects in the development of literacy skills. Although the research appears to lean towards phonological and linguistic areas as the principal difficulty relating to dyslexia (Stanovich et al., 1997; Snowling and Nation, 1997; Snowling, 2000; Hatcher and Snowling, 2002), there is a body of opinion that highlights the visual areas and recommends strategies to help deal with such difficulties (Lovegrove, 1996; Stein, 1994, 2008; Wilkins, 1995, 2003; Irlen, 1983, 1989).

Research has been conducted on eye dominance and binocular control (Stein and Fowler, 1993; Stein, 2008; Everatt, 2002) and eye-tracking has also been the subject of some research (Blau and Loveless, 1982). Pavlidis (1990) suggests that children with dyslexia have less efficient control over eye movements.

Singleton (2009) presents a strong case for the impact of visual stress on reading and how this can affect children with dyslexia. He argues that studies have revealed that the prevalence of visual stress is considerably higher in children and adults with dyslexia than in the rest of the population (Singleton and Trotter, 2005; Singleton and Henderson, 2006). Using percentage increase in rate of reading with a coloured overlay as the criterion for assessing susceptibility to visual stress, Kriss and Evans (2005) found that 45% of dyslexic children read 5% faster with an overlay, compared with 25% of non-dyslexic control children; when a more conservative criterion of 8% increase in reading speed with an overlay was applied, these figures dropped to 34%

and 22%, respectively. Using ViSS, a computer-based screening tool for visual stress, Singleton and Henderson (2007) found that 41% of dyslexic children in their sample showed high susceptibility to visual stress; the corresponding figure for the non-dyslexic control group was 23%.

There is also research evidence relating to the visual magnocellular system, which consists of large cells used for depth perception, which indicates that these cells appear to be more disorganised and smaller among dyslexics (Galaburda, 1993). This would mean that stimuli would need to be delivered more slowly in order to be accurately processed.

Stein (1994, 2008) argues that a number of children with dyslexia have binocular instability and suggests that this can be remedied through short-term use of monocular occlusion. Bishop (1989) argues that practice in reading can develop binocular stability, but Stein and Fowler (1993) suggest that this is not the case and that short-term use of monocular occlusion will result in binocular stability and should thus help promote significant gains in reading. Furthermore, Cornelissen et al. (1994) found that children who experienced visual confusion of text during reading, because of unstable binocular control, were less likely to incorporate visual memories for letter strings into their spelling strategies, relying instead on sound–letter conversion rules, thus spelling words phonologically. This supports the view, therefore, that unstable binocular control not only affects how children read but also how they spell.

Stein and Walsh (1997) have linked control of eye movement with the magnocellular pathway deficit hypothesis. They suggest that movements of the eyes may be controlled primarily by areas of the brain that receive input from the magnocellular pathway. Stein and Walsh (1997) also suggest that impaired magnocellular pathway functioning might destabilise binocular fixation, as it has a dominant role in the control of eye movements. Irlen (1991) has made claims for a scotopic sensitivity syndrome that can affect the child in terms of light sensitivity, the ability to see print clearly without distortions, the ability to perceive groups of words at the same time and the ability to sustain focus for a period of time.

Irlen (www.irlen.com) recommends the use of coloured Perspex overlays or tinted lens treatment to help overcome these difficulties. According to the website, the Irlen Method is a research-based colour method backed by over 4,000 school districts in the USA. Rosner and Rosner (1987), however, reviewed the majority of studies of the tinted lens treatment and found significant problems in experimental design, and Moseley (1990) found that any significant effect of coloured overlays was due to the reduction in light rather than to any specific colour. Studies, however, by Richardson (1988) and Wilkins (1991, 1993) have shown some significant improvement in children using overlays and lenses, particularly in visual activity and muscle balance, and subsequent reading attainments.

Kyd et al. (1992) used the Irlen overlays for children with specific learning difficulties and found significant improvements in reading rate. They are currently involved in follow-up studies examining the effect of the overlays on reading comprehension and accuracy. The results of this study are consistent with the findings from a project in Norfolk (Wright, 1993), which also provides impressive data for reading rate progress. In fact, Wright (2001, personal communication) supports the use of coloured overlays for a range of specific learning difficulties. Wilkins (1993, 2003), following extensive research, has developed a set of materials called Intuitive Overlays that can be used in both assessment and learning situations.

Furthermore, Wilkins et al. (1996) have developed a Rate of Reading test designed to assess the effects of coloured overlays. It is claimed this test has some advantages over conventional tests in that it actually tests the linguistic and semantic aspects of reading at least as much as the visual. Additionally, with conventional tests performance is limited by a reader's vocabulary. The Rate of Reading test therefore seeks to minimise the linguistic and semantic aspects of reading and maximises the visual difficulties. The same 15 common words are used in each line in a different random order. The words were selected from the 110 most frequent words in a count of words in children's reading books. The text is printed in small typeface at an optimal level for visual distortion. The test is scored by noting the total number of words in the passage read correctly and calculating the average number correctly read per minute. Wilkins et al. (1996) found the test both reliable and valid, and it successfully predicted the individuals who, when offered a coloured overlay, continued to use it. They also show that the use of the overlays had an effect on reading speed and did so immediately. The authors also report on a study in which 93 children in primary school and 59 in the first-year intake of a secondary school reported an improvement in perception of text with a particular colour, and the 22% of the sample who continued to use them for 10 months demonstrated a mean improvement of 14% in reading speed with their overlay. This improvement was not seen in children who had failed to persist in using the overlay.

Mailley (1997), however, suggests that the present system of vision-testing in school and the community does not address the diversity of the difficulty. She suggests (Mailley, 2001) that a comprehensive visual screening procedure is necessary to identify those children at risk and that schools and colleges should consider how to manage this procedure.

The Use of Visual Skills

It has been argued (Bell, 1991a) that, although programmes directed at enhancing alphabetic and phonological skills are essential, one has to be wary of the 'cognitive cost' of such programmes—a cost that is reflected in a weakening of the gestalt, right hemispheric skills. The gestalt hemisphere is usually associated with visual imagery, creativity and comprehension.

The stress and effort that is necessary for children with dyslexia to fully engage their cognitive resources and to develop phonological skills is so great, according to Bell, that a weakening of the gestalt hemisphere results as resources are diverted from the right hemispheric functions to concentrate on the left hemispheric skills of decoding and phonological processing. Not only does this result in a restriction in the use of visual imagery but also in a stifling of the development of skills in comprehension and perhaps in creativity.

Bell (1991b) has developed a programme 'Visualising and Verbalising for Language Comprehension and Thinking'. This programme provides a comprehensive procedure for the use of visualising to promote and enhance reading and comprehension. The stages outlined by Bell include picture imagery, word imagery, single sentence, multiple sentence, whole paragraph and whole page.

Additionally, the programme provides an understanding of the functions of the gestalt hemisphere and useful strategies for classroom teaching.

MOTOR ASPECTS

There are a number of user-friendly practical activities that have been developed by practitioners. McIntyre (2000, 2001) has developed handbooks of approaches on motor development, particularly for children from the early years to 11. The work of Sugden and Kirby has made significant impact in relation to motor difficulties and particularly developmental coordination difficulties, Kirby, 2006. Portwood (1999, 2001) has produced excellent guides for parents and teachers on dyspraxia that contain a number of practical suggestions. Furthermore, she has also produced a text on understanding developmental dyspraxia (Portwood, 2000), which can be a useful source for staff development in this area. Russell (1988) developed a set of graded activities for children with motor difficulties that is very teacher-friendly and contains clearly illustrated activities.

The programme consists of 14 sections including gross-motor, balancing, catching, throwing, kicking and jumping, directional orientation, visual–motor coordination and handwriting activities. These activities, though essentially directed at children with motor problems, can be extremely useful for a number of dyslexic children.

There has been considerable interest in the whole area of motor development and how it relates to other cognitive factors (Blythe, 1992, 2001, personal communication; Blythe, 2001; McPhillips et al., 2000) in relation to programmes relating to inhibition of primitive reflexes (Dennison and Hargrove, 1985; Fox, 1999; Longdon, 2001; Taylor, 2002) and to educational kinesiology (Brain Gym®; Fox, 1999). Reynolds and Nicolson provided research support to the series of exercises (partly influenced by the research conducted by Fawcett and Nicolson (1994) on the cerebellum) called the Dyslexia, Dyspraxia, Attention Disorder Treatment (DDAT; Reynolds and Nicolson, 2007). This programme brought considerable controversy and intellectual debate (see Reynolds and Nicolson, 2007).

Although the rationales for all these programmes vary in both the research supporting the programmes and the theoretical roots that have influenced them, they do serve to reinforce the concept of the link between motor development and learning in general.

ASSISTED LEARNING

Assisted learning approaches are essentially teaching approaches that require considerable interaction between the learner and others. This interaction may take the form of some kind of participant modelling or indeed reciprocal teaching (Palincsar and

Brown, 1984; Thomson, 2007). There may be an element of repetition in participant modelling approaches but they can facilitate the learning process and can be successfully utilised with reading, writing and spelling.

Paired-reading, peer-tutoring, cued spelling and the apprenticeship approach to reading are examples of this kind of approach. Metacognitive approaches can also come under this category, as such approaches can be based on interaction between teacher and student, and this interaction can help the student acquire concepts and knowledge of the learning process. Metacognitive approaches will be dealt with in some detail in the following chapter.

As an example of assisted learning, paired-reading will be described and discussed below.

Paired-reading

Paired-reading was originally devised to meet the need for a reading approach that could be both applied generally and utilised by non-professionals with a minimum of training (Morgan, 1976). Studies have shown (Neville, 1975; Wilkinson, 1980; Bell, 1991a) that releasing children from the burden of decoding can facilitate or enhance comprehension.

This is highlighted in a study examining the decoding processes of slow readers (Curtis, 1980), which found that the cognitive applications to decoding reduced the amount of attention available for other reading processes. This resulted in deficits in comprehension of text. Emphasis, therefore, can be placed on the use of context rather than the skill of decoding, but the question remains whether poor readers are able to utilise context as successfully as proficient readers. Clark (1988) observed an inefficient use of context among dyslexic children, although she noted that dyslexic children utilised a wide variation of strategies and preferences in an attempt to use context to aid comprehension. Lees (1986), however, in an examination of the data from four different studies, concluded that poor readers had similar capabilities to good readers in the utilisation of context to aid word recognition. Evans (1984b) reported on two studies using paired-reading for dyslexic children, both of which showed significant gains in reading comprehension and vocabulary.

Topping and Lindsey (1992) and Topping (2001) argue that the evidence suggests that poor readers have an over-dependence on decoding strategies at the expense of developing skills in comprehension, using contextual cues. This is a practice reinforced by many teaching programmes that over-emphasise analytical decoding approaches, resulting in sequential decoding processes that can inhibit full use of comprehension skills.

This is indeed consistent with the literature on learning styles (Carbo, 1987), which suggests that young children tend to have a preference for processing information globally rather than analytically. Yet, one must be cautious of fostering global processing methods such as the whole-word method at the expense of analytical methods such as phonics, since the teaching approaches that combine both these approaches are arguably more effective (Vellutino and Scanlon, 1986; Reason et al., 1988).

Paired-reading may be particularly useful for children with specific learning diffi-culties since it provides both visual and auditory input simultaneously. It is a simple technique that focuses on the following:

- parent and child reading together;
- programme to be carried out consistently;
- child selects reading material;
- as few distractions as possible;
- use of praise as reinforcement;
- discussion of the story and pictures (Figure 13.1).

The two principal stages of paired-reading are reading together and reading alone.

Reading together is when the parent/teacher and child read all the words aloud, with the adult adjusting the speed so that the pair are reading in harmony. The adult does not allow the child to become stuck at a word and if this happens will simply say the word to the child. This process, together with discussion, can help the child obtain meaning from the text and therefore enjoy the experience of language and of reading.

Reading alone occurs when the child becomes more confident at reading aloud. The adult can either read more softly, thus allowing the child to take the lead, or remain quiet. This can be done gradually to allow the child's confidence to build up (Topping, 1996). When the child stumbles at this stage, the adult immediately offers the word and then continues reading with the child again, until he or she gains enough confidence to read unaided.

Evaluation of Paired-reading as a Strategy

Topping (2002) has extended the strategy of paired-reading to include paired-spelling and paired-thinking. The evaluations of these, like paired-reading, are promising (Topping and Lindsey, 1992; Topping, 2001, 2002).

Paired-reading may well help children with dyslexia develop a desire to read. Clearly, an adult model or indeed a peer in the case of peer-tutoring (Topping, 2001; Topping and Bryce, 2002) can act as a good reinforcer. Other factors have also been attributed to the success of paired-reading. These include pacing the text, which helps to regulate the child's reading flow and may help to overcome the segmentation and syllabification problems outlined by many researchers (Bradley, 1990; Snowling, 1993). The fact that it is multi-sensory, particularly utilising the combination of visual and auditory modalities, may also be significant. It may also help to provide weaker read-ers with a global strategy through the practice of non-interruption of the reading flow. The value of paired reading in enhancing self-image should also not be ignored. The importance of this for children with reading problems (Lawrence, 1985, 1987) is well documented in the literature.

Some other advantages of paired-reading are:

- Failure is not an evident factor because if the child 'sticks' at a word the adult saysthe word almost immediately.

Figure 13.1 Paired-reading.

- The experience of gaining enjoyment from the language of the text helps reading become pleasurable and increases the desire to read.
- Children are provided with an example of how to pronounce difficult words and can simultaneously relate the auditory sound of the word with the visual appearance of that word.
- Children can derive understanding from the text because words are given expression and meaning by the adult and discussion about the text follows at periodic intervals.

Paired-reading, it can argued, is useful as:

- a strategy to develop motivation and confidence in reading;
- an aid to the development of fluency and expression in reading;
- a technique that could also enhance comprehension on the part of the reader.

Paired-reading, however, is seen as complementary to other strategies, such as structured language teaching and phonics skills, and does not attempt to replicate or replace this dimension of learning to read. However, it utilises the participation of parents, and this is clearly a great advantage both for the child and for the school.

Topping (1996) and Topping and Hogan (1999) suggest that paired-reading can reduce the anxieties of reading for dyslexic children, reduce their all-consuming fear of failure, and encourage motivation and reading practice.

The approach is essentially one that can effectively combine the psycholinguistic aspects of the use of context with the phonic skills associated with word attack. This, coupled with parent or peer support and appraisal, may well account for its success.

Comment

Assisted learning implies that learning, quite rightly, is an interactive process and the role of peers and adults is of great importance. This form of learning in many ways minimises the adverse effects of failure, because if the child cannot respond to a particular text or situation then assistance is provided. The important point, however, is that assistance is not necessarily provided because the child is not succeeding, but because it is built into the reading or learning strategy. The learner, therefore, is not necessarily obtaining the sense of failing, but rather of working cooperatively with another person.

SUMMARY

This chapter on teaching has sought to describe the range of different types of approaches to support literacy development for children with dyslexia. It is fair to say that no one single approach holds the key to completely dealing with dyslexic difficulties and many of the programmes and strategies described in this chapter can be used together and can be complementary to other teaching and curriculum approaches. Irrespective of the type of provision that is being provided for dyslexic children, it is important that at all times every opportunity is taken to help access the full curriculum. This can present real difficulties for some dyslexic children, but this challenge can be met through careful planning, utilising the skills of teachers and being aware of the abundance of approaches and strategies available.

One of the most important considerations when selecting an appropriate teaching approach(s) for students with dyslexia relates to issues concerning the context and the curriculum. Teaching approaches, such as those discussed here, should not be seen in isolation and need to be linked to the curriculum and the student's current work in the classroom. Specialised teaching approaches therefore should be part of an overall programme that includes differentiation as a means of curriculum access. There are many examples of differentiated texts and these, together with pre-planning and curriculum development with the dyslexic learner in mind, can provide a comprehensive and effective form of intervention. One of the key points about differentiation as a means of curriculum access is that it is seen as a way of supporting all students, thus minimising any stigma that might be felt by the student who is receiving a different type of programme from others in the class (DfES, 2001). It is important, however, to ensure that differentiation is not merely a reduction in the content coverage to release more time for literacy development. Effective differentiation should incorporate principles and practices, such as those advocated by Visser (1993), that see differentiation as a process whereby teachers meet students' needs for curriculum progression by selecting appropriate teaching methods that match an individual child's learning strategies, within a group situation. As Philips (1999) points out, differentiation must build on past achievement, present challenges to enable further achievement and provide opportunities for success. Wearmouth et al. (2003) note that differentiation is linked to text readability.

Considerations, therefore, such as the interest level of text, sentence length, complexity, word familiarity and step-by-step explanations of difficult concepts, can all be accommodated in a differentiated approach, as well as the visual aspects of presentation and the individual student's learning style. Although it is tempting, in terms of time-saving, to rely on a packaged programme, the benefits from this may not be readily transferred to other areas of the child's class work. For that reason it is crucial that any approach is seen as being part of an overall programme that should be closely matched to curriculum objectives.

According to Tod (2002), individual education programmes can provide a means of achieving this. Tod, however, acknowledges that there needs to be some clarity about the educational purpose of an IEP both for the individual student and as part of whole-school planning and provision. She suggests that IEPs cannot be divorced from the context in which they have been developed and that 'targeted, focused, additional, phonological support offered via the IEP needs to be housed within a rich interactive effective literacy curriculum' (Tod, 2002, p. 264). Perhaps this is the key to dealing with the challenges experienced by learners with dyslexia—to ensure that literacy takes on a different meaning—and not be seen as a chore or a challenge but as a motivator to obtain information and to acquire pleasure and enjoyment in learning.

POINTS FOR REFLECTION

- Reflect on some of the approaches mentioned in the chapter—consider which ones appeal to you and why.
- You will note that many of the support approaches are phonically based—reflect on some of the other approaches such as the visual supports

continued

mentioned and the need for language experience and differentiated texts. Consider how useful you may find these in your work.

- Consider the use of the paired-reading approach for students with dyslexia.

- Reflect on the statement made in the chapter that 'it is fair to say that no one single approach holds the key to completely dealing with dyslexic difficulties and many of the programmes and strategies . . . can be used together and can be complementary to other teaching and curriculum approaches'. Do you agree with this? Consider how you may integrate approaches with students.

Chapter 14

Supporting Learning

When considering the most effective way to develop the learning skills of students with dyslexia, it is important to attend to the factors that can make learning more effective for all students. Quite often the best practices for students with dyslexia are in fact best practice for all. This point is relevant to this chapter as it will focus on effective learning. There are, however, some special considerations that need to be taken into account for students with dyslexia, such as metacognitive awareness, processing speed and individual differences. These will also be referred to in this chapter.

EFFECTIVE LEARNING

Effective learning involves a number of interactive cognitive activities and processes. The learner can control these activities and processes to make learning efficient and effective. This, however, can be difficult for students with dyslexia as often they become too dependent on a teacher or support teacher. It is crucial, therefore, that the skills required for effective learning are acquired at an early age. It is surprising and perhaps alarming that often these skills do not warrant a discrete strand in the school curriculum.

There are, however, some common strands in relation to effective learning that need to be considered by teachers. These include:

- *Understanding*—the learner needs be able to understand the requirements of the task.
- *Planning*—the learner needs to be able to identify the key points and be able to work out a learning plan.
- *Action*—the learner needs to have the resources and the skills to carry out the task.
- *Transfer of learning*—previous learning should help to provide a plan and strategies for tackling new tasks.

Some important factors to consider include:

1. the need to anticipate the barriers to learning the student with dyslexia may encounter;

2. the need to accumulate knowledge of the learners individual learning preferences;
3. the need to differentiate the task through presentation and through outcome;
4. the important consideration of assisting students with dyslexia to take responsibility for their own learning and to be able to monitor their own progress.

These points above are important for learners with dyslexia because it is possible to prevent failure from occurring if these points are adhered to. For example, it is possible to anticipate the barriers to learning for students with dyslexia—for instance, in relation to memory, students with dyslexia can have difficulty with the following:

- remembering instructions;
- remembering sequences;
- remembering equipment;
- confusing time, dates and days of the week;
- remembering rules and patterns.

It is therefore possible to prevent memory from being a problem by ensuring that when setting tasks any undue burden on memory is minimised.

The same considerations apply to processing speed. The following can be challenging for students with dyslexia, so this should be taken into account when planning learning and developing materials for them. Students with dyslexia have difficulty with the following:

- handling time pressures;
- working at a fast pace;
- using efficient methods of learning;
- completing work without the need to check, and re-check;
- keeping on track and keeping the purpose of task in mind.

It should be possible to take these factors into account and therefore minimise the possibility of the learner with dyslexia failing.

KEY POINTS ABOUT LEARNING

It is also important to consider some of the key points that can be taken into account when planning learning for students with dyslexia. These include the following:

1. *Learning is a process*—it is important to consider this as it implies that learning will take place in a series of steps and, importantly, these steps have to be explicitly presented for students with dyslexia.
2. *Learning takes place over time*—this implies that students with dyslexia will need sufficient time to complete tasks and in many cases may need more time than others in the class.
3. *Learning requires a period of consolidation*—this is important for students with dyslexia as it implies that over-learning is necessary. Often students with dyslexia

may appear to have learnt something new—but they may not have consolidated that new piece of learning. This means that they require a period of over-learning in order to ensure they have automaticity in the use of that new learning. This means that often learning will take longer for students with dyslexia because they need longer to acquire automaticity.

4. *Learning is more effective when the content is familiar*—this is very important for students with dyslexia. One of the most effective means of achieving this is through pre-task discussion. This will ensure they have a good grasp of the concepts and a background understanding. Students with dyslexia need to engage in pre-task discussion before they can embark on a task independently.

5. *Over-learning needs to be planned*—over-learning is essential for students with dyslexia. This should not happen by accident; it needs to be planned and it is important to present the materials that have to be learnt in different teaching contexts and also to present them over a period of time. This enhances the opportunities for retention and understanding.

6. *Learning is holistic*—it is important to consider the emotional and social needs of students with dyslexia. Environmental factors are important and these should be considered in a learning programme for students with dyslexia.

THE LEARNING PROCESS

What does one mean when using the term 'the learning process'? This implies that learning will take place over time and involves a number of cognitive and thinking activities. There are three principal elements to learning: the input, the cognition and the output (Figure 14.1).

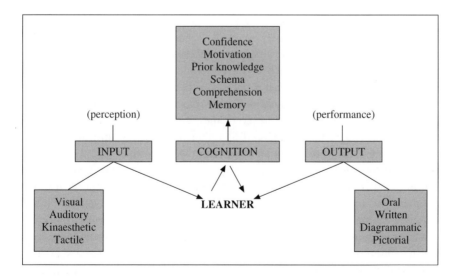

Figure 14.1   The process of learning.

- The input can be absorbed in various forms (e.g., by hearing or speaking; seeing events, print or illustrations; writing or experiencing through whole-body activities).
- Cognition occurs when the material is undergoing some form of change as the learner attempts to make sense of it.
- The output indicates the level of understanding that the learner has achieved with the new material.

Consideration needs to be given to the learner's progress at all stages of these processes. This is particularly important for dyslexic learners as they can display particular difficulty in the input and output stages, and this can influence the 'cognition' process, thus preventing the learner from obtaining a full understanding of the learning task. In order that the dyslexic child can effectively access the curriculum, it is important that these three dimensions are matched to the learner—a mismatch would obviously result in increased stress being placed on the learner with an accompanying degree of de-motivation and possible task failure. There is no one single recipe for success. All the modes of input of information are important in learning, although very young children are inclined to respond best to input of a tactile or kinaesthetic nature, and not necessarily of a visual or auditory nature (indeed, very few students prefer learning by listening). It is necessary, therefore, to consider each child individually in relation to the components of the learning process; individual preferences may be evident and these will influence the success or otherwise of both teaching and learning.

Burden (2002) suggests that learning difficulties may arise at the input phase of information-processing because the learner may have an impulsive learning style or may suffer from a blurred or sweeping perception of incoming stimuli. This means that at the initial, vital stage of learning there is a breakdown in the learning process, which can therefore affect attention and make effective learning at this important input stage less efficient. Burden also suggests that during the elaboration or cognitive phase, the learner may be unable to discriminate between relevant and irrelevant cues in defining a problem. This has been noted both among students in school and in tertiary education (Reid and Kirk, 2001) and can result in inappropriate responses to a problem or excessive elaboration, much of which is unnecessary. This excessive elaboration is often a compensatory mechanism because the student has not been able to grasp or access the key points. Burden further emphasises the potential difficulties at the output stage of the learning cycle. He suggests that people with dyslexia may have difficulty being aware of the needs of the audience or the purpose of the activity. This can also be seen in writing where there may well be redundant pages of information.

Vygotsky (1962, 1978) differentiated between the 'cognitive' (i.e., learning how to do things) and the 'metacognitive' (i.e., a gradual conscious control over knowledge and learning), and being able to use that knowledge to help with further learning. Both cognitive and metacognitive aspects are important in Vygotsky's model, and both have been applied to many areas of assessment and learning. In particular, the cognitive aspect of learning and how it relates to the theory of social constructivism has been given some prominence. This essentially means that one needs to look at not only cognitive, within-child factors but also how the child's understanding of language and learning is mediated by the learning context and the classroom environment.

Burden (2002) suggests that the cultural and social context within which learning takes place is crucial in mediating how a child learns. This implies that learning involves more than just presentation of information but embraces factors relating to the whole child and particularly the child's previous cultural and learning experiences as well. Previous experiences and learning can make new learning meaningful, and it is important to establish these before or as new learning is being presented. This process has been named as reciprocal teaching (Palincsar and Brown, 1984), where the interaction between learner and teacher can establish a scaffold to help the child bridge between his or her existing knowledge and experiences, and the new learning. Essentially, this is achieved through effective question-and-answer interaction between teacher and child, which should build on the child's response in order to extend his or her thinking.

Some suggestions for scaffolding are shown below:

- *Introductory activities*—these are essential lead-in activities and provide the means of understanding new learning. Pre-task discussion is one example of a lead-in activity.
- *Recap activities*—these are important for effective learning. Recap activities should highlight the key points. Many students have real difficulty in recapping and can find it difficult to identify the main points in a new piece of learning. Recapping is probably under-rated and under-used in learning. It is also important to allow time to revisit previous work and draw on prior knowledge.
- *Bridge-building activities*—one of the most essential aspects of learning is the skill in making connections. This is important, as often learners with dyslexia have difficulty with this. Effective learning depends to a great extent on how readily the learner can make connections between the ideas and the content of the material to be learnt and also between the new learning and previous learning.
- *Using to prevent losing*—it is important that the learner with dyslexia have opportunities to practise the knowledge and skills gained from new learning. It is this practice that leads to automaticity and it is automaticity that demonstrates that the learner has acquired competence and will be able to use this new skill to help with new learning. Often learners with dyslexia take longer to acquire automaticity.
- *Consolidation activities*—these are important, and each lesson, or period of learning, needs to finish with a summary of possible consolidation activities. This is essentially over-learning and is part of the process that can lead to automaticity.

Scaffolding therefore is process by which the teacher has to respond appropriately to the learner's behaviour in a learning situation. It is a form of guided participation and the interactions and these actions shape children's acquisition of the new material. This type of procedure is essential for learners with dyslexia as they need this guided participation to keep them on track. An important element of this learning process is self-reflection and this should be encouraged with students with dyslexia. Self-reflection and self-assessment are the essence of metacognition—that is, knowledge on how the learning has to be tackled.

REALISING POTENTIAL

Bruner (1965) also has had a significant impact on education and on our understanding of the learning process (Donaldson, 1978). One of the key principles advocated by Bruner is that of readiness. This implies that teaching must be concerned with the experiences and contexts that make the student willing and able to learn. The student needs to be cognitively and emotionally ready for the new learning.

Bruner also suggests that teaching needs to be structured so that it can be easily grasped by the student. This organisation of learning should be done at the planning stage so that the structure is in place before learning commences. This is important for students with dyslexia as they need a structure to be imposed at all stages of learning.

At the same time it is important that this structure is not restrictive. Bruner suggests that we often do not give children credit for what they are capable of and, as such, we can unwittingly restrict their progress. He suggests that teaching should be designed to facilitate extension and/or fill in the gaps in the students' understanding. It is this factor of extending learners and going beyond their current levels that is crucial for effective learning. The work of Vygotsky and Bruner is important in helping to determine the supports within the learning process that can be used by the learner with dyslexia and also in helping to realise and extend their potential for learning.

These factors also help us become aware of the notion of 'learned helplessness'. If the supports and the scaffolds are not in place then the student may fail the task and this failure can be translated into 'learned helplessness'. That is when the learner perceives his or her own abilities as not being sufficient to carry out the task without support or indeed even with support. That is why it is important to recognise the role of the foundations of learning and the teacher–learner interaction throughout the learning process. This should help to equip the learner with self-knowledge of learning and it is this that promotes independence in learning.

ZONE OF PROXIMAL DEVELOPMENT

The procedure described above—reciprocal teaching—is essentially the same as what Vygotsky describes as the Zone of Proximal Development (ZPD) and acknowledges as an important aspect of learning. This refers to the interaction between the teacher and the child and how much of the learning can be independently accessed by the child and how much requires the teacher to mediate in order for the child to access full understanding and develop further related concepts.

Burden (2002) describes the ZPD as the zone where learning can be scaffolded by others, and then when independent cognitive activity takes place the scaffolding is gradually removed at appropriate moments. This can be seen as active rather than passive learning as it is a dynamic process, and the child can actually determine the nature and extent of the learning experience. This has considerable implications for children and adults with dyslexia as they benefit from active learning, and the scaffolding experience can also help to clarify and establish concepts before the child moves on to further learning. This process can be metacognitive because it involves learners' thinking about their own thinking processes.

DEVELOPING LEARNING SKILLS

The development of skills in learning is particularly important for children with dyslexia as often they may have difficulty in identifying key points and developing efficient learning strategies. Indeed, it has been noted (Tunmer and Chapman, 1996) that children with dyslexia can have poor metacognitive awareness, which means that they may select inappropriate strategies for reading (very likely on account of their difficulties in phonological awareness) and have difficulty in unlearning once a method has been utilised over time. This can be noted, for example, in spelling when a word is habitually misspelt even after the correct spelling has been shown to the child. Additionally, children and indeed adults with dyslexia can often take inefficient routes when solving problems. They may use, for example, many different steps to get to the same end as someone who can achieve the answer using a more direct process. In some mathematical problems, children with dyslexia may take twice the number of steps to get the correct response as other children (Chinn, 2002). This means that they may lose track of the actual problem, and certainly the additional time needed to solve problems in this tangential manner can be disadvantageous. Leather and McLoughlin (2001) suggested that people with dyslexia appear to have some difficulty developing metacognitive skills for some tasks—especially those dealing with information-processing. They suggest that people with dyslexia have difficulty identifying demands and selecting the most appropriate strategy because of an overload of information, which can account for learning tasks being misdirected, which in turn leads to wrong strategy selection.

It has been noted, however (West, 1997), that this tangential problem-solving process may well enhance creativity. Nevertheless, this emphasises the importance of developing effective learning skills and strategies at an early age. This can be achieved through study skills and through developing concepts and schema, using strategies such as scaffolding and comprehension-building exercises. There is a significant role, therefore, for study skills, metacognition, learning to learn and learning styles in relation to dyslexia.

LEARNING STRATEGIES

1. *Metacognition*, which essentially means thinking about thinking, has an important role in how children learn, and this can be vital to help dyslexic children clarify concepts, ideas and situations and therefore make reading more meaningful. This also helps in the transfer of learning from one situation to another. Flavell (1979) greatly influenced the field of metacognition and its applications to the classroom, and since then metacognition has been given considerable prominence in schools and in assessment and curriculum activities.

There have been a number of models implemented in relation to metacognition. One that is well established and relevant to the learning of dyslexic children is that proposed by Brown et al. (1986). This model contains four main variables relevant to learning:

- text—the material to be learnt;
- task—the purpose of reading;
- strategies—how the learner understands and remembers information;
- characteristics of the learner—prior experience, background knowledge, interests and motivation.

2. *Children's knowledge* of their metacognitive activity, which can be achieved through thinking aloud as they perform particular tasks.

3. *The encouragement of conscious awareness* of cognitive activity such as self-questioning. Have I done this before? How did I do it? Is this the best way to tackle this problem?

4. *The encouragement of control over learning.* To develop particular strategies for dealing with a task, whether it be reading, spelling or creative writing.

5. *Comprehension-monitoring behaviour*—Wray (1994) reports on a study by Ekwall and Ekwall (1989) that defines differences between good and poor readers. The researchers suggest that the main difference relates to comprehension-monitoring behaviour. For example, good readers generate questions while they read, are able to transfer what they read into mental images, reread if necessary and actively comprehend while they read. Poor readers, on the other hand, lack a clear purpose of reading, view reading as essentially a decoding task and seldom reread or actively comprehend while they read.

6. Wray (2009) further suggests that many teachers already use discussion to *activate prior knowledge* and this can enhance metacognitive skills, but he argues that this may not be the best way of enhancing comprehension—unless it is undertaken carefully. He suggests that if prior knowledge is to be made explicit, it may be helpful to record it in some way as this has the added advantage of giving the teacher some record of the child's knowledge and, importantly, access to gaps in that knowledge and any misconceptions the child may hold.

7. *Visual imagery*—strategies such as visual imagery, obtaining the main ideas from text, developing concepts through strategies such as Mind Maps® or webbing and self-questioning, which attempt to relate previous knowledge to the new material to be learned. It is important that dyslexic students are encouraged to use these strategies, otherwise they may become too entrenched in the actual process of reading rather than in the meaning and purpose of the activity.

8. *Meaningful experiences*—Wray (1994) suggests that teachers should teach metacognitive strategies directly and always within the context of meaningful experiences (e.g., within children's project work). Cue cards that contain ideas for thinking aloud are also suggested as being useful to stimulate self-questioning during creative writing. Metacognition, therefore, should be an integral part of the learning process, and to be an effective component it should be embedded within the curriculum and within curricular activities.

9. *Reciprocal teaching*—Reciprocal teaching refers to a procedure that both monitors and enhances comprehension by focusing on processes relating to questioning, clarifying, summarising and predicting (Palincsar and Brown, 1984). This is an interactive process. Brown (1993) describes the procedure for reciprocal teaching as one that is initially led by the teacher. The teacher leads the discussion by asking questions, this generates additional questions from participants, and the questions are then clarified by teacher and participants together. The discussion is then summarised by the teacher or participants, following which a new 'teacher' is selected by the participants to lead the discussion on the next section of the text.

10. *Think to read*—Oczkus (2004) cites McLaughlin and Allen's (2002) example of the broad framework of eight strategies that they feel is essential for teaching students to understand what they are reading:
    1. Pre-viewing—activating prior knowledge, predicting and setting a purpose.
    2. Self-questioning—generating questions to guide reading.
    3. Making connections—relating reading to self, text and world.
    4. Visualising—creating mental pictures.
    5. Knowing how words work—understanding words through strategic vocabulary development, including the use of graphophonic, syntactic and semantic cueing systems.
    6. Monitoring—asking whether text makes sense and clarifying by adapting strategic processes.
    7. Summarising—synthesising important ideas.
    8. Evaluating—making judgements. (Quoted in www.think2read.co.uk/reciprocal-reading-framework.htm

11. *Scaffolding*—Scaffolding is described earlier in this chapter and refers to supports that are built to develop the understanding of text or some other area of learning. This may be in the form of the teacher either providing the information or generating appropriate responses through questioning and clarifying. The supports are then withdrawn gradually, when the learner has achieved the necessary understanding to continue with less support. Cudd and Roberts (1994) observed that poor readers were not automatically making the transfer from book language to their own writing. As a result, the students' writing lacked the precise vocabulary and varied syntax that was evident during reading. To overcome this difficulty Cudd and Roberts introduced a scaffolding technique to develop both sentence sense and vocabulary. They focused on sentence expansion by using vocabulary from the children's readers, and using these as sentence stems encouraged sentence expansion. Thus, the procedure used involved:
    • selection of vocabulary from basal reader;
    • embedding this vocabulary into sentence stems;
    • selecting particular syntactic structures to introduce the stem;
    • embedding the targeted vocabulary into sentence stems to produce complex sentences;
    • discussing the sentence stems, including the concepts involved;
    • completing a sentence using the stems;

- repeating the completed sentence, providing oral reinforcement of both the vocabulary and the sentence structure;
- encouraging the illustration of some of their sentences, helping to give the sentence a specific meaning.

Cudd and Roberts (1994) have found that this sentence expansion technique provides a 'scaffold' for children to help develop their sentence structure and vocabulary.

12. *Transfer of skills*—Transfer of skills can best be achieved when emphasis is firmly placed on the process of learning and not the product. This encourages children to reflect on learning and encourages the learner to interact with other learners and with the teacher. In this way, effective study skills can help to activate learning and provide the student with a structured framework for effective learning. Nisbet and Shucksmith (1986) describe one example of such a framework that focuses on preparation, planning and reflection. Preparation looks at the goals of the current work and how these goals relate to previous work. Planning looks at the skills and information necessary in order to achieve these goals. The reflection aspect assesses the quality of the final piece of work, asking such questions as: 'What did the children learn from the exercise and to what extent could the skills gained be transferred to other areas?'

13. *Encourage the use of self-assessment*—when tackling a new task, does the child demonstrate self-assessment by asking questions such as:
- Have I done this before?
- How did I tackle it?
- What did I find easy?
- What was difficult?
- Why did I find it easy or difficult?
- What did I learn?
- What do I have to do to accomplish this task?
- How should I tackle it?
- Should I tackle it the same way as before?

14. *Retelling*—Ulmer and Timothy (2001) developed an alternative assessment framework based on retelling as an instructional and assessment tool. This indicated that informative assessment of a child's comprehension could take place by using criteria relating to how the child retells a story. Ulmer and Timothy suggested the following criteria: textual (what the child remembered); cognitive (how the child processed the information); and affective (how the child felt about the text). Their two-year study indicated that all the teachers in the study assessed for textual information, but only 31% looked for cognitive indicators and 25% for affective. Yet, the teachers who did go beyond the textual found rich information. Some examples of information provided by the teachers indicated that, by assessing beyond the textual level, the use of the retelling method of assessment could provide evidence of the child's 'creative side', and teachers discovered that children could go 'beyond the expectations when given the opportunity'. This is a good example of how looking for alternative means of assessing can link with the child's understandings of text and promote development thinking. It can be suggested that

assessment instruments are often based on restrictive criteria, examining what the child may be expected to know, often at a textual level, but may ignore other rich sources of information that can inform about the child's thinking, both cognitive and affective, and provide suggestions for teaching.

MULTIPLE INTELLIGENCES

Ever since Howard Gardner wrote *Frames of Mind* (Gardner, 1983), the concept of intelligence and its applicability to education has been re-examined. Before then, there was a commonly held view of intelligence as a unitary concept, although that was constantly being re-examined during the second half of the twentieth century. Gardner suggests that when Binet attempted to measure intelligence in the early part of the 20th century there was indeed an assumption that intelligence was a single entity and an assumption that this entity could be measured by a single paper-and pencil test (Gardner, 1999). This, of course, had considerable implications for how children were assessed and taught during the mid-20th century and was particularly influential in streaming and in deciding the most appropriate education provision for children. Gardner himself acknowledges, however, that there has been considerable movement away from this view about intelligence, greatly supported by his attempts to highlight the need to 'pluralise the notion of intelligence and to demonstrate that intelligences cannot be adequately measured by short answer paper and pencil tests' (p. vii).

Gardner also acknowledges that his conceptualisation of intelligence is part of a larger effort to examine and define the concept and pluralisation of intelligence. At present, the multiple intelligence concept developed originally by Gardner involves eight intelligences.

Since the publication of *Frames of Mind*, Gardner has developed his concept of multiple intelligences and now no longer sees intelligence as a set of human potentials, but rather 'in terms of the particular social and cultural context in which the individual lives.' According to Gardner, this means that a significant part of an individual's intelligence exists outside his or her head, and this therefore broadens the notion of assessing intelligence by involving many different aspects of a person's skills, thoughts and preferences. The notion of multiple intelligences therefore sits well with this contextualisation view of intelligence and because of this can be more comfortably applied to educational settings. Gardner accepts that intelligences do not work in isolation, but are usually interactive and combine with other intelligences, and where one differs from another is in that combination and how that combination works for the learner. Gardner suggests that all possess these intelligences in some combination and all have the potential to use them productively. This has clear implications for the classroom and indeed for children with dyslexia as they will possess these intelligences. Although perhaps in a different combination from some others, they will still have the same potential to develop these intelligences in classroom activities. It is important, therefore, that the notion of multiple intelligences is incorporated not only into assessment but also into the teaching and learning process in schools.

Lazear (1999) has made considerable effort to incorporate Gardner's model of intelligence into both assessment and teaching. Each of the eight intelligences (Figure 14.2)

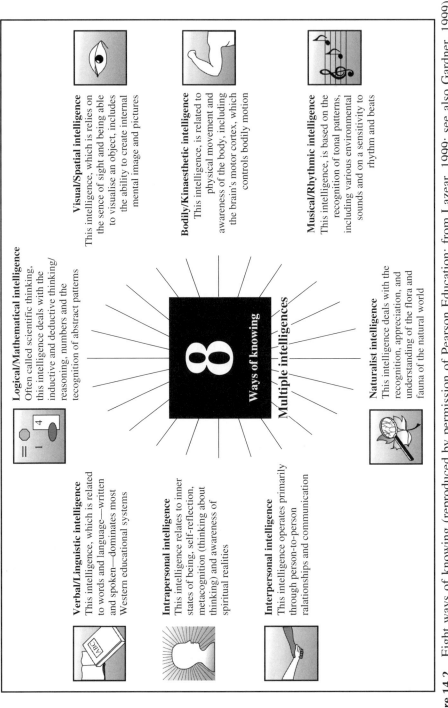

Logical/Mathematical intelligence
Often called scientific thinking, this intelligence deals with the inductive and deductive thinking/reasoning, numbers and the recognition of abstract patterns

Visual/Spatial intelligence
This intelligence, which is relies on the sence of sight and being able to visualise an object, includes the ability to create internal mental image and pictures

Bodily/Kinaesthetic intelligence
This intelligence, is related to physical movement and awareness of the body, including the brain's motor cortex, which controls bodily motion

Musical/Rhythmic intelligence
This intelligence, is based on the recognition of tonal patterns, including various environmental sounds and on a sensitivity to rhythm and beats

8 Ways of knowing

Multiple intelligences

Naturalist intelligence
This intelligence deals with the recognition, appreciation, and understanding of the flora and fauna of the natural world

Verbal/Linguistic intelligence
This intelligence, which is related to words and language—written and spoken—dominates most Western educational systems

Intrapersonal intelligence
This intelligence relates to inner states of being, self-reflection, metacognition (thinking about thinking) and awareness of spiritual realities

Interpersonal intelligence
This intelligence operates primarily through person-to-person ralationships and communication

Figure 14.2 Eight ways of knowing (reproduced by permission of Pearson Education; from Lazear, 1999; see also Gardner, 1999).

can be incorporated in this way, and if this is achieved within one's teaching and in curriculum development then children who may have weakness in some aspects of language or other processing, such as dyslexic children, will benefit.

This essentially turns the concept of deficits on its head, and, as Gardner points out, every child has the potential for effective learning, but their learning preferences and strengths need to be accessed. The eight intelligences can be summarised as follows: verbal–linguistic involves language processing; logical–mathematical is associated with scientific and deductive reasoning; visual–spatial deals with visual stimuli and visual planning; bodily–kinaesthetic involves the ability to express emotions and ideas in action such as drama and dancing; musical–rhythmic is the ability to recognise rhythmic and tonal patterns; interpersonal intelligence involves social skills and working in groups; intrapersonal intelligence involves metacognitive-type activities and reflection; and naturalist intelligence. This relates to one's appreciation of the natural world around us, the ability to enjoy nature and to recognise different species and how we incorporate and react emotionally to natural environmental factors such as flowers, plants and animals. Each of these intelligences can be incorporated into teaching and learning and into curriculum development. It is important, therefore, that the skills and preferences of, for example, children with dyslexia are utilised within a multiple intelligences curriculum. Lazear (1999) has made considerable effort to highlight the potential of multiple intelligences within daily classroom activities. For example, the verbal–linguistic mode can incorporate creative writing, poetry and storytelling; the logical–mathematical mode involves logic and pattern games and problem-solving; the visual–spatial mode can involve guided imagery, drawing and design; the bodily–kinaesthetic mode involves drama, role play and sports; the musical–rythmic mode involves classroom activities that can relate to tonal patterns and music performance; the intrapersonal intelligence mode can involve classroom activities on thinking strategies, metacognition and independent projects; and naturalist intelligence can take the form of fieldwork as well as projects on conservation, evolution and the observation of nature. Multiple intelligences, as a guide to classroom practice, can be very helpful in ensuring that the curriculum, learning and teaching provide the opportunity for the child to display and extend his or her natural abilities in many areas.

Historically, there has been considerable preoccupation with the verbal–linguistic aspects of intelligence, and this has resulted in a curriculum and examination system that appears to give a preferential status to these areas. This can be disadvantageous to children with dyslexia. It is interesting to note the comment by Pringle-Morgan as long ago as 1896, when he suggested that there is a group of otherwise intelligent people who have difficulty in expressing their understanding of a situation in writing and if this group were provided with the opportunity to present their knowledge in some other form (such as orally) they would score considerably higher in examinations. Over 100 years later the message is beginning to get through, but there have been many casualties along the road and children with dyslexia can account for some of them.

The eight intelligences can be summarised as follows:

- *verbal–linguistic*—this involves language processing;
- *logical–mathematical*—is associated with scientific and deductive reasoning;

- *visual–spatial*—deals with visual stimuli and visual planning;
- *bodily–kinaesthetic*—involves the ability to express emotions and ideas in action such as drama and dancing;
- *musical–rhythmic*—is the ability to recognise rhythmic and tonal patterns;
- *interpersonal intelligence*—involves social skills and working in groups;
- *intrapersonal intelligence*—involves metacognitive-type activities and reflection;
- *naturalist intelligence*.

Each of these intelligences can be incorporated into teaching and learning and into curriculum development. It is important, therefore, that the skills and preferences of, for example, children with dyslexia are utilised in a multiple intelligences curriculum. For example:

- *Verbal–linguistic*—creative writing, poetry and storytelling.
- *Logical–mathematical*—logic and pattern games and problem solving.
- *Visual–spatial*—can involve guided imagery, drawing and design.
- *Bodily–kinaesthertic*—drama, role play and sports.
- *Musical–rhythmic*—involves classroom activities which can relate to tonal patterns and music performance.
- *Intrapersonal intelligence*—can involve classroom activities on thinking strategies, metacognition and independent projects.
- *Interpersonal intelligence*—involves activities relating to discussion, group projects, sharing and working together.
- *Naturalist intelligence*—can take the form of fieldwork as well as projects on con- servation, evolution and the observation of nature.

STUDY SKILLS

Study skills are an essential component of any programme that aims to access the curriculum for dyslexic children. There is some evidence that dyslexic children require particular help in this area, owing to their problems with organisation. A well-constructed study skills programme is therefore essential and can do much to enhance concept development, metacognitive awareness, transfer of learning and learner autonomy. Study skills programmes will vary with the age and stage of the learner. A programme for primary children would be different from that which may help students cope with examinations at secondary level. Well-developed study skills habits at the primary stage, however, can provide a sound foundation for tackling new material in secondary school and help equip the student for examinations. Some of the principal factors in a study skills programme that should be considered include:

- *Sequencing information*—Dyslexic children may have some difficulty in retelling a story or giving information orally in the correct sequence. It is important that sequencing of information should be encouraged, and exercises that help facilitate this skill can be developed. Thus, in the retelling of a story, children should be provided with a framework that can take account of the sequence of events. Such a framework could include:

- How did the story start?
- What happened after that?
- What was the main part?
- How did it end?

- *Using context*—context can either be syntactic or semantic. In study skills, semantic context can be particularly valuable as a learning and memory aid. If the learner is using or relying on semantic context, this provides some indication that the material is being read and learnt with some understanding. The context can therefore help to:

  - retain information and aid recall;
  - enhance comprehension;
  - transfer learning to other situations.

- *Developing schema*—the development of schemata helps the learner organise and categorise information. It also ensures the utilisation of background knowledge. This can aid comprehension and recall. When children read a story or a passage, they need to relate this to their existing framework of knowledge (i.e., their own schema). So, when coming across new knowledge, learners try to fit it into their existing framework of knowledge based on previous learning, which is the schema they possess for that topic or piece of information. It is important for the teacher to find out how developed a child's schema is on a particular topic before providing more and new information. Being aware of this will help the teacher ensure that the child develops appropriate understanding of the new information. Thus, some key points about the passage could help the reader understand the information more readily and provide a framework into which the reader can slot ideas and meaning from the passage. Schemata, therefore, can help the learner:

  - attend to the incoming information;
  - provide a scaffolding for memory;
  - make inferences from the passage that also aid comprehension and recall;
  - utilise his or her previous knowledge.

- *Provide a framework*—this can include providing a the structure of the story such as

  - background;
  - context;
  - characters;
  - beginning;
  - main part;
  - events;
  - conclusion

- *Develop imaginative and visual skills*—this can involve the student developing ideas from visualising or imagining details that may be inferred but not explicitly shown. For example, in a story they may be asked to imagine the following:

  - What might the weather have been like?
  - Where do you think the story took place?

- Describe the scene.
- What were the main colours?
- Describe the main characters

SET GOALS

It is important to set the learner goals that they have to strive to achieve. If a goal is too easy it may belittle the achievement and may not stimulate the learner. Goals must be realistic, but at the same time they must be challenging. It is this balance between what is realistic and what is challenging that is the crucial factor. It is important to have knowledge and insights into the learner's style and preferences for learning.

FEEDBACK

In order for the learner with dyslexia to develop learning skills, feedback is important. Feedback should be provided throughout the task as well as at the end of the task and should offer:

- *Guidance*—the key point of any feedback is to provide the learner with guidance to ensure that he or she is progressing towards achieving the task. Guidance can and should be framed in a positive way for students with dyslexia.
- *Positive reinforcement*—it is important to start with positive comments and then some points for development can be mentioned—it is important that positive comments are made both initially and at the end of any feedback session.
- *Assessment of progress*—ideally this should be done by the learner and the key point of this is to attempt to empower the learner sufficiently so that he or she can take on the responsibility of self-monitoring their own work. This highlights the need for learners to gain some control over their own learning.
- *Suggestions for further work*—it is also important that the learner is left with a framework and suggestions for development. Further reading, additional resources that can be accessed and other points that can be made are all important.
- *Opportunities to develop self-monitoring and self-assessment*—essentially this is what feedback is all about—empowering the learner to take control over his or her own learning. Constructive teacher feedback framed in a positive tone can help the learner achieve this.

MEMORY—SOME STRATEGIES

- *Chunking*—place all similar pieces of information into one group. For example, if you are studying the geography of a country, make a chunk of all the facts relating to climate. You should be able to chunk at least four items together, so find at least four items that have a strong connection.

- *Visualise*—it is more effective to use all your senses when learning. This means using the visual modality, and for some learners this is very important. Even if you do not feel you are a visual person, a graphic or a symbol can help to strengthen the memory trace.
- *Imagine*—one of the important aspects about memory is that it is very personal. Memory is individual and the more individual it is the more effective retention can be. That is why imagination can be useful. The use of imaginative images or connections can stamp a personal identity on the information to be remembered.
- *Repetition and over-learning*—short-term memory difficulties can be overcome by repetition and rehearsal of materials. This form of over-learning can be achieved in a variety of ways and not necessarily through conventional, and often tedious, rote learning. In order to maximise the effect of repetition of learning it is important that a multi-sensory mode of learning is utilised. Students with dyslexia usually will not remember information first time around and rote repetition is not always effective. Information should be repeated in a range of different ways. Memory cards, visuals, headings, summaries, notes and discussion are all helpful for over-learning. All these can be repeating the same information but use various means to do this. This is how information is consolidated and mastered. Mastery is the aim of learning and that will take time and considerable over-learning.
- *Active learning*—This can help the learner retain and understand the new information to be learnt. The more active the learner is, the more likely the information is understood and retained. This activity could be in the form of discussion but it could also be in drama form and first person speech. This can be done more easily in some subjects such as History where first person and drama can be used to re-enact historical events.
- *Discussion*—for many learners with dyslexia, discussion is the most effective means of retaining and understanding information. Discussion can make the information meaningful and can help learners experiment with ideas and views. It is this experimentation that helps learners extend their thinking and learning. For some learners discussion can be like thinking aloud.
- *Mnemonics*—This can be auditory or visual, or both auditory and visual. Auditory mnemonics may take the form of rhyming or alliteration, while visual mnemonics can be used by relating the material to be remembered to a familiar scene, such as the classroom.
- *Mind Mapping®*—This was developed by Buzan (1993) to help children and adults develop their learning skills and utilise as much of their abilities as possible. The procedure is now widely used and can extend one's memory capacity and develop lateral thinking (Buzan, 1993). It can be a simple or a sophisticated strategy depending on how it is developed and used by the individual. It is used to help the learner to remember a considerable amount of information and encourages students to think of, and develop, the main ideas of a passage or material to be learnt. It adopts in many ways some of the principles already discussed in relation to schemata theory.

Essentially, Mind Maps® are individual learning tools, and someone else's mind map may not be meaningful to you. It is important, therefore, that children should create their own, in order to help with both understanding of key concepts and in the retention and recall of associated facts. Mind mapping® can help not only to remember information but also to help organise that information, and this exercise in itself can aid understanding. Elaborate versions of Mind Maps® can be constructed using pictorial images, symbols and different colours.

According to Buzan (1993), a Mind Map® is an expression of 'Radiant Thinking and is therefore a natural function of the human mind. It is a powerful graphic technique which provides a universal key to unlocking the potential of the brain.... Mind Maps help you to make a distinction between your mental storage capacity, which your Mind Map will help you demonstrate, and your mental storage efficiency, which your mind map will help you achieve' (pp. 59–60). Buzan suggests that storing data efficiently multiplies your capacity. This clearly has considerable implications for students with dyslexia as they may have considerable capacity for learning, but lack efficiency. Buzan suggests that a Mind Map® has four essential characteristics: a central image that is the main subject; the main themes of the subject that radiate from the central image; associated topics to the main theme; and a connected 'nodal' structure that connects the associated topics and its branches to the main theme. It is best to practise Mind Maps® with a simple topic such as 'a football game' or 'weekend activities'. For 'weekend activities' the associated topics might be sport, school work, money, friends, family, television and these can be divided into further sub-themes or branches. Mind Mapping® does require practice, but once mastered it can be used for note-taking in lectures, from videos and films, planning revision and structuring and organising essays. Developing this skill, therefore, can prove to be extremely helpful for the student with dyslexia. Mind Mapping® is also a visual and graphic strategy, and this can favour the person with dyslexia. Mind Mapping® therefore can be seen as both a metacognitive strategy, as it helps the learner become aware of planning how to use their knowledge, and a study skill strategy, as it helps with learning efficiency as well as learning capacity.

THE ROLE OF SELF-ESTEEM

One of the most important ingredients in any intervention programme for children with dyslexia is self-esteem—without a positive self-concept children with dyslexia will soon opt out of learning. It is important, therefore, that all teaching should be directed to enhancing self-esteem. There are several ways of achieving this. There are some programmes that have been specifically developed to boost self-esteem, and others that can indirectly boost self-esteem through the student's achievements. Among the first type are those programmes that focus directly on self-esteem, and some of the best known are the circle time programmes (Mosley, 1996). There have been many deviations of these programmes, but essentially they involve a degree of positive feedback and place a high regard on the individual person. They also promote group work, peer support and conflict resolution. These can be particularly suitable for children with dyslexia because they are whole-class activities, and although these can be beneficial in boosting the self-esteem of children with dyslexia they have the added benefit of all children working together and no one is excluded or withdrawn from class.

CREATIVITY AND THE 'GIFTED' DYSLEXIC STUDENT

One of the pitfalls about teaching a structured reading programme to dyslexic children is that the programme can often be so structured that it stifles creativity and perhaps comprehension. It is important that teachers are aware of this and establish teaching procedures that can accommodate to the 'gifted' dyslexic to ensure that a preoccupation with decoding does not result in a restriction of thinking and comprehension skills. See www.gifteddevelopment.com and www.visualspatial.org.

The area of giftedness focusing on the learning needs of children with dyslexia is very much the focus of the work of Yoshimoto (2005), who has developed programmes and strategies for the gifted dyslexic following the Orton–Gillingham (OG) programme. This ensures that crucial thinking and learning skills are developed alongside the basic decoding skills needed by all dyslexic students and essential for reading fluency. Yoshimoto suggests that gifted dyslexic learners can have:

- superior listening skills;
- expansive vocabulary;
- excellent general knowledge;
- good abstract reasoning skills;
- unusual capacity for processing information;
- good problem solving skills;
- can be creative, original thinkers;
- may be artistically/musically talented.

At the same time Yoshimoto claims that they:

- have a low self-concept;
- use humour to divert attention away from perceived failure;
- have a low frustration tolerance;
- react poorly to criticism;
- avoidance of failure can result in refusal to perform tasks.

It is important, therefore, to ensure that differentiation caters for all abilities as dyslexia students can be well above average in terms of their intellectual functioning and potential.

SUMMARY

Supporting the learning of students with dyslexia is an important consideration. Specific teaching approaches are certainly necessary, particularly for literacy, but dyslexia can be more than a difficulty with literacy—it can affect learning. Study skills approaches and metacognitive skills are important to consider in a learning programme. These should be afforded a high priority for children with dyslexia. It is also important to personalise study skills approaches for the individual. This means that different learners will adopt different ways of learning and remembering materials, but the responsibility to allow the learner to do this and to understand the principles associated with study skills rests with the teacher.

POINTS FOR REFLECTION

- Reflect on what you understand by effective learning. Consider how learning can be made more effective for students with dyslexia.

- Consider why the learning process can go wrong for so many students with dyslexia.

- Consider the 14 learning strategies outlined in this chapter. Which do you think would be most useful for students with dyslexia? Reflect on how you might use these in your teaching.

- Consider the importance of providing feedback to the student. Reflect on the different ways of doing this.

- Consider the importance of self-esteem in learning. Consider the strategies you might use to develop self-esteem.

- Reflect on the role of creativity in learning for students with dyslexia. Consider how you might develop this with your students.

Chapter 15

Inclusion: Curriculum Access

THE CONTEXT

There is an ongoing debate in relation to the nature of provision for students with dyslexia. There are a number of different perspectives on the most effective provision. These can range from full inclusion with some in-class support to a totally discrete educational environment quite separate from mainstream school. There is, of course, a substantial area of middle ground where there may be some separate provision but a desire to achieve eventual inclusion. This middle ground is realistic as it emphasises the view that inclusion is a process and that the process will take place over time.

The General Statement on Inclusion (QCA, 2000) on 'providing effective learning opportunities for all students' sets out three 'key principles for inclusion':

- setting suitable learning challenges;
- responding to students' diverse learning needs;
- overcoming potential barriers to learning and assessment for individuals and groups of students.

These three points will be referred to in this chapter.

The view that a distinct provision needs to be in place for students with dyslexia can be found in the criteria of The Council for the Registration of Schools Teaching Dyslexic students in the UK (CReSTeD) (see www.crested.org.uk). According to CReSTeD, the majority of schools on their register are mainstream schools that offer appropriate provision for dyslexic students covering a wide range, from students who need only a small amount of extra tuition each week to those who require substantial support. CReSTeD support and have criteria for four different types of provision: specialist provision schools; dyslexia unit; specialist classes; and withdrawal system. It can be noted that there is no category for in-class support but this can provide an important support for dyslexic students in the mainstream classroom (see categories in Table 15.1).

Table 15.1   Categories of provision

Specialist provision schools	The school is established primarily to teach pupils with dyslexia. The curriculum and timetable are designed to meet specific needs in a holistic, coordinated manner, with a significant number of staff qualified in teaching dyslexic pupils.
Dyslexia unit	The school has a designated unit or centre that provides specialist tuition on a small group or individual basis, according to need. The unit or centre is an adequately resourced teaching area under the management of a senior specialist teacher, who coordinates the work of other specialist teachers and ensures ongoing liaison with all mainstream teachers. This senior specialist teacher will probably have Head of Department status, and will certainly have significant input into the curriculum design and delivery.
Specialist classes	Schools where dyslexic pupils are taught in separate classes within the school for some lessons, most probably English and mathematics. These are taught by teachers with qualifications in teaching dyslexic pupils. These teachers are deemed responsible for communicating with the pupils' other subject teachers.
Withdrawal system	Schools where dyslexic pupils are withdrawn from appropriately selected lessons for specialist tuition from a teacher qualified in teaching dyslexic pupils. There is ongoing communication between mainstream and specialist teachers.

Source: Reproduced with permission from the Council for the Registration of Schools Teaching Dyslexic Pupils, www.crested.org.uk/pages/criteria.htm. A list of approved schools may be obtained free of charge by contacting CReSTeD (www.crested.org.uk).

Table 15.2   Index for inclusion

Inclusion in education

Inclusion in education involves:
- valuing all students and staff equally;
- increasing the participation of students in, and reducing their exclusion from, the cultures, curricula and communities of local schools;
- restructuring the cultures, policies and practices in schools so that they respond to the diversity of students in the locality;
- reducing barriers to learning and participation for all students, not only those with impairments or those who are categorised as 'having special educational needs';
- learning from attempts to overcome barriers to the access and participation of particular students to make changes for the benefit of students more widely;
- viewing the difference between students as resources to support learning, rather than as problems to be overcome;
- acknowledging the right of students to an education in their locality;
- improving schools for staff as well as for students;
- emphasising the role of schools in building community and developing values, as well as in increasing achievement;
- fostering mutually sustaining relationships between schools and communities;
- recognising that inclusion in education is one aspect of inclusion in society.

Source: www.csie.org.uk/publications/inclusion-index-explained.shtml

Table 15.3   Inclusion quality mark criteria

Pupils' progress
Pupils' attitudes, values and personal development
Leadership and management
Staffing systems and organisation
The learning environment
Teaching and learning
Resources and ICT
Parents and carers
Governors, external partners and local authority
The community

Source: Reproduced with permission from Inclusion Quality Mark, www.inclusionqualitymark.co.uk

The question and the issues to emerge from the categories above is to what extent can these accommodate the inclusive process. To answer this we need to ask some searching questions about what exactly constitutes inclusion. It is customary to set criteria for inclusion, for example the Inclusion Index (see Table 15.2) which is discussed later in this chapter and the Inclusion Quality Mark (IQM) (see Table 15.3). At the same time it might be argued that schools may well have this criteria in place but this does not guarantee that the student with dyslexia sitting in the History or English classroom will have their needs met.

RESPONDING TO THE DIVERSE NEEDS OF STUDENTS

According to the Centre for Studies in Inclusive Education in the UK (www.csie. org.uk/inclusion), inclusion is founded upon a moral position which values and respects every individual and welcomes diversity as a rich learning resource. They suggest that at a time when the educational landscape is rapidly changing, with schools having to provide for learners of increasingly diverse abilities and family, ethnic and cultural backgrounds, respect and equal commitment to all learners seem more important than ever. This is certainly a commendable statement and most would accept this as desirable. But the issue that is often raised is to what extent these can be translated into practice and, in particular, how they can be contextualised to meet the needs of students with dyslexia. It is crucial that the diverse needs of students with dyslexia are noted and understood and that schools are able to accommodate to these within the criteria set for inclusion. Inclusion is therefore about practice and not just criteria. It is important to view the term 'diverse needs' in as a broad a way as possible to ensure that the holistic needs of all students, including students with dyslexia, are met. Wedell (2000) proposes a broad concept of understanding and dealing with diverse needs. He proposes an 'interactive' model of difficulties in learning. In this model the barriers to students' learning arise as a result of the interaction between the characteristics of the child and what is offered through the pedagogy and supporting resources. This implies that one has to have knowledge of the child's characteristics as well as of the means to support that student. This means that it is important to look beyond the label and not teaching to the 'syndrome' or group. Inclusion therefore can be tackled from both the macro level, focusing on the system, and from the micro level, focusing on the individual child and his or her needs.

THE CHALLENGES

Wearmouth (2001) argues that a number of factors make schools, as institutions, incapable of responding to the learning needs of all students:

- regimentation of students;
- lack of individuality and personal recognition;
- chronological age grouping;
- inappropriate model of child-as-learner;
- within-school power relationships;
- authoritarianism.

If this is the case, developing inclusive practices to meet individual needs will be extremely challenging. The above list in fact can pave the way for alienation and exclusion rather than inclusion. It can be argued, therefore, that as school traditions stand at present, meeting the diverse needs of all will be challenging and may result in the needs of some students being overlooked. This can be a potentially vulnerable situation for children with dyslexia unless there are opportunities for planning and training for all teachers.

The following are some of the considerations that teachers and school systems have to make to accommodate to the individual needs of students with dyslexia in an inclusive school environment and the challenges inherent in pursuing an inclusive educational environment:

- *Diversity*—the student population is continuing to become less and less homogeneous and it is important, therefore, that the diverse learning styles of all students are recognised.
- *Collaboration*—teachers planning together can create more effective problem-solving strategies and can help to create approaches that can be used in the whole school. Meeting the needs of students with dyslexia in an inclusive school is not the responsibility of one teacher.
- *Flexibility*—schools and teachers need to be adaptable to the wide range of student needs.
- *Assessment*—it is important that students are able to demonstrate competence in a variety of ways and not be restricted to a formal written examination.
- *Integrity*—it is also important that the students' needs are placed before policy implementation and administrative obligations.

- *Ambition*—the needs of all need to be catered for, including the most able. All students need to be set goals that will extend them and their horizons and goals.
- *Harmony*—all organisations work and function more effectively when there is harmony. Inclusion can generate some tension and conflict and it is important that this does not prevent collaboration nor affect the school climate and ethos. These factors are essential for a smooth-running, efficient and effective school.

MEETING CURRICULUM OBJECTIVES

One of the key aspects to ensuring that inclusion is effective in terms of practice is to ensure that the tasks that are set for students and the objectives that have to be met actually match the students' needs and, importantly, that the students have the means to achieve these needs and outcomes. Often children with dyslexia fail because of unrealistic objectives and ambitious learning outcomes. That is because objectives are not set for individual needs but for curriculum or examination practicalities, and are geared more to the community of learners rather than individuals. Simpson and Ure (1993) describe some statements on matching tasks to students' needs. They found that teachers who effectively manage the match:

- share the management of learning with students;
- promote the belief that things can improve by demonstrating that agreed learning strategies work;
- use a wide range of sources of information;
- give and receive continuous feedback in terms of how students are getting on.

These statements confirm the need to incorporate students' perspectives into the practical development of inclusive practices. Each of these statements can also be consistent with the need to acknowledge learning styles in the classroom.

Sharing the management of learning with students is a good example of this. In acknowledging students' individual needs one is essentially working collaboratively with the students and helping to mange the students' learning. Moreover, this implies that students are encouraged to be reflective in relation to their own learning. This self-reflection is helpful in developing students' responsibility over their own learning.

INDEX FOR INCLUSION

In the UK a set of materials known as the Index for Inclusion (Booth et al., 2000) was developed to support the process of inclusion in schools. The Index was distributed to 26,000 primary, secondary and special schools in a government-funded initiative.

Three key areas are described in detail in the Index for Inclusion (Booth et al., 2000). These relate to inclusive cultures, inclusive policies and inclusive practices. These three areas have considerable relevance for successful inclusion, but also for students with dyslexia, as each can have a role to play in helping to meet diverse individual needs and recognising individual preferences for learning within an inclusive educational setting.

Inclusion does not happen—it is a process. Inclusion develops over time and the success of inclusion depends on the preparation and the foundations that have been put in place. It is also important to have an understanding of dyslexia, what that means and the individual profiles and variations among those identified as dyslexic.

Tomlinson (1997) defines inclusion as matching the resources we have to the learning styles and educational needs of the students. This definition recognises the need for student-centred approaches if inclusion is to be successful. At the same time, while the aim of inclusion is to cater for all, it is important that the individual needs of children, particularly those children with 'additional' and special educational needs, are not overlooked. Florian (2005) suggests that 'inclusive education is not a denial of individual difference, but an accommodation of it within the structures and processes that are available to all learners' (p. 96). While children with dyslexia might benefit from an inclusive setting, they will require some additional considerations in terms of the structures and processes of meeting their educational, social and emotional needs.

This can include ensuring that:

• they have opportunities to work in groups;
• the group dynamics are positive for students with dyslexia;
• the tasks are appropriately differentiated;
• the presentation of materials is varied and includes visual and kinaesthetic;
• learning outcomes are achievable;
• there is acknowledgement of the social and emotional needs of the child;
• there is multi-agency involvement if appropriate;
• parents' views are considered and they are kept informed of progress;
• students are given responsibility for their own learning as much as possible.

Effective inclusion for students with dyslexia therefore involves a number of areas such as:

• one's understanding of the concept of inclusion;
• how to achieve the objective of equality of learning opportunities;
• the implications for assessment and defining learning outcomes;
• differentiation and staff development;
• the management of learning for all students with dyslexia;
• accessing specialised resources.

This presents a challenge to educators: teachers, management, administrators and support staff. The challenge is how effectively teachers and other professionals can meet the needs of students with dyslexia within an inclusive environment. Giorcelli (1995, 1999) suggests that the controversy surrounding the inclusion movement is due to a number of factors, including the lack of preparedness of teachers in mainstream schools for students with high support needs and the adoption of inclusion practices without a rigorous focus on educational outcomes and, in particular, the problems that can be experienced by older students.

It is important, therefore, to address some of these challenges by examining the tensions and contradictions, and principles and practices, of inclusion, including the nature of interventions and, in particular, how they may apply to children with dyslexia. This, along with student advocacy, will be discussed in this chapter as well as the crucial role of staff support and training.

TENSIONS AND CONTRADICTIONS

Wearmouth et al. (2002) suggest that the UK national context is one that attempts to reconcile the principles of individuality, distinctiveness and diversity with inclusion and equal opportunities. There are inherent conflicts in this, and therefore tensions and contradictions will be evident. Wearmouth et al. (2003) suggest that these tensions and contradictions permeate policy and practice throughout the whole education system in the UK. There is a drive to raise the learning and achievement standards of all students through whole-class and whole-group teaching, standardised assessment and the encouragement of competition between schools through a focus on league tables based on academic performance. Yet, there is a statutory obligation to acknowledge the principle of inclusion for all students, including those with significant difficulties in the development of literacy skills such as children with dyslexia.

The revised National Curriculum for England and Wales (QCA, 2000) contains a statutory General Statement on Inclusion about providing effective learning opportunities for all students. This sets out three key principles for inclusion: setting suitable learning challenges; responding to students' diverse learning needs; and overcoming potential barriers to learning and assessment for individuals and groups of students. Wearmouth (2001) indicates that these statements can provide complex challenges for those who are planning programmes to address the learning needs of children with dyslexia. She suggests that to achieve the aims of the inclusion statement it is necessary to focus on ways in which the learning environment can potentially create barriers to literacy development. It is significant that Wearmouth identifies the learning environment as a crucial factor in achieving inclusion. Many educators would immediately focus on the child's specific difficulties and specific teaching programmes designed to deal with these difficulties. It is interesting that Wearmouth chose to identify the learning environment as one of the most influential factors. She also suggests that it is important to engage in multidisciplinary assessment and to plan programmes that take account of these perspectives, and that these should be embedded in the whole-school curriculum. Wearmouth argues that the complexity of the issues relating to inclusion must be tackled and that policy-makers need to understand the long-term nature of embedding change of this nature in relation to teacher development and the provision of resources and technology. While inclusion can be seen as a desirable outcome in terms of equity, it can also be seen as a threat and a potential conflict between meeting the needs of individuals and establishing a framework that has to meet the needs of all.

ASSESSMENT, NEED AND ACCOUNTABILITY

One of the key features of educational provision in most countries involves the concept of accountability. Governments demand results, schools want results and parents
expect results. How these results are measured is a matter of debate. The government's
expectations may be measured differently by schools and by parents—the measure
of progress can depend on how one views the purpose of education and the means of
achieving that purpose. These two variables—purpose and means—may differ, even
within an inclusive setting. Inclusion, therefore, is not the educational product but the
educational vehicle that can contain the methods, means and purposes of the educational experience for all students. That experience, however, can depend on and even
be restricted by the need for accountability, as it attempts to define the educational
experience as a measurable commodity. National testing, government benchmarks and
league tables to identify 'high performing' and 'low performing' schools are examples
of political pressures on an education system that seeks to serve 'all', but recognises
that the individual differences in children mean that 'all' will not progress in the same
way and at the same rate. An enlightened education system would not expect that, but
the reality of market forces and accountability of the public purse may determine the
nature of the educational process in schools and the educational experience of children
in the classrooms.

Some groups of learners may be a casualty of this drive to measure achievement.
Viall (2000) argues, for example, that this practice of 'high stakes assessment' in the
USA, which is intended to measure and enhance student progress, can in fact be discriminatory in relation to students with dyslexia. These 'high stakes' tests are usually
standardised, as is also the case in the UK with national testing, and many of these
types of tests do not accommodate the needs of dyslexic students, nor in fact the needs
of students from different cultures. Moreover, Viall argues that this practice carries a
risk of the teacher teaching to the tests and neglecting the importance of critical thinking and the metacognitive aspects of learning. One of Viall's suggestions to overcome
this potentially discriminatory practice is that there should be meaningful alternative
assessments that take into account the types of difficulties experienced by students
with dyslexia. This is different from providing support or examination allowances in
conventional examination systems to aid the student with dyslexia—alternative assessment means 'different' assessment. This would need a complete rethink of the aims
and objectives of the examination system, coupled with the need to identify exactly
what are the important elements to assess and how that assessment could be performed
in an equitable fashion. There has been some evidence of this in examples of portfolio assessment that have the potential to examine the performances of students with
dyslexia in a much fairer way than a one-off test or national examination.

REMOVING BARRIERS TO ACHIEVEMENT

This is the title of the UK's strategy document for the Statement of Educational
Needs (SEN; DfES, 2003)—removing barriers to achievement. This document set

out a blueprint for effective inclusion and, in particular, meeting the needs of all children, including those with SEN. The document stated that there is an 'increasing emphasis on personalised learning in the national strategies for schools, which emphasise pace and progression in learning according to students' individual needs' (p. 19). The report also stated that to help schools become more effective at responding to the needs of individual students the government will launch an Inclusion Development Programme. The programme will support partnership projects involving education, health and social care, voluntary organisations, higher education institutions, special and mainstream schools, and early years settings to develop and pilot effective practice. The aim is to develop an evidence base about what works and build consensus about how to implement good practice most effectively. The focus will be in a number of areas, including speech, language and communication needs (SLCN) and dyslexia. The report acknowledged that dyslexia and speech and communication difficulties are central to full curriculum access (p. 34). This type of document, although not directly related to dyslexia, does indicate a broad commitment and a recognition of the diversity of learners and the need to acknowledge individual differences. One of the worrying aspects of inclusion is that it may actually unintentionally exclude some children from full curriculum access because their specific needs have not been understood. This can be the case for children with dyslexia, but if the appropriate training is in place at an education authority and school level then this anxiety can be minimised.

INTERVENTIONS AND INCLUSION

The Debate

There is an ongoing debate regarding the special type of teaching that is required for children with dyslexia. This debate is encapsulated in the paradigm presented by Norwich and Lewis (2001). In this paper they investigate the claims that differential teaching is required for children with special educational needs, including dyslexia. They claim that the 'unique differences position' (p. 313), which suggests that differentiated teaching is needed for this group, has little supportive, empirical evidence and is in fact nothing more than adaptations to common teaching approaches.

Conner (1994) argues that specialist teaching approaches are little different from teaching literacy to any student, although arguably there seems to be more of a preference for bottom-up approaches towards phonological awareness, structure and over-learning. Reason et al. (1988) also question the differences in specialist approaches, indicating that individual differences within dyslexic students are more important in relation to utilising teaching approaches.

This point is developed in detail by Dyson (2001), who suggests that a radical rethink of categorisation-led interventions is needed. Dyson argues that what is required in order to achieve full equity—which is essentially the key aspect of inclusion—'is a move away from the individualisation of current approaches towards the development of systemic interventions embedded in mainstream schools and classrooms' (p. 99). In essence this means a shift from the practice of categorisation in order to identify interventions—moving from individual interventions, based on traditional special needs categorisations, to one of attempting to guarantee quality school provision for all, rather than case by case. Dyson's argument, which is firmly couched in equity principles as well as, he would argue, more cost- and time-effective interventions, appears to undermine the years of skill, experience, planning and development of individually based programmes that are currently used, for example, for children with dyslexia. This, however, is the key question that needs to be asked: What is the evidence that these individually based programmes are more effective than a more global, systemic, curriculum-based approach?

The British Psychological Society Report (BPS, 1999a) in the UK suggests that bottom-up approaches to achieve 'accurate and fluent word decoding is a pre-requisite for efficient reading for interest and information' (p. 65) and that 'reading development is dependent on the teaching methods deployed, and, also, the language in which children are learning to read... and the efficiency and integrity of underlying phonological abilities will determine how effectively children are able to learn through independent reading' (p. 65). This implies that some principles that are common to all need to be considered at the beginning stages of reading, but that close monitoring is required to ensure that the necessary, prerequisite, phonological skills are incorporated into the learner's reading pattern. What happens next if the learner is not acquiring these skills is the point of debate. Do they require more of the same or something quite different? The answer to that lies in both the assessment and ongoing monitoring while acknowledging the individual differences between dyslexic children as well as the common principles needed for efficient reading acquisition. Norwich and Lewis (2001), however, would argue that such an approach, which emphasises the need for more bottom-up phonological approaches to literacy, is 'not qualitatively different from teaching which involves less emphasis on these approaches' (p. 326).

Implications

The implications are that we need to justify that dyslexic children need different interventions and, second, we need to know exactly what the nature of those interventions and the implications for teaching provision should actually be. Chapter 12 provided information on an array of teaching approaches specifically designed for children with dyslexia. This would therefore imply that they do, in fact, need a different kind of intervention. Yet, there are very few studies that compare these approaches for dyslexic children with approaches normally offered to mainstream students who have no real literacy difficulties. Does the difference therefore lie in the nature of the pace of learning and the need for more time, more individual attention and more repetition, rather than production of a special programme that represents a 'dyslexia formula' for intervention?

Lewis and Norwich (1999) suggest that an analysis of their evidence rejects distinctive SEN teaching strategies and accepts that there are common pedagogic principles which are relevant to the unique differences between all students, including those designated as having SEN (p. 3).

They also suggest in relation to dyslexia that specialist approaches have much in common with teaching literacy to any student, though there is a tendency to bottom-up approaches (e.g. Synthetic Phonics). Other differences include the degree of structure, detail, continuous assessment, record keeping and over-learning (p. 39).

These differences, which are accepted by Norwich and Lewis, of structure, continuous assessment and over-learning are indeed beneficial to all, but the point is that they are crucial for children with dyslexia, and many of the specialised approaches are indeed built upon these facets. Norwich and Lewis accept that students with specific learning difficulties also generally require more practice than other students and practice that is well designed. They need, like other students, to be actively engaged in managing their learning, though they tend to have difficulties in applying learning and performance strategies. However, evidence has shown that such students can be taught to use and apply such strategies (p. 41). Therefore, while there may be similarities in the nature of the intervention, the means and rationale for a certain type of intervention will be different. Teachers' awareness of the type of difficulties experienced by children with dyslexia is also crucial to a full understanding of how 'common pedagogic principles' can be utilised for these children.

Whatever the answer to this, the fact remains that the educational systems in most countries are now committed in some fashion to inclusionary policies and practices. These present special challenges to teachers, because the teacher has to cater for a wide range of learning differences within a single class.

Whatever the arguments regarding the 'specialness' of the intervention for dyslexic children, there is little doubt regarding the difficulties they can experience and present in acquiring literacy. The development of literacy can often be restricted by cognitive factors relating to memory, organisation and metacognition. Inclusion, therefore, although in principle it aims to maintain equality and equitable distribution of teaching time and resources, in reality can be stressful for the teacher and actually become exclusionary for some students as their needs may be neglected in view of the multiple demands placed on teaching staff. It is important to ensure that this is prevented so that all students with dyslexia can obtain maximum benefit from an inclusive education system.

MAKING THE SCHOOL INCLUSIVE

The Index for Inclusion referred to earlier in this chapter suggests that an inclusive culture is crucial for an inclusive school. The indicators of an inclusive culture are that:

- everyone is made welcome;
- students help each other;
- staff collaborate with each other;
- staff and students treat one another with respect;
- there is a partnership between staff and parents (carers); and
- all local communities are involved in the school.

These points are extremely relevant to supporting students with dyslexia as they can be very sensitive to the educational environment (see Box 15.1).

- Notice on entrance door saying 'welcome' in different languages
- Children's work on walls
- Recognition of different cultures on wall displays
- Recognition of different abilities on wall displays
- Photographs of children
- Emphasis on activities
- Focus on schools achievements
- Emphasis on school's role in the community
- Indication that parents are made welcome
- Sitting room for parents
- Opportunities for parents to see teachers/management without appointment—for example a drop-in centre

Box 15.1   Criteria for the welcoming school

EQUITY

The desire to include all students within the mainstream setting and the mainstream curriculum is not only about getting the teaching right but also about measuring and assessing progress in a fair, non-discriminatory manner. It is also about political desire, financial commitment and a community embracement of the concept and the practice of including all in a culture-fair manner in all the community's activities. As well as honouring cultural diversity, inclusion has implications for gender and those who may have more than one 'disability'. It is interesting to note that, at school level, considerably more boys than girls are diagnosed as having dyslexia, yet, in higher education, females outnumber males among those identified as dyslexic for the first time (Singleton, 1999). The implication of this is that girls are not as readily identified as boys at school, and one can postulate that girls may not 'act out' and may be more accepting of the difficulties they face in certain subjects than boys—they may become proficient at compensating for their difficulties or expect less academically from themselves. Whatever the reason, the fact remains that in terms of equity and the desire for full and effective inclusion the abilities and needs of some girls may be overlooked (Lloyd, 1996). Additionally, Daniels et al. (2001) express concern with boys' underachievement and the conflicts surrounding the cultural messages of masculinity that affect boys. They found that gender was influential in the identity positions children adopted, and this had an effect on overall achievement. Furthermore, they suggest that certain types of competitive practices in schools may actually inhibit boys' performances. Delamont (2003) discusses the notion of the 'feminisation' of teaching and suggests that this has meant that school cultures can actually be partially blamed for the failing of boys. Clearly, therefore, gender issues are influential within the impetus to achieve full inclusion, and since boys seem to outnumber girls in relation to identified dyslexia at school this is a major concern.

Similarly with the needs of students who may have a visual or hearing impairment, with perhaps undiagnosed dyslexia. Their dyslexic needs may be overlooked because of the obvious needs that can stem from the presence of a sensory impairment. Inclusion, therefore, affects the whole community and requires not only political initiatives but social acceptance and community awareness as well.

Another example of an equity issue can be that of 'travelling children' who may in fact be incorporated into the 'learning opportunities' hypothesis (BPS, 1999a) as an explanation for dyslexic difficulties. Jordan (2001) suggests that the dropout rate is high for groups such as gypsies or travellers, and this can occur at an early age. Jordan shows that this can be as young as 9 years old. 'Travelling children', because of the nature of the oral culture, can also experience discrimination in terms of the comments made by Viall quoted earlier in this chapter on discriminatory practices in assessment. Jordan (2001) also supports this viewpoint and claims that 'reading, writing and other attainment levels are usually much lower than their peers yet in listening and talking they often outstripped their classmates' (p. 131).

PRINCIPLES OF INCLUSION

It may be suggested that inclusion is as much about principles as about practices. The principle of equity leads to the practice of meeting the needs of all, but often the principle can be enunciated without evidence of the accompanying practices. Principles should guide practice, and many of the statements and policies on inclusion have well-articulated principles. Many of these stem from the Salamanca Declaration, which followed a conference held in June 1994 when representatives of 92 governments and 25 international organisations formed the World Conference on Special Needs Education, held in Salamanca, Spain. They adopted a new Framework for Action, the guiding principle of which is that mainstream schools should accommodate all children, regardless of their physical, intellectual, social, emotional, linguistic or other conditions. Johnson (2001) quotes aspects from the Salamanca Declaration as a precursor to the principles of inclusion.

This statement essentially sets the path for an inclusionary school and implies that syndromes such as dyslexia need to be catered for within an inclusionary ethos. Yet, one needs to be realistic and appreciate that not all children will benefit from mainstream provision without some preparation on the part of the child and the teacher. This point is made by Johnson when he quotes an extract from the DfEE guidance on inclusion:

> *For most children (with SEN [special educational needs]) placement in a mainstream school leads naturally on to other forms of inclusion. For those with more complex needs, the starting point should always be the question: 'Could this child benefit from education in a mainstream setting?' For some children a mainstream placement may not be right, or not right just yet. (DfEE, 1998, p. 23)*

This, therefore, implies that full inclusion in a mainstream setting for some groups of children, although socially and politically desirable, may not be educationally appropriate at a given point in time. This means that, with support, all children can aspire to an inclusionary educational environment, but there should not be an assumption that, for all, this is the best practice at every point in their school career. There are examples in practice of children who have initially failed in an inclusionary setting, but after a period of supportive and appropriate teaching in a structured, dedicated resource for dyslexia are able to return to a mainstream setting and benefit more fully socially and educationally from the facilities on offer (Lannen, 2008, personal communication with Gavin Reid, Red Rose School, UK; Calder, 2001). Lannen cites the experience at the Red Rose School, a dedicated short-term provision for children with specific learning difficulties in St Annes-on-Sea. Most of the children admitted to the school have failed in the mainstream setting and have, not surprisingly, low levels of self-esteem as well as low attainments.

But, with dedicated facilities and the skills of staff combining to develop a caring learning environment, children progress, and many are able to be readmitted to mainstream schools. Even within this dedicated special provision it can be argued that the principles of inclusion are operating. All children within this environment have an entitlement to the full curriculum and to have their social, emotional and educational needs met. Calder (2001) describes an example of a specialised resource that attempts to respect the students' needs to be part of an inclusionary educational curriculum and environment. This resource is essentially a 'customised package' that aims to help students access the common curriculum. Because the package is customised to their specific needs it is possible for the students to achieve educationally. This type of provision centres on comprehensive assessment, full multi-professional and parental involvement, and appropriate differentiation as well as the building of self-esteem, the encouragement of learner autonomy and the development of necessary skills for learning and life.

According to Calder, this formula is based on 'an eclectic mix of strategies and approaches; pragmatism; customisation of the balance of the child's needs and her/his preferences and the reconciliation of a well-established collaborative approach with some specialised interventions to suit the (student's) needs.' It is clear that the example cited by Calder is the product of considerable planning and preparation—this, including the training of staff, is essential.

At the same time, one needs to be aware of parental choice and student wishes. Wearmouth et al. (2002) suggest that a powerful argument that is often made in favour of inclusion is that every child has the right to be educated in the neighbourhood school together with peers. They suggest, however, that a 'right' to be in a school does not necessarily mean that the resources will be available there to meet any particular learning need. Additionally, not every parent wishes his or her child to attend the neighbourhood school, and not every child wishes to go there. It is important, therefore, to consider the individual within the system, however well intended the system is in the desire to achieve equality.

AN INCLUSIVE SCHOOL

At school level Mittler (2000) suggests that the three principal aspects of inclusion are:

- All children attend their neighbourhood school in the regular classroom with appropriate support.
- All teachers accept the responsibility of ensuring that all students receive appropriate support and are given opportunities for professional development.
- Schools rethink their values, restructure their organisation, curriculum and assessment arrangements to overcome barriers to learning and participation, and cater for the full range of students in their school and in their community.

The three key principles here are: first, that all children are included; second, that staff need to accept this premise; and, third, that this can have implications for the values/attitudes of the school and the community.

HEALTHY SCHOOLS

Peacey (2001) suggests that inclusion has a much broader base than curriculum factors and relates to the health of the school. He cites the National Healthy Schools Standard, which, as well as healthy eating, emphasises the emotional well-being of students, including those with disabilities. Peacey makes an interesting point regarding pressure and the stress that normally accompanies excessive work pressure, by challenging the assumption that stress automatically follows pressure and that pressure is therefore something to avoid. He suggests that the issue is not whether we should be applying pressure, rather it is the appropriateness of the support that accompanies any perceived pressure. Of course, if the support is not forthcoming then by applying any form of pressure, such as that involved in meeting the needs of children with dyslexia, we will in fact be creating stress. Therefore, for inclusion to be successful in terms of student and teacher outcomes, support needs to be available.

SUPPORTING INCLUSION

The exact nature of that support, of course, is a matter of debate, but perhaps it also rests on the crucial question presented at the start of this chapter regarding the 'specialness' of teaching approaches for dyslexic children. Diniz and Reed (2001) put forward some questions that a school should ask in relation to support:

- What are the underlying assumptions that underpin the support system?
- Who gets support and who does not?
- What are the operational strategies in providing support?

These questions clearly need to be answered. The assumption that underlies the support system relates to the quest to achieve equality, but to do this some children will require more support and maybe a different form of support than others. This seems a perfectly reasonable assumption to make and should not run contrary to the principles of equity inherent in inclusionary practices. The question of how this support should be divided and distributed is much more contentious.

Pumfrey (2001) infers that definitions of dyslexia can be used, and misused, for resource allocation purposes. This does occur, but it is controversial as it assumes that particular cut-off points can be identified and that children's needs can be measured in terms of discrepancies and attainments. One of the contentious aspects of providing a 'special' approach for children identified with disabilities is that some form of segregation of need has to take place, and this is usually in the form and extent of the support offered. This can be divisive and can lead to unfair practices, disparity and inconsistencies in different areas of the country.

Support should not be measured in terms of 'extra hours' of tuition, funding for resources or additional personnel—certainly, these will help, but can also be wasted and squandered if they are not focusing on the real difficulty and not leading to full inclusion.

Support is as much about attitudes as about materials, recognition of the difficulty as much as resources and, above all, the need to utilise effective communication between all involved in the educational well-being of children. These factors should therefore govern operational strategies in the provision of support. Support should be available to all, not a few. The challenge for educators is to establish a means to ensure that support systems are in place so that any who require it will be able to access it without passing through many of the hoops currently in place.

Peacey (2001) contends that appropriate support in terms of materials, ideas and cultures is important as they enable people to build and grow, and this will contribute to the success of an inclusionary school. But, according to Peacey, it is also important to address issues regarding the health and well-being of the school. He suggests that it is no accident that concern for the well-being of schools (i.e., both students and staff) goes hand in hand with high attainment in schools.

STAFF SUPPORT AND TRAINING

Training to support students in an inclusive school is essential. The key question is how the training can be targeted to inclusion, since in the case of children with dyslexia there are so many different areas of training, from literacy to understanding dyslexia and, of course, the overlap between dyslexia and other syndromes. The training can be:

1. Targeted training in areas of need:
   - phonics;
   - reading fluency;
   - paired-reading;
   - spelling programmes;

- computer programmes for literacy;
- reading comprehension;
- writing skills;
- memory and study skills strategies;
- building self-esteem e.g. circle time; and
- other areas of need.

The problem with this approach is that the list is endless and the selection tends to emerge from a reaction to a crisis situation. This is a reactive programme of staff development.

2. Training to fulfil requirements of a checklist for an inclusive school. This can be proactive as the criteria or benchmark is set before training and the training is developed to fit into the criteria that have been thought out beforehand and based on the needs of staff.

In a major study in the USA, Adrienne (2002) developed a needs assessment instrument containing indicators of recommended practice for pre-school children with disabilities in inclusive natural settings. It was designed to be used by early intervention personnel to identify their needs for training. Seventy-two benchmark indicators of recommended practice were developed and these were grouped into five areas. These were:

- collaborative practices—involving the use and accessing of other agencies and links with home and the pre-school setting;
- environmental strategies—strategies used to promote learning in a range of environments;
- learning strategies—a focus on group learning experiences;
- family-centred practices—working with families in an inclusive setting;
- administrative practices—materials and organisation of learning in an inclusive setting.

This set of benchmarks was appropriate for this particular setting and for the purpose that the authors intended. What is commendable is that it is a preconceived and detailed plan using consumer wishes and needs to develop a programme of training for staff in an inclusive setting. The idea was that each staff member recorded his or her own learning plan from the benchmarks that were set.

This is similar to the use that can be made of the Index for Inclusion in the UK. For example, the following can be used as a benchmark for training:

- valuing all students and staff equally;
- increasing the participation of students in, and reducing their exclusion from, the cultures, curricula and communities of local schools;
- restructuring the cultures, policies and practices in schools so that they respond to the diversity of students in the locality;
- reducing barriers to learning and participation for all students, not only those with impairments or those who are categorised as 'having special educational needs';
- learning from attempts to overcome barriers to the access and participation of particular students to make changes for the benefit of students more widely;

- viewing the difference between students as resources to support learning, rather than as problems to be overcome;
- acknowledging the right of students to an education in their locality;
- improving schools for staff as well as for students;
- emphasising the role of schools in building community and developing values, as well as in increasing achievement;
- fostering mutually sustaining relationships between schools and communities;
- recognising that inclusion in education is one aspect of inclusion in society.

It is then possible to target specific areas of training from these benchmarks. This would ensure that the needs and the voices of staff were considered and furthermore that the training was consistent with the overall aims of the school in relation to inclusion.

STUDENT ADVOCACY

The equity principles inherent in an inclusive setting need to be extended to students. In many societies and education systems such advocacy is not evident or, if it is, it usually appears in a superficial way—perhaps through student consultation. But, there are very few examples of full and effective student advocacy. This is particularly important for students with dyslexia.

Crombie (2002c) suggests that dyslexia can be redefined in the early stages by focusing on criteria-learning and multidisciplinary early intervention. This, she argues, would make the concept less stigmatic and less 'special' in later primary and secondary schools. In fact, what Crombie is advocating is a normalisation of dyslexia. This would have important effects on the self-advocacy of students and would work only if both school and the workplace accept such normalisation.

Dyson and Skidmore (1996) also suggest that dyslexia needs to be reconceptualised so that a shift in conceptualisation can occur from that of 'diagnosis, intervention and remediation to circumvention, coping, participation and achievement' (p. 478). They argue that this reconceptualisation can contribute to the four main strands that provision should fulfil: differentiation, building self-esteem, building learner autonomy and developing skills. It might be argued that the debates over what dyslexia is, best provision, resources and intervention can leave the student less empowered.

Self-advocacy: Challenge or Threat

Developing self-advocacy for students in schools can be both challenging and threatening to staff. Essentially, self-advocacy is built on a foundation of enquiry and self-identification of students' rights and needs. This is a shift from the traditional role of teachers, which rests on the premise of transmitter of knowledge. Garner and Sandow (1995) suggest that this development of the teacher's role may be uncomfortable as self-advocacy may run contrary to the traditional models of learning often seen in schools. These models usually depend on teaching and learning, which reinforce desired behaviours and inhibit undesired behaviour as perceived by the teacher.

Wearmouth (2001) believes that, following on from the views of Garner and Sandow, it is possible that some teachers may view certain students as either undeserving of the right to self-advocacy or incapable of contributing rationally to decisions about their own lives. Self-advocacy, Wearmouth suggests, may be threatening because it can provide a challenge, and perhaps a verbal challenge, to teachers' authority as well as to the structure and organisation of the school.

Lannen (2008, personal communication) argues that the success of a school rests on the degree of exploration of student perspectives, as this helps teachers understand the motivating factors associated with a student's perception of success or failure. Wearmouth (2001) cites the work of Gersch (2001), which reports on a project that aimed to enhance the active participation of students in school through encouraging self-evaluation and advocacy. The dilemmas encountered in the project are shown in Box 15.2.

The questions listed in the box are of fundamental importance and indicate that the success of student advocacy rests on the assumptions that potential conflicts can be resolved and that attitude shifts will occur.

- How does one deal with other colleagues who might feel that children should be seen and not heard?

- Are some children not mature or capable enough to participate?

- How does one deal with parent–child dislike?

- What about scope needed for children to negotiate, try things and change their minds?

- How do adults distinguish what a child needs from what he or she prefers or wants?

Source: from Gersch (2001), quoted in Wearmouth (2001), p. 118

Box 15.2   Dilemmas encountered in a project to enhance the active participation of students

DYSLEXIA AND SELF-ADVOCACY

While self-advocacy is important for the development of independence and self-esteem in students, it is vitally important in the case of students with dyslexia. If dyslexic people are to be fully included in school and in society, they need to be able to assert their rights, identify their feelings and express their intent. These factors require practice, but often such practice is not encouraged and the scenario can occur when students with dyslexia, through sheer frustration, assert their rights in an inappropriate manner by acting out. There are many examples of this, and usually the result of such actions is expulsion or disaffection on the part of the students. Kirk and Reid (2003), in a study of people in a young offenders' institution, found that when some were identified as dyslexic their immediate reaction was one of anger, and they seized the opportunity to talk about a denial of their educational rights. Many adults with dyslexia have described how they moved from school to school in an attempt to have their needs met and to be able to express themselves in a non-threatening situation ('Genius, Criminals and Children', Channel 4, 1999; Kirk and Reid, 2001).

An example of a student talking about his rights and the need for self-advocacy was recorded for a staff development programme on literacy (Open University, 2002). This interview highlights factors associated with communication, self-advocacy and self-esteem as crucial in terms of developing positive student perceptions of dyslexia.

STAFF SUPPORT

If inclusion is to be successful and achieve its aims of equality and meeting the diverse learning needs of individuals and groups of students as indicated in the general inclusion statement discussed earlier in this chapter (QCA, 2000), then considerable emphasis will be required in the area of staff support. Giorcelli (1999) supports this view from her experience in Australia. She noted that the move towards a merged special and regular education system has changed the face of schooling and has forced all teacher preparation and development programmes to prepare teachers to accommodate students with disabilities and learning differences in regular school environments and to equip support or specialist teachers for consultation and teaming functions as well as for direct specialist teaching functions (p. 269).

This view therefore suggests that training and supporting staff for an effective role in an inclusive school rests on building and developing existing knowledge bases and ensuring that the expertise that has been accumulated among specialists over a number of years is not lost, but forms the basis of staff development for mainstream teachers. While it is accepted that the label of specialist may run counter to the concept of inclusion, the expertise that specialists can bring to mainstream schools needs to be appreciated. This expertise, however, should not be seen as a 'how to', but rather as a 'what if'. This means that specialists are not the purveyors of knowledge, but the catalysts for attitude change, confidence-building and ongoing consultation.

It seems that a balance between the effective use of specialist knowledge and the development of teacher skills to respond to student diversity is needed, without the need to retreat to the extreme positions often echoed in the categorisation and anti-categorisation argument.

KEY FACTORS

Some of the key factors in relation to successful inclusion and, in particular, in relation to children with dyslexia include: a commitment by the education authority and the school to an inclusive ideal; a realisation by staff of the widely embracing features of inclusion and the equity issues inherent in these features; awareness of the particular specific needs associated with children with dyslexia and the requirement to accommodate to these through curriculum and teaching approaches; acceptance that inclusion is more than integration in that it embraces social, cultural and community equity issues as well as educational equality; regard for the cultural differences in communities and families and acknowledgement that children with dyslexia require flexible approaches in assessment and teaching; and honouring not only children's individual rights, but also their individual differences.

POINTS FOR REFLECTION

- Reflect on how criteria such as the Index for Inclusion can be supportive of students with dyslexia.

- Consider the challenges and the tensions in achieving full inclusion for students with dyslexia.

- Consider how you might justify the idea that learners with dyslexia need a different type of approach from some other children.

- Reflect on how inclusive your own practice is. Consider how it might become more inclusive.

- Reflect on the advantages and disadvantages of inclusion for learners with dyslexia.

- Consider the importance of student advocacy. How might you facilitate this?

Chapter 16

Inclusion in Secondary Education: Accessing the Curriculum

In order to achieve an inclusive secondary school, every subject teacher has to be responsible for developing and providing suitably differentiated curriculum materials, accessible to all students. These materials should provide all students, including students with dyslexia, with the opportunity to develop their individual strengths. Thomson (2007) suggests that most secondary teachers' training and expertise are specific to their subjects and that many will not be aware of the specific needs of students with dyslexia. Thomson notes that dyslexia is often hidden, masked by a student's high ability or by distracting behaviour patterns, even deliberately concealed by teenagers who are desperate not to be 'different' from their peers. This can be a real issue in secondary school and one that can have a detrimental affect on students' performance in class and indeed their behaviour. She suggests that dyslexic students can achieve quite well in some subjects, so their 'additional needs' may not be observed for some time. This often means that the student with dyslexia will experience failure in the secondary school before their additional needs are noted.

Once the student has been identified as having additional needs on account of his or her dyslexia, the dilemma then facing teachers is how to select the most appropriate intervention. Many of the approaches suggested for children with dyslexia appear to be more appropriate for the primary than the secondary stage. Many phonics programmes, for example, are not really suitable in content for children of secondary age. This can present a difficulty and a challenge to those working in the secondary sector. Although some structured programmes have been used successfully with adolescents and indeed adults, such as Toe by Toe (Cowling and Cowling, 1998), there has also been a considerable thrust in secondary schools towards learning skills, study skills, and curriculum access through examining potential difficulties in different subject areas and through differentiation. These factors are very appropriate and can help to meet the needs of students with dyslexia. This chapter will therefore look at some of the challenges facing staff in secondary schools and how these challenges may be met, with examples of some of the responses that have been established by teachers and education authorities.

RESPONSIBILITY

It is necessary for teachers, management and policy-makers to acknowledge that, in order to meet the needs of secondary age children, it is necessary to embark on whole-school approaches and a comprehensive programme of staff development. This can help subject staff realise the responsibility they have for students with dyslexia and not pass that responsibility to learning support or other specialists. For too long now, the responsibility to deal with the challenges presented by students with dyslexia have rested with the specialist teacher. This type of model lends itself to the possibility that subject teachers may opt out of providing for students with dyslexia by acknowledging that it is a specialist area in which they have no expertise and that therefore it should be left to specialists.

One of the key issues, therefore, in secondary schools relates to the notion of responsibility. Peer and Reid (2002, 2003) suggest that the ethos of the school should be supportive and that all staff need to be made aware of the type of difficulties in different subject areas that may be displayed by students with dyslexia. It is important that departments tackle this through discussion with specialists, if available, and through differentiation. They also suggest that whole-school approaches to issues such as marking should be put in place—where children can receive a high mark for understanding and knowledge, rather than always being marked down for poor presentation skills, spelling, punctuation and grammar.

FEATURES OF SECONDARY SCHOOLS

There are some factors that are inherent in secondary schools that can present the student with dyslexia with some difficulty. It will be beneficial, therefore, if subject teachers are aware of these potential difficulties so that they can anticipate them before they do become a problem for the student. What can compound the situation, of course, is that some students have not been identified as dyslexic, even after a few years in secondary school, but have to persist and compensate for these difficulties.

One of the key points relating to the debate on dyslexia (Nicolson, 1996, 2001) is that dyslexia can be seen as being more than a difficulty with reading. Yet, many teachers, particularly those in secondary schools, have a perception of dyslexia as being a difficulty with reading. There are many other factors associated with dyslexia that can disrupt learning for the student with dyslexia, including cognitive factors such as memory, speed of processing, possibly coordination, identification of the main points in text, and organisation and study skills. These should be part of a staff development programme. Thomson and Chinn (2001) provide an overview of some of the difficulties relating to the secondary school situation for students with dyslexia.

They divide these into organisational, coordination, note-taking and project work. For example, some students with dyslexia may need additional help in finding their way around the school, even after they have been at the school for some time. There are many ways of helping with this, but providing a colour-coded map of the school may be useful.

Coordination difficulties, if present, will likely be noted in sports, although many students with dyslexia can also excel at sport; in fact, it provides an outlet for frustration and a refreshing respite from the challenges of some academic subjects.

Thomson and Chinn also suggest that difficulties in taking notes can be evident and that the pressures inherent in this type of activity can easily be avoided. Typed notes in colour with large, user-friendly fonts such as Sassoon or Comic Sans are preferable.

Students with dyslexia can also have difficulty with extraction of information, and this can be a particular feature of secondary schools where much of the work is done through independent study. Thomson and Chinn therefore suggest that it is necessary for the teacher not only to anticipate these potential difficulties but also to be aware of the positive aspects relating to dyslexia. For example, the secondary school teacher can note how students with dyslexia could apply more global thinking to a problem and, therefore, be able to develop unusual and creative solutions to some problems. Essentially, besides indicating the need to provide strategies for students, the secondary school curriculum can also be analysed and made more dyslexia friendly, at least in its presentation. Thomson and Chinn suggest that there is a need for additional high/low material that would allow information to be presented at a reading level commensurate with the student's decoding skills, but at an informative and inquiry level, in keeping with the student's actual abilities. This, of course, is a challenge, but there are a number of good examples of how this can be done with readers in primary schools, such as the high/low series (LDA) and the series of novels published by Barrington Stoke. Indeed, Barrington Stoke have also launched a special series of high/low readers on teenage fiction, which are written with the secondary school student in mind.

Thomson and Chinn (2001) suggest that, with some minor adjustments and recognition of the difficulties associated with dyslexia, teachers can make a considerable difference. They suggest the following: help being given discreetly to individuals; additional time being provided to complete a task; printed handouts being provided together with summaries of the work; students working together in small groups; grades and marking that show individual improvement so that it is meaningful for that individual student; marking that is constructive; and work judged for content not spelling. While training is important, it is also important that the subject teacher should have knowledge and understanding of dyslexia and how this knowledge can be applied to their specific subject area. The strategies mentioned above need little training, only recognition of the difficulties that may be experienced by students with dyslexia.

Some excellent work has been carried out by Renaldi (2008), who has developed a dyslexia-friendly glossary for secondary school. This is essentially a dictionary of specialist terms for the student's own use. Many of the words are represented in visual format (see Figure 16.1) and they can help to provide an explanation, an aid to memory and understanding. This type of aid can help with development of concepts and schema as well as the meaning of the term.

Figure 16.1   Visual Elements.

DIFFERENTIATION AND CURRICULAR DEVELOPMENT

Differentiation and curricular development are both challenges and responses to meeting the needs of students with dyslexia in the secondary school. Kirk (2001) suggested that the subject-based curriculum of the secondary school, in which subjects are pursued in isolation, could leave students with a highly fragmented educational experience. It is important that these experiences are contextualised and made meaningful. Differentiation can help to make subject content meaningful, and curriculum development such as developing thematic units of work can make it less fragmented. Kirk suggests that it is important that the common features that most subjects share be utilised to help the student develop concepts and automaticity.

For example, she argues that all subjects should foster the capacity to think, to communicate, to solve problems, to engage with others, and to acquire important skills of various kinds, and that failure to recognise these features can lead to a limitation of the educational experiences for students with dyslexia.

Dargie (2001) maintains that secondary teachers need to be aware of the need to structure materials provided for students with dyslexia to meet their specific needs. He suggests that long, multi-clausal sentences and the use of metaphorical language should be avoided.

There are many examples of differentiation that have been the product of consultative collaboration within school departments (Dodds, 1996). Ideally, the needs of students with dyslexia should be met in this way and the resources and guidance on differentiation can provide a framework for the development of a differentiated approach. One of the important points to consider is that, although the language and sentence structure may be different and the overall plan of the page designed in a user-friendly fashion in a differentiated text, the underlying concepts that are to be taught should be the same. Therefore, the cognitive demands and the learning outcomes should be the same in text and tasks for all learners—differentiation only implies that the means of achieving these outcomes will be different, but not the conceptual outcomes.

DIFFERENTIATION AND ASSESSMENT

Dargie (2001) suggests that subjects such as History need to be assessed in a differentiated mode for students with dyslexia. He argues that students with dyslexia need opportunities to talk extensively in the History classroom. This can allow them to engage in 'print-free' debate and utilise their strengths in oral discussion. He suggests that talking about an issue can help students develop a theme in sequence, and this can be useful for students with dyslexia. Additionally, practice in discussion can also have an impact on the student's ability to question, infer, deduce, propose and evaluate.

Differentiation, therefore, is not only about making the work and the texts more accessible for students with dyslexia but also about making the assessment more appropriate and effective. This latter aspect is often overlooked owing to the restrictions imposed by national examinations on the nature of the support that can be offered in assessment. It can be argued that traditional forms of assessment can disadvantage the dyslexic student because usually there is a discrepancy, and this may be a significant discrepancy, between their understanding of a topic and how they are able to display that understanding in written form. This may be overcome through continuous and portfolio assessment in most subject areas.

Dodds and Lumsden (2001) point out that the deficit may not lie with the student with dyslexia, but with an assessment process that is unable to accommodate to the diversity of learners. They strongly advocate, therefore, that both teaching and assessment should be differentiated and diversified. This can be achieved through use of the multiple intelligence paradigm, which avails itself of Gardner's eight intelligences (Lazear, 1999) (see Chapter 14 of this book). This includes formal speech, journal-keeping, creative writing, poetry, verbal debate and storytelling as a means of assessing the verbal–linguistic modality. While we are still a long way from a dynamic assessment paradigm that focuses on metacognitive strategies and views assessment as a teaching rather than a testing tool, such assessment is reported as being used in some classroom contexts.

Metacognitive assessment can be informative, as it can provide information about children's actual levels of understanding and can be used to develop the most effective teaching approaches for students, which can strengthen the link between assessment and teaching.

SUBJECT AREAS

Mathematics

There are some excellent texts in the area of Mathematics for dyslexic students.

These include: the excellent practical guide *Working with Dyscalculia* by Anne Henderson, Fil Came and Mel Bough (Learning Works International) and also *Maths and Dyslexics* by Anne Henderson (1998), which is a practical guide with illustrations indicating ways to tackle complex concepts; and Steve Chinn's excellent book *The Trouble with Maths* (Routledge), which also offers many practical suggestions.

Chinn (2001) suggests that learning style is an important factor in assisting the student deal more effectively with mathematical problems. Although Riding and Rayner (1998) suggest that 'a person's cognitive style is a relatively fixed aspect of learning performance . . .', Chinn urges teachers to view learning styles, certainly from the Mathematics view, with more flexibility and states that learning styles can be modified and adapted with teaching. Chinn suggests that much of the individuality associated with learning styles can be managed in a classroom setting. He does acknowledge, however, that teachers need to recognise the differences in strategies and in presentation preferences selected by different learners. Some learners, therefore, prefer oral instruction while others need visual input; some will need concrete materials while others find them unnecessary.

Chinn (2001) describes some of the learning styles that have been associated with Mathematics. The research from Bath et al. (1986) and Chinn (2000) describes cognitive style in Mathematics by describing the characteristics of 'inchworms' and grasshoppers'. The inchworm [a caterpillar of a geometrid moth] would focus on parts and detail of a mathematical problem while the grasshopper would view the problem holistically; so, while the inchworm would be orientated towards a problem-solving approach and examine the processes needed to solve the problem, the grasshopper would be answer-orientated and very likely use a flexible range of methods. The inchworm would prefer to use paper and pen while the grasshopper would rarely document the method used. Marolda and Davidson (2000) also describe the characteristics of Mathematics. They describe these as Mathematics Learning Style I and Mathematics Learning Style II. The former is highly reliant on verbal skills and prefers the how to the why, while the latter prefers perceptual stimuli and often reinterprets abstract situations visually or pictorially, preferring the why to the how. Similarly, Chinn (2004) describes two learning personalities: the qualitative style, which is characterised by sequential processing from parts to whole and is procedurally oriented; and the quantitative method, which is characterised by visual processing from whole to parts. This type of student would generally approach problems holistically, may be good at identifying patterns and is more comfortable with mathematical concepts and ideas.

Music

Difficulties Associated with Music

Ditchfield (2001) suggests that Music can present a different type of challenge to students with dyslexia from that faced in other subjects. Yet, it can be noted that some dyslexic students can be very musical and find music relaxing and a natural outlet for the difficulties experienced in literacy. The reading of music can relate to learning a new language. Students have to learn the meaning of symbols, some with only subtle differences between them, and know when and how to use them.

Visual difficulties and music

Ditchfield suggests that because reading music requires visual as well as memory skills, this can put some additional burden on the visual processing system. There is evidence that some students with dyslexia may have a degree of unstable vision relating to convergence difficulties (Stein et al., 2001), other difficulties relating to visual sensitivity (Mailley, 2001) and visual processing difficulties relating to the magnocellular visual system (Everatt, 2002; Stein et al., 2001; Eden et al., 1996). These difficulties can result in visual disturbances, especially when one considers the nature of music scores. Lines are positioned close together, and visual blur may occur as well as omissions and additions due to eye-tracking difficulties; indeed, in some cases the lines in a music score may close up and appear distorted.

Processing difficulties

Ditchfield also identifies a number of potential complexities such as the need to convert the language of music, which is essentially drawn on a vertical plane, to a horizontal plane for such instruments as keyboards. The difficulties associated with working and short-term memory have already been noted elsewhere in this book, and these difficulties can also be challenging for the student reading Music. Sight reading in Music can therefore be difficult for the student with dyslexia, as different forms of information have to be processed simultaneously. Essentially, the student has to read the score, reintepret it for his or her instrument and reproduce it in a different form in the instrument being played. There are at least three simultaneous tasks in that activity, and these will present some difficulties for the student with dyslexia and impose a burden on working memory. Additionally, these activities have to be carried out at some speed. It has already been noted that dyslexia can be associated with speed of processing difficulties, which means that the person with dyslexia may require more time to process the different aspects of the information compared with someone who

Symbol	Name	Meaning
(bass clef)	Bass clef	
(treble clef)	Treble clef	
(crochet) or	Crochet	1 beat
(quaver) or or	Quaver	½ beat
(semibreve)	Semibreve	4 beats
(minim) or	Minim	2 beats
	Middle C	
(stave lines)	Manuscript or Stave	5 lines
(notes on stave) or	NB Stems go up or down depending on where they are written on the stave	

Figure 16.2 Musical symbols.

is not dyslexic. Additionally, the student has to keep in time with other instruments in the orchestra and, perhaps, also watch the conductor.

There are, therefore, considerable simultaneous processing activities occurring when the person with dyslexia is reading Music and playing an instrument at the same time.

Coordination difficulties and music

There is also a view that there may be an overlap between dyslexia and dyspraxia (Peer, 2001; Portwood, 2000) and that the person with dyslexia may have eye–hand coordination difficulties or experience other motor difficulties that can account for difficulties in processing and conducting different tasks simultaneously (Dore and Rutherford, 2001; Fawcett and Nicolson, 2001). This can result in coordination diffi-culties and affect the performance of the student.

Strategies

It is important that effort is made to provide the student with some strategies that can help overcome these difficulties in Music. Ditchfield (2001) suggests that relatively simple procedures such as enlarging a normal size score and using coloured paper may help. Some dyslexic people find that it helps if scores are printed on tinted paper and if coloured overlays are used. The important point is that strategies should be individualised for each student—not all students with dyslexia will benefit from the use of colour. It is necessary, therefore, to adapt specific strategies to suit individual needs.

Hubicki and Miles (1991) recommend the use of coloured staves as these can help students identify and decipher particular notes and patterns. The use of computer technology will also help some students, and there are some excellent programs to help individuals learn conventional notation and other aspects of theory and practice. Ditchfield actually suggests that it is possible to dispense with traditional methods that use ink and manuscript paper when recording musical scores. Computer technology may be used as an aid to composing and in helping students learn musical notation.

The main points regarding music and dyslexia are that, first, the student with dyslexia may have considerable natural musical ability, but not be able to read or copy music scores. Second, this can be frustrating for the student, and it is important that strategies are put in place to help the student overcome these difficulties. It is important to appreciate that students with dyslexia will have other associated difficulties in addition to reading, and this can result in time management and organisational difficulties as well as speed of processing and coordination factors.

Science Subjects

General Science

Hunter (2001) argues that for many students with dyslexia science subjects are areas of the curriculum where they can excel. Usually, the need for extended writing is less than in English or social subjects, and they are able to focus on content to a greater extent without finding the writing demands overpowering. Additionally, assessment is often by multiple choice or short answers rather than lengthy essays, and this can be advantageous to the student with dyslexia. Hunter also makes the point that communication within the school is of vital importance in helping to assist the student with dyslexia in all subjects, but particularly those subjects where supports can be provided. However, it is necessary for the teacher to know which supports would be most beneficial. She argues that it is not enough to note that a student is dyslexic: the individual strengths and weaknesses need to be detailed. For example, she suggests that information should be available on whether the student can make use of a laptop or use the computer in the classroom.

Details on the student's familiarity with technology, with reading accuracy and spelling, particularly when under time pressure, should be provided to the subject teacher. It is also important to know how the student may respond to the help available. Not all students with dyslexia accept support readily, as some like to manage discreetly as best they can. It is also important for the subject teacher to recognise that self-esteem can often be affected after many years of struggling with literacy in school. As in most teaching programmes, it is important to ensure that the student will achieve some success. However slight that may seem to the teacher, it can be an enormous leap for the student. Hunter also recognises that the learning environment in Science can be quite different from that found in other classrooms, such as the English classroom, and the student may need time to adjust to this: a detailed and labelled plan of the science laboratory can be helpful.

Strategies (such as the use of Mind Maps®) can be helpful as they provide a visual plan that is meaningful for the student and can make notes more meaningful as well as helping with organisation and recall. The use of technology, Hunter argues, can be of considerable benefit in conducting and reporting on experiments in Science. Often, the student with dyslexia may not complete his or her experiment in normal class time and may not be able to access the information needed outside the laboratory.

However, by networking computers via an intranet, or Internet, system the student can finish work after class and utilise the supports available in the school. Notes can also be put on the internal school intranet, so that they can be fully accessed by students with dyslexia. This can also help to encourage and establish independent learning.

It is important that students with dyslexia enjoy some success. Hunter therefore suggests that clear, logical, short, achievable targets are necessary. It is important that students are aware of exactly what is expected from the unit of work and should also be in a position to assess whether they are on target to achieve those outcomes. Self-esteem can be enhanced in science subjects by developing students' abilities in group work and ensuring that some of the responses are provided orally. Hunter argues that if this is done, the problems often experienced in recording and accessing information can be overshadowed by the successes experienced by the student in Science.

Biology

Howlett (2001) argues that, compared with other subjects, Biology involves a considerable amount of factual detail. Additionally, there are many technical words that are rarely used in everyday speech. In this subject, therefore, students with dyslexia will come across new words and combinations of letter and sounds that may still have Latin or Greek spellings—some of these words may also look and sound similar, but yet have entirely different meanings. She also suggests that many of the words and concepts are abstract, such as 'homeostasis', 'ecosystem' and 'respiration', and that it is important that the student has a clear idea of these abstract words, has developed a visual representation of them and has an accurate schema. For example, when remembering particular parts of plants or animals most of the words will be new, but the function of the words can apply across most species of plants and animals. It is therefore important, for example, that the student has understood the concept of respiration in both plants and animals, as this can help in the understanding of the concept of breathing. It may be necessary to highlight this transfer of learning to students with dyslexia, as they may not note this without assistance. A great deal of the work in science subjects such as Biology involves practical experiments and assignments based on practical work. There are certain skills associated with practical work, such as understanding the instructions, that in fact may be quite complex: organising the experiment, ensuring that all the information and components are at hand and reporting on the experiment in a clear manner. Howlett (2001) provides a summary of the types of difficulty that dyslexic students may experience in Biology. These include remembering and recalling 'names' accurately (both in text and labelling of diagrams), spelling of technical words, learning a considerable quantity of factual information, understanding abstract concepts, remembering and following instructions accurately in practical work and recording observations accurately.

Diagrams

Thomson (2007) suggests that many students with dyslexia have poor fine motor skills and handwriting is slow, laboured and non-automatic, lacking fluency. They may be unable to write continuously without frequent rests. There may be unusual spatial organisation of the page with words widely spaced or tightly squashed together with margins ignored and writing off the line.

It is therefore worthwhile spending some time on diagram construction and presentation. Diagrams are important for students with dyslexia, and they are also an important part of science and particularly Biology. Howlett (2001) suggests that it is useful to spend a little time on the mechanics of producing diagrams, as this will have long-term benefits and be helpful in other subjects, such as Geography. She suggests that before making a detailed diagram it is preferable to make a plan that will serve as a rough draft. Other factors that should be considered include deciding how much of the page is to be used, as often the drawing may extend to a larger area than first thought, and using colour purposefully, which means only using it if it will help the student understand the diagram better. It is important, therefore, to have a consistent colour key. Additionally, since it is acknowledged that dyslexia can be associated with word-finding and word retrieval, it is important that labels are used clearly and accurately—the use of labels together with a diagram, if clearly presented, can help to reinforce the organisation, understanding and retrieval of information.

Practical tasks such as measuring and cutting out can be a source of difficulty for students with dyslexia in subject classes. Some students may have motor-planning problems affecting the ability to predict or follow a series of steps in the right order; others have fine/gross motor problems affecting ability to manipulate objects and write, affecting the completion of practical tasks—they may have a strange/awkward way of holding tools and equipment. In some practical activities it is a good idea to pair them with a buddy and they can complete the activities together. Thomson suggests that they often have little or no understanding of scale, experience confusion about appropriate measures for different tasks and are unable to complete practical activities involving direction.

Biology can have a number of practical activities that can confuse the learner with dyslexia but it can also lend itself to multi-sensory learning using the tactile and kinaesthetic modalities. This in fact applies to all subjects and many of the barriers experienced by students with dyslexia can be overcome if activities are presented in a multi-sensory manner.

Physics

It can be argued that much of the subject content of secondary school subjects is determined by examination considerations. This can make it extremely difficult for the class teacher. At the same time, there are many examples of good practice using the principles of differentiation and acknowledging the nature of the difficulties that can be experienced by students with dyslexia (Brice, 2001; Dodds and Lumsden, 2001). One example of this in relation to Physics has been described by Holmes (2001). Physics is a subject that can present some difficulties to dyslexic students because of the abstract nature of its concepts and sequential logic as well as the memorising of formulae, but it is also one of the subjects in which they can do well because, like some of the other science subjects, it may involve less reading than some of the social science subjects. Holmes suggests a top-down approach that provides a whole-school awareness of dyslexia and allows subject teachers to reflect on the implications of providing for dyslexic students in their own subject. Other factors that Holmes considers include: building a bank of support materials that can become a whole-school resource and recognising the implications of secondary difficulties that can affect a student's performance in subjects such as Physics. There is also scope for cross-curricular transfer, such as the relationship between Mathematics and Physics, which could mean that the student's difficulties in Physics are a consequence of Mathematics difficulties. This emphasises the need for a whole-school approach to dealing with the needs of students with dyslexia.

English

Thomson (2006) developed an ambitious yet very successful project on meeting the needs of learners with dyslexia in the secondary school (Thomson, 2006). This project comprises of a series of booklets for each of the subject areas in the secondary school as well as some general points underpinning assessment and support. Some of the suggestions made for specific subjects can in fact be utilised in most of the other subject areas as they represent dyslexia-appropriate approaches.

For example, in relation to English the following can be observed and implemented in the classroom:

- Issue writing guidelines and paragraph headings to support the structure of extended writing.
- Provide a framework for extended writing and model different types of subject writing.
- Use Mind Mapping®, bullet points etc. to help with planning and structure.
- Encourage students to work in note form, concentrating on key words or terms.
- Provide ICT for written work and make sure that the editing features and spellchecker are used.
- Allow rests when extended writing is required.
- Permit alternatives to extended writing, e.g., charts, diagrams, pictorial representations.
- Permit the use of tape/digital recorders to be saved as voice files or transcribed later.
- Highlight errors in writing and suggest possible corrections/amendments for redrafting (from Thomson, 2006, www.dyslexiascotland.org.uk)

An interesting observation is that despite the general perception that students with dyslexia would find English challenging and would try to avoid that subject, when given a choice, this does not in fact appear to be the case. There is a considerable percentage of students with dyslexia who undertake English as the main topic in further and higher education courses. Although the 'grammar' aspects of English can be challenging for dyslexic students, the critical thinking associated with English literature is often stimulating. Turner (2001) suggests that many dyslexic students derive great enjoyment from studying literary works, and accessing age- and ability-appropriate literature. She suggests, however, that this still needs careful handling, since many students with dyslexia will very likely not have much background reading to refer to, and this can account for gaps in knowledge that make it extremely important for teachers to explain all concepts to them. Turner also emphasises that teaching the language of literature is important. She believes that all students in a class need to be given vocabulary support, since poetry, novels and prose can be tackled with more ease when students have this background knowledge about literature.

Many literature classics are now available in video and audio, and this can help the student develop a picture of the scene and the situational context of the novel or play. Turner rightly suggests that using video or audio materials should not be considered a 'short cut'. They are, in fact, a real alternative and can be more in keeping with the student's learning style than reading the novel, when first introduced to the theme. It may be better to commence any theme with background discussion to develop ideas and concepts and then present the theme for the novel in visual or drama form, before the student actually commences to read the book. Turner suggests that strategies such as pointing out underlying themes, encouraging the use of Mind Maps® to plan an overview and observing the connections between characters and the main ideas of the novel are support techniques that the English teacher can use.

One of the difficulties, apart from grammar and spelling, that may be experienced by students with dyslexia is the construction and structuring of written work. They may have numerous ideas, but lack of structure can mean that some key points may be omitted or that much redundant information will be included. Additionally, the argument may be jumbled and confusing. Clearly, the student with dyslexia may benefit from some assistance in essay writing. Although this may come under more general study skills, strategies such as those described below can be contextualised for essay-writing and, indeed, for a specific essay.

Essay and Report-writing

Thomson, in her significant contribution to supporting students in secondary school, suggests the following additional support strategies that can be used to assist students with dyslexia:

- Provide printed or electronic notes in advance.
- Identify a partner whose notes can be photocopied.
- Have copying done as soon as possible after a lesson.
- Allow the use of a recorder (digital or tape) so that dictated notes are accurately taken.
- When dictating, spell out any technical or difficult words for all students.

- Provide summaries of chapters of books to support students' note-taking skills.
- Provide a framework for note taking to help dyslexic students organise their own notes.
- Teach the use of bullet points and summaries for note taking.
- Allow the use of Mind Maps®, charts and diagrams for note taking.

Stages of Report-writing

Some stages that may be useful to consider in report writing are outlined in the following subsections.

Preparation

This can involve the following examination of the question or topic, and the student can ask himself or herself the following questions:

- What does the question mean?
- What do you already know about the topic?
- What do you still have to find out?
- At this initial stage what do you think is the answer to the question?
- What kind of detail do you think you may need to support your answer?

Information

- What sort of information do you need?
- Where will you find it?
- What are the key points?
- How did you identify the key points?
- Are there any other points you may wish to consider?
- Keep a note of where you obtained information you are using—this includes references and quotes.
- Organise your notes into headings and subheadings, or use a Mind Map® strategy.

Constructing

- Write a draft essay plan identifying the purpose of each section or paragraph.
- Identify the key points that you will use in the introduction—these should be general points, but you need to write beside them the specific detailed points that will form the main part of your essay.
- Check that you have interpreted the question accurately—often there may be more than one way to interpret a question.
- From the general key points in your introduction, note down the specific points and examples you will use to support your points.
- Try to ensure you have a coherently developed argument.

- The conclusion should provide a firm answer to the question. Try to avoid flowery and elaborate language in your conclusion—this takes time and is often unnecessary as it may not add anything to your answer.
- Your conclusion should relate to your introduction.

Writing

- Use short sentences when constructing arguments and ensure that you have used evidence to support your assertions.
- Try to ensure that each paragraph has a specific focus, is self-contained and does not repeat what you have already said.
- Proof-read for meaning first and then, very importantly, for grammar and spelling.

Reviewing

- Have you identified the key points and the appropriate sub-points that fit into these key points?
- Write them out in note form and check them against the key points in your essay.
- Have you included the implications of your key points in your essay?
- Check your presentation and then submit it.

While the above framework can be useful, it is important that it is contextualised for the subject and topic that is being studied. This means that the teacher can give examples at each of the main stages on what is meant and how it may relate to the topic.

Additional Language Learning

Schneider (2009) suggests that two main factors make foreign language learning difficult for individuals with dyslexia. The first is the nature of the disability itself; the second is the way that foreign languages are traditionally taught in public schools and at universities. She argues that the instructional practices commonly used to teach foreign languages in schools can be put forward as a reason why students with dyslexia do not succeed in foreign languages. Methods of teaching, she suggests, are insensitive to dyslexic students' needs for explicit, direct and metacognitive instruction because they are based on theoretical concepts that do not consider significantly struggling learners. Foreign language teaching and research are still largely based on ideal foreign language learners who possess a natural *language acquisition device* and a *universal grammar* that allow them to succeed in learning other languages without great difficulties. This is not the case for students with dyslexia and Schneider argues that the problem is that current foreign language teacher education programmes do not prepare teachers adequately to meet the needs of dyslexic students.

It has also been suggested by Crombie and McColl (2001) that children with dyslexic difficulties may find modern languages quite challenging. There are a number of reasons for this: the need to learn new vocabulary; the new grammatical structure to be learnt; the tendency for the teaching of foreign languages to be verbal, auditory and usually at a pace that is too fast for the student with dyslexia to assimilate.

Crombie and McColl (2001) make some suggestions that can help make modern languages more dyslexia-friendly:

- Use charts and diagrams to highlight the bigger picture, add mime and gesture to words.
- Add pictures to text.
- Use colour to highlight gender and accents.
- Label diagrams and charts.
- Use games to consolidate vocabulary, make packs of pocket-size cards, use different colours for different purposes.
- Combine listening and reading by providing text and tape.
- Use Mind Maps® and spidergrams.
- Allow the student to produce own tape.
- Present in small amounts, using a variety of means, giving frequent opportunities for repetition and revision.
- Provide an interest in the country concerned and show films, etc.
- Rules and other information about the language should be provided in written form for further study and future reference.

In terms of intervention for additional language learning Schneider suggests that instruction should follow eight principles. These are:

1. Multi-sensory—students use all learning channels simultaneously, particularly the kinaesthetic–tactile one.
2. Structured—the teacher breaks content down into small steps and sequences tasks carefully from less to more complex to assure mastery.
3. Metacognitive—the teacher models for students how and why certain procedures/ rules are necessary for success in foreign language reading, writing, spelling, pronunciation and listening.
4. Repetitive—students engage in multiple forms of multi-sensory structured practice because understanding a concept guarantees the ability to apply language concepts or study/test-taking strategies correctly.
5. Explicit—the teacher models concretely how to use certain language concepts to help the foreign language student understand the mechanisms that characterise appropriate use in the new language.
6. Analytic–synthetic—through explicit instruction and practice, students who learn an alphabet language become versed in breaking words, syllables, sentences, and paragraphs apart to be able to analyse and understand their components. Students also learn how to synthesise these parts back together into meaningful whole units.
7. Diagnostic—while students practise new language concepts, the teacher informally assesses the degree of understanding through dynamic assessment procedures.

8. Prescriptive—the teacher adapts instructional procedures according to the diagnostic findings both during remaining class time and in preparation for subsequent lessons (adapted from Schneider, 2009).

Schneider (2009) also suggests that when students, their parents and teachers, as well as the administration, collaborate effectively, individuals with dyslexia receive a realistic opportunity to succeed in another language and learn about multicultural issues. This is a significant message as the responsibility for ensuring that the full curriculum is accessible for students with dyslexia is as much a management responsibility as a teacher one. Collaboration and cooperation with a focus on sharing is an important factor that can contribute to successful outcomes in the learning of additional languages.

Social Subjects

Social subjects such as History, Geography and Modern Studies usually involve a considerable amount of reading and writing. This can be challenging for students with dyslexia, and can also be challenging for the teacher to present the subject in an accessible manner. Dargie (2001) suggests that discussion is a good reinforcing vehicle, and that this should always be used as a follow-up to the study of history texts. He provides examples of discussion and problem-solving activities on, for example, the Act of Union in 1707 and shows how this can relate to current developments in parliament and to topics and themes on devolution that have universal currency. The key point is that subjects such as History can be broadened and incorporate current events that can make it more meaningful for the student. Learners with dyslexia will understand more fully if the information is relevant and meaningful. This is the key to accessing subjects such as History for students with dyslexia. This would also mean that they would not need to read every word in a text as they would be able to utilise contextual cues. This would certainly be the case if the student had a sound background in the topic and contextual knowledge and understanding of the principal ideas and concepts relating to that historical period. This can also be achieved through group discussion as well as visually through films and videos. In relation to Geography, Williams and Lewis (2001) emphasise the importance of differentiation. They suggest that differentiation does not mean developing worksheets with reduced or simplified content. To embark on differentiation effectively, teachers need to undertake considerable preparatory work. They need to consider factors such as readability levels, how resources will be designed, how diagrams will be labelled, the use of colour, the provision of printed materials such as notes and maps to prevent tracing and excessive note-taking as well as the provision of keywords and specialised vocabulary. Williams and Lewis also suggest that differentiation by task should be considered. This will provide the student with dyslexia with a choice of tasks from which to select. They also emphasise that the outcome of the learning experience and student assessment can be differentiated without diluting the quality of the task or assessment procedure. This would also mean that a range of assessment strategies need to be considered in order that dyslexic students can demonstrate their knowledge and understanding of the subject. Dodds (1996), using Modern

Studies as an example, shows how worksheets can be created using visual examples to support the text and the tasks, together with the use of appropriate language that can be easily understood by the student. The higher-order thinking and problem-solving skills, however, are the same for all students. It is important that accessibility does not compromise the need to develop critical thinking in social subjects.

MULTIPLE INTELLIGENCES IN SECONDARY SCHOOLS

Multiple intelligences were discussed in the previous chapter and they can have particular applicability for the secondary school. Subjects such as History and Geography can involve the eight intelligences quite readily. Lazear (1999) highlights how they can be used not only in individual subjects but also across the whole curriculum to ensure metacognitive transfer. One example of this can be the use of visual imagery combined with music—practice at this can help the student develop visual abilities, and, if she or he were to verbalise them, they can have a spin-off effect on language and storytelling. He also indicates how the reverse can apply when students try to impose appropriate sound into a story they have read. Similarly, bodily–kinaesthetic intelligence can be applied in all subjects: in History a dramatic account of a historical incident can help develop kinaesthetic–bodily intelligence, as can learning particular folk dances from different cultures or a different historical period. Bodily–kinaesthetic intelligence is one modality that is often overlooked in class subjects because it usually involves movement in class and perhaps some disruption. This, however, can be brought into all subjects: Science, in terms of measurement or practical activities, and English, in relation to drama and performing plays. Role-playing activities that can be used in all subjects can also capitalise on most of the eight intelligences. Not only does a multiple intelligence framework ensure that students have opportunities to develop their skills as well as work on their weaknesses, but multiple intelligence approaches are usually multi-sensory by nature as well. This means that all modalities will be used either in learning or in assessment, and this is beneficial for students with dyslexia.

Most subjects, such as Modern Foreign Languages, English, Art and Drama, which may be challenging in terms of the amount of reading students need to complete, can lend themselves to kinaesthetic approaches by focusing on experiential learning activities. This, therefore, is the very essence of multiple intelligence—to ensure access to all components of the curriculum and ensure that all the student's modalities are being utilised. This will also help the student become familiar with his or her preferred choice of learning, and therefore go some way towards promoting self-sufficiency in learning.

PHYSICAL EDUCATION

Physical education is a subject that can have applicability to a multiple intelligence framework as well as implications for other areas of learning across the curriculum. It is a subject that can be crucial in the metacognitive aspects of transferring learning. Some students with dyslexia can have coordination difficulties, and these should be known to the physical education (PE) specialist. This, however, should not deter the student from fully participating in the PE curriculum. Exercise and sport can be beneficial not only in acting as a stress reducer, but also may have a spin-off to other skills such as reading. There have been a number of different types of exercise programmes established for students with dyslexia, and although these may have a specific rationale (Dore and Rutherford, 2001; Longdon, 2001), they do utilise physical factors for the cognitive development of the individual. Specific exercises have also been developed as part of PE programmes involving specially tailored programmes for children with specific difficulties (Portwood, 2001; McIntyre, 2001; Russell, 1988) and relaxation exercises such as yoga. The important point is that PE teachers should be aware of the important role they can play in dealing with the difficulties associated with dyslexia and the overlap between the benefits of an exercise programme and the development of skills such as reading.

At the same time, some students with dyslexia can in fact excel at sport and PE. This is important, as it may be the only component of the curriculum in which they can achieve any success. If this is the case, then it may well have a positive spin-off to other curricular areas. The relationship between physical activity and learning should therefore not be overlooked, and this can have implications for teacher training and staff development in general.

STAFF DEVELOPMENT

In order to achieve a whole-school awareness of dyslexia and the needs of students with dyslexia, it is crucial that staff development is given a high priority. Ideally, this should be a whole-staff initiative and not one from which individual teachers can opt out. Although different subject teachers may have different needs relating to dyslexia, it is important that some of the general principles are discussed and that this is followed up with activities involving individual subject areas.

Thomson (2006) suggests that staff should be aware of the following points:

- Always give 'thinking time' to allow dyslexic students to process input and construct an appropriate response.
- Set up a gesture code so that dyslexic students know when they will be called upon to answer.
- Ask students to repeat aloud the question you have just asked.
- Encourage the use of physical prompts, e.g., listing items using fingers.
- Provide an attention focus for listening that is directly relevant to lesson content.
- Always summarise any discourse and use questioning to support dyslexic students to fill gaps.

C. Palmer (2001) reports on developments in training and provision for secondary students with dyslexia in Somerset. The system developed in Somerset involves monitoring and evaluating schools' special educational needs provision through a process called 'A Framework for Supported Self-Review' that deals with systems and provision for special educational needs in mainstream schools. This initiative commenced in September 2000 and involves a rolling programme of specialist training for teachers, ongoing professional development, Special Educational Needs Coordinator (SENCO) training and a certificate course—Special Needs in Mainstream Schools. Palmer also reports on the local education authority's policy document, 'Specific Learning Difficulties—Policy Document: Policy into Practice'. There are a number of authority- and county-wide initiatives in the UK on dyslexia. Many describe the development and implementation of training programmes for specialist and mainstream teachers (Reid, 1998, 2001a).

CHALLENGES: KEY AREAS

Peer and Reid (2002) suggest some key areas that can present a challenge to teachers in their efforts to provide effectively for students with dyslexia in the secondary school:

- the subject content;
- subject delivery;
- assessment;
- cross-curricular aspects;
- metacognitive factors;
- learning styles/multiple intelligences; and
- initial teacher education and staff development.

Thomson (2002) reported on these developments by asserting that the difficulties experienced by students with dyslexia at secondary school were rooted in the curriculum.

She suggests that the need to inform subject teachers of a range of aspects on dyslexia, such as the characteristics, the skills often possessed by students with dyslexia and the difficulties which can be associated with dyslexia, was paramount.

Thomson advocates a curriculum perspective in dealing with dyslexia and views the curriculum as the vehicle for change and support. She relates this to the development of 'coordinated support plans' that have been developed to help ensure that all students are 'included' and that all subject teachers are aware of how to support students with dyslexia in the classroom. She further advocates that subject teachers should be aware of issues relating to dyslexia in the whole-school assessment process, in curriculum-planning and in the selection and the appropriate use of resources. As Kirk (2001) points out, however, cross-curricular staff development requires a considerable investment in time, particularly from the learning support staff, and, additionally, it may be necessary to convince senior management of the need for such initiatives.

It is important that these issues are responded to in order that the student with dyslexia can achieve some success in different subject areas. Some of the implications of these factors relating to assessment, teaching and learning are discussed elsewhere in this book, but this chapter has presented an overview of how these challenges and responses to them may help students with dyslexia to access the full curriculum. Many subject areas of the curriculum appear to be content-driven. The 'content' therefore dominates the teaching methods and the pace of learning, and this can be detrimental to the potential success of students with dyslexia. It might even be argued that subject-teaching in the secondary school is dominated by examinations, and this would also dictate the pace of learning. This means that aspects such as learning styles and the cognitive and metacognitive aspects of learning are dwarfed by the need to absorb vast quantities of information for examinations. It is crucial, therefore, that subject teachers have an accurate learning profile of the student as this can at least make the subject teacher aware of the individual student's particular strengths and weakness. Often, when the pace of learning is dominated by examinations the individual's specific needs can be overlooked.

POINTS FOR REFLECTION

- Reflect on the notion of dyslexia as a hidden disability and how this may be dealt with in the secondary school.

- Consider what you feel represent the key elements in differentiation. What factors would you note when differentiating materials for students with dyslexia?

- Consider the need to ensure that the student with dyslexia has full access to each subject of the curriculum. Reflect on the common principles that may be applied to all subjects and those that are subject specific.

- Reflect on the challenges that can be evident in trying to ensure that all school subjects are accessible for students with dyslexia.

Chapter 17

Inclusion: Further and Higher Education and the Workplace

One of the major advances to benefit people with dyslexia in recent years has been the increased access to further and higher education. All universities and colleges in the UK and in many other countries now have to provide for the needs of students with dyslexia. The Disability Discrimination Act (1995) in the UK has helped to prevent discriminatory practices in the workplace and in education. At universities support is now available for students with dyslexia through the Special Educational Needs Disability Act (SENDA) (part iv of the DDA (DfES, 2001)). Similarly, in the USA, Canada, New Zealand and Australia there are many examples of good practices, particularly in providing support for students with dyslexia.

In the UK the Dyslexia in Higher Education working party report (Singleton, 1999) provided clear guidelines on assessment and support for students with dyslexia as well as guidelines for disability staff and course tutors. Subsequently, a number of informative texts have been available, aimed directly at dyslexia in adults (Reid and Kirk, 2001; Bartlett and Moody, 2000; Morgan and Klein, 2000; McLoughlin et al., 2002; Jamieson and Morgan, 2008). In addition, a number of reports have been commissioned and published—such as the Moser report on adult literacy (Moser, 2000), the Adult Dyslexia for Employment, Practice and Training (ADEPT) report on best practice in assessment and support for adults with dyslexia focusing particularly on the unemployed (Reid et al., 1999) and The BDA Employers Guide (British Dyslexia Association, 2005).

In the USA, legislation such as the Americans with Disabilities Act (1994) can also provide a framework and opportunities for employees with dyslexia to resolve work disputes, although Gerber (1997) suggests that the ongoing reference to case law is still a powerful influence.

This chapter will deal with some of these issues, particularly in relation to the identification of students with dyslexia, accessibility of further and higher education for dyslexic students, the support that can be provided to help ensure the successful completion of the course of study and some suggestions that may be useful for students themselves. Additionally, this chapter will also focus on the needs of people in employment as well as employers in relation to dyslexia. These may also provide pointers to the development of similar practices in other countries.

FURTHER AND HIGHER EDUCATION

Identification and Assessment

One interesting point to note is the high percentage of students with dyslexia identified for the first time after entering university. In a UK study of over 100 institutions, 43% of the total dyslexic student population were diagnosed as 'dyslexic' after admission to university (Singleton, 1999). There are likely a number of reasons for this, but in the course of time this number should be reduced as more students are identified at school level. Young people with dyslexia can be quite adept at developing coping strategies to compensate for their difficulties.

This may be satisfactory at school, especially as there is usually an imposed structure, and even if they have not been diagnosed as dyslexic there is still very often support available to assist them. At university or college, however, the picture can be quite different. Very often students have to structure and organise their own work, and usually time limits are imposed in submitting completed work. It is this type of situation that can be daunting for the undiagnosed dyslexic person, and this usually prompts them to seek some help, perhaps for the first time in their educational career.

Assessment: the Context

An assessment should not be carried out in isolation. The assessment needs to be contextualised for the course of study and for the needs of the student. The demands and the skills needed for different courses can vary considerably.

The demands of training in nurse-training will be quite different from those experienced in some science, engineering or teacher-training courses. Additionally, the person conducting the assessment needs to know about some of the other factors that may influence the outcome of the assessment and the student's performance in the course. Factors such as English being a second language and factors relating to the student's school and life experiences may also influence course performances. It is also important to recognise that dyslexia is about how reading difficulties affect individuals and how this can contribute to low self-esteem and other difficulties. It is for this reason that constructive feedback following an assessment is beneficial for the student. Such feedback can make a considerable difference to the self-esteem of the student, if handled sensitively.

Assessment: the Process

There are several procedures that can be used by colleges and universities to identify students. In practice, in the UK this is usually by referral to an educational psychologist who has experience of assessing dyslexia in adults. This latter point is very important because not all educational psychologists have experience of assessing for dyslexia and fewer have experience with adults. An examination of the UK Directory of Chartered Psychologists (BPS, 1999b) shows that only 27% of those providing educational psychology services indicated that they can perform dyslexia assessments on adults (Reid et al., 1999).

Since 2005 (DfES report, 2005) a system has been developed indicating that specialist teachers with approved qualifications (usually Associate Member of the British Dyslexia Association (AMBDA)) in Dyslexia and/or specific learning difficulties are eligible to apply to be an assessor and from September 2007 these specialist teacher-assessors were required to obtain a practising certificate. The certificate is issued for a set period and renewable on evidence of a continuous professional development (CPD) record. This system complements the assessments undertaken by educational psychologists who still seem to be in demand as key personnel in the assessment process at universities.

Additionally, many universities and colleges in the UK have implemented screening procedures before undertaking a full psychological assessment. Indeed, some of these screening procedures are quite sophisticated, and tests such as the Dyslexia Adult Screening Test (DAST) can provide much of the information needed for a diagnostic evaluation of the student's needs.

Moody (2009) argues that when it comes to literacy, there is an even greater problem about which 'bits' of literacy to assess. The following need to be included:

- Reading single words
- Spelling
- Reading comprehension
- Reading speed

Traditionally, she argues that the comparison has been made between IQ and the level of single-word reading and spelling. But she maintains this can be misleading. An intellectually able dyslexic person who has had a reasonably good education may have compensated well enough for his difficulties to score well on simple tests of basic reading and spelling. By contrast, he/she may score badly on tests of higher-level literacy skills, such as silent reading comprehension and structuring written work; and the reading and writing speeds may be below average. Moody also suggests that some assessors have decided to take flight altogether from a comparison of IQ with literacy and base a diagnosis of dyslexia simply on literacy skills, maintaining that if these are below average a person is dyslexic irrespective of the level of their overall intellectual ability. There are dangers in this approach as it is important to identify if there is any discrepancy between reasoning skills and processing skills and this can best be achieved with reference to an IQ test. A customized checklists and screening procedures therefore can be used only as a starting point.

In addition to customised checklists and screening procedures, the Dyslexia Adult Screening Test (Fawcett and Nicolson, 1997) and other computer screening procedures for dyslexia such as Lucid Adult Dyslexia Screening (LADS; Singleton et al., 2002) are also available. Computer-based assessment can be the first line in identification; although it may not give a definitive diagnosis, it can be useful as an initial screening. It is feasible that students can access computer-screening from a central database within the college or university (Kirk, 2002). Additionally, checklists can be used. Computer-screening or a checklist will provide the student with feedback that may prompt him or her to make an appointment with the university support services to discuss further assessment. As mentioned above, this could be in the form of a psychological assessment or through the use of diagnostic screening procedures, such as DAST (Fawcett and Nicolson, 1998), as well as attainment tests. Additionally, a structured interview with the student is extremely valuable. Jamieson and Morgan (2008) provide an example of a student questionnaire that can glean a considerable amount of background information on the student. This includes:

- information on previous assessments,
- medical history and early development,
- speech and language development,
- education and current difficulties.

By far the most important aspect is the section on current difficulties and this aspect should be structured for the student to ensure that they are able to articulate their current difficulties accurately. This might include areas such as:

- Remembering timetable
- Essay deadlines
- Researching and using library facilities
- Planning for tutorials
- Summarising information
- Writing lecture notes
- Understanding what questions are really asking
- Planning and organisation
- Spelling and handwriting.

Factors to Consider

Ideally, a structured system of identification and assessment should be developed and contexualised for each college or university.
   This could include:

- initial screening and interview;
- cognitive assessment;
- diagnostic assessment;
- workplace and course needs assessment;
- implications for the course, student and/or workplace;
- recommendations for support;
- user-friendly report, which should have a clear summary attached.

There are a number of factors that need to be considered in an assessment and in the provision of support and feedback to the student. One of those factors involves organisational aspects, including how notes and information are organised, the organisation of work diary and timetable, and an examination revision programme. These aspects can often present difficulties for students with dyslexia and can also be very time-consuming and, indeed, time-wasting. Other factors that are important include cognitive aspects such as memory and processing speed. These aspects have considerable implications for study and for examinations and would need to be considered in the support that is offered to the student. Metacognitive aspects that relate to the efficiency of learning, including transferring learning to new situations, are important for effective learning. Study skills, therefore, are important and some time needs to be spent with the student in exploring the most effective methods of studying for that particular student. Often, studying is very individual and strategies can vary depending on the student and, indeed, the nature of the course.

In general, students with dyslexia will display some difficulties in literacy. This may not be in reading accuracy, but very likely in speed of reading. Indeed, they may show a reluctance to read in general, and 'weighty' textbooks can be daunting.

However, if the reading is structured this can make a considerable difference to the student's motivation to read. It should, however, be considered that the student will require additional time to complete some reading tasks.

Kirk and Reid (2003) identified some of the difficulties associated with dyslexia in students—these can be used as a guide in the development of a checklist of study factors for students in further and higher education:

- difficulties in reading accuracy;
- speed-of-reading difficulties;
- persistent spelling errors;
- difficulties with grammatical structure;
- sequencing difficulties in words and in ideas;
- need to reread text;
- difficulties planning and organising written work;
- difficulty memorising facts;
- difficulty memorising formulae;
- taking notes in lectures;
- planning essays;
- study skills;
- transferring learning from one situation to another;
- noting inferences in texts;
- written examinations, particularly if timed;
- difficulty with technical words;
- difficulty identifying main points;
- short attention span;
- difficulty with proof-reading;
- unable to read aloud;
- poor sequencing, history, events, ordering information.

Assessment: the Effect

One of the objectives of conducting an assessment is to identify whether or not the student has dyslexia. This is important in terms of securing the additional allowances to which students with dyslexia are entitled, such as extra time for examinations.

Additionally, however, an assessment needs to provide students with some specific strategies that may be appropriate in relation to their profile and the needs of their course.

Feedback

It is also important to spend some time after the assessment ensuring that the student is clear on the results and the implications of the assessment. It can be quite daunting for students to be assessed for a 'disability', and the results may come as a surprise to some students. Often, however, many students who are diagnosed as dyslexic for the first time at university usually, though not always, have a suspicion that they have dyslexic difficulties. Nevertheless, it is still important to provide full and informative feedback, which may well take the form of a counselling session. It is important that feedback should be clear and jargon-free. It may be necessary at this point to provide the student with encouragement; they may wish to meet other students with dyslexia, perhaps in the form of a study skills group. It is important also to emphasise that dyslexia is simply a difference in how information is processed and that in some situations it may be a disability, but that the disability aspect does not need to take prominence.

There are many encouraging accounts from students with dyslexia who are now employed in a range of occupations, and there are many examples of successes (Reid and Kirk, 2001). For example, Reid and Kirk record how one student, who still experienced anxiety over his studies, commented on the positive aspects of tutorials.

Indicating that he likely over-prepared for tutorials and read too much, he found that his experiences in life and in coming to terms with his dyslexia helped him in tutorials. He felt this gave him a balanced perspective on some issues. At the same time, it is important to learn from unfortunate experiences endured by some students with dyslexia. Reid and Kirk (2001) report on one student, Vanessa, who 'received a computer, but little else' (pp. 168–170). She indicated that she was not shown how to use it, and indeed the computer that she received was not the most appropriate for the course. To make matters worse, she did not actually receive the computer until the start of her second year. The message here is the need to ensure that there is effective communication and follow-up after the assessment. The student needs to be in open and accessible contact with those who can provide advice and support throughout the whole period of the student's studies, not just immediately after the assessment. It is also important that dyslexia does not represent being given a computer—this can be an easy option and, while a computer can be helpful in most instances, it is important that the other needs of the student, including emotional needs, are not forgotten. Additionally, the student needs to have the opportunity to speak with a member of the computer staff who can advise on the most appropriate computer and software. Jamieson and Morgan (2008) quote a student who remarks that a mixture of anger and relief was felt when a diagnosis of dyslexia was given. This can be quite common and it is important to provide appropriate, perhaps informal counselling to students who experience these emotions.

Experience of Further and Higher Education

For some students, entry into further and higher education can present a challenge to their long-standing perception of themselves (McLoughlin and Leather, 2009). As Kirkland (2009) points out, often students in higher education do not ask for help until it is too late. Many are not accustomed to requesting help as it has often been provided for them at school and others can be intimidated by 'academia', and their self-esteem can be adversely affected. It is important, therefore, that course tutors and all teaching staff are familiar with dyslexia and how dyslexia may affect a person's self-esteem. This is important when the tutor is giving feedback to students following an assignment, as often the student with dyslexia has very likely spent more time than others in the preparation of the essay and will become very discouraged if the results do not equate with this effort. For that reason it is crucial that students are aware of how they performed and how they can develop their skills for subsequent assignments.

One-to-one feedback is essential in order to highlight the strengths and the weaknesses of the written assignment. Some aspects of the written assignment that may need to be commented on are:

- spelling;
- grammar;
- organisation;
- introduction;
- relevance of argument;
- use of evidence;
- the extent to which the question has been answered;
- examples of how the arguments could be developed.

Throughout the feedback an opportunity should also be provided for dyslexic students to develop the essay and the arguments orally. This can boost their confidence for subsequent essays.

It is important for the tutor to appreciate that dyslexic students will often take longer than other students to plan and complete a written piece of work. A pre-assignment discussion to help the student talk through some of the main issues would be helpful, as would an interim discussion on progress. The student may need some precise guidance on reading, as it is important that the dyslexic student does not waste time in reading aspects of a book that are not totally relevant.

Pollak (2001a) refers to both the views and feelings of the students and the challenges facing academic institutions. He suggests that it is necessary to consider the self-image of the student with dyslexia, but that this also presents a challenge to the higher education sector to accommodate to students whose sense of identity is challenged not only by the label 'dyslexic' but also by academic writing in general.

Models of Supports

There are different models of supports that can be utilised at colleges and universities.

The social model of perceiving disability in terms of accommodation and supports is quite prevalent. This means that the responsibility is be shared by the institution and the staff. Courses, course presentation and the assessment criteria will be dyslexia-friendly. Many students with dyslexia find written assignments, note-taking in lectures and the pace of study in some courses quite challenging. Academic writing can be a difficult skill for the student with dyslexia to acquire, although with practice and full and constructive feedback over time this skill can be acquired.

Pollak (2001a) refers to the different models of perceiving academic writing developed by Lea and Street (2000), such as the 'study skills' model, which proposes that there is a potential student deficit in the technical skill of writing; and the 'academic socialisation' model, which implies that students can be acclimatised into academic discourse. Pollak suggests these models can be related to different perspectives of support offered to students with dyslexia. Yet, as Jamieson and Morgan (2008) point out, the term 'disability' has to be used in order for the university to gain support funding for the student—even though the student has difficulty in coming to terms with the use of the term 'disability'.

Pollak (in press) undertook interviews of students in higher education who were receiving support. One theme, according to Pollak, running through the interview data was the extent to which the higher education experiences of students identified with many types of learning difference were similar; another was the need for greater staff awareness of learning differences in general and inclusive practices in particular. Pollak argues that this data reinforces the concept of neurodiversity. This is an interesting concept (www.neurodiversity.com) and one which can move the thinking around deficits and support one stage further.

Grant (in press) suggests that by undertaking an assessment within a framework of neurodiversity, the narrowness of specific diagnostic categorisation can be overcome. Rather than perceiving this difference as a dysfunctional one requiring 'curing', Grant argues that this difference will to be appreciated and accepted. He argues that the concept of neurodiversity can be adopted as being one that also includes a wide range of specific learning differences, including dyslexia, dyspraxia, dyscalculia, attention deficit (hyperactivity) disorder (AD(H)D) and Tourette's syndrome. He suggests that neurodiversity is:

> an umbrella term…that encompasses a range of specific learning differences, including dyslexia, dyspraxia, dyscalculia, ADD/AD(H)D, and Asperger's. One or more specific learning differences may be present simultaneously, and it is possible for some forms of neurodiversity, such as a weakness only in working memory, to lack a well-known diagnostic category, such as dyslexia…Neurodiversity is a positive statement of differentiation, for while it explicitly refers to individuals whose everyday ways of thinking and behaving differ in certain key aspects from the majority of people, it rejects the assumption that these differences are dysfunctional and are to be 'cured'. Instead, there is a societal obligation that others make suitable adjustments and accommodations to enable inherent potential to be fully realised.

This view accepts there are difficulties but seems to move away from artificial or overlapping labels to one of similarities and support. Pollak suggests that it may be that eventually a 'grand unifying theory' of neurodiversity will be formulated. He also suggests that one can recognise neurodiversity as types of brain which are currently identified as disabled and are extremely common, so common in fact as to form part of the natural diversity of human beings.

One of the responses to this, according to Pollak, is for higher education institutions to offer central funding to help them provide an inclusive learning and teaching experience for all. He cites an example from Canada, where the University of British Columbia (UBC) has a suite of recording booths; students can take printed material and be given a CD containing a recording of the text being read aloud by a volunteer. Pollak argues that university libraries remain inaccessible to many students, because trying to extract meaning from printed pages (even where the text is not small and the page is not white) is extremely slow and laborious. A way forward must be found for students to be provided with scanned versions of key texts, and for all new acquisitions to come with CDs containing the entire book.

Self-disclosure

Self-disclosure is an important factor if students are to develop a healthy perception of their dyslexia and the associated challenges. It is also important for achieving self-advocacy. Yet often self-disclosure can present dilemmas for students with dyslexia. Price and Gerber (2008) provide some insights into self-disclosure. These are summarised below.

1. Self-disclosure is driven by context and situation. It is important that dyslexia is disclosed at the right time and in the right place.
2. Self-disclosure is the management of personal information. All information pertaining to disability is private and confidential. Whether all or part of that information is shared, and how it is shared, is at the discretion of the person with the (learning) disability.
3. Self-disclosure is nestled in the larger concept of self-determination. Disclosure is just one part of self-determination that empowers persons with learning disabilities to have control over the choice of disclosure.
4. There is risk to self-disclosure. There are no guarantees in disclosure. It can be a plus but it can be a negative when disclosure produces misunderstanding, stigma or bias.
5. Disclosure must include information and not just the label. The term learning disabilities lacks specificity and even has different meanings in different countries such as the United States and UK. It is helpful if disclosure is accompanied by the challenges the adult faces and the accommodations that are necessary.
6. Disclosure is just the beginning. When the decision to disclose is made, it is important to consider that it is the beginning of a dynamic process that will necessitate self-advocacy skills.

The points made by Price and Gerber are extremely relevant as they do show how self-disclosure can be advantageous but that certain conditions at the university in the students' experiences and in society can restrict and prevent students from disclosing their dyslexia.

At this point, when considering self-disclosure it is important to recognise the different agendas adopted by those at university; for example, management, course tutors and students each can have different priorities. Kirkland (2009) argues that institutions have their own priorities regarding how they fit in to a wider landscape. She maintains that institutions' strategic plans, action plans and objectives will influence the priorities of their schools, faculties and departments and how they prioritise their resources. She argues that it is necessary to develop a consistent and uniform university-wide protocol for assessing students with dyslexia in each university. The actual details of the protocol can be different for different universities but the principle of a system that is open and transparent and can be understood by management, tutors and students is paramount.

She argues that workload issues should be seen as a tutor's priority and effort should be made to ensure that the course is presented in a manner that can meet the needs of the student with dyslexia.

Self-disclosure can be influenced by the need for the student to be accepted and 'fit in' to the student group. This can be made more challenging when the student has perceptions of his or her dyslexia as a disability and this can be exacerbated by the stresses of meeting deadlines and undertaking examinations, both of which can be demanding for students with dyslexia.

Study Skills Models

There is a view that the 'study skills' model reinforces the view that the difficulties the student experiences is a 'disorder' within the student which needs to be treated (Pollak, 2005). Pollak argues that this view can be equated to the 'disability model' noted in many academic institutions. This notion of disability is further emphasised through the funding arrangements in the UK, which usually see learning support staff in higher education placed within a 'disability office' or unit. Additionally, support for students is usually arranged through the Disability Students Allowances Scheme, and this further emphasises the notion of disability.

The 'academic socialisation' model, on the other hand, according to Pollak, focuses on the role of a student's learning strategies or style in the process of acculturation into academic discourse. This, Pollak suggests, parallels the discourse of dyslexia that sees it as a 'difference' rather than a deficit.

Jamieson and Morgan (2008) indicate that the academic tutor has a role to play in terms of presentation of the topic and clarity of the assignment. This view suggests that universities and colleges can redefine their perceptions of 'study skills' and focus more on student adjustment to learning or interpretation of the learning task. This places responsibility for supporting students with dyslexia on course tutors, the academic tutor, the management and those developing the programme of study and the assessment criteria.

This is similar to the paradigm identified by Reid and Kirk (2001) that highlights the individual and the social model of perceiving dyslexia. The 'individual model' focuses on the individual and the individual's difficulties, such as the inability to undertake certain tasks such as note-taking, proof-reading, following instructions, meeting deadlines, using libraries, accuracy in typing and poor organisation. On the other hand, the 'social model' implies that adaptations can be made to tasks and the study environment to make the course and the institution dyslexia-friendly.

This means that the dyslexic person would cope without necessarily accessing additional support, such as open learning, materials written in a dyslexia-friendly style, information provided in a variety of means, oral assessment rather than written examinations, and lecture theatres, libraries and other facilities that have been made dyslexia-friendly.

Perceptions of Support

It is certainly necessary for universities and colleges to make support provision available for students, but it is often a concern of students that, although they may get the support throughout their course, their eventual aim to secure employment may be compromised by declaring their dyslexia. While this is a legitimate concern, it is fair to say that many employers now have more enlightened perceptions of dyslexia (British Dyslexia Association, 2005).

Yet, attitudes can take a long time to change and, although some professions have moved forward, there are still examples of young people with dyslexia experiencing difficulty in the few professions where attitudes appear more inflexible.

Riddick (2001) interviewed a number of practising teachers and trainee teachers with dyslexia about their experiences of teaching, teacher training and the specific coping strategies they have adopted in the classroom. They were all asked if (and how) their own experiences of literacy difficulties had influenced the way they teach children, and especially those with literacy difficulties. All the participants reported using a number of effective coping strategies and felt that, on balance, the advantages of being dyslexic outweighed the disadvantages in terms of giving them greater empathy and understanding of children's problems. The majority felt that their own very negative experiences of school had been a strong motivating factor in wanting to teach in order to give children a better educational experience than their own.

Yet, despite that, many trainee and new teachers were reluctant to admit to being dyslexic. Riddick (2009) argues that in a climate of inclusion a more enabling and open attitude to teachers with dyslexia should be adopted in order that trainee teachers do not harbour a fear that they are in some way inferior to colleagues because of their dyslexia. Riddick points out that in the USA similar concerns have been expressed about the conflict between making accommodations for student teachers with learning disabilities and the demand for teachers with high literacy and numeracy standards. She suggests that it is not surprising that there is a high percentage of trainee teachers who are dyslexic not declaring their disability on application, because of fear of rejection. However, it is the policy in all institutions in the UK not to discriminate against an applicant on the basis of any disability, including dyslexia. Nevertheless, Riddick's findings suggest that a substantial proportion of students feel that they need to hide their disability, perhaps also feeling that their employment prospects may be disadvantaged by revealing their dyslexia. At the same time, there are many examples of students, including trainee teachers, obtaining support and empathy both in training and in the profession (Reid and Kirk, 2001).

Coping Strategies

Help Lines

People with dyslexia, whether students or in the workplace, usually find their own way of coping with situations that can put demands on them. Many of these coping strategies are individual for that person, but it is often informative to learn from the experiences of others in similar positions. Support groups can therefore be of some benefit to the adult with dyslexia. Usually, local organisations have help lines and these can often provide on-the-spot advice (for example, the BDA help line, www.bdadyslexia.org.uk, 0845 251 9002; the Adult Dyslexia Organisation, www.adult-dyslexia.org; Dyslexia Scotland, www.dyslexiascotland.org.uk, 0844 800 84 84; International Dyslexia Association (IDA), www.interdys.org; and the Center for Child Evaluation and Teaching, Kuwait (www.ccetkuwait.org, +965 832 000).

Jameson (1999) suggests that support groups should have a programme encapsulating four choices: a discussion group for adult dyslexic people only; an open discussion group that welcomes partners and friends; a programme of invited speakers; or a mixture of the above. She also suggests that a support group should have a development plan that encapsulates a mission statement, keeps a record of activities and obtains charitable status.

Self-esteem

Riddick (2008) suggested that dyslexic adults have relatively low self-esteem and, significantly, that this low self-esteem is not confined to academic self-esteem. This would imply that support may be needed in relation to a number of life and family factors. This means that literacy is only one aspect of a much bigger picture, and low self-esteem can affect performance in a range of life skills. One student quoted by Jamieson and Morgan (2008) said that 'being dyslexic is a fundamental part of who I am. There are many things beside reading and writing that I find difficult' (p. 43).

Often, people with dyslexia will expend more effort perhaps than is necessary for a task and, in fact, over-prepare. This was the view of a student interviewed by Reid and Kirk who suggested that he over-prepared for tutorials and did not use all the materials he had prepared. Often, in fact, this is due to poor organisation—perhaps the difficulty in identifying the key points. The student may have notes of relevant information, but lacks the general headings—the key points within which to contextualise these notes. This makes retrieval difficult, especially in a tutorial situation where it can involve a free-flow type of discussion.

Riddick (2009) asked teachers about the kind of coping strategies they used in the classroom. They stressed the importance of extra preparation and advance preparation.

She cites one trainee teacher remarking that 'preparation is power'. Many, however, always carried a spellchecker or dictionary with them. She comments that, although all the trainee teachers had developed effective coping strategies, they were fearful of negative reactions from schools and would have welcomed support, such as mentoring or advice from experienced teachers with dyslexia.

THE WORKPLACE

The models of support that can be adopted in the workplace also follow the same pattern and come up against the same kind of issues that are found in education settings. Employers can make adaptations to tasks, provide dyslexia-friendly equipment and make the work environment dyslexia-friendly, which will benefit all employees, or they may make 'special arrangements' for dyslexic people, which often leaves individuals with dyslexia feeling that they have been provided with favours and privileges. If special arrangements are put in place for the person with dyslexia, it is important that the individual should not be reminded of this even if they make a dyslexic-type error. Often, people with dyslexia can be quite sensitive, and some work tasks, particularly those that may require a degree of sequencing and accuracy, can be stressful.

Tasks that could be demanding for people with dyslexia in the workplace include:

- difficulty following a number of instructions if given at the same time;
- following a technical manual;
- reading reports quickly;
- writing short memos;
- recalling telephone numbers;
- remembering what was said at meetings;
- filing documents;
- tasks involving hand–eye coordination difficulties, which may result in poor presentation of work;
- reporting at meetings;
- diary-keeping;
- difficulty doing more than one task at the same time, such as speaking on the phone and writing messages.

Many of these may result in frustration, anger or embarrassment in the workplace but they can be overcome by careful and sensitive management, which would ensure that the person with dyslexia is not overexposed to these situations. In fact Jameson (2009) argues that at an employment tribunal a dyslexic person is so hampered by their communication difficulties that they give the impression of being uncooperative and obstructing justice. She indicates that it is vital that the legal profession are made aware of dyslexic problems. McLoughlin and Leather (2009), quoting a judicial outcome analysis, show that many disabled employees have been prevented from gaining the protection offered by legislation. They suggest that the evidence shows 63% of Tribunal decisions favouring employers.

Moody (2009) explains that the weaknesses of people with dyslexia that can affect efficiency at work include:

- literacy skills—following a technical manual, reading reports quickly and writing memos in clear English;
- memory—remembering telephone numbers and recalling what was said at meetings;
- sequencing ability—difficulty in filing documents in the correct place and looking up entries in dictionaries and directories;
- visual orientation—may have difficulty dealing with maps;
- hand–eye coordination—can result in poor presentation of written work and figures;
- speech—may talk in a disorganised way, especially at meetings and on the telephone;
- organisational skills—may miss appointments and their work area can look disorganised;
- emotional factors—may display anger, embarrassment and anxieties.

McLoughlin and Leather (2009) suggest that if dyslexic people are to be fully included in society, the emphasis should be on empowerment or enablement rather than a model of disability that perceives the 'dyslexic as a victim'.

They suggest that empowerment comes from:

- Self-understanding—dyslexia is often referred to as a 'hidden disability'. Dyslexic people therefore have to advocate for themselves, and can only do so if they have a good understanding of the nature of their difficulty, how it affects them and what they need to do to improve their performance.
- Understanding by others, particularly employers—if dyslexic people have to deal with managers and colleagues whose understanding of the nature of dyslexia is limited, it is likely the dyslexic person will be excluded rather than included.

If employers are enlightened and informed, discriminatory practices should be minimised. This paves the way for rethinking the concept of disability along the lines of the social model of disability. Mc Laughlin and Leather argue that employers need to understand dyslexia in its broadest context. In particular, it is important that they acknowledge that life transitions can undermine a dyslexic person's performance and highlight their difficulties. Some of the transition situations they suggest include:

- job redefinition;
- change of job;
- promotion;
- work back to training/education;
- change of personnel.

They also suggest that employers can help dyslexic individuals by arranging a work skills evaluation which should look at the whole person, including their skills and abilities. They argue that this should be flexible, individualised and provide a wide variety of solutions and suggestions for skill development. It is important that the results of this type of evaluation should help to develop independence in order that the person with dyslexia can feel more fulfilled and more in control over their role in the workplace.

CONCLUDING COMMENT

There a number of key factors that affect adults with dyslexia in both education and the workplace, many of which are very similar. The situations may differ, but the need for support, for a common understanding and for a positive and constructive attitude towards dyslexia is the same, irrespective of the setting. It is too easy to become complacent when supports have been set and funding secured—these aspects are by no means the answer, but can provide a pathway towards equality and success for all adults with dyslexia. It is important, however, to consider 'dyslexia' within the wider notion of equality, whether it be gender, race or culture, and ensure that, in fact, equality does prevail. The key factor in relation to the implications of disability legislation, workplace policies and course arrangements on dyslexia is that there should be understanding and an acknowledgement on the part of all employers, course managers and administrators that adults with dyslexia are not being supported, but, in fact, are being accepted. Only with this acceptance can real equality be achieved.

POINTS FOR REFLECTION

- Consider how legislation has facilitated support for students in post school establishments. How has this translated into practice?

- Consider the challenges students with dyslexia experience in post-school education. Consider:

  i) how these may affect their performances in courses;

  ii) how they may be dealt with by the college./university and by the student.

- How important do you consider self-disclosure? How can this be encouraged in the work or post-school setting?

- Reflect on the type of workplace accommodations that can be made for adults with dyslexia.

Chapter 18

Issues and Concerns

Although much progress has been made in the whole area of dyslexia over the past 20 years, there are still a number of significant issues that can cause concern to practitioners and to parents.

These include the area of dyslexia in different languages and particularly children who are exposed to more than one language at home and school. Multilingualism has been an issue for a number of years. This was raised internationally at the BDA's first international conference on multilingualism in 1999. The momentum was carried through at the follow-up conferences in Washington, DC in 2001 and in Cyprus in 2004. Other issues which will be discussed in this chapter are those relating to the overlap between dyslexia and other syndromes such as dyspraxia, dyscalculia, specific language disorders and ADHD (attention deficit hyperactivity disorder) in particular. This also has been a long-standing issue which has perplexed practitioners and caused some anxiety to parents. The other issue which will be tackled in this chapter is that of teacher training. There has been a call for training of teachers at undergraduate and post-graduate level since 1990 and there have been pockets of success (Reid, 2001a), but progress has been patchy with no real universal acceptance of this need.

ISSUE 1. MULTILINGUALISM

Multilingualism is an area that can present a challenge to those involved in assessment and teaching of children and adults with dyslexia. Recently, there has been much interest in this area, and many writers, researchers and teachers have put forward opinions on what can and should be done. This area presents a challenge because it has been neglected for too long. Additionally, although considerable advances were being made during the 1990s in teacher-friendly assessment and teaching materials based on current research on dyslexia, it was in many cases assumed that these materials would be suitable for all children with dyslexic difficulties, irrespective of their cultural and social background.

The British Psychological Working Party Report (BPS, 1999a) emphasises the importance of culturally relevant materials for children with dyslexia and, particularly, culture-fair assessment. Dyslexia, the report suggests, may be 'masked by limited mastery of the language of tuition' (p. 60). It is acknowledged in the report that dyslexia can occur across languages, cultures, socio-economic status, race and gender. Yet, the report notes that the tools needed to uncover the masking of dyslexic difficulties are not readily available. Furthermore, the message that this gives to teachers is that the key reason why a child is not acquiring literacy skills in the language being taught is because of the bilingual dimension, and not due to any other factor such as dyslexia.

The MacPherson Report in the UK (MacPherson of Cluny, 1999) draws attention to the unconscious norms that continue to operate within our society, which can exclude and certainly disadvantage people from ethnic groups. The Report comments on institutional racism and suggests that this can be detected in processes, attitudes and behaviours that amount to discrimination through unwitting prejudice and ignorance. This can certainly apply to the identification of dyslexia, as the knowledge of how to assess children from ethnic backgrounds is not widely available and the prevalent use of tests that are standardised on monolingual populations illustrates this.

There are, therefore, a number of key issues that need to be addressed in terms of policy and practice before teachers can feel adequately prepared to meet the diverse needs of diverse groups of children who may have 'masked' dyslexic difficulties. There is also a responsibility to prevent a child being misdiagnosed (false positive) by describing the child as having a learning difficulty when one is not present (Peer and Reid, 2000). This chapter, therefore, will discuss some of the issues raised above and provide some pointers and principles for teachers in order to acknowledge and appreciate the role of the dual dimensions of dyslexia and multilingualism.

Cultural Factors

Often, approaches that exist to meet their needs are considered to be separate and 'specialist' in nature, and this has the effect of excluding mainstream teachers from accepting the responsibility to meet the needs of bilingual learners alongside, and together with, the needs of monolingual learners. Kelly (2002) suggests that teachers need to consult and collaborate with people who have a sound knowledge of the cultural background of the students in order to avoid confusing common second-language errors of bilingual students with indicators of dyslexia. She suggests that these can sometimes overlap: as in the case of left–right confusion in Urdu, which is written from right to left; and with auditory discrimination with Punjabi speakers, who may have difficulty with 'p' and 'b'. Kelly suggests that it is important to consider information from parents as they will have a more complete picture of their child in a range of settings, including those not involving language skills. Kelly therefore suggests that teachers should be alerted if the child has a lack of interest in books, discrepancy between listening comprehension and reading skills, difficulties in acquiring automaticity or difficulties with balance, as well as persistent problems in phonological awareness despite adequate exposure to English.

In New Zealand, Macfarlane et al. (2000) suggest that there is little evidence that dyslexia is more or less prevalent among Maori than in any other ethnic group. They concede, however, that it is possible that some Maori have been wrongly labelled 'dyslexic', when they may have no or some other learning difficulty that could be better ascribed to other sources. They cite the research from Spreen (1988), which indicates that movement in and out of the 'dyslexic group' is due to a large number of variables that can potentially affect reading development: family background, behaviour variables and cognitive variables. Additionally, this view is further supported by the views of McNaughton (1995) on socialisation values which, he suggests, match home culture. Berryman and Wearmouth (2009) argue that dyslexia is commonly understood as an explanation of difficulties in literacy from a cognitive psychology perspective. This level of explanation, they argue, ignores the impact of culture. They suggest that research shows the benefits to literacy learning that accrue when schools work to address issues of cultural understandings between themselves and their home communities and therefore dyslexia should be seen in a broader, more culturally aware perspective. This is relevant to all countries today, as virtually every country is exposed to a multicultural environment. Bishop et al. (2007) tested the impact of working with a wide range of teachers across all curriculum areas in Years 9 and 10 to embed culturally responsive pedagogies in their classrooms as a means to raising the achievement of Maori students in New Zealand. They found that teachers' perceptions of Maori students were a key issue. They found that with specific training, teachers learnt to develop a greater awareness of the behaviours in language and literacy that students come to school with, and they were able to help students make connections between their own diverse communities and experiences and school literacy experiences.

Identification

One of the key challenges facing educators in relation to bilingualism and dyslexia is that of identification. This is a challenge because syndromes such as dyslexia do not occur for only one reason—usually, there are a number of factors that contribute to the presence of this type of literacy difficulty, and if a child is also bi/multilingual then this will be an added factor that needs to be taken into account throughout the assessment. As indicated earlier, many assessment strategies and tests do not explicitly take this into account. It has been noted that cultural and language factors in many standardised tests (Everatt et al., 2000) can militate against the child whose first language is not English. Many standardised assessment strategies have been developed for use with a monolingual population, and this can account for the underestimation or, indeed, the misdiagnosis of dyslexia in bilingual children. Landon (2001) addresses this by asking, 'what factors appear to lead to low rates of detection of dyslexia amongst bilingual learners and could the same factors also explain the poor standards of literacy amongst many learners of English as an Additional Language (EAL learners)?' The importance of these questions is that they actually investigate the issues and provide a good example of the types of question teachers need to ask when assessing children who are bilingual. To answer the questions presented by Landon one must consider the range of factors that contribute to dyslexia. It is important to acknowledge that culture-fair assessment can be of two types. It is important to develop assessment materials in the language being taught, but to make those materials culture-fair, and this may also involve a heavy visual emphasis. Additionally, it may be necessary to develop assessment materials in the first language of the child to assess whether dyslexia is present and affecting the development of skills in literacy in that first language.

Although there are a number of screening and diagnostic tests used to assess dyslexic children, these are essentially directed at the monolingual population of dyslexic children, and particularly in the English language.

Some assessment procedures have been developed specifically for the bilingual learner (Sunderland et al., 1999). These focus on checklists, interview guidelines, diagnostic tests, and cultural and linguistic factors that may affect diagnosis. For example, they have developed an interview form for bilingual students that looks at: language history; schooling (primary and secondary); language-listening behaviours; reading (approaches used by the student); writing and spelling (planning strategies used and spelling approaches); Mathematics; memorisation difficulties; and spatial–temporal factors such as difficulties following directions, map-reading and following oral instructions. The interview schedule is extremely comprehensive and includes such aspects as visual and motor factors. Essentially, this process is a diagnostic interview and notes any considerations that should be put in place for the student, such as extra time in examinations. These procedures are extremely useful, not least because they are dedicated to assessing the bilingual learner but also because they provide follow-up guidance for teaching, which is a crucial element in all forms of assessment.

Some key issues in relation to assessing bi- or multilingual children are:

- *Screening*—when should this take place and what is the nature of, and the criteria for, screening?
- *Diagnosis*—can adapted, formal standardised tests be used successfully? How valid can they be with different populations of children?
- *Language*—should we be focusing on dynamic rather than static assessment for bilingual children? This takes into account elements of the test situation, such as language and links with teaching in scaffolding and building language concepts.
- *Learning style*—it is important to view the bilingual child as an individual learner and to take into account the particular learning styles of each individual and context. Is the learning environment conducive to the learner's cultural experiences and her or his cognitive style of learning? This can have implications for different cultures, as often there is a culture-dominant learning style.

Macfarlane et al. (2000) discuss the learning style of the Maori people in New Zealand and suggest that Maori people view learning as a natural consequence of one's interaction with people and the environment. They have an oral tradition and the notion of the written counterpart to learning is a relatively recent phenomenon in Maori culture. Macfarlane et al. argue that allowances must be made for different learning and teaching styles to ensure that the student's *mana* (integrity) is not devalued. Macfarlane and Glynn (1998) contend that it is the right of Maori students to see their language, cultural knowledge and preferred learning styles legitimated within the classroom.

Culture-fair Assessment

According to Cline (1998), this may represent the 'holy grail', but analysis of test performance within specific cultural and linguistic groups is important, as this can help to identify particular test items that consistently lead to cultural confusion or misperception.

Macfarlane et al. (2000) report on the New Zealand Literacy Taskforce (set up in March 1999), which made it clear that student achievement is influenced by personal, cultural, family and school factors. They report that the Taskforce was adamant that the expectations of the achievement of all children should be the same, regardless of the language of instruction or their ethnicity. This group also agreed that, although the goal is relevant and appropriate to children in Maori-medium education, the procedures and approaches for achieving the goal may well be different from those in English-medium education. This is a clear statement that makes no apologies for upholding the cultural and the linguistic needs of a specific group within society.

Macfarlane et al. suggest that there are many general features of learning to read and write that apply across countries, but some of these are specific to New Zealand, as the cultural context within New Zealand includes recognition of the educational and language needs of both Maori and non-Maori (deriving from obligations of the Treaty of Waitangi and such official policies as the recognition of both English and Te Reo Maori as official languages). It was interesting to note, therefore, that the Literacy Taskforce endorsed 11 principles of best practice of instruction, significant among which is the one that refers to teaching that takes account of children's linguistic and cultural backgrounds.

Macfarlane et al. (2000) suggest that the complexity of human communication can lead to problems in accurately diagnosing actual linguistic difficulties in such groups as Maori children. In some cases, Maori children may have been assessed as experiencing literacy difficulties, yet can excel in reciting intricate and lengthy *waiata moteatea* (ancient song and verse), *whaikorero* (speech-making) and *karakia* (incantations).

Additionally, they comment on the role of linguistic and cultural features of Maori communication as a factor that needs to be considered in a culture-fair assessment. Communication can operate through verbal units of sounds, syllables, words, sentences and discourses, but, they argue, non-verbal behaviours that have a cultural basis also need to be considered. Such non-verbal signals include facial expression, eye contact, proximity, tone of voice, pitch of voice, gestures, body movements and speech pace. These may have a more prominent role and communicative function in some cultural groups than others.

Focusing on the Welsh language, Forbes and Powell (2000) describe some of the language issues encountered when developing literacy assessment measures for a population, such as that in parts of Wales, who are exposed to two different languages at levels that may vary widely both within and between home and school. They suggested, therefore, that test materials for young students should not contain items that might discriminate against some children because of their unfamiliarity with language forms more prevalent in other parts of Wales, particularly across the North–South dialectal divide. Some of the key factors to emerge from the subsequent development and piloting of the test included the need to use a 'comic' format, a storyline that involves school, appropriate print size and inclusion of as many pictures as possible.

Teaching

Teaching approaches should consider the child's strengths as well as noting the difficulties experienced by the child. Additionally, it is important that any Individual Educational Programme (IEP) that is developed is a result of wide-ranging deliberation between professionals and parents. Many of the teaching approaches advocated will be an adaptation of those suggested earlier in this book for monolingual dyslexic learners, and it is important that this adaptation occurs following consultation with school staff, support staff and specialist teachers. This type of programme should contain many different strands, including phonological awareness and reading through analogy. Although these approaches can be offered within a programme for the whole class, it is important that they are contextualised for the bilingual child.

It is important to consider the development of higher-order thinking skills when teaching children with dyslexia. This equally applies to dyslexic children who are bilingual as well as those who are not. Programmes involving thinking skills are important elements in this, and there may be a tendency to overlook these types of programme in preference for a more direct decoding–literacy acquisition type of intervention. Dynamic assessment offers an opportunity to utilise a thinking skills paradigm, as it encourages responses relating to what the child does know and how the learner actually processes information, as well as the level and type of conceptual knowledge the learner has acquired. This approach essentially links assessment and teaching and highlights the child's learning process. Usmani (1999) suggests the bilingual, bicultural child may have a broad range of thinking skills, which may go undetected if the professional is unaware of the cultural values or fails to understand them in relation to the assessment and teaching programme.

One example of a programme that takes community and cultural values into account is the 'Pause Prompt Praise' (PPP) programme which was designed to raise Maori student literacy achievement in mainstream settings (Glynn, Wearmouth and Berryman, 2006). This technique, originally devised by Glynn and McNaughton (1985), was designed to be used with parents of students experiencing difficulties in literacy acquisition. The programme contained a booklet that offered advice about arranging a time and place for reading; selecting suitable books at the appropriate level; supporting children to become independent readers; using praise to support children's reading development; and monitoring progress in reading. It can be argued that these suggestions represent good practice in any reading programme. What is unique about Pause Prompt Praise is the manner in which it was developed and introduced to parents and schools. It took account of cultural needs and parents' perspectives.

Key Principles

The key principles in the teaching of children with dyslexia, such as multi-sensory, cumulative and sequential, and over-learning to achieve automaticity, are equally important for learners who are bilingual. Therefore, information needs to be presented to the dyslexic learner on different occasions and in different ways to help consolidation of the information or task. This also helps to strengthen short-term memory, and by using the information in different contexts long-term memory can also be strengthened.

A range of activities—both computer and game—are also useful for bilingual children. Computer games can be multi-sensory and give some responsibility to the learner. Although additional language learners may need support, it is important that they are not over-supported. Children when learning need practice at making decisions and taking responsibility for their own learning, which is why it is often best to adapt a programme so that it can be used flexibly by the teacher and the child.

Metacognitive Awareness/Schema

There is a view that children with dyslexia may have poor metacognitive awareness, particularly in relation to print and literacy (Tunmer and Chapman, 1996). When children are learning to read words, they develop 'recognition', then 'understanding' and then 'transferable' skills, which means that they need to develop concepts and an understanding of the text before they can use the new word or text in other contexts—this transferring of skills is crucial to the development of metacognitive awareness. To achieve metacognitive awareness, children usually develop schemata (children's specific understanding, from their perspective, of a situation or text). To achieve schemata of a situation, children need to be able to express their understanding of the situation verbally or in written form, and identify the specific concepts and how these relate to the overall picture. The teacher, through a process called scaffolding, helps to build up this understanding and the conceptual and schematic development of the child.

The awareness of schemata is important to the understanding of text for all children, but this particularly applies to children with dyslexia and can also have important implications for children who have a bilingual background. Therefore, the child who for some reason activates inappropriate schemata will not fully understand the text and, in fact, may elicit the wrong meaning from a piece of text.

Consideration of schemata, therefore, is particularly important for learners who are dyslexic and bilingual, as often their experiences are socially, culturally and perhaps linguistically different from their monolingual peers.

One of the most effective means of developing schemata and ensuring that the child has an appropriate schema is through pre-reading discussion. This sets the scene, introduces the characters, describes the situation and provides some of the key words and concepts for the child. Pre-reading discussion can involve the parents and can be initially in the child's first language, particularly with children whose English is not well developed. Texts relating to the cultural experiences of bilingual learners will assist in the development of schemata and the subsequent development of metacognitive awareness. This strategy of using the parents for pre-reading discussion may also help in the development of short-term memory and visualisation.

Stamboltzis and Pumfrey (2000) also recommend the Multisensory Structured Language (MSL) approach for teaching first language skills to dyslexic students. Grammar, syntax and phonology are taught through a programme that emphasises hearing, seeing, speaking and writing. Another major source of information on how to teach bilingual students, according to Stamboltzis and Pumfrey, comes from genre-based approaches to literacy. Genre-based ideas have implications for the selection of reading materials and the adaptation of reading instructions for the various groups of students. They suggest that genre theory can be useful, since it suggests that pictures, captions and labels can enhance the decoding and comprehension of text for bilingual students who learn to read by extensive use of visual material, and this would clearly be very helpful.

They also suggest that listening to stories can help children develop vocabulary, concepts, oral fluency and sense of story and that this can be particularly effective for bilingual students. All types of listening activities and role-playing provide exposure to natural, English-speaking situations, and these should be incorporated into a teaching programme.

As far as possible the teaching of reading to bilingual learners should be based on top-down strategies, otherwise described as language experience approaches. It is also important to ensure that the programme has a clear structure and that the child should be aware of that structure—this can also help the child view the programme or task in a holistic way, providing a complete picture of the activity.

ISSUE 2. THE USE OF COMPUTERS AND TECHNOLOGY

Dimitriadi (2000) suggests that technology can facilitate access to the curriculum for bilingual children. She suggests that equipment and programmes can support simultaneous input from different languages in oral, written or visual format and provide bilingual learners with the opportunity to enrich the curriculum with their diverse cultural experiences. There is little doubt that Information and Communication Technology (ICT) has transformed the educational experiences of children in schools. Technology offers the opportunity to enhance conceptualisation and expression of ideas, and Dimitriadi suggests that it can be used both as a means to approach regional culture and to promote the differentiation in learning styles as a norm in the educational process (Dimitriadi, 1999). She suggests that technology can help to reinforce alphabet skills by establishing correspondence between phonemes and graphemes in one language, and making the necessary connections between the way in which apparently similar graphemes have different sounds in other languages. She suggests that technology can help to reinforce alphabet skills by establishing correspondence between phonemes and graphemes in one language, and making the necessary connections between the way in which apparently similar graphemes have different sounds in other languages.

She suggests that a voice recognition system, programmed to understand regional accents and problematic utterance, will encourage the input of speech and translate it into script. This can help with spelling and allow the opportunity to self-check and to construct simple sentences. Spellcheckers with phonically constructed word banks facilitate the writing process by generating lists of possible alternatives.

It is possible, therefore, according to Dimitriadi, to include simultaneously an oral and written translation of the rule into another language. Talking word processors with pre-recorded word banks can provide immediate aural feedback to users by repeating each word or sentence typed and by prompting the learner to self-correct the sentence by seeing their spelling mistakes in the form of highlighted words. Dimitriadi (1999) discusses the versatility of speech word processors and, particularly, how they can be programmed to repeat each phoneme typed, which provides users with constant practice of exploring the relationships between graphemes and phonemes in the target language.

Dimitriadi suggests that computers can help with some of the difficulties related to the directional flow of the learner's written language structure, such as in Cantonese Chinese or in Arabic scripts where the characters follow a different course from that of European languages. She suggests that a multimedia computer allows learners to record their voices, instead of typing the information, and, temporarily, they overcome the burden a new script might pose.

Gregg and Baner (2009) suggest that there is no doubt that the Internet and other information and communication technologies are shaping new theoretical perspectives on literacy. She quotes the statistic that in 1994 the percentage of classrooms in the USA with at least one computer with Internet access was 3%; in 2002, it went up to 92% (NCREL, 2003). But she suggests that electronic formats alone do not provide accessibility to print, unless they are used in conjunction with cognitive/metacognitive strategies. This can result in print becoming more available to students with dyslexia. She also argues that according to a report by the National Council on Disability in the USA (2000), use and adoption of technology by individuals with dyslexia is often shaped by lack of trained professionals to evaluate the rapidly changing array of assistive technologies. This means that the advances in technology can actually restrict its impact. She concludes that technology alone is not the solution to enhancing the reading comprehension performance of students with dyslexia. However, she argues that teaching cognitive/metacognitive reading strategies without serious consideration of the digital reading world of today leaves many students with dyslexia missing effective solutions for reading success.

ISSUE 3. OVERLAP, CONTINUUM AND INTERVENTION

One of the major issues facing teachers is the dilemma concerning the overlap between the various syndromes that can be associated with learning difficulties. The term normally used in the UK is specific learning difficulties while in the USA it is learning disabilities. Within these broad terms there are a number of more specific labels such as dyslexia, dyspraxia, attention difficulties, dyscalculia and specific language disorder. Yet in reality there will very likely be overlap between these and the student identified as dyslexic may well have some of the characteristics of the other syndromes such as attention difficulties or dyscalculia. In fact, Weedon and Reid (2002, 2005) identified 17 specific learning difficulties during the development of a screening procedure for identifying a user-friendly matrix for specific learning difficulties. It was indicated during the piloting of the instrument that at least seven of these had strong correlations (Weedon and Reid, 2003).

Like dyslexia, many of the other specific learning difficulties can be seen within a continuum. The term comorbidity is now used to describe the overlap between the different specific learning difficulties. This is an acknowledgement that specific learning difficulties can be found within a continuum and that there is likely to be some overlap between several of these as they tend to be factors associated with left hemisphere, language-associated functioning. Moreover, since neurological processing activities tend to be interactive rather than independent, it is likely that, for example, children with dyslexia may share some of their characteristics with children diagnosed as having a specific language impairment.

Came and Reid (2008) propose the view that teachers should focus on a core of common concerns. This implies that many children will share some of the same difficulties even though they have been identified with different syndromes. For example, many will have:

- attention difficulties;
- memory problems;
- organisational difficulties;
- difficulties with processing speed.

They propose, therefore, that tackling those four areas alone will help to meet the needs of most children identified with dyslexia, dyspraxia, ADHD and dyscalculia. So rather than focus on the label, they suggest that teachers should be focusing on a core of common concerns. This means that teachers will not feel de-skilled (often, when faced with children with labels, teachers who have not been on any specialist training courses can easily feel de-skilled).

It is not unusual for dyslexia, dyspraxia and, to a certain extent, ADHD to share some common factors.

Developmental Coordination Disorders (DCD)

According to Jones (2005), many terms have been used to describe DCD—these include 'clumsy', motor coordination problems, motor impairment, movement difficulties, developmental dyspraxia, minimal brain dysfunction and congenital maladroitness. The work of Henderson and Sugden (1992; Sugden and Wright, 1996) has been influential in relation to highlighting this syndrome. The term DCD appears in both the American Psychiatric Association (APA) *Diagnostic and Statistical Manual of Mental Disorders* (DSM-IV, 1994) and the World Health Organization (WHO) *Classification of Diseases and Related Health Problems* (ICD-10, 1993).

DCD is essentially a motor coordination difficulty but it can be seen within a continuum from mild to severe and can affect fine-motor activities, such as pencil grip, and gross-motor activities, such as movement and balance.

Some researchers and practitioners prefer to use the term dyspraxia and Portwood (2001) describes dyspraxia as 'motor difficulties caused by perceptual problems, especially visual–motor and kinaesthetic–motor difficulties'. The definition of dyspraxia provided by the Dyspraxia Trust in England is an 'impairment or immaturity in the organisation of movement which leads to associated problems with language, perception and thought' (Dyspraxia Trust, 2001).

Jones suggests that there is also a lack of agreement of what is necessary for a child to be categorised as having DCD, and to what extent the condition coexists alongside other 'specific' learning difficulties. Kaplan et al. (1998) challenge the view of focusing on syndromes. Kaplan's research suggests that there are no pure diagnosis categories of developmental disorders, but rather 'semi-random clusters of symptoms related to motor coordination, autism, learning and processing factors. For example out of a study measuring 162 children for DCD, reading difficulties and ADHD, 53 children obtained scores which classified them for "pure" cases, 47 children did not meet the criterion for any of the 3 conditions and 62 were classified as "comorbid" cases.' Kaplan et al. suggest comorbidity as being the rule rather than the exception.

Attention Deficit Disorders (ADHD)

There has been considerable debate regarding the concept of attention disorders. A number of perspectives can be noted, ranging from the medical to educational and social. It is, however, interesting to note that in the American Psychiatric Association's *Diagnostic and Statistical Manual of Mental Disorders* (DSM-IV; APA, 2000), ADHD is noted as the most prevalent neuro-developmental disorder of childhood. DSM-IV provides such criteria for diagnosis as factors relating to inattentiveness, hyperactivity and impulsivity—'often runs about or climbs excessively' and 'often interrupts or intrudes on others'. To qualify as ADHD these factors need to have persisted for at least six months to a degree that is maladaptive and inconsistent with developmental level. Although there has been a considerable amount of literature on ADHD, there is still controversy regarding the unitary model of ADHD as a discrete syndrome. There is also some debate on the nature of the syndrome and, particularly, its primary causes. For example, Barkley (1997) suggests that it is a unitary condition and that the primary impairment relates to behaviour inhibition, which has a cascading effect on other cognitive functions. This view is, however, countered by Rutter (1995), who suggests that a cognitive deficit specific to ADHD has still to be determined and that even if the majority have cognitive impairments the trait is not common to all children with ADHD. It is perhaps useful at this point to attempt to place the symptoms and characteristics of ADHD into some form of framework to help understand the different strands and various characteristics that can contribute to ADHD.

Framework for Attention Difficulties

The causal modelling framework used to describe dyslexia in Chapter 2 (Morton and Frith, 1995) can actually be applied to ADHD. Their framework focuses on the neurological, cognitive, behavioural and environmental levels. These categories can be applied to all of the specific learning difficulties, as it does present an overview that highlights both the different dimensions that can impact on the child and also the notion of how the impact of these can overlap—e.g., attention/impulsivity can be due to all four of the dimensions. This will have some impact on intervention. It indicates that even if the cause may be found to be neurobiological, the behaviours can be controlled through intervention at the cognitive or classroom (educational) level.

Neurological level

At the neurological level, in relation to attention difficulties, the following factors may be relevant:

- *Hemispheric preferences*—usually, a child with ADHD would be a right hemisphere processor.
- *Saliency determination*—that is, recognising what is relevant. Often, a child with ADHD would have difficulty in recognising the relevant features of conversation or written work.
- *Auditory distractibility*—this would imply that they would be easily distracted by noise of some sort.
- *Tactile distractibility*—similarly, touch could be distracting, and, often, the child with ADHD may want to touch in order to be distracted.
- *Motor inhibition*—often, children with ADHD may have difficulty in inhibiting response and may react impulsively in some situations.

Cognitive level

In relation to the cognitive dimensions, the following factors may be significant:

- *Depth of processing*—if the child is not attending to a stimulus then it is likely that the processing will be at a shallow as opposed to a deep level. Clearly, if this is the case then the child will not gain much from the learning experience, either in understanding or in pleasure—therefore, the learning experience will not be automatically reinforced.
- *Information-processing*—just as in the case of dyslexia, the information-processing cycle of input, cognition and output can be influential in identifying the types of difficulties that may be experienced by children with attention difficulties. This would therefore have implications for teaching.
- *Metacognitive factors*—these are important for reinforcing learning, for transferring learning and for developing concepts. It is likely the child with attention difficulties will have poor metacognitive skills, and this will also make learning less meaningful and have a negative effect on attention span.

Classroom factors

In relation to educational or classroom factors, the following can be considered:

- Factors associated with free flight—this means that the child will have little control over the thinking process (essentially, what may be described as a right hemisphere processing style). This would mean that the individual would require some structure to help to direct their thinking processes.

- Unpredictability, inconsistency and impulsivity—this again indicates that there is little control over learning and that many actions would be impulsive.
- Pacing skills and on-task factors—these again indicate a lack of control over learning and that students with attention difficulties have a problem with pacing the progress of work and, therefore, may tire easily or finish prematurely.

Identifying and Defining Attention Difficulties

Examining the factors described above would lead one to believe that attention difficulties and ADHD can be easily confused and that the syndrome would be difficult to identify as a discrete syndrome.

It is not surprising, therefore, that a number of definitions of ADHD are currently used and a considerable amount of literature on the subject has expounded different views and a variety of interventions. Essentially, however, identification seems to be through the use of diagnostic checklists or observations, such as the Brown Rating Scale (Brown, 1996, 2001) and the Conners scale (Conners, 1996). These are widely used, but they do demand an element of clinical judgement on the part of the assessor. The important aspect about them is not so much whether they give a diagnosis, but rather that these instruments provide a list of definable and observable characteristics that can inform a teaching programme, irrespective of the diagnosis.

It is therefore feasible to identify attention difficulties within an education setting, although in practice much of this type of diagnosis appears to be undertaken by medical professionals—even though presenting difficulties are usually more obvious in school. If a child is said to have attention difficulties, then these should be obvious in every subject and in all activities. In practice, this is rarely the case and must cast some doubt on the validity of the diagnosis.

Criteria

The criteria for ADHD are noted in DSM-IV and usually the accepted criteria are those shown below.

Behaviour symptoms

- Can be noted in more than one setting
- Be more severe than in other children the same age
- Start before the age of 7
- Be prolonged over a period of time
- Make it difficult for the child to fit in and function effectively at school, home and/or other social situations

Inattention

- Easily distracted by external stimuli
- Fails to give close attention to details
- Has difficulty organising class work and activities

- Has difficulty organising class work and activities
- Often loses things necessary for tasks or activities
- Difficulty sustaining attention in tasks or play activities
- Does not seem to listen when spoken to directly
- Does not follow through on instructions, fails to finish homework
- Superficial processing is evident and voids engaging in tasks that require sustained mental effort

Hyperactivity/impulsivity

- Often fidgets with hands or feet or squirms in seat
- Requires a lot of mobility—has difficulty sitting for sustained periods
- Has difficulty playing or engaging in leisure activities constructively
- Often talks excessively and switches from topic to topic
- Often blurts out answers before questions have been completed
- Difficulty waiting his or her turn

Intervention

Intervention for ADHD can take a number of forms: These can include:

- medical in the form of drugs, such as Ritalin;
- educational in relation to classroom adaptations, task analysis and investigation of the student's learning preferences; or
- dietary in relation to examining children's reactions to certain foods.

There is also a view (Lloyd and Norris, 1999; Lloyd, 2006) that ADHD is a social construction. There is certainly a strong commercial basis to ADHD, and this may have fuelled the impetus for acceptance of ADHD as a discrete specific difficulty.

Indeed, there is a view that special educational needs, whatever they might be, can be approached from a situation-centred perspective (Frederickson and Cline, 2002). They quote Deno (1989), who argues that proponents of this view believe that special educational needs 'can only be defined in terms of the relationship between what a person can do and what a person must do to succeed in a given environment' (Frederickson and Cline, 2002, p. 40). This view indicates that learning difficulties are in fact environmental and a construction of the education system. This would imply that teaching and curriculum approaches hold the key to minimising the effect on the child of what may be termed a 'special educational need'. Along the same continuum of the environmentally focused approach, one can also view the interactional approach to SEN. Frederickson and Cline suggest this is the 'complex interaction between the child's strengths and weaknesses, the level of support available and the appropriateness of the education being provided' (p. 420). This can be viewed in the form of three components—the task, the child and the environment—and assessment should include all three aspects.

Adopting a contextual/environmental perspective to assessment and intervention can be just as beneficial as that of focusing on the child's deficits.

In terms of intervention the following can be beneficial:

- Working in groups
- Including lots of discussion
- Allowing scope for creativity but providing some kind of structure
- Ensuring active and interactive learning
- Providing 'why' questions
- Providing a lot of visuals, colour, music.

Hughes and Cooper (2007), in their book on teaching approaches for ADHD, suggest the following:

- Avoid confrontational situations.
- Show the child respect.
- Listen to the child's concerns.
- Avoid distraction.
- Keep instructions to a minimum—one at a time.
- Provide reassurance on tasks.
- Split tasks up into shorter tasks with breaks.
- Enable them to complete tasks.
- Scaffold the child's work.
- Provide routine.
- Provide outlets for active behaviour.
- Provide a clear structure in the class.

The overwhelming reaction when one examines this list is very positive. Clearly all of these points will benefit children with ADHD and help to minimise anxiety and disruption in the classroom. Yet one must consider a fundamental truth—each of these points will also be beneficial for children with dyslexia, dyspraxia and indeed, it might be argued, all children! This emphasises in many respects the futility of teaching to syndromes and the efficiency and potential effectiveness of identifying the presenting characteristics and the barriers to learning and attempting to restructure the learning experience to help to meet those individual needs.

Tridas (2007) emphasises the importance of the environment in children with ADHD. Environmental adaptations should be seen as a part of the accommodation put in place and these should be communicated to the home. This is essential to ensure success. Some strategies suggested by Tridas include:

- Establish routines.
- Create task lists.
- Organise the child's study area.
- Break routines and tasks down into small chunks to make them easier to accomplish.
- Sit child as close to the teacher as possible.
- Sit the child away from large windows or open doors.
- Use study carrels rather than desks.
- Avoid open plan classrooms.
- Set realistic expectations.

ISSUE 4. ALTERNATIVE THERAPIES

One of the areas that may have far-reaching political, social, educational and financial considerations is that known as 'alternative therapies'. These tend to be popular, innovative and often have media appeal and in some cases extravagant claims of success. That is not to say they are not helpful—some of the evidence, in fact, seems to support the benefits of some alternative forms of intervention.

One of the reasons why there has been a spate of alternative therapies in the field of learning disabilities and dyslexia is that although dyslexia has been recognised for many years, there is still no real agreement on the most effective way to remediate dyslexia and even traditional phonological-based interventions have not proved as successful in developing reading fluency as one might hope (National Reading Panel, 2000). Fawcett and Reid (2009) suggest that the problem is that alternative approaches are attractive to parents and to schools, because of the state of 'unreadiness' of the current administrative and school system to provide informed and consistently applied identification and classroom-based intervention focusing on individual needs. If provision and practice were informed and consistent then alternative approaches would not be able to penetrate into the traditional educational area. Fawcett and Reid point out that the main concern is that alternative approaches have often not undergone stringent and robust clinical trials.

Fawcett and Reid suggest that the gold standard in experimental design for evaluating interventions is the double blind placebo controlled study. It is taken from the medical field where it is widely used to evaluate the effectiveness of new drugs, and whether or not they have harmful side effects. A double blind approach means that neither the experimenter, the child, the teacher nor the family know which approach the child is receiving, either the therapy which the study is testing, or whether they have been given an alternative known as a placebo. It is important to make sure that studies are double blind, to overcome any tendency for performance to improve simply because the child or the experimenter expects this or wants this to happen. In some studies, a cross-over technique is used. This means that half the children receive the placebo in the first set of trials. This is held to be ethically sound, because no one is deprived of an intervention thought to be beneficial. A stringent and well-controlled system would mean that the trial supervisor was not aware of who received placebo and who received treatment. This approach is relatively easy within a medical setting, but is less easy to adhere to in an experimental educational setting. There has been considerable debate on whether or not the approaches typically used in the education system, for both traditional and alternative interventions, have been sufficiently researched. Improvements made using a specific method may actually reflect the commitment of the teacher rather than the effectiveness of the intervention. (For a review of some of the issues arising in the methodology of interventions see the special issue of *Dyslexia*, 2007, 13, 4, pp. 231–256). The IDA position statement Dyslexia Treatment Programs (www.interdys.org) contains helpful advice for teachers and parents (March 2009) which states "IDA cautions parents who are looking for instructors, clinicians, schools, and programs to be very thorough in their review of programs and services that claim to treat dyslexia or "cure" dyslexia. In this era of internet advertising, claims are frequently made about therapies and treatment programs that have little or no scientific merit. Claims about the effectiveness of some widely advertised programs and/or their components may be unsubstantiated by objective, independent research, and the practitioners of those programs and methods may not have met customary standards for training in the field" (p. 2). They also suggest that educational diagnostic evaluation should be used to pinpoint children's instruction and treatment needs.

Dietary Approaches

There has been considerable popular coverage of the use of food additives, and much anecdotal evidence to support the view that these may have an adverse affect on learning, particularly for children with ADHD. Richardson (2001) suggests that there is a wide spectrum of conditions in which deficiencies of highly unsaturated fatty acids appear to have some influence. Further, Richardson argues that fatty acids can have an extremely important influence on dyslexia, dyspraxia and ADHD. Richardson argues that it is not too controversial to suggest that there is a high incidence of overlap between these three syndromes. In fact, she suggests that the overlap between dyslexia and ADHD can be around 30–50% and even higher in the case of dyspraxia. Richardson also argues that the truly essential fatty acids (EFA), which cannot be synthesised by the body, must be provided in the diet—these are linoleic acid (omega 6 series) and alpha-linoleic acid (omega 3 series). She suggests that the longer-chain highly unsaturated fatty acids (HUFA) that the brain needs can normally be synthesised from EFAs, but this conversion process can be severely affected and limited by dietary and lifestyle factors. Some of the dietary factors, for example, which can block the conversion of EFA to HUFA include excess saturated fats, hydrogenated fats found in processed foods and deficiencies in vitamins and minerals, as well as excessive consumption of coffee and alcohol, and smoking. Richardson suggests that the claims connecting hyperactivity and lack of EFA are not new. Colquhoun and Bunday (1981) noted various clinical signs of possible EFA deficiency in a survey of hyperactive children, and Richardson reports on further studies that support these early claims (Stevens et al., 1996; Richardson and Puri, 2000). Furthermore, studies on dyspraxia have highlighted the possibility of links with EFA and suggested that fatty acid supplements can be beneficial (Stordy, 1995, 1997). In relation to dyslexia and ADHD, Richardson suggests that fatty acid supplements have also been shown to be successful, and supplementation has been associated with improvements in reading. She further reports on school-based trials, indicating that this intervention can be realistically applied in schools (Richardson, 2002; Portwood, 2002). More recently, Richardson and her colleagues (Cyhlarova et al., 2007) have shown that reading performance in both dyslexics and controls is linked to higher total omega-3 concentration, and that for dyslexic subjects was negatively related to omega-6 concentration, suggesting that it is the balance between the two which is relevant to dyslexia.

Dietary approaches have popular appeal as well as the effect of other environmental influences on children's learning. This latter point has been taken up in detail in Sue Palmer's book *Toxic Childhood* (Palmer, 2007). Essentially, focusing on environmental influences and a healthy diet is beneficial and may make the conditions for learning more effective. It should be considered, however, that this is no substitute for effective intervention. It may enhance the success of an intervention but it is not a replacement.

Approaches Using New Technology

There is a spate of new technology bombarding the educational market. While in the main this is advantageous, the use of technology needs to be handled sensitively and appropriately. A computer and software programs with ambitious claims will not in themselves make significant differences. They can, however, be an essential accompaniment to an appropriate learning programme. One example of this is given by Tallal and Merzenich (1993), who have claimed that, like language disordered children, children with dyslexia take longer to process sounds that change rapidly. This is test with high and low tones, or the sounds ba and da, which are only different in the first few milliseconds. Children with dyslexia (and specific language impairment) cannot tell the difference between the sounds if they are presented close together, and this means that they are likely to have problems with phonological awareness. This theory has been under development for the past 30 years. In terms of intervention, the Fast ForWord® program has been designed to train children in just those changes which prove most difficult for them. In order to help them to be successful, the sounds they hear are drawn out by 50% so that they sound like whale noises, and with this prolonged presentation children learn to complete the task.

In a controlled study, Hook et al. (2001) found that their Fast ForWord® group showed significant gains in phonemic awareness following intensive training, but after 2 years, gains in spoken language and reading were no greater than those of a control group which received no intervention, and not as good as children undertaking a more traditional intervention. It is claimed that a major drawback is the lack of flexibility in the Fast ForWord® system, which means that it is not possible to vary the program systematically to check which aspects are helpful. Evaluations of the suite of Fast ForWord® products, drawn from the IeS US Department of Education website (July, 2007; ies.ed.gov/ncee/wwc/pdf/WWC_Fast_Forword_070907.pdf; What Works Clearinghouse, 2007), have identified five studies from the 115 which they reviewed which meet their stringent criteria for evidence standards, based on randomised controlled trials. More than half of the studies reviewed were reports from the Scientific Learning Corporation, which distribute Fast ForWord®. These studies, including 587 children from kindergarten to third grade, show that there were positive effects on alphabetics (mean improvement 8 percentile points) and mixed effects on comprehension (mean improvement 1 percentile point), but the website considers the evidence for improvement to be small. None of the studies meeting the criteria address fluency or general reading achievement.

Fast ForWord® is used widely in the USA, with over 570 000 students using the program in 3700 schools nationwide.

There are a number of other programmes that rely on computer technology and often the selection of these is problematic for teachers. The golden rule is—try to get a demo disc and try it out first. Additionally, check the credentials of the company and the other products they have produced. Of course, word of mouth is the best recommendation. Seek out people who have actually used the product.

Exercise and Movement

There has been long-standing interest in exercise and therapies based on movement for children with specific learning difficulties. Fitts and Posner (1967) provided an account of the learning stages in motor skill development and, particularly, the development of automaticity. Denckla and Rudel (1976) found that children with dyslexia had a deficit in rapid, automatised naming, and Denckla (1985) suggested that children with dyslexia are characterised by a 'non-specific developmental awkwardness' that is irrespective of athletic ability. In terms of intervention, Doman and Delacato (see Tannock, 1976) through a series of exercises related motor development to the development of other cognitive skills, and this aspect can also be noted in the work of Ayres (1979) and has been developed considerably by Blythe (1992), Blythe and Goddard (2000), Goddard Blythe and Hyland (1998), Dobie (1996) and McPhillips et al. (2000).

The work of Dennison (1981; Dennison and Hargrove, 1985) and Dennison and Dennison (1997, 2001) in relation to the Brain Gym and Hannaford (1995, 1997) on the importance of dominance and laterality and, particularly, the influence of dominance patterns on learning has also been influential in classrooms, especially for children with dyslexia.

There are a number of programmes that involve movement and claim to have beneficial cognitive and learning effects for children with a range of specific learning difficulties.

The Inhibition of Primitive Reflexes

Blythe (1992) found that 85% of those children who have specific learning difficulties and do not respond to various classroom intervention strategies have a cluster of aberrant reflexes. He argues that as long as these reflexes remain undetected and uncorrected the educational problems will persist. These reflexes should only be present in the very young baby and become redundant after about six months of life. But, if these reflexes continue to be present after that time, Blythe argued, the development of the mature postural reflexes is restricted, and this will adversely affect writing, reading, spelling, copying, Mathematics, attention and concentration.

Blythe (1992) and Goddard Blythe (1996) have developed a programme—the Developmental Exercise Programme, an assessment and intervention programme—for assessing the presence of these reflexes and a series of exercises designed to control primitive reflexes and release postural reflexes. Argument in favour of the effect of uninhibited primitive reflexes on learning has been supported by other studies (Bender, 1976; Ayres, 1979; Mitchell, 1985). McPhillips et al. (2000) suggested that foetal movements, which form the basis of the Institute for Neuro-Physiological Psychology's (INPP) reflex inhibition programme (Blythe, 1992; Goddard Blythe, 1996), may play a critical role in the maturational processes of the development of the infant's brain and that this can have implications for cognitive development and subsequent skills involved in, for example, the reading process. In fact, Goddard Blythe and Hyland (1998) found birth complications to be the single most significant factor in children who later went on to develop specific learning difficulties.

Goddard Blythe (2005) investigated the extent of improvements using the INPP approaches in a study with 810 children with special educational needs and specifically assessed whether neurological dysfunction was a significant factor underlying academic achievement. The progress of 339 children aged 4 to 5 years of age was tracked through the school year to see whether children with higher scores on the INPP Developmental Test Battery (indications of neurological dysfunction) performed less well academically at the end of the school year and 235 children aged 8–10 years undertook a specific programme of developmental exercises (The INPP Schools' Developmental Exercise Programme) for 10 minutes a day under teacher supervision over the course of one academic year. The results showed that the children who participated in the daily INPP exercises made significantly greater improvement on measures for neurological dysfunction, balance and coordination when compared to a control group. Children who had scores of more than 25% on tests for neurological dysfunction and whose reading age was less than their chronological age at the outset also showed small but significantly greater progress in reading than children who did not take part in the programme. Goddard Blythe and Bythe have published a considerable amount of data to support the programme and have engaged heavily in training programmes, and the recipients of this training are actively engaged in implementing this form of treatment in clinics and in schools.

Educational Kinesiology

Educational kinesiology is a combination of applied kinesiology and traditional learning theory, although some aspects of yoga and acupressure are also evident in the recommended programme.

Kinesiology is the study of muscles and their functions with particular attention paid to the patterns of reflex activity that link effective integration between sensory and motor responses. It has been argued (Mathews, 1993) that children often develop inappropriate patterns of responses to particular situations and that these can lock the child into inappropriate habits.

Dennison and Dennison (1997, 2001) have produced a series of exercises (Brain Gym®) from which an individual programme can be devised for each child according to the assessment. Many of these exercises include activities that involve crossing the midline, such as writing a figure eight in the air, or cross-crawling and skip-across activities that require crossing the midline of the body to help achieve hemispheric integration. The aim is to achieve some form of body balance so that information can flow freely and be processed readily. This programme, known as the Brain Gym®, has been widely and successfully implemented in the school setting (Fox, 1999; Longdon, 2001; Taylor, 1998). Dennison and Dennison (1989, 2000) developed a system called Brain Organisation Profile (BOP) to visually represent their theory. Taylor (2002) examined the basis and application of this profile with children with ADHD and was able to develop a useful BOP for each child in the research sample. Taylor found that children with ADHD did show more evidence of mixed laterality processing than the control group.

However, despite the wide use and the beneficial effects echoed by teachers using the programme (Lannen, 2008, personal correspondence), in a review of the research in the area Hyatt (2007) concluded that both the theory and the experimental evidence provided do not support the current wide use in the school environment. This might be one of the situations where teachers have to try the approach and if it seems to be benefiting the child then it should be continued.

Comment on Alternative Interventions

There are many views on the efficacy of alternative programmes of treatment. These programmes are usually not harmful, and indeed those reported here appear to hold much promise. Many may appear different, but actually arise from similar causal concerns relating to the neurological–biological developmental processes and, indeed, may be complementary to each other.

Most, however, can be costly and some risk is attached to engaging wholeheartedly in any one programme. For example, one such programme, the Dore approach, was largely based on the cerebellar deficit of dyslexia (Nicolson et al., 1995; Reynolds and Nicolson, 2007). It claimed that the problems in learning to read are part of a brain-based problem in learning to become automatic in any skill and that these problems can be traced to differences in the cerebellum in dyslexia. The Dore programme is no longer available. It was expensive to deliver, employing psychologists and medically trained personnel and using large-scale technical equipment to measure progress, and the approach fuelled considerable controversy (Reynolds and Nicolson, 2007; Fawcett and Reid, 2009).

It is important, however, that enthusiasm for any particular treatment or intervention does not minimise the effect of good classroom teaching. There is an abundance of well-researched teaching and learning programmes, and the strategies reported in this book have been developed following years of practice and research. I recall speaking at a conference on dyslexia and being the only speaker to focus on what actually happens in the classroom. That is not to minimise the contributions from the other speakers—far from it—but rather to highlight that an essentially educational problem requires an educational solution.

Certainly, the theoretical justifications of various approaches are important, as are treatments supporting the foundations of learning, such as those reported in this section; but it is also important to strive for a comprehensive view and multidisciplinary approach to supporting children and adults with dyslexia and other learning difficulties. Without collaboration and cooperation between all the professionals involved in seeking to help people with learning difficulties, confusion, concern and anxiety may well arise and reach exaggerated proportions.

Silver (2001) makes illuminative comments on 'controversial therapies' and suggests that the process from initial concept to acceptance of a particular treatment approach is slow and can take years. Research needs to support a particular approach and the results need to be published in peer-reviewed journals. There is a great deal of anecdotal evidence that often convinces parents of the value of certain approaches. These usually stem from people who have benefited from the treatment or whose children have—these views are not to be discounted, although it must be acknowledged that what works for one child may not be successful for another.

There are many other alternative treatments that have not been discussed here, but are popular with parents. They include the Davis Dyslexia Correction Method, which involves orientation and symbol mastery (Davis and Braun, 1997); Sound Therapy (Johanson, 1997), which is based on frequency-specific, left hemisphere auditory stimulation with music and sounds (Auditory Discrimination Training); visual approaches such as the Meares–Irlen method which refers to the presence of a visual defect that can be related to difficulties with light source, glare, wave length and black and white contrast; the range of precision-tinted Haploscopic Filters of a specific density and hue—individually prescribed for patients—that are worn as either contact lenses or spectacles called ChromaGen™; and the process using computer software—TintaVision—that can identify the colour of filter that maximises the rate of reading and edge detection for individual learners. It can be suggested the there are too many innovations for the parent or teacher to handle or understand. This further underlines the need for collaboration between parents and professionals—perhaps the approach that always works is one that which involves 'effective communication'!

ISSUE 5. TRAINING AND PROFESSIONAL DEVELOPMENT

In 1988 I wrote an article for the *Times Educational Supplement* entitled 'Dyslexia: A Suitable Case for Training'. This was an appropriate heading because at the time there was little training of teachers in the field of dyslexia and in fact little widespread acceptance of the notion of dyslexia as being a valid condition that could be considered appropriate for a teacher training programme. Since then, however, there have been significant developments. Most of these developments have been in the area of continuous professional development (CPD) and little real progress has been made in the undergraduate initial teacher education programmes, although there have been pockets of exceptions such as the integration of dyslexia into B.Ed. modules (Johnson, 2000, personal correspondence) and the impetus from the Moray House project funded by the Scottish Dyslexia Trust and the then Scottish Education Department in the 1990s (Reid, 2001a).

There has, however, been significant progress since then and this can be noted in the vast increase of university-validated courses that have been accredited by the British Dyslexia Association (BDA), for example the Open University (www.open. ac.uk), and a number of independent training organisations have also emerged running fully accredited courses. These include Learning Works International (www.learning-works.org.uk), Dyslexia Action (www.dyslexiaaction.org.uk) and the Center for Child Evaluation and Teaching in Kuwait (CCET; www.ccetkuwait.org).

It is creditable that the BDA have set standards on these courses, and the BDA also have quality mark criteria for education authority training courses for teachers, often linked to their dyslexia-friendly schools initiative. These have made a significant

Table 18.1   AMBDA criteria

The course must provide a minimum of:

- 90 hours of lectures, seminars and guided learning hours plus private study time. It should include 12 hours of lectures and tutor led seminars devoted to the study of psychometric testing.
- 30 hours of evaluated specialist teaching, a minimum of 12 hours of which must be with the same pupil. The remaining 18 hours may be with two different pupils, one of which could be taught in a group.
- 3 hours of teaching to be observed and assessed by a course tutor who holds AMBDA.
- 3 diagnostic assessment reports stemming from three different assessments carried out under supervision and demonstrating a range of assessment experience. These must include:
  - supporting assessment plans;
  - working papers; and
  - related tutors' reports.
- 1 hour of one of the above diagnostic assessments must be observed and assessed by a course tutor who holds AMBDA.
- Observation of the 3 hours of evaluated specialist teaching for the purposes of both formative and summative assessment. This should be split into 1 hour segments and should take place at appropriate points during 30 hours of teaching.
- Teaching should be evaluated by formal and informal means of observation, teaching diaries and the monitoring of pupils' progress. The teaching programme should be discussed and approved by the supervisor or tutor. Progress should be monitored with a final report on the quality of teaching.

(Reproduced by permission of British Dyslexia Association).

difference to the awareness and acceptance of the area of dyslexia. An example of the AMBDA criteria, shown in Table 18.1, can vouch for the extent of care and consideration that has gone into ensuring the quality of such courses (see BDA website, www.bdadyslexia.org.uk).

Some of the issues that can cause some anxiety, however, are the perspectives and the philosophy of these courses. Some of the issues discussed throughout this book in terms of identification and intervention can feature in training courses. For example, to what extent do they promote individual one-to-one programmes that may not be easily applied in mainstream settings as opposed to inclusive approaches that can be carried out in a mainstream classroom? But the positive view is that there is a motivation to develop courses and clearly a positive response to them from teachers and education authorities.

The situation with undergraduate training is less promising. Often teacher education programs are very content loaded, with little scope for specialisms such as dyslexia. There is, however, evidence that many universities do have some input in the field of dyslexia, often within an SEN or Additional Support Needs in Scotland (ASN) (www.additionalsupportneeds.org.uk), but practical course components are needed to more fully equip teachers with the skills to implement programmes in the classroom.

Yet it is encouraging that major conferences such as the International Dyslexia Association (IDA) commit to a whole-day symposium of teacher education programmes entitled 'Quality Teacher Preparation Reading Programs: A Pre-requisite for Effective Reading Teachers' (IDA, 29 October 2008, Seattle, USA).

There is a view that initial teacher education programmes do not have sufficient input in the teaching of reading. This point has been made by many newly qualified teachers. One of the individual programmes recommended by the IDA is the Orton–Gillingham Approach, which is an intensive and detailed phonically based approach to teaching literacy skills to children with dyslexia. Green (2008, personal correspondence), an author in the area of dyslexia and an International Orton–Gillingham trainer, suggested that this is exactly the type of focus that teacher education programmes should be adopting. This view was supported by speakers in a symposium at the International Dyslexia Association (November 2008) on Teacher Education and Reading.

Although there have been many promising developments in the area of training, there are still a number of unresolved issues, particularly in the area of initial teacher education.

As Sir Jackie Stewart indicated in the foreword to this book, 'the teacher-training colleges (need to be) prepared to restructure their curriculum, to ensure that every single new teacher that qualifies into the profession has the skills for the early recognition of children with learning disabilities, and knows how to progress them on to more developed specialists in the field, (otherwise) we are not going to fully deal with, or resolve, the problem'. (p. xvii)

COMMENT ON ISSUES

There are a number of issues that remain unresolved in the field of dyslexia. To resolve these it is crucial for educators, teachers, parents and psychologists to be aware of the needs of young people with dyslexia, and indeed adults in relation to college and university support and support in the workplace. Yet considerable progress has been made in awareness of the needs, at both a political and a social level, but it is still important that agendas are shared, that different perspectives are communicated and that joint action and effective collaboration result. Sharing of information, dissemination of ideas and listening and appreciating different viewpoints and agendas are crucial but often, in an area where anxieties and emotions run high, this can be difficult to accomplish.

POINTS FOR REFLECTION

- Reflect on the issues relating to multilingualism. What do you consider are the key issues and challenges that need to be addressed in relation to this?

- What do you understand by the term 'culture-fair assessment'?

- Reflect on the criteria for intervention for children who are bi- or multilingual.

- Consider the role of technology for students with dyslexia. Reflect on the advantages and disadvantages of this.

continued

- Consider the overlap between dyslexia and other specific learning difficulties. What challenges does this present to educators?

- What is meant by the term 'alternative therapies'? Reflect on some of the alternative therapies you are familiar with. How useful might they be for schools?

- Consider some reasons for adopting a cautious approach when dealing with alternative interventions.

- From those mentioned in this chapter, which do you find most appealing and how might they be used in the classroom situation?

- Consider the issue of teacher education and dyslexia. Reflect on the components that newly qualified teachers would find useful.

- Reflect on the AMBDA criteria. What would you consider to be the vital elements for specialist training? Consider what other factors might be important.

Chapter 19

The Role of Parents

The role parents can play in helping their child(ren) deal with the difficulties associated with dyslexia is of far-reaching importance. In fact, the role played by parents' associations in helping to bring attention to the needs of young people with dyslexia has also been considerable. Parents have informed successive governments and participated in policy-making forums at local and national levels that have had a significant effect on practice. While thriving organisations such as the British Dyslexia Association (BDA), International Dyslexia Association (IDA) and the European Dyslexia Association (EDA) exist and continue to have an impact on policy and practice in the UK, Europe and the USA, there are other means open to parents in order to help their child fulfil his or her potential. By far the most accessible and potentially rewarding means is through direct communication with the school. This, without doubt, needs to be the parents' first port of call, as communication at this level has the potential to quell anxieties and maximise the skills of both parents and teachers. Yet, in practice this may be difficult. Some parents, rightly or wrongly, are still reluctant to approach the school and may therefore find it difficult to openly consult with the school regarding any difficulties their child may be experiencing. In fact, Mittler (2000) suggests that the whole basis of home–school relationships need to be reconceptualised. Although, as he suggests, schools have undergone considerable transformation in both accountability and accessibility over the last generation, many parents, who had little direct experience of this during their own schooldays, are still more familiar with an outdated model of home–school links. Mittler talks of a 'velvet curtain between home and school...and there is an unavoidable underlying tension that arises from the imbalance of power between them' (p. 151). Mittler therefore suggests that every school needs to have its own home–school policy that goes beyond 'fine words' (p. 153). In England and Wales the Ofsted (Office for Standards in Education) frameworks for inspection indicate that inspectors must evaluate and report on the effectiveness of the school's partnership with parents, including parental involvement with the school and the school's links with the community. The Special Educational Needs and Disability Act (DfEE, 2001) outlines steps that aim to enhance parent–school partnerships by ensuring that all local education authorities (LEAs) make arrangements for parent partnership services and by encouraging LEAs to work with voluntary associations if necessary to achieve this. Frederickson and Cline (2002) suggest that the steps indicated in this legislation could prevent many cases of dispute from going to a tribunal. Similarly, in Scotland there has been a considerable thrust towards parent partnerships, particularly in the area of dyslexia. There have been several instances of parents being involved in the development of policy documents and in dissemination (Fife Education Authority, 1996; Edinburgh City Council, 2002). There is also evidence of ministerial interest in dyslexia, with government ministers and inspectors involved in conferences and seminars (Scottish Dyslexia Forum, 2002), and parents and parents' associations have been involved in government consultation papers on a range of special educational needs (Scottish Parliament, 2001).

It is essential, therefore, that schools develop proactive working policies to promote home–school partnerships, particularly in relation to parents of children with dyslexia. Not only will this help to utilise the skills of parents but it will also avoid potential legal wrangles and the tribunals that have been evident in the past 10 years.

PARENTAL CONCERNS

Concerns experienced by parents are usually about either the lack of diagnosis or a feeling that their child's needs are not being met. Understandably, there is strong belief among parents that a label (identification of the special need) is necessary in order for their child to get appropriate help. While this may well be true in some instances, particularly if the child is significantly lagging in attainments and additional resources or a review of provision is needed, in many cases the label is not the most essential factor. The most essential factor is for the school to be aware of the child's progress in all aspects of the curriculum, to communicate this to parents and together discuss how the school (and parents) plan to deal with any lack of progress.

A comment often made by parents is that the school may not outwardly acknowledge the label 'dyslexia' or may in fact be waiting for a more formal diagnosis from an educational psychologist. This, of course, can be frustrating for parents, and while this is unfortunate it is not the 'end of the world', because the school will accept responsibility for the child's progress and will investigate, by whatever means, the child's progress and seek to find an explanation for any lack of progress. All this will be done without any recourse to a label. A label, of course, is helpful and in some situations, such as examination support, essential. In fact, Heaton (1996) found that many parents felt considerable relief when the label 'dyslexia' was provided. She quotes one parent as saying, 'I was so relieved to know that it had a name' (p. 15), and another saying, 'my family had begun to hint she might be mentally retarded because she was illiterate. I could never explain why I knew she wasn't, so the diagnosis helped me a lot' (p. 16). It is important, therefore, to consider that a label can often be accompanied by acceptance, and this can pave the way for constructive collaboration between home and school. Fawcett (2001), in fact, suggests that anxieties can arise from the potential conflict between the views of individuals and interest groups who may have different agendas. This potential conflict can be noticed between parents and teachers, in particular, and indeed this may force parents and LEAs into opposition.

This should be avoided, as anxieties and stresses can usually be felt by the child. It is important, therefore, to ensure that the aims of the school in relation to any particular child are made clear to the parents and that both parents and teachers share a common agenda in relation to the child's progress and level of work.

Crombie (2002b) suggests that cooperation and collaboration between school and parents is at the heart of the dyslexia policy and practice established in East Renfrewshire. She believes that teachers were often hesitant to label a child dyslexic. She suggests, though, that good communication with parents and an understanding of dyslexia will enable teachers to discuss with parents the reasons for their reluctance to label before the child has had the chance to make a real effort to learn to read.

Mittler (2000) maintains that when parents and practitioners work together in early years settings, the results have a positive impact on the child's development and learning. It is important, therefore, at an early stage to seek an effective partnership with parents. This, in fact, is the rationale behind the many early intervention initiatives in education (Fraser, 2002). Frederickson and Cline (2002) comment on the findings of Wolfendale (1989) that parent–school partnerships had made little impact.

PARENTAL SUPPORT

Effective communication can provide a strong platform for parental support. It has also been noted that actual diagnosis and, if appropriate, a label can also be welcome and provide some reassurance and, indeed, relief on the part of the parents. It can also be noted that a label can in fact make a difference to the child. A further example of this is the case of Philip, a day student at a school for children with specific learning difficulties in England (Open University, 2002). In the interview with Philip, he quickly pointed out that it was a relief for him to get the label 'dyslexic' because it meant, 'I was not stupid.' It can also provide children and young people with some indication of what dyslexia is and how it might affect them—positively as well as negatively. It can also make them develop skills in self-advocacy that can be extremely useful beyond school, particularly in the workplace.

Heaton (1996) provides an indication of the kinds of issues and strategies that parents need to be familiar with. For example, one of parents' most frequently asked questions is how much homework should the child with dyslexia undertake. This anxiety can stem from the fact that it may take him or her much longer than others in the class to complete the same exercise. Heaton interviewed parents on this subject who had tried a variety of strategies to make this issue as comfortable as possible for the child. She found that parents felt it was effective in some cases to use colour-coding for different subjects. This helped to save time when the child was packing for school, and it was easier to access the homework for that subject. Heaton also reports on the issue of time spent doing homework. It was indicated that some parents felt that a compromise was necessary: if the child had spent a given amount of time on the homework it should be stopped at a prearranged time, even if the homework was not fully finished.

It is important to maintain the motivation of children with dyslexia, and poring over arduous homework nightly may not be the most effective way to achieve this.

Heaton also suggests that parents should not spend too much time thinking about the extent of their child's difficulties, as this can become an obsession and eventually counterproductive.

There are a number of activities that parents can utilise to help their child with literacy. However, whatever the parent is doing should be communicated to the school and vice versa, without exception. Some programmes lend themselves more to be used by parents in conjunction with school than some others.

Many parents interviewed in Heaton's research vouched for the beneficial effects of technology and, in particular, laptop computers. One parent said, 'the computer is the best thing we ever bought, but you need to make sure you get the right one'. This is very important, as the choice and the advances in computer technology can be confusing. The BDA has a well-established computer committee which has provided advice to parents and professionals in this area (Crivelli, 2001). There are also some reading programmes that have been well received by parents and can be used in conjunction with schools, such as Toe by Toe. The programme called 'Paired Reading' is another good example of a joint school–home programme in literacy (Topping, 1996). He suggests that paired-reading is a very successful method that involves the parent (tutor) and the child (tutee) reading aloud at the same time. It is, however, a specific, structured technique. Both parent and child read all the words out together, with the tutor modulating the speed to match that of the child and acting as a good model of competent reading. The child must read every word, and when the child says a word incorrectly the tutor just tells the child the correct way to say the word. The child then repeats the word correctly, and the pair carry on. Saying 'no' and giving phonic and other prompts is forbidden. However, tutors do not jump in and correct the child straight away. The rule is that tutors pause and give the child four or five seconds to see if they will put it right by themselves. It is intended only for use with individually chosen, highly motivating, non-fiction or fiction books that are above the independent readability level of the tutee. Topping suggests, however, that the name has been a problem—the phrase 'paired-reading' has such a warm, comfortable feel to it that some people have loosely applied it to almost anything that two people do together with a book. One of the important aspects of paired-reading and, indeed, any reading activities is praise—the parent should look pleased when the child succeeds using this technique.

Topping indicates that paired-reading is suitable for children 'of all reading abilities' and can help to avoid stigmatisation. Reid (2002) suggests there are many teaching programmes, many of which will be useful for children with dyslexia. It may be misguided for parents or for teachers to pin their hopes on any one programme.

The key issue is that programmes and teaching approaches should be considered in the light of the individual child's learning profile. The school should have a good knowledge of both the child and specific teaching approaches. Again, because there is such a wealth of materials on the market, it is important to monitor and evaluate the approach and the progress periodically. It is also important that parents share in this monitoring with schools.

In relation to support, it is important to recognise that support should not be measured in terms of hours or days. It is difficult to quantify the optimum length of support for any individual young person with dyslexia. Consistency is important, and frequent periodic reviews should provide guidance on the effectiveness of the approaches being used and whether particular approaches should be continued.

It is also important to recognise that such monitoring need not be in terms of reading and spelling ages. These are important, of course, but it is also necessary to obtain information and assess performances on particular aspects of curriculum work, such as comprehension, problem solving and other activities that embrace much more than reading and spelling accuracy.

PARENTS' CHALLENGES

It is important for educators to appreciate the agenda of parents. For many parents dyslexia can be an unknown condition and anxiety can result, particularly in the face of conflicting advice and opinions. Reid (2004) interviewed a number of parents on the issues they had to deal with on discovering their child was dyslexic. Some of the responses included the need to:

- maintain the child's self-esteem;
- help the child start new work when he or she had not consolidated previous work;
- protect the dignity of the child when dealing with professionals/therapists;
- help in the child's personal organisation;
- peer insensitivity;
- misconceptions of dyslexia.

These responses touch on some of the key areas, particularly the emotional aspect of dyslexia. They also touch on the misunderstandings and misconceptions of dyslexia that can exist. Some of the other key issues that parents have to deal with include the following.

Frustration

Without question, all schools and all teachers want to do their best for all children. Schools, however, have to meet the needs of individuals as well as the needs of all learners. Teachers have also to meet the demands placed on them by the management and the education system. These demands are often based on principles relating to accountability and results. These principles can present a difficulty in relation to dyslexia because progress made by children with dyslexia may not always be easily measured, and certainly not by conventional means. For example, for some children with dyslexia, merely attending school can be a measure of success, but schools may not record this as progress and would rather focus on progress on attainments such as reading, spelling and writing. This is perfectly reasonable, but children with dyslexia may not make significant progress in this area, not at least in the short term. This can lead to some frustration on the part of parents and highlight very clearly the different agendas that can be seen between home and school. This underlines the importance of effective and shared communication.

Trust

Not all staff in schools are familiar with dyslexia. It can sometimes be difficult for parents to place their trust in a system that may not even seem to recognise dyslexia, but this is exactly what they have to do! Parents can have a role to play in providing information on dyslexia to schools—it does not need to be the other way round.

Understanding

The knowledge and awareness of dyslexia can vary from country to country and indeed within countries and school districts. Having spoken on dyslexia to parents' associations in many different countries, this is becoming very apparent and almost without exception a scheduled and advertised talk to a parents' association will include many teachers in the audience. It is important that parents understand what dyslexia is, and this should be explained to them as soon as their child is assessed; it is equally important that teachers are also aware of the different dimensions of dyslexia.

Emotional Aspects

If a child is failing in literacy or finds some aspects of learning challenging, then he or she may be affected by this emotionally. It is important that this is addressed and preferably prevented.

There are a number of ways of helping to maintain and to boost children's self-esteem but one of the most obvious and most effective ways is to ensure that they achieve some success and genuine praise. In order for praise to be effective the child has to be convinced that the praise is worthy of their achievements. When children feel a failure, it is difficult to reverse these feelings and often they need to change their perceptions of themselves. This can be a lengthy process and ongoing support, praise and sensitive handling are necessary.

Some parents have indicated that the following can be useful for developing self-esteem:

- paired-reading;
- mind mapping, including software mapping;
- memory games;
- learning styles;
- opportunity for the child to use to use verbal ability and to benefit from discussion and to focus on areas of success.

Alexander (2007) suggests that parents can serve as cheerleaders for their child. This includes:

- advocating for children when they are younger;
- teaching them to be their own advocates;
- encouraging the child when he or she hits an obstacle;

- developing their strengths and talents;
- developing their child's work habits.

PARENTS AS PARTNERS

The role parents can play in helping their child deal with the difficulties associated with dyslexia is of far-reaching importance. Parents are the first 'port of call', particularly in the kindergarten and the early years. Communication at this level has the potential to minimise anxieties and maximise the skills of parents and teachers, as well as assisting in the identification of the difficulties associated with dyslexia.

It is important to consider how parents may help at home. One of the key aspects is communication, and particularly communication with the school. This chapter ends on a positive note by suggesting that, despite the anxieties and the difficulties faced by parents, and children themselves, there have been considerable developments in schools in awareness of, and in support for, children with dyslexia. There is a great deal of support available. No parent of a child with dyslexia should feel isolated.

POINTS FOR REFLECTION

- Reflect on how schools can develop proactive working policies with parents.
- Consider the concerns experienced by parents. How might schools help to assist parents deal with these concerns?
- How can schools develop effective and constructive links with parents?

Appendix 1

Some Tests for Dyslexia that Can Be Used by Teachers

TEST OF PHONOLOGICAL AWARENESS-SECOND EDITION: PLUS (TOPA-2+)

Joseph K. Torgeson and Brian R. Bryant

- Ages: 5 through 8 years.
- Testing time: Kindergarten—30–45 min.; Early Elementary—15–30 min.
- Administration: Group or individual.

This is a group-administered, norm-referenced measure of phonological awareness for children ages 5 through 8 years. The scale, which can also be administered individually, has demonstrated reliability and the test yields valid results that are reported in terms of percentile ranks and a variety of standard scores.

COMPREHENSIVE TEST OF PHONOLOGICAL PROCESSING (CTOPP)

Richard Wagner, Joseph Torgeson and Carol Rashotte

- Ages: 5;0 through 24;11.
- Testing time: 30 minutes.
- Administration: Individual.

The Comprehensive Test of Phonological Processing (CTOPP) assesses phonological awareness, phonological memory and rapid naming. Persons with deficits in one or more of these kinds of phonological processing abilities may have more difficulty learning to read than those who do not.

LAUNCH INTO READING SUCCESS—TEST OF PHONOLOGICAL AWARENESS

Lorna Bennett and Pamela Ottley

Phonological awareness programme designed just for young children. Can prevent reading failure at an early stage if it is identified and intervention with the right programme is used. *Launch Into Reading Success* is a phonological skills training programme designed for use by teachers and other professionals in schools and for parents at home. Can provide an effective first step for a child to take in the pursuit of literacy.

GORT-4: GRAY ORAL READING TESTS, FOURTH EDITION

J. Lee Wiederholt and Brian R. Bryant

- Ages: 6;0 through 18;11.
- Administration time: 20–30 minutes.
- User qualification: Level B.

The Gray Oral Reading Tests, Fourth Edition (GORT-4) is an individually administered test of oral reading ability that provides an efficient and objective measure of growth in oral reading and an aid in the diagnosis of oral reading difficulties. Five scores give you information on a student's oral reading skills in terms of:

- *rate*—the amount of time taken by a student to read a story;
- *accuracy*—the student's ability to pronounce each word in the story correctly;
- *fluency*—the student's rate and accuracy scores combined;
- *comprehension*—the appropriateness of the student's responses to questions about the content of each story read;
- *overall reading ability*—a combination of a student's fluency (i.e., rate and accuracy) and comprehension score.

TOWRE—TEST OF WORD READING EFFICIENCY

Authors: Joseph Torgeson, Richard Wagner, and Carol Rashotte

- Ages: 6;0 through 24;11.
- Testing time: 5–10 minutes.
- Administration: Individual.

The *Test of Word Reading Efficiency* (TOWRE) is a nationally normed measure of word reading accuracy and fluency.

WIST (WORD IDENTIFICATION AND SPELLING TEST)

Barbara Wilson

Many teachers who are O-G trained use this test. Can pinpoint whether O-G would help the student (can also be done in a group).

DIBELS

dibels.uoregon.edu/

The Dynamic Indicators of Basic Early Literacy Skills (DIBELS) are a set of standardised, individually administered measures of early literacy development. They are designed to be short (one minute) fluency measures used to regularly monitor the development of pre-reading and early reading skills.

The tests above available from PRO-ED, Inc.—leading publisher of nationally standardised tests (www.proedinc.com/customer/default.aspx)

BANGOR DYSLEXIA TEST

LDA, Cambridge, www.LDAlearning.com

This is a commercially available short screening test developed from work conducted at Bangor University (Miles, 1983a). The test is divided into the following sections:

- left–right (body parts);
- repeating polysyllabic words;
- subtraction;
- tables;
- months forward/reversed;
- digits forward/reversed;
- b–d confusion;
- familiar incidence.

DYSLEXIA SCREENING TEST (DST)

Fawcett and Nicolson (1996)

The screening instrument can be used for children between 6;6 to 16;5 years of age, although there is also an alternative version developed by the same authors for younger children, Dyslexia Early Screening Test, and also an adult version (Nicolson and Fawcett, 1996). The test consists of the following attainment tests:

- one minute reading;
- two minutes spelling;
- one minute writing;

and the following diagnostic tests:

- rapid naming;
- bead threading;
- postural stability;
- phonemic segmentation;
- backwards digit span;
- nonsense passage reading;
- verbal and semantic fluency.

The Dyslexia Screening tests can be accessed by all teachers and are available from the Psychological Corporation, 24–28 Oval Road, London NW1 1YA; e-mail cservice@harcourtbrace.com.

COGNITIVE PROFILING SYSTEM (CoPS)

Lucid Creative Ltd, Beverley, Yorkshire, UK

This is a computerised screening programme and constitutes a user-friendly package, complete with facilities for student registration, graphic report and printout of results. CoPS is used in over 3500 primary schools in the UK and elsewhere in the world.

SPECIAL NEEDS ASSESSMENT PROFILE (SNAP Version 3)

Weedon and Reid (2003, 2005, 2008)

The Special Needs Assessment Profile (SNAP) is a computer-aided diagnostic assessment and profiling package that makes it possible to 'map' each students' own mix of problems on to an overall matrix of learning, behavioural and other difficulties. From this, clusters and patterns of weaknesses and strengths help to identify the core features of a student's difficulties—visual, dyslexic, dyspraxic, phonological, attentional or any other of the 17 key deficits targeted—and suggests a diagnosis that points the way forward for that individual student. It provides a structured profile which yields an overview at the early stages of 'School Action' in the Code of Practice—and also informs the process of external referral, at 'School Action Plus'.

SNAP involves four steps:

Step 1 *(Pupil Assessment Pack)*—structured questionnaire checklists for completion by class teachers and parents give an initial 'outline map' of the child's difficulties.

Step 2 *(CD-ROM)*—the SENCO or Learning Support staff charts the child's difficulties, using the CD-ROM to identify patterns and target any further diagnostic follow-up assessments to be carried out at Step 3.

Step 3 *(User's Kit)*—focused assessments from a photocopiable resource bank of quick diagnostic 'probes' yield a detailed and textured understanding of the child's difficulties.

Step 4 *(CD-ROM)*—the computer-generated profile yields specific guidance on support (including personalised information sheets for parents) and practical follow-up.

The kit helps to facilitate collaboration between different groups of professionals and between professionals and parents, which is vital in order to obtain a full picture of the student's abilities and difficulties. There is a dedicated website, freely accessible, that contains a number of ideas on teaching to cover difficulties associated with 17 different specific learning difficulties. The website address is www.SNAPassessment.com.

SNAP is available from Hodder and Stoughton (www.hoddertests.co.uk) and also at www.SNAPassessment.com.

WECHSLER INDIVIDUAL ACHIEVEMENT TEST (WIAT-11)

This is a comprehensive measurement tool useful for achievement skills assessment, learning disability diagnosis, curriculum planning, and suitable from pre-school children to adults. New norms also allow for the evaluation of and academic planning for college students with disabilities.

The test includes reading and listening comprehension, word reading and pseudoword reading, spelling and written expression as well as oral expression. There are also sub-tests on numerical operations and mathematical reasoning.

WIAT-11 is available from www.pearsonassess.com.

WIDE RANGE ACHIEVEMENT TEST (WRAT 4)

The WRAT 4 includes the following four subtests:

- Word Reading—measures letter and word decoding through letter identification and word recognition
- Sentence Comprehension—measures an individual's ability to gain meaning from words and to comprehend ideas and information contained in sentences through the use of a modified close technique

- Spelling—measures an individual's ability to encode sounds into written form through the use of a dictated spelling format containing both letters and words
- Maths Computation—measures an individual's ability to perform basic mathematic computations through counting, identifying numbers, solving simple oral problems, and calculating written maths problems.

Appendix 2

Further Contacts

N. AND S. AMERICA AND CANADA

USA

International Dyslexia Association (IDA)   www.interdys.org
Learning Disabilities Association of America   www.ldaamerica.org

Caribbean

Caribbean Dyslexia Association, Haggart Hall, St. Michael, Barbados

Argentina

APHDA   aphda@hotmail.com

Canada

Canada Dyslexia Association 495 Richmond Road, Suite 200, Ottawa, Ontario K2A
4B2, Canada; Tel: 613-722-2699; Fax: 613-722-4799;
E-mail: info@dyslexiaassociation.ca

International Dyslexia Association   www.interdys.org/Branchdetail.aspx?bid=17
  British Columbia Branch
The International Dyslexia   www.idaontario.com/dyslexia_ONBIDA_
  Association Ontario Branch   resources.html
Canadian Academy of Therapeutic   www.ogtutors.com
  Tutors

AUSTRALIA AND NEW ZEALAND

Australia

The Australian Federation of SPELD Associations	www.auspeld.org.au/2006_lavoie_tour.html
SPELD Victoria Inc.	www.speldvic.org.au
SPELD South Australia	www.speld-sa.org.au
SPELD NSW	www.speldnsw.org.au
SPELD (TAS) Inc	www.speldtasmania@bigpond.com
SPELD WA	speld@opera.iinet.net.au
	www.dyslexia-speld.com
SPELD Queensland Inc.	www.speld.org.au

New Zealand

SPELD New Zealand Inc.	www.speld.org.nz
Learning and Behaviour Charitable Trust	www.lbctnz.co.nz

EUROPE

European Dyslexia Association (EDA), E-mail: eda@kbnet.co.uk,
Website: www.dyslexia.eu.com

DITT   www.ditt-online.org/About.htm

Denmark

Danish Dyslexia Association   www.ordblind.com

Greece

Greek Dyslexia Association   www.dyslexia.gr

Hungary

Hungarian Dyslexia Association   www.diszlexia.hu

Italy

Associazione Italia Dislessia   www.dislessia.it

Luxembourg

Dyspel asbl   www.dyspel.org

Republic of Ireland

Dyslexia Association of Ireland   www.dyslexia.ie

Sweden

The Swedish Dyslexia Association – dyslexiforeningen.se

UK

British Dyslexia Association   www.bdadyslexia.org.uk
Dyslexia Scotland   www.dyslexiascotland.org.uk
Welsh Dyslexia Project   www.welshdyslexia.info

MIDDLE EAST

Israel

www.orton-ida.org.il

Kuwait

www.ccetkuwait.org
www.kuwaitdyslexia.com

ASIA

Hong Kong

Dyslexia Association (Hong Kong)   www.dyslexia.org.hk
Hong Kong Association for Specific Learning Difficulties   www.asld.org.hk

Japan

Japan Dyslexia Society   info@npo-edge.jp

Singapore

Dyslexia Association of Singapore   www.das.org.sg

AFRICA

Egypt

Learning Resource Center (LRC) Cairo, Egypt   www.lrcegypt.com

Gambia

Madonna Jarret Thorpe Trust, P.O. Box 4232, The Gambia, West Africa; Tel: 00220 9902099; E-mail: mjtt@airtip.gm. A dyslexia charity, aimed to create awareness of dyslexia to the public, schools and teaching colleges. Offers regular teacher and parent workshops. Organises conferences about dyslexia. Campaigns for the implementation of special education needs in schools curriculum. Promotes multi-sensory teaching methods in schools. Promotes specialist dyslexia teachers and holds after-school clubs.

Ghana

Crossroads Dyslexic Centre at U2KAN, P. O. Box KD525 Kanda, Accra, Ghana, West Africa; Tel: 00233-21-230391/020 811 6198; E-mail: joybanad@yahoo.com. One of the functions of a local dyslexic centre is to support and empower people with dyslexia and their families.

South Africa

SAALED, PO Box 2404, Cape Town 7740, South Africa
The Remedial Foundation, PO Box 32207, Braamfontein 2017, Johannesburg, SA

Uganda

Rise and Shine Dyslexia Organization (RASDO), P.O. Box 2882, Kampala, Uganda

OTHER WEBSITES

Dr Gavin Reid   www.drgavinreid.com
Red Rose School   www.redroseschool.co.uk   Provides for the educational,
                                                    emotional and social needs of
                                                    no greater than 48 boys and
                                                    girls, aged between 7 and
                                                    16 years, of average and above
                                                    average intelligence who
                                                    experience Specific Learning
                                                    Difficulties and/or experiences
                                                    which cause them to become
                                                    delicate and vulnerable in a
                                                    mainstream setting.

Dr. Steve Chinn, International Maths and Dyslexia expert www.stevechinn.co.uk author award winning The Trouble with Maths.

Center for Child Evaluation and Teaching (CCET), Kuwait www. ccetkuwait.org

CCET is a non-profit organization established in 1984. It is the oldest and largest charity in Kuwait dedicated to supporting individuals with learning disabilities, their families, teachers and other professionals on how to overcome the challenges they face. Provides scientific-based information on learning disabilities in both English and Arabic so as to raise awareness, build capacity and share knowledge on best practices (see website for DVD and magazine on LD).

Fun Track Learning Centre, Unit 2, 590 Stirling Highway, Mosman Park, Western Australia 6012; P.O. Box 134, Mosman Park, WA 6912

www.funtrack. com.au

ORGANISATIONS

Arts Dyslexia Trust www.sniffout.net

Learning Works International www.learning-works.org.uk

Focus on learning and motivating learners whatever their shape, size or ability! Specialise in designing professional development courses, team challenges and learning resources to meet the needs of staff, pupils and parents. Has built a reputation for high quality, inspiring training.

Creative Learning Company New Zealand www.creativelearning centre.com

CoPS www.lucid-research.com

Co:Writer, Earobics www.donjohnston.co.uk

Dyslexia Association of Ireland	www.dyslexia.ie/third.htm; www.dyslexia.ie/res.htm
Northern Ireland Dyslexia Association	www.nida.org.uk
Dyslexia Action	www.dyslexiaaction.org.uk
Dyslexia Online Magazine	www.dyslexia-parent.com/ magazine.html

ARTICLES AND REVIEWS ABOUT DYSLEXIA

Dyslexia Online Journal	www.dyslexia-adults.com/ journal.html	Articles and research for professionals working in the field of dyslexia.
Dyslexia Parents Resource	www.dyslexia-parent.com	Information and resources about dyslexia for parents of children who are, or may be dyslexic.
Family Onwards	www.familyonwards.com	
Helen Arkell Dyslexia Centre	www.arkellcentre.org.uk	
I am dyslexic - a site put together by an 11 year old dyslexic boy	www.iamdyslexic.com	
Institute for Neuro-Physiological Psychology (INPP)	www.inpp.org.uk	
Dr. Loretta Giorcelli – well-known international consultant	www.doctorg.org	
Dyslexia North West registered charity based at the Red Rose School, 28–30 North Promenade, St. Annes on Sea, Lancashire, FY8 2NQ	www.redroseschool.co.uk	
PenFriend	www.penfriend.biz	
School Daily New Zealand up to date educational news and debate	www.schooldaily.com	
SNAP assessment	www.snapassessment.com	
TextHelp	www.texthelp.com	
THRASS	www.thrass.co.uk	

Lexia-Herman Method	store.cambiumlearning. com/ProgramPage. aspx?parentId= 019005474&functionID= 009000008&pID= &site=sw	
World Dyslexia Network Foundation	web.ukonline.co.uk/wdnf/ advice.html	A series of advice and help sheets have been written by leading experts in their fields
World of Dyslexia	www.dyslexia-parent.com/ world_of_dyslexia.html	for useful links

LITERACY

The National Literacy Strategy site	www.standards.dfes.gov.uk/ literacy	
Centre for Early Literacy Univ. of Maine.	www.umaine.edu	Links to Reading Recovery project and literacy for primary children
Paired-reading, writing and thinking	www.dundee.ac.uk/ psychology/TRW	Keith Topping
Buzan Centres Ltd, 54 Parkstone Road, Poole, Dorset BH 15 2 PG	www.Mind-Map.com	
Crossbow Education, 41 Sawpit Lane, Stafford, Staffordshire ST17 OTE	www.crossboweducation.com	Games for learning
Iansyst Ltd.	www.dyslexic.com	
THRASS	www.thrass.co.uk	
PRO-ED, Inc. is a leading publisher of nationally standardized tests	www.proedinc.com/customer/ default.aspx	
Pearson Assessment	www.pearsonassess.com	
European Dyslexia Association	www.dyslexia.eu.com	
Dyslexia International Tools and Technology (DITT)	www.dyslexia- international.org	
SEN Marketing/Egon Publishers	www.senbooks.co.uk	

References

Aaron, P. G. (1989) *Dyslexia and Hyperlexia.* Boston, Kluwer.

Aaron, P. G. (1991) Can reading disabilities be diagnosed without using intelligence tests? *Journal of Learning Disabilities,* **245**, 178–186.

Aaron, P. G. (1994) Differential diagnosis of reading disabilities. In: G. Hales (ed.), *Dyslexia Matters.* London, Whurr.

Aaron, P. G. and Joshi, R. M. (1992) *Reading Problems: Consultation and Remediation.* New York, Guilford Press.

Abu-Rabia, S., Share, D. and Said, M. (2003) Word recognition and basic cognitive processes among reading-disabled and normal readers in Arabic. *Reading and Writing: An Interdisciplinary Journal,* **16**, 423–442.

Acalin, T. A. (1995) A comparison of Reading Recovery to Project READ (unpublished doctoral dissertation, California State University, Fullerton).

Adamik-Jászò, A. (1995) Phonemic awareness and balanced reading instructions. In: P. Owen and P. Pumfrey (eds), *Children Learning to Read: International Concerns. Vol. 1. Emergent and Developing Reading: Messages for Teachers.* London, Falmer Press.

Adams, M. (1990a) *Beginning to Read: Thinking and Learning about Print.* Cambridge, MA, MIT Press.

Adams, M. J. (1990b) *Beginning to Read: The New Phonics in Context.* Oxford, Heinemann.

Adrienne, F. (ed.) (2002) *Successful Inclusion of Infants and Toddlers with Disabilities in Natural Settings.* Child Development Resources, P.O. Box 280, Norge, VA.

Alexander, A. W. (2007) Developmental dyslexia. In: E. Q. Tridas (ed.), *From ABC to ADHD: What Parents Should Know About Dyslexia and Attention Problems* (pp. 57–102). Baltimore, MD, The International Dyslexia Association.

Alston, J. (1993) *Assessing and Promoting Writing Skills.* Tamworth, UK, NASEN.

Alston, J. (1996) Assessing and promoting handwriting skills. In: G. Reid (ed.), *Dimensions of Dyslexia, Vol. 2, Literacy, Language and Learning.* Edinburgh, Moray House.

Alton-Lee, A. (2006) How teaching influences learning: Implications for educational researchers, teachers, teacher educators and policy makers. *Teaching and Teacher Education,* **22**, 612–626.

Americans with Disabilities Act (1994) United States Federal Law, Washington, DC.

APA (1994) *Diagnostic and Statistical Manual of Mental Disorders* (4th edn). Washington, DC, Author.

APA (2000) *Diagnostic and Statistical Manual of Mental Disorders* (DSM-IV TR, 4th edn). Washington, DC, American Psychiatric Association.

Aram, D. M. and Healy, J. M. (1988) Hyperlexia: A review of extraordinary word recognition. In: L. K. Obler and D. Fein (eds), *Exceptional Brain.* New York, Guilford Press.

Archer, A. (1981) Decoding of multisyllable words by skill deficient fourth and fifth grade students (unpublished doctoral dissertation, University of Washington, Seattle).

Archer, A., Gleason, M. and Vachon, V. (2000) *REWARDS: Reading Excellence: Word Attack and Rate Development Strategies.* Longmont, CO: Sopris West.

Arnold, H. (1992) *Diagnostic Reading Record.* London, Hodder & Stoughton.

Atkinson, P., Davies, B. and Delamont, S. (eds) (1994) *Discourse and Reproduction: Essays in Honour of Basil Bernstein.* Cresskill, NJ, Hampton Press.

Au, K. H. and Raphael, T. E. (2000) Equity and literacy in the next millennium. *Reading Research Quarterly,* **35**(1), 143–159.

Augur, J. and Briggs, S. (1992) *The Hickey Multisensory Language Course.* London, Whurr.

Ayres, A. J. (1979) *Sensory Integration and the Child.* Los Angeles, Western Psychological Services.

Baddeley, A. (1986) Working memory. *Science,* **255**, 556–559.

Badian, N. A. (1997) Dyslexia and the double deficit hypothesis. *Annals of Dyslexia,* **47**, 69–87.

Baker, J., Dreher, M. and Guthrie, J. (2000) *Engaging Young Readers.* New York, Guilford.

Bakker, D. J. (1979) Hemispheric differences and reading strategies: Two dyslexias? *Bulletin of the Orton Society,* **29**, 84–100.

Bakker, D. J. (1990) *Neuropsychological Treatment of Dyslexia.* New York, Oxford University Press.

Barkley, R. A. (1997) *ADHD and the Nature of Self-control.* New York, Guilford Press.

Bartlett, D. and Moody, S. (2000) *Dyslexia in the Workplace.* London, Whurr.

Bath, J. B., Chinn, S. J. and Knox D. E. (1986) *The Test of Cognitive Style in Mathematics.* East Aurora, NY, Slosson (now out of print, see Chinn, 2000).

Bell, N. (1991a) Gestalt imagery: A critical factor in language comprehension (a reprint from *Annals of Dyslexia,* **41**). Baltimore, MD, Orton Dyslexia Society.

Bell, N. (1991b) *Visualizing and Verbalizing for Language Comprehension and Thinking.* Paso Robles, CA, Academy of Reading Publications.

Bell, N. (1992) *Visualizing and Verbalizing for Language Comprehension and Thinking.* Paso Robles, CA, Academy of Reading.

Bender, M. L. (1976) *The Bender–Purdue Reflex Test.* San Rafael, CA, Academic Therapy Publication.

Bergeron, B. (1990) What does the term 'whole-language' mean? Constructing a definition from the literature. *Journal of Reading Behaviour,* **22**, 301–329.

Berninger, V. (2004) Brain-based assessment and instructional intervention: understanding and changing the constraints in functional reading and writing systems. In: G. Reid and A. Fawcett (eds), *Dyslexia in Context: Research and Practice.* London, Whurr.

Berninger, V. W. (2007) *Process Assessment of the Learner (PAL-11) Assessment for Reading and Writing.* San Antonio, TX, Psychological Corporation.

Berninger, V., Vaughan, K., Abbott, R., Brooks, A., Abbott, S., Reed, E., Rogan, L. and Graham, S. (1998) Early intervention for spelling problems: Teaching spelling units of varying size within a multiple connections framework. *Journal of Educational Psychology,* **90**, 587–605.

Berryman, M. and Wearmouth, J. (2009) Responsive approaches to literacy learning within cultural contexts. In: G. Reid (ed.), *The Routledge Dyslexia Companion.* London, Routledge.

Bishop, D. V. M. (1989) Unstable vergence control and dyslexia: A critique. *British Journal of Ophthalmology,* **73**, 223–245.

Bishop, D. V. M. and Snowling, M. J. (2004) Developmental dyslexia and specific language impairment: Same or different. *Psychological Bulletin,* **130**, 858–886.

Bishop, R. (2003) Changing power relations in education: Kaupapa Maori messages for 'mainstream' education in Aotearoa, New Zealand. *Comparative Education,* **39**(2), 221–238.

Bishop, R., Berryman, M., Powell, A. and Teddy, L. (2007). *Te Kotahitanga: Improving the educational achievement of Māori students in mainstream education Phase 2: Towards a whole school approach.* Report to the Ministry of Education. Wellington, Ministry of Education.

Blau, H. and Loveless, E. J. (1982) Specific hemispheric routing: TAKV to teach spelling to dyslexics: VAK and VAKT challenged. *Journal of Learning Disabilities,* **15**(8), 461–466.

Blythe, P. (1992) *A Physical Approach to Resolving Specific Learning Difficulties.* Chester, UK, Institute for Neuro-Physiological Psychology.

Blythe, P. and Goddard, S. (2000) *Neuro-physiological Assessment Test Battery.* Chester, UK, Institute for Neuro-Physiological Psychology.

Blythe, S. G. (2001) Neurological dysfunction as a significant factor in children diagnosed with dyslexia. Paper presented at the 5th International British Dyslexia Conference, University of York, April.

Booth, T., Ainscow, M., Black-Hawkins, K., Vaughn, M. and Shaw, L. (2000) *Index for Inclusion: Developing Learning and Participation in Schools.* Bristol, Centre for Studies in Inclusive Education (CSIE).

Bowers, P. G. and Wolf, M. (1993) Theoretical links among naming speed, precise timing mechanisms and orthographic skill in dyslexia. *Reading and Writing: An Interdisciplinary Journal,* **5**, 69–85.

BPS (1999a) *Dyslexia, Literacy and Psychological Assessment.* Leicester, UK, British Psychological Society.

BPS (1999b) *The Directory of Chartered Psychologists.* Leicester, UK, British Psychological Society.

Bradley, L. (1989) Specific learning disability: Prediction-intervention-progress. Paper presented to the Rodin Remediation Academy International Conference on Dyslexia, University College of North Wales.

Bradley, L. (1990) Rhyming connections in learning to read and spell. In: P. D. Pumfrey and C. D. Elliott (eds), *Children's Difficulties in Reading, Spelling and Writing.* London, Falmer Press.

Bradley, L. and Bryant, P. (1991) Phonological skills before and after learning to read. In: S. A. Brady and D. P. Shankweiler (eds), *Phonological Processes in Literacy.* London, Lawrence Erlbaum.

Bradley, L. and Huxford, L. M. (1994) Organising sound and letter patterns for spelling. In: G. D. Brown and N. C. Ellis (eds), *Handbook of Normal and Disturbed Spelling Development, Theory, Processes and Interventions.* Chichester, John Wiley & Sons.

Bramley, W. (1996) *Units of Sound.* Staines, UK, The Dyslexia Institute.

Breznitz, Z. (2008) The origin of dyslexia: The asynchrony phenomenon. In: G. Reid, A. Fawcett, F. Manis and L. Siegel (eds), *The Sage Dyslexia Handbook.* London, Sage.

Breznitz, Z. and Horowitz, T. (2007) All the wrong and rights moves: A comparison of cerebral activity during accurate and erroneous reading performance among dyslexics and regular readers, an ERP study (manuscript submitted for publication).

Brice, M. (2001) Good practice framework of support for pupils and dyslexia in secondary schools. Paper presented at the Fifth BDA International Conference, York, April.

British Dyslexia Association (2005) *The Employers Guide to Dyslexia*, BDA, Sundial Events, Key 4 Learning, UK.

Brooks, G. (2002) *What Works for Children with Literacy Difficulties: The Effectiveness of Intervention Schemes.* London: DfES research report 380.31.

Brooks, G. (2007) *What Works for Children with Literacy Difficulties: The Effectiveness of Intervention Schemes* (3rd edn). Slough, DfCSF/NfER.

Brooks, G., Pugh, A. K. and Schagen, I. (1996) *Reading Performance at 9.* Slough, UK, NFER and the Open University.

Brown, A., Armbruster, B. and Baker, L. (1986) The role of metacognition in reading and studying. In: J. Oraspinu (ed.), *Reading Comprehension from Research to Practice.* Hillsdale, NJ, Lawrence Erlbaum.

Brown, M. (1993) Supporting learning through a whole-school approach. In: G. Reid (ed.), *Specific Learning Difficulties (Dyslexia) Perspectives on Practice.* Edinburgh, Moray House.

Brown, T. E. (1996) *Brown Attention-Deficit Disorder scales.* London, Psychological Corporation.

Brown, T. E. (2001) *Brown Attention Deficit Disorder Scales (BADDS).* San Antonio, TX, PsychCorp.

Bruck, M. (1993) Component spelling skills of college students with childhood diagnosis of dyslexia. *Learning Disabilities Quarterly,* **16**, 171–184.

Bruner, J. (1990) *Acts of Meaning.* Cambridge, MA, Harvard University Press.

Bruner, J. S. (1965). *The Process of Education.* Cambridge, MA, Harvard University Press.

Bruner, J. S. (1986) *Actual Minds, Possible Worlds.* Cambridge, MA: MIT Press.

Brunswick, N., McCrory, E., Price, C. J., Frith, C. D. and Frith, U. (1999) Explicit and implicit processing of words and pseudowords by adult developmental dyslexics: A search for Wernicke's Wortschatz? *Brain, 122*, 1901–1917.

Bryant, P. (1994) Children's reading and writing. *The Psychologist,* **7**(2), 61.

Bryant, P. and Bradley, L. (1985) *Children's Reading Problems.* Oxford, Blackwell.

Burden, B. (2002) A cognitive approach to dyslexia: Learning styles and thinking skills. In: G. Reid and J. Wearmouth (eds), *Dyslexia and Literacy, Theory and Practice.* Chichester, John Wiley & Sons.

Burroughs-Lange, S. (2008) *Comparison of Literacy Progress of Young Children in London Schools: A Reading Recovery Follow up Study.* Institute of Education, University of London, www.ioe.ac.uk/schools/ecpe/readingrecovery/London%20eval%20follow%20up%20May%2008.pdf, accessed September 2008.

Buzan, T. (1993) *The Mind Map Book: Radiant Thinking.* London, BBC Books.

Calder, I. (2001) Dyslexia across the curriculum. In: L. Peer and G. Reid (eds), *Dyslexia: Successful Inclusion in the Secondary School.* London, David Fulton.

Came, F. and Reid, G. (2008) *CAP It All: Concern, Assess, Provide: Practical Tools and Techniques to Identify and Assess Individual Needs.* Learning Works International Ltd, Wiltshire, UK.

Campione, J. C. and Brown, A. L. (1989) Assisted assessment: A taxonomy of approaches and an outline of strengths and weaknesses. *Journal of Learning Disabilities,* **22**(3), 151–165.

Carbo, M. (1987) De-programming reading failure. Giving unequal learners an equal chance. *Phi Delta Kappa,* November, 196–200.

Carver, R. P. (1998) Predicting reading level in Grades 1 to 6 from listening level and decoding level: Testing theory relevant to simple view of reading. *Reading and Writing: An Interdisciplinary Journal,* **10**, 121–154.

Castles, A., Datta, H., Gayan, J. and Olson, R. K. (1999) Varieties of developmental reading disorder: Genetic and environmental influences. *Journal of Experimental Child Psychology,* **72**, 73–94.

Catts, H. W. and Kamhi, A. G. (2005) Causes of reading disabilities. In: H. W. Catts and A. G. Kamhi (eds), *Language and reading disabilities* (pp. 94–126). Boston, MA, Allyn & Bacon.

Cazden, C. B. (1999) The visible and invisible pedagogies of Reading Recovery. In: A. J. Watson and L. R. Giorcelli (eds), *Accepting the Literacy Challenge.* Sydney, Scholastic.

CBI (2008) *Educations and Skills Survey 'Taking Stock'.* Glasgow, CBI Scotland.

Chall, J. (1967) *Learning to Read: The Great Debate.* New York, McGraw-Hill.

Chall, J. S. and Popp, H. M. (1996) *Teaching and Assessing Phonics: Why, What, When, How? A Guide for Teachers.* Cambridge, MA, Educators.

Channel 4 (1999) *Genius, Criminals and Children.* Twenty Twenty Television for Channel, 4 July.

Chapman, J. W., Tunmer, W. E. and Prochnow, J. E. (1999) Success in Reading Recovery depends on the development of phonological processing skills (revised research report for phase three of contract ER35/299/5, Palmerston North, New Zealand: Massey University).

Chinn, S. (2001) Learning styles and Mathematics. In: L. Peer and G. Reid (eds), *Dyslexia: Successful Inclusion in the Secondary School.* London, David Fulton.

Chinn, S. (2002) 'Count me in.' A comparison of the demands of numeracy and the problems dyslexic learners have with Maths. Paper presented at North Kent Dyslexia Association 13th One Day Conference for Teachers, Greenwich, London, October.

Chinn, S. (2004) *The Trouble with Maths: A Practical Guide to Helping Learners with Numeracy Difficulties.* Abingdon, RoutledgeFalmer.

Chinn, S. J. (2000) *Informal Assessment of Numeracy Skills.* Mark, UK, Markco.

Chomsky, N. (1986) *Knowledge of Language.* New York, Praeger.

Clark, D. B. (1988) *Dyslexia: Theory and Practice of Remedial Instruction.* Parkton, MD, York Press.

Clark, K (Ed.) (2003) *Count Me In: Responding to Dyslexia.* Glasgow/Edinburgh: University of Strathclyde/SEED.

Clay, M. (1985) *The Early Detection of Reading Difficulties: A Diagnostic Survey with Recovery Procedures.* Auckland, Heinemann Educational.

Clay, M. (1992) *Reading: The Patterning of Complex Behaviour.* London, Heinemann.

Clay, M. (1993) *An Observational Survey of Early Literacy Achievement.* London, Heinemann Educational.

Clay, M. and Cazden, C. B. (1990) A Vygotskian interpretation of Reading Recovery. In: L. Moll (ed.), *Vygotsky and Education* (pp. 114–1350). New York, Cambridge University Press (reprinted in C. B. Cazden 1992) *Whole Language Plus: Essays on literacy in the United States and New Zealand.* New York, Teachers College Press).

Cline, T. (1998) The assessment of special educational needs for bilingual children. *British Journal of Special Education,* **25**(4), 159–163.

Colquhoun, I. and Bunday, S. (1981) A lack of essential fatty acids as a possible cause of hyperactivity in children. *Medical Hypothesis,* **7**, 673–679.

Coltheart, M. (1978) Lexical access in simple reading tasks. In: G. Underwood (ed.), *Strategies of Information Processing* (pp. 151–216). London, Academic Press.

Combley, M. (2001) *The Hickey Multisensory Language Course* (3rd edn). London, Whurr.

Conner, M. (1994) Specific learning difficulties (dyslexia) and interventions. *Support for Learning,* **9**(3), 114–119.

Conners, C. K. (1996) *Conner's Rating Scales Revised.* London, Psychological Corporation.

Cooke, A. (2002) *Tackling Dyslexia* (2nd edn). London, Whurr.

Cooper, C. (1995) Inside the WISC-III UK. *Educational Psychology in Practice,* **10**(4), 215–219.

Cornelissen, P. L., Richardson, A. R., Mason, A., Fowler, M. S. and Stein, J. F. (1994) Contrast sensitivity and coherent motion detection measured at photopic luminance levels in dyslexics and controls. *Vision Research,* **315**, 1483–1494.

Cowling, H. and Cowling, K. (1998) *Toe by Toe: Multisensory Manual for Teachers and Parents.* Bradford, UK, Toe by Toe.

Cox, A. R. (1985) Alphabetic Phonics. An organisation and expansion of Orton–Gillingham. *Annals of Dyslexia,* **35**, 187–198.

Cox, A. R. (1992) *Foundations for Literacy. Structures and Techniques for Multisensory Teaching of Basic Written English Language Skills.* Cambridge, MA, Educators.

Crivelli, V. (2001) ICT across the curriculum. In: L. Peer and G. Reid (eds), *Dyslexia and Inclusion.* London. David Fulton.

Croft, S. and Topping, K. (1992) *Paired Science: A Resource Pack for Parents and Children.* Centre for Paired Learning, Dundee, UK, University of Dundee.

Crombie, M. (2002a) Dyslexia: A new dawn (unpublished PhD thesis, University of Strathclyde, Glasgow).

Crombie, M. (2002b) Dealing with diversity in the primary classroom: A challenge for the class teacher. In: G. Reid and J. Wearmouth (eds), *Dyslexia and Literacy: Theory and Practice.* Chichester, John Wiley & Sons.

Crombie, M. (2002c) Early screening policy and practice. Paper presented at 'Practice Makes Perfect' Conference held by Dyslexia in Scotland, Edinburgh, 28 September 2002.

Crombie, M. and McColl, H. (2001) Dyslexia and the teaching of modern foreign languages. In: L. Peer and G. Reid (eds), *Dyslexia: Successful Inclusion in the Secondary School.* London, David Fulton.

Cudd, E. T. and Roberts, L. L. (1994) A scaffolding technique to develop sentence sense and vocabulary. *The Reading Teacher,* **47**(4), 346–349.

Curtis, M. E. (1980) Development of components of reading skills. *Journal of Educational Psychology,* **72**(5), 656–669.

Curtis, P. (2008) 'Education: Primary pupils without basic skills highlight Labour's biggest failure, says schools minister'. *The Guardian,* Thursday August 21 (www.guardian.co.uk/education/2008/aug/21/primaryschools.earlyyearseducation).

Cyhlarova, E., Bell, J. G., Dick, J. R., Mackinlay, E. E., Stein, J. F. and Richardson, A. J. (2007) Membrane fatty acids, reading and spelling in dyslexic and non-dyslexic adults. *European Neuropsychopharmacology,* **17**, 116–121.

Dal, M. (2008) Dyslexia and foreign language learning. In: G. Reid, A. Fawcett, F. Manis and L. Siegel (eds), *The Sage Dyslexia Handbook.* London, Sage.

Dal, M., Arnbak, E. and Brandstätter, H. (2005) *Dyslexic Students and Foreign Language Learning.* Reykjavik, Iceland University of Education.

Daly, K. A. (1997) Definition and epidemiology of otitis media. In: J. E. Roberts, I. F. Wallace and F. W. Henderson (eds), *Otitis Media in Young Children: Medical, Developmental and Educational Considerations* (pp. 14–15). Baltimore, MD, Brookes.

Daniels, H., Creese, A., Hey, V., Leonard, D. and Smith, M. (2001) Gender and learning: Equity, equality and pedagogy. *Support for Learning,* **16**(3), 112–116.

Dargie, R. (1995) *Scotland in the Middle Ages.* Fenwick, UK, Pulse.

Dargie, R. (2001) Dyslexia and History. In: L. Peer and G. Reid (eds), *Dyslexia: Successful Inclusion in the Secondary School.* London, David Fulton.

Davis, R. D. and Braun, E. M. (1997) *The Gift of Dyslexia. Why Some of the Smartest People Can't Read and How They Can Learn.* London, Souvenir Press.

de Jong, P. F. and van der Leij, A. (2003) Developmental changes in the manifestation of a phonological deficit in dyslexic children learning to read a regular orthography. *Journal of Educational Psychology,* **95**, 22–40.

Deacon, S. H., Parrila, R. and Kirby, J. R. (2008) A review of the evidence on morphological processing in dyslexics and poor readers: A strength or weakness? In: G. Reid, A. Fawcett, F. Manis and L. Siegel (eds), *The Sage Dyslexia Handbook.* London, Sage.

Delamont, S. (2003) *Feminist Sociology.* London, Sage.

Denckla, M. B. (1985) Motor co-ordination in dyslexic children: Theoretical and clinical implications. In: F. H. Duffy and N. Geschwind (eds), *Dyslexia: A Neuroscientific Approach to Clinical Evaluation.* Boston, Little Brown.

Denckla, M. B. and Rudel, R. G. (1976) Rapid 'automatised' naming (RAN): Dyslexia differentiated from other learning disabilities. *Neuropsychologia,* **14**, 471–479.

Dennison, G. E. and Dennison, P. E. (1989) *Educational Kinesiology Brain Organisation Profiles.* Glendale, CA, Edu-Kinesthetics.

Dennison, G. E. and Dennison, P. E. (1997) *The Brain Gym® Handbook.* Glendale, CA, Edu-Kinesthetics.

Dennison, G. E. and Dennison, P. E. (2000) *Educational Kinesiology Brain Organisation Profiles (Teacher's training manual, 3rd edn).* Glendale, CA, Edu-Kinesthetics.

Dennison, G. E. and Dennison, P. E. (2001) *Brain Gym® Course Manual.* Glendale, CA, Edu-Kinesthetics.

Dennison, P. E. (1981) *Switching On: The Holistic Answer to Dyslexia.* Glendale, CA, Edu-Kinesthetics.

Dennison, P. E. and Hargrove, G. (1985) *Personalized Whole Brain Integration.* Glendale, CA, Edu-Kinesthetics.

Deno, S. L. (1989) Curriculum based measurement and special education services: A fundamental and direct relationship. In: M. R. Shinn (ed.), *Curriculum-based Measurement: Assessing Special Children.* New York, Guilford Press.

DES (1975) *A Language for Life* (Report of the Committee of Inquiry—chair: Sir Alan Bullock for the Department for Education and Skills). London, HMSO.

DfEE (1998) *Framework for Teaching.* London, Department for Education and Employment.

DfEE (2001) *Bridging the Gap.* London, Department for Education and Employment.

DfES (2001) *Special Education Needs Code of Practice.* London, Department for Education and Skills.

DfES (2003) *Excellence and Enjoyment: A Strategy for Primary Schools.* London, DfESDfES0377/2003.

DfES (2005) *PATOSS Working Group 2005/DfES Guidelines.* www.patoss-dyslexia.org/DSA22.html.

DfES (2006) *The Independent Review of the Teaching of Early Reading (Rose Report).* London, Department for Education and Skills. www.standards.dcsf.gov.uk/phonics/report.pdf.

Dimitriadi, P. (1999) Multimedia authoring and specific learning difficulties (dyslexia): A single case study. Paper delivered at CAL99, London, Institute of Education, 29–31 March.

Dimitriadi, Y. (2000) Using ICT to support bilingual dyslexic learners. In: L. Peer and G. Reid (eds), *Multilingualism, Literacy and Dyslexia. A Challenge for Educators.* London. David Fulton.

Diniz, F. (2002) Interview for audio E 801: *Difficulties in Literacy Development.* Milton Keynes, Open University.

Diniz, F. A. and Reed, S. (2001) 'Inclusion': Issues. In: L. Peer and G. Reid (eds), *Dyslexia: Successful Inclusion in the Secondary School.* London, David Fulton.

Ditchfield, D. (2001) Dyslexia and Music. In: L. Peer and G. Reid (eds), *Dyslexia: Successful Inclusion in the Secondary School.* London, David Fulton.

Dobie, S. (1996) Perceptual motor and neurodevelopmental dimensions in identifying and remediating developmental delay in children with specific learning difficulties. In: G. Reid (ed.), *Dimensions of Dyslexia.* Edinburgh, Moray House.

Dodds, D. (1996) Differentiation in the secondary school. In: G. Reid (ed.), *Dimensions of Dyslexia. Vol. 1: Assessment, Teaching and the Curriculum.* Edinburgh, Moray House Publications.

Dodds, D. and Lumsden, D. (2001) Examining the challenge: Preparing for examinations. In: L. Peer and G. Reid (eds), *Dyslexia: Successful Inclusion in the Secondary School.* London, David Fulton.

Dombey, H. (1992) Reading Recovery: A solution to all primary school reading problems? *Support for Learning,* **7**(3), 111–115.

Donaldson, M. (1978) *Children's Minds.* Glasgow, Fontana/Collins.

Dore, W. and Rutherford, R. (2001) Closing the gap. Paper presented at the BDA 6th International Conference on Dyslexia, York.

Dyson, A. (2001) Special needs education as the way to equity: An alternative approach? *Support for Learning,* **16**(3), 99–104.

Dyson, A. and Skidmore, D. (1996) Contradictory models: The dilemma of specific learning difficulties. In: G. Reid (ed.), *Dimensions of Dyslexia, Vol. 2: Literacy, Language and Learning.* Edinburgh, Moray House.

Dyspraxia Trust (2001) *Praxis Makes Perfect.* Hitchin, UK, Dyspraxia Trust.

Eames, F. H. (2002) Changing definitions and concepts of literacy: Implications for pedagogy and research. In: G. Reid and J. Wearmouth (eds), *Dyslexia and Literacy: Theory and Practice.* Chichester, John Wiley & Sons.

Eden, G. F., VanMeter, J. W., Rumsey, J. M., Maisog, J. M., Woods, R. P. and Zeffiro, T. A. (1996) Abnormal processing of visual motion in dyslexia revealed by functional brain imaging. *Nature,* **382,** 67–69.

Edinburgh City Council (2002) Dyslexia—'Good Practice' Conference for Parents, King's Manor Hotel, Edinburgh, 22 March 2002.

Ehri, L. (1992) Reconceptualizing the development of sight word reading and its relationship to recoding. In: P. Gough, L. Ehri and R. Treiman (eds), *Reading Acquisition* (pp. 107–143). Hillsdale, NJ, Lawrence Erlbaum.

Ehri, L. (1995a). Phases of development in learning to read words by sight. *Journal of Research in Reading,* **18,** 116–125.

Ehri, L. (1995b) The emergence of word reading in beginning reading. In: P. Owen and P. Pumfrey (eds), *Children Learning to Read: International Concerns. Emergent and Developing Reading: Messages for Teachers.* London, Falmer Press.

Ehri, L. (1999) Phases of development in learning to read words. In: J. Oakhill and R. Beard (eds), *Reading Development and the Teaching of Reading: A Psychological Perspective* (pp. 79–108). Oxford, Blackwell.

Ehri, L. (2005) Learning to read words: Theory, findings, and issues. *Scientific Studies of Reading,* **9**(2), 167–188.

Ehri, L. and McCormick, S. (1998) Phases of word learning: Implications for instruction with delayed and disabled readers. *Reading and Writing Quarterly,* **14,** 135–163.

Ehri, L. C. (2002) Reading processes, acquisition, and instructional implications. In: G. Reid and J. Wearmouth (eds), *Dyslexia and Literacy: Theory and Practice.* Chichester, John Wiley & Sons.

Ehri, L. C. and Robbins, C. (1992) Beginners need some decoding skill to read words by analogy. *Reading Research Quarterly,* **21**(1), 13–26.

Ekwall, E. and Ekwall, C. (1989) Using metacognitive techniques for the improvement of reading comprehension. *Journal of Reading Education,* **14**(3), 6–12.

Elbaum, B., Vaughn, S., Hughes, M. T. and Moody, S. W. (2000) How effective are one-to-one tutoring programs in reading for elementary students at risk for reading failure? A meta-analysis of the intervention research. *Journal of Educational Psychology,* **92**(4), 605–619.

Elbeheri, G. and Everatt, J. (2008) Dyslexia in different orthographies: Variability in transparency. In: G. Reid, A. Fawcett, F. Manis and L. Siegel (eds), *The Sage Dyslexia Handbook.* London, Sage.

Elbro, C., Nielsen, I. and Petersen, D. K. (1994) Dyslexia in adults: Evidence for deficits in non-word reading and in the phonological representation of lexical items. *Annals of Dyslexia,* **44,** 205–226.

Elbro, C., Rasmussen, I. and Spelling, B. (1996) Teaching reading to disabled readers with language disorders: A controlled evaluation of synthetic speech feedback. *Scandinavian Journal of Psychology,* **37,** 140–155.

Elley, W. B. (1992) *How in the World Do Students Read?* The Hague, International Association for the Evaluation of Educational Achievement.

Elliott, J. (2007) Dyslexia: A label to get you off the hook. 27 May, quoted in Bee, P. (2007) www.timesonline.co.uk/tol/life_and_style/health/features/article1847619.ece.

Ellis, N. C. and Large, B. (1981) The early stage of reading: A longitudinal study. *Applied Cognitive Psychology,* **2,** 47–76.

Evans, A. (1984b) Paired reading: A report on two projects (unpublished paper, Division of Education, University of Sheffield).

Evans, T. L. P. (1996) *I can read deze books.* A qualitative comparison of the Reading Recovery program and a small group reading intervention (unpublished doctoral dissertation, Auburn University, Auburn, Alabama).

Everatt, J. (2002) Visual processes. In: G. Reid and J. Wearmouth (eds), *Dyslexia and Literacy, Theory and Practice.* Chichester, John Wiley & Sons.

Everatt, J. and Elbeheri, G. (2008) Dyslexia in different orthographies: Variability in transparency. In: G. Reid, A. Fawcett, F. Manis and L. Siegel (eds), *The Sage Dyslexia Handbook.* London, Sage.

Everatt, J. and Reid, G. (2009) An overview of recent research. In: G. Reid (ed.), *The Routledge Dyslexia Companion.* London, Routledge.

Everatt, J., Adams, E. and Smythe, I. (2000) Bilingual children's profiles on dyslexia screening measures. In: L. Peer and G. Reid (eds), *Multilingualism, Literacy and Dyslexia. A Challenge for Educators.* London, David Fulton.

Fawcett, A. (1989) Automaticity: A new framework for dyslexic research. Paper presented at the 1st International Conference of the British Dyslexia Association, Bath.

Fawcett, A. (2001) A parent's perspective: A personal account. In: L. Peer and G. Reid (eds), *Dyslexia and Inclusion.* David Fulton, London.

Fawcett, A. (2002) Dyslexia and literacy: Key issues for research. In: G. Reid and J. Wearmouth (eds), *Dyslexia and Literacy, Theory and Practice.* Chichester, John Wiley & Sons.

Fawcett, A. and Reid, G. (2009) Dyslexia and alternative interventions. In: G. Reid (ed.), *The Routledge Dyslexia Companion.* London, Routledge.

Fawcett, A. J. and Nicolson, R. (2008) Dyslexia and the cerebellum. In: G. Reid, A. Fawcett, F. Manis and L. Siegel (eds), *The Sage Dyslexia Handbook.* London, Sage.

Fawcett, A. J. and Nicolson, R. I. (1992) Automatisation deficits in balance for dyslexic children. *Perceptual and Motor Skills,* **75**, 507–529.

Fawcett, A. J. and Nicolson, R. I. (1996) *The Dyslexia Screening Test.* London, The Psychological Corporation.

Fawcett, A. J. and Nicolson, R. I. (1997) *The Dyslexia Early Screening Test.* London, The Psychological Corporation.

Fawcett, A. J. and Nicolson, R. I. (1998) *Dyslexia Adult Screening Test.* London, The Psychological Corporation.

Fawcett, A. J. and Nicolson, R. I. (2001) Dyslexia: The role of the cerebellum. In: A. J. Fawcett (ed.), *Dyslexia: Theory and Good Practice.* London, Whurr.

Fawcett, A. J. and Nicolson, R. I. (eds) (1994) *Dyslexia in Children: Multidisciplinary Perspectives.* Hemel Hempstead, UK, Harvester Wheatsheaf.

Fennema-Jansen, S. (2001) Measuring effectiveness: Technology to support writing. *Special Education Technology,* January/February, 16–22.

Feuerstein, R. (1979) *The Dynamic Assessment of Retarded Performers: The Learning Potential Assessment Device, Theory, Instruments and Techniques.* Baltimore, MD, University Park Press.

Fife Education Authority (1996) *Partnership: Parents, Professionals and Pupils.* Fife, UK, Fife Education Authority.

Fill, M., Gips, M. and Hosty, K. (1998) The Phono-Graphix method for teaching reading and spelling. *The Clinical Connection,* **11**, 4.

Fitch, R. H., Miller, S. and Tallal, P. (1997) Neurobiology of speech perception. *Annual Review of Neuroscience,* **20**, 331–353.

Fitts, P. M. and Posner, M. I. (1967) *Human Performance.* Belmont, CA, Brooks Cole.

Flavell, J. H. (1979) Metacognition and cognitive monitoring. *American Psychologist,* October, 906–911.

Florian, L. (2005) 'Inclusion', 'special needs' and the search for new understandings. *Support for Learning,* **20**(2), 96–98.

Forbes, S. and Powell, R. (2000) Bilingualism and literacy assessment. In: L. Peer and G. Reid (eds), *Multilingualism, Literacy and Dyslexia. A Challenge for Educators.* London, David Fulton.

Fox, A. (1999) An evaluation of the contribution of a Brain Gym® intervention programme on the acquisition of literacy skills in a mainstream primary school setting (unpublished M.Ed. dissertation, University of Edinburgh, August).

Frankiewicz, R. G. (1985) *An Evaluation of the Alphabetic Phonics Program Offered in the One-to-One Mode.* Houston, TX, Neuhaus Education Center.

Fraser, I. (2002) *Difficulties in Literacy Development* (interview in ED 801 course video). Milton Keynes, UK, Open University.

Frederickson, F., Frith, U. and Reason, R. (1997) *The Phonological Abilities Battery.* London, NFER-Nelson.

Frederickson, N. (1999) The ACID test—or is it? *Educational Psychology in Practice,* **15**(1), 2–8.

Frederickson, N. and Cline, T. (2002) *Special Educational Needs, Inclusion and Diversity: A Textbook.* Buckingham, UK, Open University Press.

Friel-Palti, S. and Finitzo, T. (1990) Language learning in a prospective study of otitis media with effusion in the first two years of life. *Journal of Speech and Hearing Research, 33*, 188–194.

Frith, U. (1985) Beneath the surface of developmental dyslexia. In: K. E. Patterson, J. C. Marshall and M. Coltheart (eds), *Surface Dyslexia*. London, Routledge & Kegan Paul.

Frith, U. (1995) Dyslexia: Can we have a shared theoretical framework ? *Educational and Child Psychology,* **12**(1), 6–17.

Frith, U. (2002) Resolving the paradoxes of dyslexia. In: G. Reid and J. Wearmouth (eds), *Dyslexia and Literacy, Theory and Practice*. Chichester, John Wiley & Sons.

Galaburda, A. (1993) Cortical and sub-cortical mechanisms in dyslexia. Paper presented at 44th Annual Conference, Orton Dyslexia Society, New Orleans.

Galaburda, A. M. and Rosen, G. D. (2001) Neural plasticity in dyslexia: A window to mechanisms of learning disabilities. In: J. L. McClelland and R. S. Siegler (eds), *Mechanisms of Cognitive Development: Behavioral and Neural Perspectives* (pp. 307–323). Mahwah, NJ, Lawrence Erlbaum.

Gallagher, A., Frith, U. and Snowling, M. (2000) Precursors of literacy: Delay among children at genetic risk of dyslexia. *Journal of Child Psychology and Psychiatry,* **41**, 203–213.

Gardner, H. (1983) *Frames of Mind. The Theory of Multiple Intelligences*. New York, Harper & Row.

Gardner, H. (1985) *Frames of Mind*. New York, Basic Books.

Gardner, H. (1999) Foreword. In: D. Lazear, *Eight Ways of Knowing Teaching for Multiple Intelligences* (3rd edn, pp. vii–viii). Arlington Heights, IL, Skylight Professional Development.

Garland, J. (1997) Phelps v The Mayor and Burgesses of the London Borough of Hillingdon.

Garner, P. and Sandow, S. (1995) *Advocacy, Self-advocacy and Special Needs*. London, David Fulton.

Gerber, P. J. (1997) Life after school: Challenges in the workplace. In: P. J. Gerber and D. S. Brown (eds), *Learning Disabilities and Employment*. Austin, TX, Pro-Ed.

Gersch, I. (2001) Listening to children. In: J. Wearmouth (ed.), *Special Educational Provision in the Context of Inclusion*. London, David Fulton.

Geschwind, N. and Galaburda, A. (1985) Cerebral lateralisation biological mechanisms associations and pathology: A hypothesis and a programme for research. *Archives of Neurology,* **42**, 428–459.

Gilger, J. W., Pennington, B. F. and De Fries, J. C. (1991) Risk for reading disability as a function of parental history in three family studies. *Reading and Writing,* **3**, 205–218.

Gilger, J. W. (2008) Some special issues concerning the genetics of dyslexia: Revisiting multivariate profiles, comorbidities, and genetic correlations. In: G. Reid, A. Fawcett, F. Manis and L. Siegel (eds), *The Sage Dyslexia Handbook*. London, Sage.

Giorcelli, L. R. (1995) An impulse to soar: Sanitisation, silencing and special education. The Des English Memorial Lecture given at the Australian Association of Special Education Conference, Darwin (reproduced in SPELD Celebration of Learning Styles Conference Proceedings, 1996). Christchurch, New Zealand, SPELD.

Giorcelli, L. R. (1999) Inclusion and other factors affecting teachers' attitudes to literacy programs for students with special needs. In: A. J. Watson and L. R. Giorcelli (eds), *Accepting the Literacy Challenge*. Gosford, Australia, Scholastic.

Given, B. K. and Reid, G. (1999) *Learning Styles: A Guide for Teachers and Parents*. St Annes-on-Sea, UK, Red Rose.

Glynn, T. and McNaughton, S. (1985) The Mangere home and school remedial reading procedures: Continuing research on their effectiveness. *New Zealand Journal of Psychology,* **15**(2), 66–77.

Glynn, T., Crooks, T., Bethune, N., Ballard, K. and Smith, J. (1989) *Reading Recovery in Context* (a report). Wellington, New Zealand, New Zealand Department of Education.

Glynn, T., Wearmouth, J. and Berryman, M. (2006) *Supporting Students with Literacy Difficulties: A Responsive Approach*. Milton Keynes, Open University Press/McGraw-Hill Education (ISBN: PB 13-978-0335-21915-0).

Goddard Blythe, S. (1996) *Developmental Exercise Programme*. Chester, UK, Institute for Neuro-Physiological Psychology.

Goddard Blythe, S. (2005) Releasing educational potential through movement. *Child Care in Practice,* **11**(4), 415–432.

Goddard Blythe, S. and Hyland, D. (1998) Screening for neurological dysfunction in the specific learning difficulties child. *British Journal of Occupational Therapy,* **61**(10), 459–464.

Goodman, K. (1976) Reading—a psycholinguistic guessing game. In: H. Singer and R. B. Ruddell (eds), *Theoretical Models and Processes of Reading*. Newark, NY, International Reading Association.

Gorrie, B. and Parkinson, E. (1995) *Phonological Awareness Procedure*. Ponteland, UK, Stass.

Goswami, U. (1990) A special link between rhyming skills and the use of orthographic analogies by beginning readers. *Journal of Child Psychology and Psychiatry*, **31**, 301–311.

Grant, D. (in press) The psychological assessment of neurodiversity. In: D. Pollak (ed.), *Neurodiversity in Higher Education*. Wiley, Chichester.

Gravel, J. S. and Wallace, I. F. (1995) Early otitis media, auditory abilities and educational risk. *American Journal of Speech-Language Pathology*, **4**, 89–94.

Green, S. (2006) Reciprocal reading and comprehension monitoring. Paper presented at South African Association of Learning Disabilities Conference, April.

Green, S. (2008) Is there a need for the development of a customized protocol for communication between home, school and REACH Learning Center and can this protocol have a perceived positive impact on support for students who experience difficulties with literacy? (unpublished dissertation E 801, Milton Keynes, Open University).

Gregg, N. and Baner, M. (2009) Reading comprehension solutions for college students with dyslexia in an era of technology: An integrated approach. In: G. Reid (ed.), *The Routledge Dyslexia Companion*. London, Routledge.

Hagtvet, B. E. (1997) Phonological and linguistic–cognitive precursors of reading abilities. *Dyslexia*, **3**(3), 163–177.

Hales, G. (2001) Self-esteem and counselling. In: L. Peer and G. Reid (eds), *Dyslexia: Successful Inclusion in the Secondary School*. London, David Fulton.

Hall, K. (1998) 'Our nets define what we shall catch': Issues in English assessment in England. In: G. Shiel and U. Ni Dhalaigh (eds), *Developing Language and Literacy: the Role of the Teacher* (pp. 153–167). Dublin, Reading Association of Ireland.

Hannaford, C. (1995) *Smart Moves. Why Learning Is Not All in Your Head*. Arlington, VA, Great Ocean.

Hannaford, C. (1997) *The Dominance Factor. How Knowing Your Dominant Eye, Ear, Brain, Hand and Foot Can Improve Your Learning*. Arlington, VA, Great Ocean.

Harker, R. (2007) *Ethnicity and School Achievement: Some Data to Supplement the Biddulph et al.* (2003) Best Evidence Synthesis: Secondary analysis of the Progress at School and Smithfield (1994) data sets for the iterative Best Evidence Synthesis Programme. Wellington: Ministry of Education.

Harris, C. (1993) *Fuzzbuzz Books/Spell/Words/Letters*. Oxford, Oxford University Press.

Harrison, C. (1994) *Literature Review: Methods of Teaching Reading*. Edinburgh, Scottish Office Education Department.

Hasbrouck, J. E., Ihnot, C. and Rogers, G. H. (1999) 'Read Naturally': A strategy to increase oral reading fluency. *Reading Research and Instruction*, **39**, 27–38.

Hatcher, J. and Snowling, M. J. (2002) The phonological representations hypothesis of dyslexia: From theory to practice. In: G. Reid and J. Wearmouth (eds), *Dyslexia and Literacy, Theory and Practice*. Chichester, John Wiley & Sons.

Hatcher, P. (1994) *Sound Linkage. An Integrated Programme for Overcoming Reading Difficulties*. London, Whurr.

Hatcher, P. (2001) *Sound Linkage* (2nd edn). Chichester, Wiley.

Healy, J. (1982) The enigma of hyperlexia. *Reading Research Quarterly*, **17**, 319–338.

Healy, J. M. (1991) *Endangered Minds*. Touchstone, NJ, Simon & Schuster.

Heaton, P. (1996) *Dyslexia: Parents in Need*. London, Whurr.

Henderson, A. (1998) *Maths for the Dyslexic (A Practical Guide)*. London, David Fulton.

Henderson, S. and Sugden, D. (1992). *Movement Assessment Battery for Children*. Sidcup, Kent.

Henry, M. (1996) The Orton–Gillingham approach. In: G. Reid (ed.), *Dimensions of Dyslexia*, Vol. 1: *Assessment, Teaching and the Curriculum*. Edinburgh, Moray House.

Henry, M. K. (2003) *Unlocking Literacy: Effective Decoding and Spelling Instruction*. Baltimore, MD, Brookes.

HMIE (2008) 'Education for Learners with Dyslexia' Inspectorate Report. Scottish Executive, October 2008.

HMSO (2004) *The Children's Act—Every Child Matters: Change for Children*. London, HMG.

Holloway, J. (2000) *Dyslexia in Focus at 16 Plus: An Inclusive Teaching Approach.* Tamworth, UK, NASEN.

Holmes, P. (2001) Dyslexia and physics. In: L. Peer and G. Reid (eds), *Dyslexia: Successful Inclusion in the Secondary School.* London, David Fulton.

Hook, P. E., Macaruso, P. and Jones, S. (2001) Efficacy of Fast ForWord training on facilitating acquisition of reading skills by children with reading difficulties. *Annals of Dyslexia,* **51**, 73–96.

Hornsby, B. and Farmer, M. (1990 and 1993) Some effects of a dyslexia centred teaching programme. In: P. D. Pumfrey and C. D. Elliott (eds), *Children's Difficulties in Reading, Spelling and Writing.* London, Falmer Press.

Hornsby, B. and Miles, T. R. (1980) The effects of a dyslexic-centred teaching programme. *British Journal of Educational Psychology,* **50**(3), 236–242.

Hornsby, B. and Shear, F. (1980) *Alpha to Omega: The A–Z of Teaching Reading, Writing and Spelling.* London, Heinemann Educational.

Houston, M. (2002) *Dyslexia: Good Practice Guide.* City of Edinburgh Council, UK.

Howlett, C. A. (2001) Dyslexia and Biology. In: L. Peer and G. Reid (eds), *Dyslexia: Successful Inclusion in the Secondary School.* London, David Fulton.

Hubicki, M. and Miles, T. R. (1991) Musical notation and multi-sensory learning in child language. *Child Language Teaching and Therapy,* **7**(1), 61–78.

Hughes, L. A. and Cooper, P. (2007) *A Teacher's Guide for ADHD.* London, Sage.

Hunt, G. (2002) Critical literacy and access to the lexicon. In: G. Reid and J. Wearmouth (eds), *Dyslexia and Literacy: Theory and Practice.* Chichester, John Wiley & Sons.

Hunter, V. (2001) Dyslexia and General Science. In: L. Peer and G. Reid (eds), *Dyslexia: Successful Inclusion in the Secondary School.* London, David Fulton.

Hyatt, Keith J. (2007) Brain Gym®: Building stronger brains or wishful thinking? *Remedial and Special Education,* **28**, 117–124.

Hynd, G. W., Hall, J., Novey, E. S., Eliopulos, D., Black, K., Gonzales, J. J., Edmonds, J. E., Riccio, C. and Cohen, M. (1995) Dyslexia and corpus callosum morphology. *Archives of Neurology,* **52**, 32–28.

Irlen, H. L. (1983) Successful treatment of learning. Paper presented at the 91st Annual Convention of the American Psychological Association, Anaheim, CA.

Irlen, H. L. (1989) *Scotopic Sensitivity Syndrome Screening Manual* (3rd edn). Long Beach, CA, Irlen Institution.

Irlen, H. L. (1991) *Reading by the Colors: Overcoming Dyslexia and Other Reading Disabilities through the Irlen Method.* New York, Avebury.

Jameson, M. (1999) Setting up support groups. Workshop presented at Dyslexia into the Year 2000 Conference, 12 June, Dundee, Scotland.

Jameson, M. (2009) Dyslexia on trial. In S. Moody (ed.), *Dyslexia: Scenes from Working Life.* Oxford, Wiley-Blackwell.

Jamieson, C. and Morgan, E. (2008) *Managing Dyslexia at University: A Resource for Students, Academic and Support Staff.* London, David Fulton.

Jeffries, S. and Everatt, J. (2004) Working memory: Its role in dyslexia and other learning difficulties. *Dyslexia,* **10**, 196–214.

Johanson, K. (1997) Left hemisphere stimulation with music and sounds in dyslexia remediation. Paper presented at the 48th Annual Conference of the International Dyslexia Association (formerly the Orton Dyslexia Association). Baltimore, MD, International Dyslexia Association.

Johnson, M. (2001) Inclusion: The challenges. In: L. Peer and G. Reid (eds), *Dyslexia: Successful Inclusion in the Secondary School.* London, David Fulton.

Johnson, M., Philips, S. and Peer, L. (1999) *Multisensory Teaching System for Reading.* Didsbury, UK, Special Educational Needs Centre, Didsbury School of Education, Manchester Metropolitan University.

Johnston, R. S. (1992) Methods of teaching reading: The debate continues. *Support for Learning,* **7**(3), 99–102.

Johnston, R., Connelly, V. D. and Watson, J. (1995) Some effects of phonics teaching on early reading development. In: P. Owen and P. Pumfrey (eds), *Children Learning to Read: International Concerns. Vol. 1. Emergent and Developing Reading: Messages for Teachers* (pp. 32–42). London, Falmer Press.

Jones, N. (2005) Including children with Special Educational Needs. In: N. Jones (ed.), *Effective Provision for Children with DCD*. London, Sage.

Jordan, E. (2001) Interrupted learning: The traveller paradigm. *Support for Learning,* **16**(3), 128–134.

Joshi, R. M. and Carreker, S. (2009) Development, assessment and instruction. In: G. Reid (ed.), *The Routledge Dyslexia Companion*. London, Routledge.

Joshi, R. M. and Aaron, P. G. (2008) Assessment of literacy performance based on the componential model of reading. In: G. Reid, A. Fawcett, F. Manis and L. Siegel (eds), *The Sage Dyslexia Handbook*. London, Sage.

Joshi, R. M., Williams, K. A. and Wood, J. (1998) Predicting reading comprehension from listening comprehension: Is this the answer to the IQ debate? In: C. Hulme and R. M. Joshi (eds), *Reading and Spelling: Development and Disorders* (pp. 319–327). Mahwah, NJ, Erlbaum.

Kaplan, B. J., Crawford, S. G., Wilson, B. N. and Dewey, D. M. (1998). DCD may not be a discrete disorder. *Human Movement Science,* **17**, 471–490.

Katusic, S. K., Colligan, R. C., Barbaresi, W. J., Schaid, D. J. and Jacobsen, S. J. (2001) Incidence of reading disability in a population-based birth cohort, 1976–1982. *Mayo Clinic Proceedings,* **76**(11), 1081–1092. Rochester, MN.

Kaufman, A. S. (1994) *Intelligent Testing with the WISC-III*. New York, Wiley.

Keene, E. and Zimmerman, S. (2007) *Mosaic of Thought: The Power of Comprehension Strategy Instruction*. Portsmouth, NH, Heinemann.

Kelly, K. (2002) Multilingualism and dyslexia. Paper presented at Multilingual Conference, IDA, Washington, DC, June.

Kirby, A. (2003) *The Adolescent with Developmental Coordination Disorders*. Jessica Kingsley.

Kirby, A. (2006) *Dyspraxia: Developmental Co-ordination Disorder*. Human Horizon Series. London, Souvenir Press.

Kirk, J. (2001) Cross-curricular approaches to staff development in secondary schools. In: L. Peer and G. Reid (eds), *Dyslexia: Successful Inclusion in the Secondary School*. London, David Fulton.

Kirk, J. (2002) *Guidelines on Dyslexia*. Edinburgh, University of Edinburgh.

Kirk, J. and Reid, G. (2001) An examination of the relationship between dyslexia and offending in young people and the implications for the training system. *Dyslexia,* **7**(2), 77–84.

Kirk, J. and Reid, G. (2003) *Adult Dyslexia Checklist: Criteria and Considerations*. BDA Handbook. Reading, UK, British Dyslexia Association.

Kirkland, J. (2009) The development of protocols for assessment and intervention at university for students with dyslexia. In: G. Reid (ed.), *The Routledge Dyslexia Companion*. London, Routledge.

Knight, D. F. and Hynd, G. W. (2002) The neurobiology of dyslexia. In: G. Reid and J. Wearmouth (eds), *Dyslexia and Literacy, Theory and Practice*. Chichester, John Wiley & Sons.

Knight, D., Day, K. and Patten-Terry, N. (2009) Preventing and identifying reading difficulties in young children. In: G. Reid (ed.), *The Routledge Dyslexia Companion*. London, Routledge.

Koop, C. and Rose, D. (2008) Reading to learn in Murdi Paaki: Changing outcomes for indigenous students. *Literacy Learning: The Middle Years,* **16**(1), 41–46.

Kriss, I. and Evans, B. J. W. (2005) The relationship between dyslexia and Meares–Irlen syndrome. *Journal of Research in Reading,* **28**, 350–364.

Kyd, L., Sutherland, G. and McGettrick, P. (1992) A preliminary appraisal of the Irlen screening process for scotopic sensitivity syndrome and the effect of Irlen coloured overlays on reading. *British Orthothalmic Journal,* **49**, 25–30.

Landon, J. (2001) Inclusion and dyslexia—the exclusion of bilingual learners? In: L. Peer and G. Reid (eds), *Dyslexia: Successful Inclusion in the Secondary School*. London, David Fulton.

Lawrence, D. (1985) Improving self-esteem and reading. *Educational Research,* **27**(3), 194–200.

Lawrence, D. (1987) *Enhancing Self-Esteem in the Classroom*. London, Paul Chapman.

Lazear, D. (1994) *Multiple Intelligence Approaches to Assessment*. Tucson, AZ, Zephyr Press.

Lazear, D. (1999) *Eight Ways of Knowing Teaching for Multiple Intelligences* (3rd edn). Arlington Heights, IL, Skylight Professional Development.

Lea, M. and Street, B. (2000) Student writing and staff feedback in higher education: An academic literacies approach. In: M. Lea and B. Stierer (eds), *Student Writing in Higher Education*. Buckingham, UK, Open University Press.

Leather, C. and McLoughlin, D. (2001) Developing task specific metacognitive skills in literate dyslexic adults. Paper presented at the Fifth International Conference BDA, York, April.

Lees, E. A. (1986) A cognitive developmental analysis of reading skills in good and poor readers. Paper presented at Annual Conference of Developmental Psychology Section, September, Leicester, UK, British Psychological Society.

Leikin, M. and Zur Hagit, E. (2006) Morphological processing in adult dyslexia. *Journal of Psycholinguistic Research,* **35**, 471–490.

Letterland (2008) www.letterland.com/teachers.

Letterland International (1997) *About Letterland '97.* Cambridge, UK, Letterland International.

Lewis, A. and Norwich, B. (1999) Mapping a pedagogy for special educational needs. *Research and Intelligence,* **69**, 6–8.

Liberman, A. (1992) The relation of speech to reading and writing. In: R. Frost and L. Katz (eds), *Orthography, Phonology, Morphology, and Meaning* (pp. 167–177). North Holland, Elsevier.

Liberman, I. Y. and Liberman, A. M. (1992) Whole language versus code emphasis: Underlying assumptions and their implications for reading instruction. In: P. B. Gough, L. C. Ehri and R. Trieman (eds), *Reading Acquisition.* London, Lawrence Erlbaum.

Lidz, C. S. (1991) *Practitioner's Guide to Dynamic Assessment.* New York, Guilford Press.

Lindamood, C. H. and Lindamood, P. C. (1998) *The Lindamood Phoneme Sequencing Program for Reading, Spelling, and Speech.* Austin, TX, Pro-Ed.

Literacy Commission in Scotland (2008) Cross-party working party on literacy. Scottish Executive.

Lloyd, G. (1996) Introduction. In: G. Lloyd (ed.), *Knitting Progress Unsatisfactory (Gender and Special Issues in Education).* Edinburgh, Moray House.

Lloyd, G. (2006) Supporting children in school. In: J. Stead, G. Lloyd and D. Cohen (eds), *Critical New Perspectives on ADHD.* Abingdon, Routledge.

Lloyd, G. and Norris, C. (1999) Including ADHD? *Disability and Society,* **14**(4), 505–517.

Longdon, W. (2001) Brain Gym® training in news and views. *Scottish Dyslexia Trust Newsletter,* Spring.

Lovegrove, W. (1993) Visual timing and dyslexia. Paper presented at Rodin Academy for the Study of Dyslexia Conference, October 1993, London.

Lovegrove, W. (1996) Dyslexia and a transient/magnocellular pathway deficit: The current situation and future directions. *Australian Journal of Psychology,* **46**, 167–171.

Luke, A., O'Brian, J. and Comber, B. (2001) Making community texts objects of study. In: H. Fehring and P. Green (eds), *Critical Literacy.* Newark, DE, International Reading Association.

Lundberg, I. (2002) The child's route into reading and what can go wrong. *Dyslexia,* **8**(1), January–March, 1–13.

Lynch, R. (2007) Enriching children, enriching the nation: Public investment in high-quality prekindergarten. Economic Policy Institute (Executive Summary). Retrieved 12 August 2008, from www.epi.org.

Lynch, R. T. and Gussel, L. (1996) Disclosure and self-advocacy regarding disability-related needs: Strategies to maximize integration in postsecondary education. *Journal of Counseling and Development, 74*, 352–358.

MacArthur, C. A. (1998) Word processing with speech synthesis and word prediction: Effects on dialogue journal writing of students with learning disabilities. *Learning Disability Quarterly,* **21**(2), 151–166.

Macfarlane, A. and Glynn, T. (1998) Mana Maori in the professional development programme for resource teachers: Learning and behaviour. Paper presented at the NZARE 20th Annual Conference, Dunedin, Hamilton, NZ, University of Waikato, 3–6 December.

Macfarlane, A., Glynn, T., Presland, I. and Greening, S. (2000) Maori culture and literacy learning: Bicultural approaches. In: L. Peer and G. Reid (eds), *Multilingualism, Literacy and Dyslexia. A Challenge for Educators.* London, David Fulton.

Mackay, T, (1997) *A Vision for Transforming the Reading Achievement of All Children.* West Dunbartonshire Council, Scotland.

MacPherson of Cluny, Sir William (1999) *The Stephen Lawrence Inquiry* (The MacPherson Report). London, Her Majesty's Stationery Office.

Mahfoudi, A. and Haynes, C. (2009) Phonological awareness in reading disabilities remediation: Some general issues. In: G. Reid (ed.), *The Routledge Dyslexia Companion.* London, Routledge.

Mailley, S. (1997) The classroom implications of visual perceptual difficulties: An exploratory study including Scotopic Sensitivity Syndrome or Irlen Syndrome (unpublished MA dissertation, University of Leicester).

Mailley, S. (2001) Visual difficulties with print. In: M. Hunter-Carsch (ed.), *Dyslexia, A Psychosocial Perspective*. London, Whurr.

Marolda, M. R. and Davidson, S. D. (2000) Mathematics learning profiles and differentiated teaching strategies. *Perspectives*, **26**(3), 10–15.

Marsh, G., Friedman, M., Welch, V. and Desberg, P. (1980) The development of strategies in spelling. In: U. Frith (ed.), *Cognitive Processes in Spelling* (pp. 339–354). London, Academic Press.

Mathews, M. (1993) Can children be helped by applied kinesiology? Paper presented at 5th European Conference in Neuro-Developmental Delay in Children with Specific Learning Difficulties, Chester.

McClelland, J. L. (1988) Connectionist models and psychological evidence. *Journal of Memory and Language*, **27**, 107–123.

McCulloch, C. (1985) The Slingerland approach: Is it effective in a specific language disability classroom? (MA Thesis, Seattle, Seattle Pacific University).

McGuinness, C., McGuinness, D. and McGuinness, G. (1996) Phono-Graphix: A new method for remediation of reading difficulties. *Annals of Dyslexia*, **46**, 73–96.

McGuinness, D. (1998) *Why Children Can't Read*. London, Penguin.

McIntyre, C. (2000) *Dyspraxia in the Early Years, Identifying and Supporting Children with Movement Difficulties*. London, David Fulton.

McIntyre, C. (2001) *Dyspraxia 5–11 (A Practical Guide)*. London, David Fulton.

McLaughlin, M. and Allen, M. B. (2002) *Guided Comprehension: A Teaching Model for Grades 3–8*. Newark, DE, International Reading Association.

McLoughlin, D. and Leather, C. (2009) Dyslexia: Meeting the needs of employers and employees in the workplace. In: G. Reid (ed.), *The Routledge Dyslexia Companion*. London, Routledge.

McLoughlin, D., Leather, C. and Stringer, P. (2002) *The Adult Dyslexic Interventions and Outcomes*. London, Whurr.

McNaughton, S. (1995) *Patterns of Emerging Literacy: Processes of Development and Transition*. Auckland, Oxford University Press.

McPhillips, M., Hepper, P. G. and Mulhern, G. (2000) Effects of replicating primary-reflex movements on specific reading difficulties in children: A randomised double-blind, controlled trial. *The Lancet*, **355**, 537–541.

Meek, M. (1985) *Learning to Read*. London, Bodley Head.

Mercer, C. D., Campbell, K. U., Miller, M. D., Mercer, K. D. and Lane, H. B. (2000) Effects of a reading fluency intervention for middle schoolers with specific learning disabilities. *Learning Disabilities Research and Practice*, **15**, 179–189.

Miles, E. (1989) *Bangor Dyslexia Teaching System*. London, Whurr.

Miles, T. R. (1983a) *Bangor Dyslexia Test*. Cambridge, Learning Development Aids.

Miles, T. R. (1996) Do dyslexic children have IQs? *Dyslexia*, **2**(3), 175–178.

Milne, D. (2006) *Teaching the Brain to Read*. Hungerford, Berkshire, UK, Smart Kids.

Mitchell, S. (1985) An investigation into the presence or absence of postural reflex abnormalities in children with speech problems (unpublished pilot study, City of Birmingham Polytechnic).

Mittler, P. (2000) *Working Towards Inclusive Education: Social Contexts*. London, David Fulton.

Mittler, P. (2002) Parents and teachers. In: J. Wearmouth, J. Soler and G. Reid (eds), *Addressing Difficulties in Literacy Development: Responses at Family, School, Pupil and Teacher Levels*, Abingdon, RoutledgeFalmer.

Moats, L. (2008) Quality Teacher Preparation Reading Programs: A Pre-requisite for Effective Reading Teachers. Symposium at the 59th annual conference International Dyslexia Association, 29 October, Seattle, USA.

Moats, L. C. (2005a) Language Essentials for Teaching of Reading and Spelling Module 4 The Mighty Word: Building Vocabulary and Oral Language. Sopris West Educational Services, Longmont, CO, USA.

Moats, L. C. (2005b) Language Essentials for Teaching of Reading and Spelling Module 9 Teaching Beginning Spelling and Writing. Sopris West Educational Services, Longmont, CO, USA.

Molfese, D. L., Molfese, V. J., Barnes, M. E., Warren, C. G. and Molfese, P. J. (2008) Familial Predictors of dyslexia: Evidence from preschool children with and without familial dyslexia risk. In: G. Reid, A. Fawcett, F. Manis and L. Siegel (eds), *The Sage Dyslexia Handbook*. London, Sage.

Moody, S (ed.) (2009) *Dyslexia and Employment: A Guide for Assessors, Trainers and Managers*. Chichester, Wiley.

Moody, S. (2009) Dyslexia: a case of mistaken identity? In Moody, S. (ed.) Dyslexia and Employment: A Guide for Assessors, Trainers and Managers. Chichester, John Wiley & Sons.

Morgan, E. and Klein, C. (2000) *The Dyslexic Adult in a Non-dyslexic World*. London, Whurr.

Morgan, R. T. T. (1976) Paired reading tuition: A preliminary report on a technique for cases of reading deficit. *Child Care, Health and Development*, 2, 13–28.

Morrow, L. M., Tracey, D. H., Woo, D. G. and Pressley, M. (1999) Characteristics of exemplary first grade literacy instruction. *Reading Teacher Journal*, **52**(5), 462–476.

Morton, J. and Frith, U. (1995) Causal modelling: A structural approach to developmental psychopathology. In: D. Cicchetti and D. J. Cohen (eds), *Manual of Developmental Psychopathology* (pp. 357–390). New York, Psychological Assessment of Dyslexia and John Wiley & Sons.

Moseley, D. (1989) How lack of confidence in spelling affects children's written expression. *Educational Psychology in Practice*, **5**(1), 42–46.

Moseley, D. and Nicol, C. (1995) *ACE (Actually Coded English) Spelling Dictionary*. Cambridge, LDA.

Moseley, D. V. (1990) Research into visual function, reading and spelling. *Dyslexia Review*.

Moser, C. (2000) *Better Basic Skills: Improving Adult Literacy and Numeracy*. London, Department for Education and Employment.

Mosley, J. (1996) *Quality Circle Time in the Primary Classroom*. Cambridge, LDA.

Moss, H. (2000), Using literacy development programmes. In: J. Townend and M. Turner (eds), *Dyslexia in Practice: A Guide for Teachers*. Dordrecht, Kluwer Academic.

Muter, V., Hulme, C. and Snowling, M. (1997) *Phonological Abilities Test*. London, Psychological Corporation.

Nagy, W., Berninger, V. W., Abbott, R. D., Vaughan, K. and Vermeulen, K. (2003) Relationship of morphology and other language skills in at-risk second-grade readers and at-risk fourth grade writers. *Journal of Educational Psychology*, **95**, 730–742.

Nation, K. and Snowling, M. J. (1998) Individual differences in contextual facilitation: Evidence from dyslexia and poor reading comprehension. *Child Development*, **69**, 996–1011.

National Council on Disability (2000). Transition and postsecondary outcomes for youth with disabilities: Closing the gap to postsecondary education and employment. Retrieved 20 April 2008 from www.ncd.gov/newsroom//2000/transition_11-01-00.htm.

National Reading Panel. (2000) *Teaching Children to Read: An Evidence-Based Assessment of the Scientific Research Literature on Reading and Its Implications for Reading Instruction*. Washington, DC, US Department of Health and Human Services, Public Health Service, National Institutes of Health, National Institute of Child Health and Human Development. www.nichd.nih.gov/publications/nrp/report.pdf, accessed 4 December 2008.

NCCA (1999) *Curriculum for Primary Schools: English Language*. Dublin, National Council for Curriculum and Assessment.

NCREL (2003). 21st century skills: Literacy in the digital age. North Central Regional Educational Laboratory (NCREL). Retrieved 2 October 2007 from www.ncrel.org/engauge/skills/skills.htm.

Neville, M. H. (1975) Effectiveness of rate of aural message on reading and listening. *Educational Research*, **1**(18), 37–43.

Newcomer, P. (1999) *Diagnostic Achievement Battery-3*. Austin, TK: Pro-ED.

Nicolson, R. I. (1996) Development dyslexia: Past, present and future. *Dyslexia*, **2**(3), 190–207.

Nicolson, R. I. (2001) Developmental dyslexia: Into the future. In: A. Fawcett (ed.), *Dyslexia, Theory and Good Practice*. London, Whurr.

Nicolson, R. I. and Fawcett, A. J. (1990) Automaticity: A new framework for dyslexia research? *Cognition*, **35**, 159–182.

Nicolson, R. I. and Fawcett, A. J. (1996) *The Dyslexia Early Screening Test*. London, The Psychological Corporation.

Nicolson, R. I., Fawcett, A. J. and Dean, P. (1995) Time estimation deficits in developmental dyslexia: Evidence for cerebellar involvement. *Proceedings of the Royal Society: Biological Sciences*, **259**, 43–47.

Nisbet, J. and Shucksmith, J. (1986) *Learning Strategies*. London, Routledge.

Norwich, B. (2009) How compatible is the recognition of dyslexia with inclusive education? In: G. Reid (ed.), *The Routledge Dyslexia Companion.* London, Routledge.

Norwich, B. and Lewis, A. (2001) Mapping a pedagogy for special educational needs. *British Educational Research Journal,* **27**(3), 313–331.

Oczkus, L. (2004) *Super Six Comprehension Strategies: 35 Lessons and More for Reading Success.* Christopher Gordon Publishers, USA, Norwood, MA

Olson, R. and Byrne, B (2005) Genetic and environmental influences on reading and language ability and disability. In: H. Catts and A. Kamhi (eds), *The Connections Between Language and Reading Disabilities* (pp 173–200). Mahwah, NJ, Erlbaum.

Olson, R. K., Forsberg, H., Wise, B. and Rack, J. (1994) Measurement of word recognition, orthographic and phonological. In: G. R. Lyon (ed.), *Frames of Reference for the Assessment of Learning Disabilities: New Views on Measurement Issues* (pp. 243–277). Baltimore, MD, Brookes.

Open University (2002) Difficulties in Literacy Development (E 801 course audio tape and study guide). Milton Keynes, UK, Open University Press.

Organisation for Economic Co-operation and Development [OECD] (2000) *Measuring Students' Knowledge and Skills: The PISA 2000 Assessment of Reading, Mathematical and Scientific Literacy.* Paris: OECD.

Osmond, J. (1994) *The Reality of Dyslexia.* London, Cassell.

Ott, P. (1997) *How to Detect and Manage Dyslexia: A Reference and Resource Manual.* Oxford, Heinemann.

Ott, P. (2007) *Teaching Children with Dyslexia: A Practical Guide.* London, Routledge.

Ottley, P. and Bennett, L. (1997) *Launch into Reading Success through Phonological Awareness Training.* Harcourt Assessment, (Pearson Education Ltd.), UK, Oxford.

Oxley, L. and Topping, K. (1990) Peer tutored cued spelling with seven to nine year olds. *British Education Research Journal,* **16**, 63–79.

Palincsar, A. and Brown, A. (1984) Reciprocal teaching of comprehension fostering and comprehension monitoring activities. *Cognition and Instruction,* **1**(2), 117–175.

Palincsar, A. and Klenk, L. (1992) Fostering literacy learning in supportive contexts. *Journal of Learning Disabilities,* **25**, 211–225.

Palmer, C. (2001) Good practice in learning support: The Somerset Learning Support Services. Paper presented at Fifth BDA International Conference, York, April.

Palmer, M. J. (2001) Handwriting and spelling achievement in children with specific language learning differences. www.slingerland.org/administration/research.html, accessed September 2008.

Palmer, S. (2007) *Toxic Childhood: How the Modern World Is Damaging Our Children and What We Can Do About It.* London, Orion Books.

Paulesu, E., De-monet, J. F., Fazio, F., McCrory, E., Chanoine, V., Brunswick, N., Cappa, S. F., Cossu, G., Habib, M., Frith, C. D. and Frith U. (2001) Dyslexia: Cultural diversity and biological unity. *Science,* **291**, 16 March (www.sciencemag.org).

Paulesu, E., Frith, U., Snowling, M., Gallagher, A., Morton, J., Frackowiak, F. S. J. and Frith, C. D. (1996) Is developmental dyslexia a disconnection syndrome? Evidence from PET scanning. *Brain,* **119**, 143–157.

Pavlidis, G. Th. (1990) *Perspectives on Dyslexia: Neurology, Neuropsychology and Genetics* (Vol. 1). Chichester, John Wiley & Sons.

Peacey, N. (2001) Inclusion and the Revised National Curriculum. In: L. Peer and G. Reid (eds), *Dyslexia: Successful Inclusion in the Secondary School.* London, David Fulton.

Peer, L. (2001) Dyslexia and its manifestations in the secondary school. In: L. Peer and G. Reid (eds), *Dyslexia: Successful Inclusion in the Secondary School.* London, David Fulton.

Peer, L. (2002) Dyslexia, multilingual speakers and otitis media (PhD thesis, University of Sheffield).

Peer, L. (2005) *Glue Ear.* London: David Fulton.

Peer, L. (2009) Dyslexia and glue ear: A sticky educational problem. In: G. Reid (ed.), *The Routledge Dyslexia Companion.* London, Routledge.

Peer, L. and Reid, G. (2002) Dyslexia and literacy: Challenges in the secondary school. In: G. Reid and J. Wearmouth (eds), *Dyslexia and Literacy, Theory and Practice.* Chichester, John Wiley & Sons.

Peer, L. and Reid, G. (2003) *Introduction to Dyslexia.* London, David Fulton.

Peer, L. and Reid, G. (eds) (2000) *Multilingualism, Literacy and Dyslexia: A Challenge for Educators.* London, David Fulton.

Perfetti, C. (1992) The representation problem in reading acquisition. In: P. Gough, L. Ehri and R. Treiman (eds), *Reading Acquisition* (pp. 107–143). Hillsdale, NJ, Erlbaum.

Peters, M. L. (1970) *Success in Spelling.* Cambridge Monographs on Education No. 4. Cambridge, Cambridge Institute of Education.

Peters, M. L. (1985) *Spelling: Caught or Taught? A New Look.* London, Routledge.

Philips, S. (1999) *Management Skills for SEN Co-ordinators in the Primary School.* London, Falmer.

Pinnell, G. S., Deford, D. and Lyons, C. A. (1988a) *Reading Recovery: Early Intervention for At-Risk First Graders* (ERS Monograph). Arlington, VA, Educational Research Service.

Pinnell, G. S., Lyons, C. A. and Deford, D. E. (1988b) *Reading Recovery* (Sopris West Educational Programmes that Work, 14th edn). Denver, CO, Sopris West in cooperation with the National Dissemination Study Group.

Pinnell, G. S., Lyons, C. A., Deford, D., Bryk, A. S. and Seltzer, M. (1991) *Studying the Effectiveness of Early Intervention Approaches for First Grade Children Having Difficulty in Reading.* Education Report No. 16. Columbus, OH, Martha L. King Language and Literacy Center, Ohio State University.

Plaut, D. C., McClelland, J. L., Seidenberg, M. S. and Patterson, K. (1996) Understanding normal and impaired word reading: Computational principles in quasi-regular domains. *Psychological Review,* **103**, 56–115.

Pollak, D. (2001a) Access to higher education for the mature dyslexic student: A question of identity and a new perspective. Paper presented at the 5th BDA Conference, York, April.

Pollak, D. (2005) *Dyslexia: The Self and Higher Education.* Stoke on Trent, Trentham Books.

Pollak, D. (ed.) (in press) *Neurodiversity in Higher Education.* Chichester, Wiley.

Portwood, M. (1999) *Developmental Dyspraxia: Identification and Intervention, A Manual for Parents and Professionals.* London, David Fulton.

Portwood, M. (2000) *Understanding Developmental Dyspraxia. A Textbook for Students and Professionals.* London, David Fulton.

Portwood, M. (2001) *Developmental Dyspraxia: A Practical Manual for Parents and Professionals.* Durham, UK, Durham County Council Educational Psychology Service.

Portwood, M. (2002) School based trials of fatty acid supplements. Paper presented at Education Conference Durham County Council, June 2002.

Pressley, M. (2006) *Reading Instruction that Works: The Case for Balanced Teaching.* New York, Guilford Press.

Price, L. A. and Gerber, P. J. (2008) Adults with learning disabilities and self disclosure: In higher education and beyond. In: G. Reid, A. Fawcett, F. Manis and L. Siegel (eds), *The Sage Dyslexia Handbook.* London, Sage.

Prifitera, A. and Dersch, J. (1993) Base rates of WISC diagnostic subtest patterns among normal learning disabled and ADHD samples. *Journal of Pyschoeducational Assessment,* WISC-III Monograph, 43–55.

Pumfrey, P. (2001) Specific developmental dyslexia: 'Basics to back' in 2000 and beyond? In: M. Hunter-Carsch (ed.), *Dyslexia, A Psychosocial Perspective.* London, Whurr.

Pumfrey, P. (2002) Specific developmental dyslexia: 'Basics to back' in 2000 and beyond? In: J. Wearmouth, J. Soler and G. Reid (eds), *Addressing Difficulties in Literacy Development, Responses at Family, School, Pupil and Teacher Levels.* London, RoutledgeFalmer.

Pumfrey, P. D. (1990) Integrating the testing and teaching of reading. *Support for Learning,* **5**(3), 146–152.

Pumfrey, P. D. (1995) The management of specific learning difficulties (dyslexia): Challenges and responses. In: I. Lunt, B. Norwich and V. Varma (eds), *Psychology and Education for Special Needs: Recent Developments and Future Directions* (pp. 45–70). London, Ashgate.

QCA (2000) *General Statement on Inclusion, Curriculum 2000.* London, Qualifications and Curriculum Authority.

Rack, J. (1994) Dyslexia: The phonological deficit hypothesis. In: R. I. Nicolson and A. J. Fawcett (eds), *Dyslexia in Children: Multidisciplinary Perspectives.* Hemel Hempstead, UK, Harvester Wheatsheaf.

Rack, J. and Walker, J. (1994) *Does Dyslexia Institute Teaching Work?* (reprinted from *Dyslexia Review,* **6**(2), Autumn). Staines, UK, The Dyslexia Institute.

Rack, J. P., Snowling, M. J. and Olson, R. K. (1992). The non-word reading deficit in dyslexia: A review. *Reading Research Quarterly,* **27**, 29–53.

Ramaswami, S., (1994) *The Differential Impact of Reading Recovery on Achievement of First Graders in the Newark School District*. Newark, NJ: Newark Board of Education, Office of Planning, Evaluation and Testing (ERIC Document Reproduction Service No. ED 374 180).

Rashotte, C. A., MacPhee, K. and Torgeson, J. K. (2001) The effectiveness of a group reading instruction program with poor readers in multiple grades. *Learning Disability Quarterly,* **24**, 119–134.

Rassool, N. (1999) Literacy: In search of a paradigm. In: N. Rassool (ed.), *Literacy for Sustainable Development in the Age of Information*, pp. 25–53, Clevedon, Multilingual Matters.

Raven, J. C. (1992, 1993) *Standard Progressive Matrices*. Oxford, Oxford Psychologists Press.

Ray, B. J. (1986) A cooperative teacher education and language retraining programme for dyslexics in West Texas. Paper presented at the Action in Research V Conference, Lubbock, TX.

Read, C. (1971) Pre-school children's knowledge of English phonology. *Harvard Educational Review,* **41**, 1–34.

Reason, R. and Boote, R. (1994) *Helping Children with Reading and Spelling: A Special Needs Manual*. London, Routledge.

Reason, R. and Frederickson, N. (1996) Discrepancy definitions or phonological assessment. In: G. Reid (ed.), *Dimensions of Dyslexia: Assessment, Teaching and the Curriculum* (Vol. 1). Edinburgh, Moray House.

Reason, R., Brown, P., Cole, M. and Gregory, M. (1988) Does the 'specific' in specific learning difficulties make a difference to the way we teach? *Support for Learning,* **3**(4), 230–236.

Reid, G. (1992) Learning difficulties and learning styles: Observational criteria. Paper presented at South East Learning Styles Conference, George Mason University, VA.

Reid, G. (1994a) Metacognitive assessment and dyslexia. Paper presented at 3rd International Conference of the British Dyslexia Association, Manchester, April.

Reid, G. (1996) *Dimensions of Dyslexia, Vol. 1: Assessment, Teaching and the Curriculum; Vol. 2: Literacy, Language and Learning*. Edinburgh: Moray House.

Reid, G. (1998) *Dyslexia: A Practitioners Handbook* (2nd edn). Chichester, Wiley.

Reid, G. (2001a) Specialist teacher training in the UK Issues, considerations and future directions. In: M. Hunter-Carsch (ed.), *Dyslexia, A Psychosocial Perspective*. London, Whurr.

Reid, G. (2001b) Dyslexia, metacognition and learning styles. In: G. Shiel and U. Ni Dhalaigh (eds), *Reading Matters: A Fresh Start*. Dublin, Reading Association of Ireland/National Reading Initiative.

Reid, G. (2002) Dyslexia: Research and implications for practice. Paper presented at the RTLB national conference, Learning to Motivate, Motivate to Learn, Dunedin, New Zealand, 18 September.

Reid, G. (2004) *Dyslexia: A Complete Guide for Parents*, Chichester, Wiley.

Reid, G. (2007a) *Motivating Learners in the Classroom: Ideas and Strategies*. London, Sage.

Reid, G. (2007b) *Dyslexia* (2nd edn). London, Continuum.

Reid, G. and Came, F. (2009) Identifying and overcoming the barriers to learning in an inclusive context. In: G. Reid (ed.), *The Routledge Dyslexia Companion*. London, Routledge.

Reid, G. and Green, S. (2007a) *100 Ideas for Supporting Pupils with Dyslexia*. London, Continuum.

Reid, G. and Green, S. (2007b) *The Teaching Assistant's Guide to Dyslexia*. London, Continuum.

Reid, G. and Kirk, J. (2001) *Dyslexia in Adults: Education and Employment*. Chichester, Wiley.

Reid, G. and Strnadova, I. (2008) Learning styles and curriculum access. In: G. Reid, A. Fawcett, F. Manis and L. Siegel (eds), *The Sage Dyslexia Handbook*. London, Sage.

Reid, G. Kirk, J., Hui, D. and Mullin, K. (1999) *Adult Dyslexia for Employment, Practice and Training* (a report on best practice in dyslexia assessment, support and training in the employment service). Sheffield, UK, Employment Service.

Reid, G., Deponio, P. and Petch, L. D. (2005) Identification, assessment and intervention: Implications of an audit on dyslexia policy and practice in Scotland. *Dyslexia,* **11**(3), 203–216.

Reid, G., Green, S. and Zylstra, C. (2008) Role of parents. In: G. Reid, A. Fawcett, F. Manis and L. Siegel (eds), *The Sage Dyslexia Handbook*. London, Sage.

Reid-Lyon, G. (1995) *Toward a Definition of Dyslexia* (reprinted from *Annals of Dyslexia,* **45**). Baltimore, MD, Orton Dyslexia Society.

Renaldi, F. (2008) *Dyslexia Friendly Teaching—a Glossary of Vocabulary*. Kinross High School, Perth and Kinross, UK.

Reynolds, D. and Nicolson, R. I. (2007) Follow-up of an exercise-based treatment for children with reading difficulties. *Dyslexia,* **13**(2), 78–96.

Richardson, A. (1988) The effects of a specific red filter on dyslexia. *British Psychological Society Abstracts,* 56.

Richardson, A. J. (2001) Dyslexia, dyspraxia and ADHD: Can nutrition help? Paper presented at 4th Cambridge Conference, Helen Arkell Dyslexia Association, Cambridge, 1 March.

Richardson, A. J. (2002) Dyslexia, dyspraxia and ADHD: Can nutrition help? Paper presented at Education Conference, Durham County Council, June.

Richardson, A. J. and Puri, B. K. (2000) The potential role of fatty acids in attention deficit/hyperactivity disorder (ADHD). *Prostaglandins, Leukotrienes and Essential Fatty Acids,* **63**, 79–87.

Riddick, B. (1995a) Dyslexia and development: An interview study. *Dyslexia: An International Journal of Research and Practice,* **1**(2), 63–74.

Riddick, B. (1995b) Dyslexia: Dispelling the myths. *Disability and Society,* **10**(4), 457–473.

Riddick, B. (1996) *Living with Dyslexia.* London, Routledge.

Riddick, B. (2001) The experiences of teachers and trainee teachers who have dyslexia. Paper presented at the Fifth International Conference, BDA, York, April.

Riddick, B. (2002) Researching the social and emotional consequences of dyslexia. In: J. Soler, J. Wearmouth and G. Reid (eds), *Contextualising Difficulties in Literacy Development: Exploring Politics, Culture, Ethnicity and Ethics.* London, RoutledgeFalmer.

Riddick, B. (2008) Dyslexia-friendly schools and universities—do they exist? How to be one. Paper presented at the Norwegian Dyslexia Association, Oslo, September.

Riddick, B. (2009) The implications of students' perspectives on dyslexia for school improvement. In: G. Reid (ed.), *The Routledge Dyslexia Companion.* London, Routledge.

Riding, R. and Rayner, S. (1998) *Cognitive Styles and Learning Strategies; Understanding Style Differences in Learning and Behaviour.* London, David Fulton.

Robertson, J. (2000) *Dyslexia and Reading: A Neuropsychological Approach.* London, Whurr.

Robertson, J. and Bakker, D. J. (2002) The balance model of reading and dyslexia. In: G. Reid and J. Wearmouth (eds), *Dyslexia and Literacy: Theory and Practice.* Chichester, John Wiley & Sons.

Roffman, A. J., Herzog, J. E. and Wershba-Gershon, P. M. (1990). Helping young adults understand their learning disabilities. *Journal of Learning Disabilities,* **27**, 413–419.

Rohl, M. and Tunmer, W. (1988) Phonemic segmentation skills and spelling acquisition. *Applied Psycholinguistics,* **9**, 335–350.

Romani, C., Ward, J. and Olson, A. (1999) Developmental surface dysgraphia: What is the underlying cognitive impairment? *Quarterly Journal of Experimental Psychology,* section A, 52, 97–128.

Rose Report (2006) www.standards.dcsf.gov.uk/phonics/report.pdf.

Rose, D., Gray, B. and Cowey, W. (1999) Scaffolding reading and writing for indigenous children in school. In: P. Wignell (ed.), *Double Power: English Literacy and Indigenous Education.* Melbourne, Languages Australia.

Rose, J., (2006) *The Rose Review into the Teaching of Reading.* London, DfES, www.standards.dfes.gov.uk/rosereview/report.

Rosner, J. and Rosner, J. (1987) The Irlen treatment: A review of the literature. *Optician,* 25 September, 26–33.

Russell, J. (1988) *Graded Activities for Children with Motor Difficulties.* Cambridge, Cambridge Educational.

Russell, S. (1993) Access to the curriculum. In: G. Reid (ed.), *Specific Learning Difficulties (Dyslexia) Perspectives on Practice.* Edinburgh, Moray House.

Rutter, M. (1995) Relationships between mental disorders in childhood and adulthood. *Acta Psychiatrica Scandinavica,* **91**, 73–85.

Savage, R. (2001) The 'simple view' of reading: Some evidence and possible implications. *Educational Psychology in Practice,* **17**, 17–33.

Sawyer, D. J. and Bernstein, S. (2008) Students with phonological dyslexia in school-based programs: Insights from Tennessee schools. In: G. Reid, A. Fawcett, F. Manis and L. Siegel (eds), *The Sage Dyslexia Handbook.* London, Sage.

Schneider, E. (2009) Dyslexia and foreign language learning. In: G. Reid (ed.), *The Routledge Dyslexia Companion*. London, Routledge.

Schneider, E. and Crombie, M. (2003) *Dyslexia and Foreign Language Learning*. London: David Fulton.

Scoble, J. (1988) Cued Spelling in adult literacy: A case study. *Paired Reading Bulletin,* **4**, 93–96.

Scottish Dyslexia Forum (2002) Dyslexia: Research and its implications for policy and practice. Paper presented at Conference, University of Stirling, 13 May.

Scottish Executive (2008) *Getting it Right for Every Child: An Overview of the Getting It Right Approach*. Scottish Executive (Web only). www.scotland.gov.uk/Publications/2008/09/22091734/0.

Scottish Parliament (2001) *Report on Inquiry into Special Educational Needs: Education, Culture and Sports Committee* (3rd report). Edinburgh, Her Majesty's Stationery Office.

Seidenberg, M. S. and McClelland, J. (1989) A distributed, developmental model of word recognition. *Psychological Review,* **96**, 523–568.

Share, D. L. (2008) On the Anglocentricities of current reading research and practice: The perils of over-reliance on an 'Outlier' orthography. *Psychological Bulletin,* **134**, 584–615.

Shaul, S. and Breznitz, Z. (2007) Asynchrony of cerebral systems activated during word recognition: A comparison of regular and dyslexic readers. Manuscript submitted for publication.

Shaywitz, S. (2003), *Overcoming Dyslexia: A New and Complete Science-Based Program for Reading Problems at Any Level*. New York, Alfred Knopf.

Shiel, G. (2002) Literacy standards and factors affecting literacy: What national and international assessments tell us. In: G. Reid and J. Wearmouth (eds), *Dyslexia and Literacy: Theory and Practice*. Chichester, John Wiley & Sons.

Shiel, G., Cosgrove, J., Sofroniou, N. and Kelly, A. (2001) *Ready for Life? (The Literacy Achievements of Irish 15-year-olds with Comparative International Data, the PISA 2000 Study)*. Dublin, Educational Research Centre.

Siegel, L. S. (1989) IQ is irrelevant to the definition of learning disabilities. *Journal of Learning Disabilities,* **22**, 469–478.

Siegel, L. S. (1992) An evaluation of the discrepancy definition of dyslexia. *Journal of Learning Disabilities,* **25**, 618–629.

Siegel, L. S. and Lipka, O. (2008) The definition of learning disabilities: Who is the individual with learning disabilities? In: G. Reid, A. Fawcett, F. Manis and L. Siegel (eds), *The Sage Dyslexia Handbook*. London, Sage.

Silver, L. (2001) *Controversial Therapies* (reprinted from *Perspectives,* **27**(3), 1–4). Baltimore, MD, The International Dyslexia Association.

Simpson, M. and Ure, J. (1993) *What's the Difference? A Study of Differentiation in Scottish Secondary Schools*. Aberdeen, UK, Northern College.

Singleton, C. (2002) Dyslexia: Cognitive factors and implications for literacy. In: G. Reid and J. Wearmouth (eds), *Dyslexia and Literacy: Theory and Practice*. Chichester, John Wiley & Sons.

Singleton, C. (2009) Visual stress and dyslexia. In: G. Reid (ed.), *The Routledge Dyslexia Companion*. London, Routledge.

Singleton, C. H. (chair) (1999) *Dyslexia in Higher Education: Policy, Provision and Practice* (report of the National Working Party on Dyslexia in Higher Education). Hull, UK, University of Hull.

Singleton, C. H. and Henderson, L. M. (2006) Visual factors in reading. *London Review of Education,* **4**, 89–98.

Singleton, C. H. and Henderson, L. M. (2007) Computerised screening for visual stress in children with dyslexia. *Dyslexia,* **13**, 130–151.

Singleton, C. H. and Trotter, S. (2005) Visual stress in adults with and without dyslexia. *Journal of Research in Reading,* **28**, 365–378.

Singleton, C. H., Horne, J. K. and Thomas, K. V. (2002) *Lucid Adult Dyslexia Screening (LADS)*. Beverley, UK, Lucid Creative Limited.

Smith, B. (1994) *Teaching Spelling*. Royston, UK, United Kingdom Reading Association (UKRA).

Smith, F. (1971) *Understanding Reading*. London, Holt, Rinehart & Winston.

Smith, P., Hinson, M. and Smith, D. (1998) *Spelling and Spelling Resources*. Tamworth, UK, NASEN.

Smythe, I., Everatt, J. and Salter, R. (eds) (2004) *The International Book of Dyslexia* (2nd edn). London: Wiley & Sons.

Snowling, M. (1993) Specific learning difficulties: A cognitive developmental perspective. Paper presented at the Two-day Conference, Edinburgh, Centre for Specific Learning Difficulties, Moray House.

Snowling, M. J. (1994) Towards a model of spelling acquisition: The development of some component skills. In: G. D. A. Brown and N. C. Ellis (eds), *Handbook of Spelling: Theory, Process and Intervention* (pp. 111–128). Chichester, John Wiley & Sons.

Snowling, M. J. (2000) *Dyslexia* (2nd edn). Oxford, Blackwell.

Snowling, M. J. (2002) Individual differences in children's reading development: Sound to meaning in learning to read. Paper given at 21st Vernon-Wall Lecture for the Annual Meeting of the Education Section of the British Psychological Society, 3 November 2001. Leicester, UK, British Psychological Society.

Snowling, M. J. and Hulme, C. (1994) The development of phonological skills. *Philosophical Transactions of the Royal Society B,* **346**, 21–28.

Snowling, M. J. and Nation, K. A. (1997) Language, phonology and learning to read. In: C. Hulme and M. J. Snowling (eds), *Dyslexia, Biology Cognition and Intervention.* London, Whurr.

Snowling, M. J., Hulme, C., Wells, B. and Goulandris, N. (1992) Continuities between speech and spelling in a case of developmental dyslexia. *Reading and Writing,* **4**, 19–31.

Soler, J. (2002) Policy contexts and debates over how to teach literacy. In: J. Soler, J. Wearmouth and G. Reid (eds), *Contextualising Difficulties in Literacy Development: Exploring Politics, Culture and Ethics.* London, RoutledgeFalmer.

Soler, J. and Smith, J. (eds) (2000) *Literacy in New Zealand: Practices, Politics and Policy since 1900.* Auckland, Addison Wesley Longman.

Southern Education Foundation (2007) *Pre-Kindergarten in the South: The Region's Comparative Advantage in Education.* Atlanta, GA.

Southern Education Foundation (2008) *Time to Lead Again: The Promise of Georgia Pre-K.* Atlanta, GA.

Sparks, R. and Ganschow, L. (1993) The effects of a multisensory structured language approach on the native and foreign language aptitude skills of high-risk, foreign language learners: A follow-up study. *Annals of Dyslexia,* **43**, 193–216.

Spreen, O. (1988) Prognosis of learning disability. *Journal of Consulting and Clinical Psychology,* **56**, 836–842.

Stainthorp, R. (1995) Some effects of context on reading. In: P. Owen and P. Pumfrey (eds), *Children Learning to Read: International Concerns. Vol. 1. Emergent and Developing Reading: Messages for Teachers.* London, Falmer Press.

Stamboltzis, A. and Pumfrey, P. D. (2000) Text genre, miscue analysis, bilingualism and dyslexia: Teaching strategies with junior school pupils. In: L. Peer and G. Reid (eds), *Multilingualism, Literacy and Dyslexia. A Challenge for Educators.* London, David Fulton.

Stanovich, K. and Stanovich, P. (1995) How research might inform the debate about early reading acquisition. *Journal of Research in Reading,* **18**(2), 87–105.

Stanovich, K. E. (1986) Matthew effects in reading: Some consequences of individual differences in the acquisition of literacy. *Reading Research Quarterly,* **21**, 360–407.

Stanovich, K. E. (1988) Explaining the difference between the dyslexic and the garden-variety poor readers: The phonological core model. *Journal of Learning Disabilities,* **21**(10), 590–604.

Stanovich, K. E. (1991) Discrepancy definitions of reading disability: Has intelligence led us astray? *Reading Research Quarterly,* **26**, 7–29.

Stanovich, K. E. (1992) Speculations on the causes and consequences of individual differences in early reading acquisition. In: P. B. Gouch, L. C. Ehri and R. Treiman (eds), *Reading Acquisition* (pp. 65–106). Hillsdale, NJ, Lawrence Erlbaum.

Stanovich, K. E., Siegel, L. S. and Gottardo, A. (1997) Progress in the search for dyslexia subtypes. In: C. Hulme and M. J. Snowling (eds), *Dyslexia, Biology Cognition and Intervention.* London, Whurr.

Stein, J. (2002) The sensorimotor basis of learning disabilities. Paper presented at New Developments in Research and Practice Conference, County Hall, Durham, 14 June 2002.

Stein, J. (2008) The neurobiological basis of dyslexia. In: G. Reid, A. Fawcett, F. Manis and L. Siegel (eds), *The Sage Dyslexia Handbook.* London, Sage.

Stein, J. and Walsh, V. (1997) To see but not to read: The magnocellular theory of dyslexia. *Trends in Neuroscience,* **20**, 147–152.

Stein, J. F. (1994) A visual defect in dyslexics? In: R. I. Nicolson and A. J. Fawcett (eds), *Dyslexia in Children: Multidisciplinary Perspectives.* Hemel Hempstead, UK, Harvester Wheatsheaf.

Stein, J. F. and Fowler, M. S. (1993) Unstable binocular control in dyslexic children. *Journal of Research in Reading,* **16**(1), 30–45.

Stein, J., Talcott, J. and Witton, C. (2001) The sensorimotor basis of developmental dyslexia. In: A. Fawcett (ed.), *Dyslexia; Theory and Good Practice.* London, Whurr.

Stevens, L. J., Zentall, S. S., Abate, M. L., Kuczek, T. and Burgess, J. R. (1996) Omega-3 fatty acids in boys with behaviour, learning and health problems. *Physiology and Behavior,* **59**, 915–920.

Stordy, B. J. (1995) Benefit of docosahexaenoic acid supplements to dark adaptation in dyslexia. *The Lancet,* **346**, 385.

Stordy, B. J. (1997) Dyslexia, attention deficit hyperactivity disorder, dyspraxia—Do fatty acids help? *Dyslexia Review,* **9**(2), 1–3.

Sugden, D. and Wright, H. (1996). Curricular entitlement and implementation for all children. In: N. Armstrong (ed.), *New Directions in Physical Education: Change in Innovation.* London, Cassell.

Sunderland, H., Klein, C., Savinson, R. and Partridge, T. (1999) *Dyslexia and the Bilingual Learner: Assessing and Teaching Young People Who Speak English as an Additional Language.* London, Borough of Southwark, Language and Literacy Unit.

Swanson, H. L. (1999) Reading research for students with LD: A meta-analysis of intervention outcomes. *Journal of Learning Disabilities,* **32**, 504–532.

Tallal, P. and Merzenich, M. (1997) Fast ForWord™ training for children with language-learning problems: Results from a national field study by 35 independent facilities. Paper presented at the 1997 annual meeting of the American Speech-Language-Hearing Association, Boston, MA, 21 November.

Tannock, R. (1976) Doman–Delacato method for treating brain injured children. *Physiotherapy,* **28**(4).

Task Force on Dyslexia (2001) Report. Dublin: Government. Available online at www.irlgov.ie/educ/pub.htm.

Taylor, M. F. (1998) An evaluation of the effects of educational kinesiology (Brain Gym®) on children manifesting ADHD in a South African context (unpublished M.Phil. dissertation, University of Exeter, UK).

Taylor, M. F. (2002) Stress-induced atypical brain lateralization in boys with attention-deficit/hyperactivity disorder. Implications for scholastic performance (unpublished PhD thesis, University of Western Australia, Perth, Australia).

Thomson M (2007) *Supporting Dyslexic Pupils in the Secondary Curriculum.* Edinburgh, Dyslexia Scotland.

Thomson, G. (1990) On leaving school, who tells? In: G. Hales (ed.), *Meeting points in Dyslexia. Proceedings of the 1st International Conference of the British Dyslexia Association.* Reading, UK, British Dyslexic Association.

Thomson, M. (2002) Access across the curriculum in secondary school. Paper presented at Dyslexia in Scotland Annual Conference, 28 September 2002, Edinburgh.

Thomson, M. (2006) *Dyslexia Friendly Guidance for the Secondary School.* Series produced and distributed by Dyslexia Scotland, Stirling, UK.

Thomson, M. and Chinn, S. (2001) Good practice in the secondary school. In: A. Fawcett (ed.), *Dyslexia: Theory and Good Practice.* London, Whurr.

Tod, J. (2002) Individual education plans and dyslexia: Some principles. In: G. Reid and J. Wearmouth (eds), *Dyslexia and Literacy, Theory and Practice.* Chichester, John Wiley & Sons.

Tod, J. and Fairman, A. (2001) Individualised learning in a group setting. In: L. Peer and G. Reid (eds), *Dyslexia: Successful Inclusion in the Secondary School.* London, David Fulton.

Tomlinson, J. (1997) Inclusive learning: The report of the committee of inquiry into the post-school education of those with learning difficulties and disabilities in England, 1996. *European Journal of Special Need Education,* **12**(3), 184–196.

Topping, K. (2001) Peer and parent assisted learning. In: G. Shiel and U. Ni Dhalaigh (eds), *Reading Matters: A Fresh Start.* St Patrick's College, Dublin, Reading Association of Ireland/National Reading Initiative, Education Research Centre.

Topping, K. J. (1996) Parents and peers as tutors for dyslexic children. In: G. Reid (ed.), *Dimensions of Dyslexia, Vol. 2: Literacy, Language and Learning.* Edinburgh, Moray House.

Topping, K. J. (2002) Paired thinking, developing thinking skills through structured interaction with peers, parents and volunteers. In: G. Reid and J. Wearmouth (eds), *Dyslexia and Literacy: Theory and Practice.* Chichester, John Wiley & Sons.

Topping, K. J. and Bryce, A. (2002) Cross-age peer tutoring of reading and thinking in the primary school: A controlled study of influence on thinking skills (paper submitted for publication).

Topping, K. J. and Hogan, J. (1999) *Read On: Paired Reading and Thinking* (video resource pack, 2nd edn 2002). London, BP Educational Services (www.bpes.com).

Topping, K. J. and Lindsey, G. A. (1992) The structure and development of the paired reading technique. *Journal of Research in Reading,* **15**(2), 120–136.

Topping, K. J. and Watt, J. M. (1992) Cued Spelling: A comparative study of parent and peer tutoring (paper submitted for publication, University of Dundee).

Topping, K. J. and Wolfendale, S. (eds) (1985) *Parental Involvement in Children's Reading.* London, Croom Helm.

Torgeson, J. K. (1996) A model of memory from an informational processing perspective: The special case of phonological memory. In: G. R. Lyon and N. A. Krasnegor (eds), *Attention, Memory and Executive Function* (pp. 157–184). Baltimore, MD, Brookes.

Torgeson, J. K. (2004) Lessons learned from research on interventions for students who have difficulty learning to read. In: P. McCardle and V. Chhabra (eds), *The Voice of Evidence in Reading Research* (pp. 355–382). Baltimore, MD, Brookes.

Torgeson, J. K. (2005) Recent discoveries on remedial interventions for children with dyslexia. In: M. J. Snowling and C. Hulme (eds), *The Science of Reading: A Handbook* (pp. 521–537). Oxford, Blackwell.

Torgeson, J. K., Morgan, S. T. and Davis, C. (1992) Effects of two types of phonological training on word learning in kindergarten children. *Journal of Educational Psychology,* **84**, 364–370.

Torgeson, J. K., Wagner, R. K. and Rashotte, C. A. (1997) Prevention and remediation of severe reading disabilities: Keeping the end in mind. *Scientific Studies of Reading,* **1**, 217–234.

Townend, J. (2000) Phonological awareness and other foundation skills of literacy. In: J. Townend and M. Turner (eds), *Dyslexia in Practice: A Guide for Teachers.* Dordreeht, Kluwer Academic.

Treiman, R. (1993) *Beginning to Spell: A Study of First Grade Children.* New York, Oxford University Press.

Tridas E. Q. (ed.) (2007) *From ABC to ADHD: What Parents Should Know About Dyslexia and Attention Problems.* The International Dyslexia Association, Baltimore, Maryland.

Tunmer, M. (1997) *Psychological Assessment of Dyslexia.* London, Whurr.

Tunmer, W. and Chapman, J. (1998) Language, prediction skill, phonological recording ability, and beginning reading. In: C. Hulme and R. Joshi (eds), *Reading and Spelling: Development and Disorders* (pp. 33–68). Mahwah, NJ: Lawrence Erlbaum.

Tunmer, W. E. (1994) Phonological processing skills and reading remediation. In: C. Hulme and M. Snowling (eds), *Reading Development and Dyslexia.* London, Whurr.

Tunmer, W. E. and Chapman, J. (1996) A developmental model of dyslexia. Can the construct be saved? *Dyslexia,* **2**(3), 179–89.

Tunmer, W. E. and Chapman, J. W. (2004) Reading Recovery: Distinguishing myth from reality. In: R. M. Joshi (ed.), *Dyslexia: Myths, Misconceptions, and Some Practical Applications* (pp. 99–114). Baltimore, MD, International Dyslexia Association.

Tunmer, W. E. and Chapman, J. W. (2006) Metalinguistic abilities, phonological recoding skills, and the use of sentence context in beginning reading development: A longitudinal study. In: R. M. Joshi and P. G. Aaron (eds), *Handbook of Orthography and Literacy* (pp. 617–635). Mahwah, NJ, Erlbaum.

Tunmer, W. E. and Greaney, K. T. (2008) Reading intervention research: An integrative framework. In: G. Reid, A. Fawcett, F. Manis and L. Siegel (eds), *The Sage Dyslexia Handbook.* London, Sage.

Tunmer, W. E., Herriman, M. L. and Nesdale, A. R. (1988) Metalinguistic abilities and beginning reading. *Reading Research Quarterly,* **23**, 134–158.

Turner, E. (2001) Dyslexia and English. In: L. Peer and G. Reid (eds), *Dyslexia: Successful Inclusion in the Secondary School.* London, David Fulton.

Turner, M. (1991) Finding out. *Support for Learning,* **6**(3), 99–102.

Turner, E. (2002) Multisensory teaching and tutoring. *The Dyslexia Handbook 2002.* Reading, UK, British Dyslexia Association.

Turner, M. (1995) Children learn to read by being taught. In: P. Owen and P. Pumfrey (eds), *Children Learning to Read: International Concerns. Vol. 1. Emergent and Developing Reading: Messages for Teachers.* London, Falmer Press.

Ulmer, C. and Timothy, M. (2001) How does alternative assessment affect teachers' practice? Two years later. Paper presented at the 12th European Conference on Reading, Dublin, Ireland, 1–4 July.

Usmani, K. (1999) The influence of racism and cultural bias in the assessment of bilingual children. *Educational and Child Psychology,* **16**(3), 44–54.

Vachon, V. (1998) Effects of mastery of multisyllabic word reading component skills and of varying practice contexts on word and text reading skills of middle school students with reading deficiencies (unpublished doctoral dissertation, University of Oregon, Eugene).

Vadasy, P. F. and Sanders, E. A. (2008) Individual tutoring for struggling readers: Moving research to scale with interventions implemented by paraeducators. In: G. Reid, A. Fawcett, F. Manis and L. Siegel (eds), *The Sage Dyslexia Handbook.* London, Sage.

Vadasy, P. F., Sanders, E. A. and Peyton, J. A. (2006) Code-oriented instruction for kindergarten students at risk for reading difficulties: A randomized field trial with paraeducator implementers. *Journal of Educational Psychology,* **98**, 508–528.

Vellutino, F. R. and Scanlon, D. M. (1986) Experimental evidence for the effects of instructional bias on word identification. *Exceptional Children,* **53**(2), 145–155.

Vellutino, F. R., Fletcher, J. M. Snowling, M. J. and Scanlon, D. M. (2004) Specific reading disability (dyslexia): What have we learnt in the past four decades? *Journal of Child Psychology and Psychiatry,* **45**(1), 2–40.

Vellutino, F. R., Scanlon, D. M., Sipay, E. R., Small, S. G., Pratt, A., Chen, R. S., et al. (1996) Cognitive profiles of difficult to remediate and readily remediated poor readers: Early intervention as a vehicle for distinguishing between cognitive and experimental deficits as basic causes of specific reading disability. *Journal of Educational Psychology,* **88**, 601–638.

Venezky, R. (1970) *The Structure of English Orthography.* The Hague, Mouton.

Venezky, R. (1999) *The American Way of Spelling: The Structure and Origins of American English Orthography.* New York, Guilford Press.

Viall, J. T. (2000) *High Stakes Assessment in Perspectives* (Summer 2000 issue, Vol. 26, No. 3, p. 3). Baltimore, International Dyslexia Association.

Visser, J. (1993) *Differentiation: Making It Work.* Tamworth, UK, NASEN.

Visser, J. (2003) Developmental coordination disorder: A review of research on subtypes and comorbidities. *Human Movement Science,* **22**, 479–493.

Vogel, S. A. and Adelman, P. B. (2000) Adults with learning disabilities 8–15 years after college. *Learning Disabilities: A Multi-Disciplinary Journal,* **10**(3), 165–182.

Vygotsky, L. S. (1962, 1986) *Thought and Language.* Cambridge, MA, MIT Press.

Vygotsky, L. S. (1978) *Mind in Society: The Development of Higher Psychological Processes.* Cambridge, MA, Harvard University Press.

Wagner, R. (2008) Rediscovering dyslexia: New approaches for identification, classification, and intervention. In: G. Reid, A. Fawcett, F. Manis and L. Siegel (eds), *The Sage Dyslexia Handbook.* London, Sage.

Wagner, R. K., Torgeson, J. K. and Rashotte, C. A. (1999) *Comprehensive Test of Phonological Processing.* Austin, TX: PRO-Ed.

Walker, J. (2000) Teaching basic reading and spelling. In: J. Townend and M. Turner (eds), *Dyslexia in Practice: A Guide for Teachers.* New York, Kluwer Academic.

Ward, S. B., Ward, T. J., Hatt, C. V., Young, D. L. and Molner, N. R. (1995) The incidence and utility of the ACID, ACIDS, and SCAD profiles in a referred population. *Psychology in the Schools,* **32**(4), 267–276.

Watkins, M. W., Kush, J. C. and Glutting, J. J. (1997) Discriminant and predictive validity of the WISC III ACID profile among children with learning disabilities. *Psychology in the Schools,* **34**(4), 309–319.

Wearmouth, J. (2001) Inclusion: Changing the variables. In: L. Peer and G. Reid (eds), *Dyslexia: Successful Inclusion in the Secondary School.* London, David Fulton.

Wearmouth, J. and Reid, G. (2002) Issues for assessment and planning of teaching and learning. In: G. Reid and J. Wearmouth (eds), *Dyslexia and Literacy, Theory and Practice.* Chichester, John Wiley & Sons.

Wearmouth, J., Soler, J. and Reid, G. (2002) *Addressing Difficulties in Literacy Development: Responses at Family, School, Pupil and Teacher Levels.* London, RoutledgeFalmer.

Wearmouth, J., Soler, J. and Reid, G. (2003) *Meeting Difficulties in Literacy Development, Research, Policy and Practice.* London, RoutledgeFalmer.

Wechsler, D. (2001) *Wechsler Individual Achievement Test-II.* San Antonio, TX: Harcourt.

Wechsler, D. (2004) *Wechsler Intelligence Scale for Children—IV.* San Antonio, TX: Psychological Corporation.

Wedell, K.(2000) Personal interview from Wearmouth, J. (2001) Inclusion: changing the variables. In: L. Peer and G. Reid (eds), *Dyslexia: Successful Inclusion in the Secondary School.* London, David Fulton.

Weedon, C. and Reid, G. (2001) *Listening and Literacy Index.* London, Hodder & Stoughton.

Weedon, C. and Reid, G. (2002) *Special Needs Assessment Portfolio (pilot version).* Edinburgh, George Watson's College.

Weedon, C. and Reid, G. (2003) *Special Needs Assessment Portfolio.* London, Hodder & Stoughton.

Weedon, C. and Reid, G. (2005) *Special Needs Assessment Profile (SNAP V2 revised).* London, Hodder Murray.

Weedon, C. and Reid, G. (2008) *Special Needs Assessment Profile (SNAP V3).* London, Hodder Murray.

Welch, A. R. (1991) Education and legitimation in comparative education. *Comparative Education Review,* **34**, 3.

Welch, A. R. and Freebody, P. (2002) Explanations of the current international 'literacy crises'. In: J. Soler, J. Wearmouth and G. Reid (eds), *Contextualising Difficulties in Literacy Development: Exploring Politics, Culture, Ethnicity and Ethics.* London, RoutledgeFalmer.

Wendon, L. (1993) Literacy for early childhood: Learning from the learners. *Early Child Development and Care,* **86**, 11–12.

West, T. G. (1997) *In the Mind's Eye. Visual Thinkers, Gifted People with Learning Difficulties, Computer Images and the Ironies of Creativity* (2nd edn). Buffalo, NY, Prometheus Books.

What Works Clearinghouse (2007, July) *Beginning Reading: Fast ForWord.* Washington, DC, US Department of Education: Institute of Education Sciences.

White, S., Milne, E., Rosen, S., Hansen, P., Swettenham, J., Frith, U. and Ramus, F. (2006) The role of sensorimotor impairments in dyslexia: A multiple case study of dyslexic children. *Developmental Science,* **9**(3), 237–269.

Whiteley, H. E. and Smith, C. D. (2001) The use of tinted lenses to alleviate reading difficulties. *Journal of Research in Reading,* **24**, 30–40.

Wiederholt, J. L. and Bryant, B. R. (2001) *Gray Oral Reading Tests—Fourth Edition (GORT-4).* Austin, TX.

Wilkins, A. (1991) Visual discomfort and reading. In J. F. Stein (ed.) *Vision and Visual Dyslexia* (pp. 155–170). Basingstoke, Macmillan.

Wilkins, A. J. (1993) *Intuitive Overlays.* London, IOO Marketing.

Wilkins, A. J. (1995) *Visual Stress.* Oxford, Oxford University Press.

Wilkins, A. J. (2003) *Reading Through Colour.* Chichester, Wiley.

Wilkins, A. J., Jeanes, J. R., Pumfrey, P. D. and Laskier, M. (1996) *Rate of Reading Test R: Its Reliability and Its validity in the Assessment of the Effects of Coloured Overlays.* Cambridge, MRC Applied Psychology Unit.

Wilkinson, A. C. (1980) Children's understanding in reading and listening. *Journal of Educational Psychology,* **72**(4), 561–574.

Williams, F. and Lewis, J. (2001) Dyslexia and Geography. In: L. Peer and G. Reid (eds), *Dyslexia: Successful Inclusion in the Secondary School.* London, David Fulton.

Wilson, J. (1993) *Phonological Awareness Training: A New Approach to Phonics.* London, Educational Psychology.

Wilson, J. and Frederickson, N. (1995) Phonological awareness training: An evaluation. *Educational and Child Psychology,* **12**(1), 68–79.

Wimmer, H. (1993) Characteristics of developmental dyslexia in a regular writing system. *Applied Psycholinguistics,* **14**(1), 1–33.

Wimmer, H. (1996) The early manifestation of developmental dyslexia: Evidence from German children. *Reading and Writing,* **8**, 171–188.

Wise, B. W., Ring, J. and Olson, R. (1999) Training phonological awareness with and without explicit attention to articulation. *Journal of Experimental Child Psychology,* **72**, 271–304.

Wolf, B. J. (1985) The effect of Slingerland instruction on the reading and language of second grade children (PhD dissertation, Seattle Pacific University, Seattle, WA).

Wolf, M. (1996) The double-deficit hypothesis for the developmental dyslexics. Paper read at the 47th Annual Conference of the Orton Dyslexia Society, November 1996, Boston.

Wolf, M. and Bowers, P. G. (1999) The double-deficit hypothesis for the developmental dyslexias. *Journal of Educational Psychology,* **91**, 415–438.

Wolf, M. and O'Brien, B. (2001) On issues of time, fluency and intervention. In: A. Fawcett (ed.), *Dyslexia, Theory and Good Practice.* London, Whurr.

Wolfendale, S. (1989) *Parental Involvement: Developing Networks between School, Home and Community.* London, Cassell.

Wood, F. B. (2000) Surprises ahead: The new decade of dyslexia, neurogenetics and education. Keynote lecture at the 51st Annual Conference of the International Dyslexia Association, Washington, DC, 8–11 November 2000.

Wood, T. A., Buckhalt, J. A. and Tomlin, J. G. (1988) A comparison of listening and reading performance with children in three educational placements. *Journal of Learning Disabilities,* **8**, 493–496.

Woodcock, R. W. (1998) *Woodcock Reading Mastery Tests—Revised.* Circle Pines, MN: American Guidance Service.

World Health Organization (1993) *Classification of Diseases and Related Health Problems (ICD-10).* Geneva: WHO.

Wray, D. (1994) *Literacy and Awareness.* London, Hodder & Stoughton.

Wray, D. (2002) Metacognition and literacy. In: G. Reid and J. Wearmouth (eds), *Dyslexia and Literacy: Theory and Practice.* Chichester, John Wiley & Sons.

Wray, D. (2006) Developing critical literacy: A priority for the 21st century. *Journal of Reading, Writing and Literacy,* **1**(1), 19–34.

Wray, D. (2009) Extending literacy skills: Issues for practice. In: G. Reid (ed.), *The Routledge Dyslexia Companion,* London, Routledge.

Wray, D. and Lewis, M. (1997) *Extending Literacy: Reading and Writing Non-fiction in the Primary School.* London: Routledge.

Wright, A. (1992) Evaluation of the first British Reading Recovery programme. *British Educational Research Journal,* **18**(4), 351–368.

Wright, A. (1993) Irlen: The never ending story. Paper presented at the 5th European Conference of Neuro-developmental Delay in Children with Specific Learning Difficulties, Chester.

Yoshimoto, R. (2005) Gifted dyslexic children: Characteristics and curriculum implications. Presentation at the 56th Annual Conference, IDA, Denver, Colorado, USA, November 9–12.

Zeffiro, T. and Eden, G. (2000) The neural basis of developmental dyslexia. *Annals of Dyslexia,* **50**, 3–30.

Zeigler, J. C. and Goswami, U. (2005) Reading acquisition, developmental dyslexia, and skilled reading across languages: A psycholinguistic grain size theory. *Psychological Bulletin,* **131**, 3–29.

Index